Jeff Duntemann Series Editor

ISAPI/ NSAPI
Web Programming

HIGH PERFORMANCE

Jeff Duntemann **Series Editor**

ISAPI/ NSAPI
Web Programming

HIGH PERFORMANCE

Tony Beveridge

Paul McGlashan

CORIOLIS GROUP BOOKS

an International Thomson Publishing company I(T)P[®]

Albany, NY • Belmont, CA • Bonn • Boston • Cincinnati • Detroit • Johannesburg • London
Madrid • Melbourne • Mexico City • New York • Paris • Singapore • Tokyo • Toronto • Washington

PUBLISHER	KEITH WEISKAMP
PROJECT EDITOR	MICHELLE STROUP
COVER ARTIST	GARY SMITH/PERFORMANCE DESIGN
COVER DESIGN	ANTHONY STOCK
INTERIOR DESIGN	NICOLE COLÓN
LAYOUT PRODUCTION	SHADY LANE GRAPHICS & EDITORIAL
COPYEDITOR	NANCY WARNER
PROOFREADER	SHELLY CROSSEN
INDEXER	CAROLINE PARKS

High Performance ISAPI/NSAPI Web Programming
ISBN: 1-57610-151-7
Copyright © 1997 by The Coriolis Group, Inc.

The Coriolis Group, Inc.
An International Thomson Publishing Company
14455 N. Hayden Road, Suite 220
Scottsdale, Arizona 85260

602/483-0192
FAX 602/483-0193
http://www.coriolis.com

Printed in the United States of America
10 9 8 7 6 5 4 3 2 1

Acknowledgments

Tony Beveridge

I would like to thank Keith Weiskamp and Anthony Potts for their initial discussions with me and allowing the book to proceed. Very special thanks to Michelle Stroup for her skilled editing, patience, good humor, and recognition that not every anthropomorphic reference needs deletion! Thanks also to Nancy Warner.

To Natasha and Alex, I don't think I could have completed this book without your support, patience, and tolerance. I know I wasn't always a darling to live with and that you let things pass (especially Natasha!) quite a few times! I hope I reciprocate often enough. You know you can always count on me—I'm just not sure for what.

To my co-author, Paul, thanks for writing half! We had an aggressive schedule and you are the only person I know whom I could count on to pull it off. Your ability to assimilate concepts is nothing short of, well, cool!

Special regards to Damien Hollis and Roger Bengtsson—geezers, we will work together one day and it will be in OO!

Optimation New Zealand, my employer, kindly gave me permission to describe the SEREF framework and include significant amounts of the source code on the CD-ROM included with this book. Our WWW site can be reached at **www.optimation.co.nz**. Thanks to Neil Butler and Paul McGlashan.

Paul McGlashan

I would firstly like to thank my most excellent colleague and holder of the OO faith Tony for conceiving the idea, and inviting me to share in making it a reality. I look forward to our next escapade! Thanks to Michelle for her encouragement, and to both Michelle and Nancy for their attention to detail and good suggestions during the copyediting process.

I would especially like to thank my wife Anne Marie and my children James, Jono, and Pat for putting up with not having me around at night and on the weekends while I was writing. To my mother Ann, and John for providing a home away from home while I worked into the wee hours. To my friends Caroline and Steve for their support and encouragement.

Contents

Introduction

The Web server has evolved considerably, both in architecture and function, since the embryonic days of the World Wide Web. The HTTP protocol that underpins a significant portion of a Web server's operation, and its gradual development, has subtly changed the model used in processing an HTTP request. Orthogonal to this evolution have been advances in contemporary operating system architecture. The proliferation of multi-threaded kernels and dynamic object loading has engendered a new attitude and design for many software architectures.

The combined effect of these changes has manifested itself in Web server technology with a shift to a multi-threaded, in-process extension paradigm. To exploit this shift, and also to expose fundamental HTTP request processing behavior, many server vendors now provide an API that will allow developers to dynamically augment the behavior the server. This book describes in detail the ISAPI and NSAPI extension APIs.

Microsoft's ISAPI provides both an extension API (called ISAPI filters) and a CGI replacement API (called ISA). When used with the IIS server, many custom schemes can be created including decryption, enterprise object instantiation, authentication, URL mapping, CGI-type servicing, logging and encryption. Chapters 7 through 10 discuss the IIS architecture, ISAPI filters, ISA DLLs, and filter and ISA DLL configuration.

Netscape's NSAPI provides an extension API that is used for both HTTP request filtering and CGI-type service. When used with Enterprise Server, alternate request processing behavior can be developed, including authentication, URL mapping, access control, MIME typing, CGI-type servicing and logging. Chapters 3, 4, and 6 discuss Netscape's Enterprise Server architecture, NSAPI extension development, and extension function configuration.

Web server extension portability, across operating systems and vendor APIs, is an important topic for the commercial software developer. Microsoft and Netscape model the temporal progression of an HTTP request's processing in quite different ways. Their proprietary APIs facilitate developer extension of their servers, but not in a common enough manner to make portability a trivial issue. Therefore, to aid developers in this area, we have created an object-oriented C++ framework that enables the use of a common model for extensions across ISAPI, NSAPI, and their supported platforms. A consequence of our design is that extensions written using the framework are instantly source code portable across all platform and API combinations. Chapters 12 through 14 discuss the architecture, design, use, and implementation of this framework called SEREF (for Server Extension Framework). Included in this description are UML notation diagrams of various kinds.

Readers with questions or comments should email the authors directly at tonyb@optimation.co.nz (Tony Beveridge) and paulm@akl.optimation.co.nz (Paul McGlashan).

HIGH PERFORMANCE

HTTP

CHAPTER

1

HTTP, the Hypertext Transfer Protocol, is a simple, client/server protocol typically layered over TCP/IP. HTTP is an application-level protocol in the style of traditional Internet application protocols such as SMTP (Simple Mail Transfer Protocol) and NNTP (Network News Transfer Protocol), but is designed to support transactional behavior between a client program (usually a Web browser) and a server connected via a network (typically the Internet).

HTTP

HTTP first appeared in prototype form on the Internet in 1990 and since then has developed in sophistication to accommodate the ever-growing functionality and performance needs of the World Wide Web. This chapter provides a gentle introduction to the protocol, beginning with a brief history of its development (including a comparison of current and pending versions) followed by a description of the version in current use—HTTP 1.0.

This chapter looks at the HTTP protocol in some detail and attempts to obtain a useful balance between a tutorial and a reference approach. We have tried to do this without replicating the entire contents of the relevant RFC documents (of which there are an increasing number). If you are already an experienced HTTP developer, we suggest you skip this chapter.

Throughout the chapter, sample sessions illustrate aspects of the protocol using a range of commercial and public domain client and server technologies. Client programs that are used include Netscape Navigator and Telnet. Servers that are used include Netscape Enterprise Server Version 2.0 and Apache Version 1.2.

> **Note:** *RFCs ("Requests for Comments") are used by the Internet community for setting new Internet standards. All the Internet protocols in use today are specified by an RFC. For example, Version 1.0 of the HTTP protocol is defined in RFC 1945. An RFC begins as a discussion document (or Internet Draft) and then, as it wins support from the Internet community, it moves through a standardization process managed by the Internet Engineering Task Force (IETF). You can find a complete list of RFCs at **info.internet.isi.edu/ 1s/in-notes/rfc**. For more information about the IETF and its working groups, visit their home page at **www.ietf.org**.*

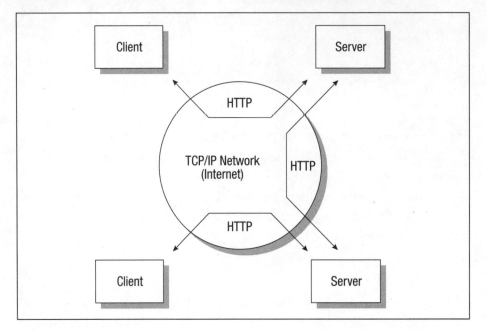

Figure 1.1
The Client/Server model.

Background

The father of the World Wide Web, Tim Berners-Lee, developed HTTP, along with the companion specifications for HTML and the URI (Uniform Resource Identifier) while he was a fellow at CERN (the European Particle Physics Laboratory in Geneva, Switzerland). Discovering that the laboratory, like most organizations, had trouble keeping track of information, Tim put forward a proposal for structuring the lab's information into a web of documents connected by hypertext links. The proposal was an instant hit at CERN.

Tim envisioned a worldwide community of people collaborating in the creation of a global store of knowledge by publishing their own hyperlinked documents. This vision finally became reality when he published his work via the Internet in 1991 and heralded a new paradigm for client/server computing over the Internet.

At this time, CERN made available its prototype Web client and server technologies along with preliminary specifications for defining communication between them. Development of HTTP, HTML, and URI specifications is now managed by working groups of the Internet Engineering Task Force (IETF).

The original HTTP protocol, Version 0.9 [Berners-Lee 1990], was implemented in the prototype software originally published by CERN. This version is a subset of the full protocol as it exists today and defines a restricted subset to which future versions will always be backward compatible.

Version 1.0, defined in RFC 1945, reflects the protocol in current usage. This version, however, has significant scalability and performance problems and is currently being revised in the form of HTTP 1.1 (RFC 2068). A next-generation protocol, HTTPng, is another proposed extension to HTTP 1.0 and provides an alternative method to resolving some of 1.0's performance problems.

HTML is just one of the data formats understood by HTTP clients and servers. (Other formats commonly used include plain text, images, audio, video, PostScript files, and the like.) HTML has been around since 1990 and is most recently described in RFC 1866, which outlines HTML Version 2.0.

The concept of a URI was first described in RFC 1630 by Berners-Lee in 1994. Since then, specifications for its derivative URL and URN forms have also been published. (Refer to section "URIs And Related Forms," later in this chapter.)

> **Note:** Tim Berners-Lee now heads up the W3 Consortium (W3C), an industry consortium including CERN, Massachusetts Institute of Technology (MIT), the Institut National de Recherche en Informatique et en Automatique (INRIA) and Keio University. W3C has taken on the mantle from CERN for promulgating standards for the World Wide Web. You can visit the W3C home page at **www.w3.org**.

HTTP 0.9

HTTP 0.9 is a simple message-oriented protocol to which the newer versions of HTTP (1.0 and 1.1) are backward compatible. The protocol describes a request/response paradigm where a client program connects to a server at a specified address and invokes a GET request to retrieve an object (typically an HTML document) located on the server. The server responds by sending back the object (or an error message) to the client program before ending the response by closing the connection.

Note: A GET request is just one of a number of different types of commands an HTTP client can perform. HTTP also provides POST and PUT commands for sending data to a server, and a HEAD command for obtaining information about an object (instead of the object itself).

HTTP 1.0

HTTP 1.0 builds on HTTP 0.9, by adding features needed to support the retrieval of many different object types over more complex network connections. Additions to the protocol include:

- Additional request types (for example, HEAD and POST requests).

- Protocol versioning of request and response messages (for example, the first line of a response message beginning with **HTTP/1.0** indicates that the server complies with Version 1.0 of the HTTP protocol).

- Server response codes indicating success or failure of request and response messages (for example, the first line of a response message ending with **200 OK** indicates that the request was successful).

- Message header and body formats based on MIME (Multipurpose Internet Mail Extensions) for defining both the data type of the retrieved object and additional metainformation (for example, a MIME header such as **Content-type: text/html** indicates that the response message contains an HTML document).

- A basic security mechanism using a challenge/response paradigm for access authentication. You may have seen this working when you have attempted to access an HTML page and been asked to enter a user name and password.

Note: MIME is an extension of the original specification for mail headers and content found in RFC 822. MIME extends RFC 822 so that mail messages can contain more complex objects than just a single plain text body. In fact, MIME allows a single message to contain multiple body parts of different types. The MIME specification has been recently updated in RFCs 2045, 2046, 2049, and RFC 2047. RFCs 2045, 2046, and 2049 supersede RFCs 1521, 1522, and 1590 respectively.

In HTTP 0.9 the interaction takes place directly between client and server. This limited view has been expanded in HTTP 1.0, which provides for connections through intermediate entities such as proxy servers. (Refer to the section *Basic Authentication Scheme* later in this chapter.)

HTTP's use of MIME to describe the data type of the object inside a message provides HTTP with a powerful and extensible way of handling almost any kind of data. This approach can be used to handle simple text and HTML as well as more sophisticated multimedia content, such as audio and video.

HTTP 1.1

HTTP 1.1 is a significant leap forward from HTTP 1.0 and attempts to address a number of its shortfalls—particularly in the areas of performance, security, data-type handling, and caching. By being more rigorous in its definition (for example in the operation of caching and proxy servers), HTTP 1.1 leaves much less room for misinterpretation. This should translate into more reliable implementations of the protocol.

HTTP 1.1's major improvements include:

- Improved performance with the introduction of Persistent Connections as the default mode of connection.

- Improved security through the introduction of a Digest Authentication scheme (refer to the section Authentication later in this chapter) that overcomes the Basic Authentication scheme's limitation of transmitting user name and password credentials **in the clear**.

  Note: *In practice, these credentials are lightly encoded using the BASE64 translation scheme. (Refer to the section "Basic Authentication Scheme," later in this chapter.)*

- A Content Negotiation mechanism that allows the client and server to agree on the best way to represent an object.

HTTP 1.1 puts forward a design for caching objects on the server and a client/server protocol for controlling the cache operation to further improve the performance of the protocol. The goal of this design is to reduce request, round-trip times, and to reduce network bandwidth by sending back full responses only when absolutely necessary.

HTTP 1.1 also overcomes HTTP 1.0's one-to-one relationship between a server and an IP address. Under HTTP 1.1, a Host header determines which server should satisfy the request by specifying the server name.

Persistent Connections

Performance has always been an issue with HTTP because each HTTP request requires its own TCP/IP connection. This can be problematic when the HTML object being retrieved contains references to other embedded objects—usually images—each of which must also be retrieved to completely satisfy the original request.

HTTP 1.1's persistent connections largely overcome this problem because the connection between client and server remains established until either the client or the server signals that the connection is to be closed. This is done through the formal introduction of the Connection header. Unlike HTTP 1.0, persistent connections are the default mode of connection.

Another benefit of persistent connections is that requests and responses can be *pipelined;* for example, a client can send a continuous string of requests without waiting for the outcome of the previous request. Also the start-up and tear-down costs of the request are reduced to that of establishing a single connection.

Some HTTP 1.0 implementations (like Netscape) support an experimental scheme in which the client specifically requests a persistent connection using the Connection: Keep-alive header. This, however, is not generally supported and can lead to problems, especially if the request is passed to a proxy server that doesn't support the Keep-alive request who then forwards it on to a server that does.

Content Negotiation

HTTP 1.1 introduces a negotiation method between clients and servers that allows the client to select the *best available* representation of a requested object when there is a choice. The protocol provides for three negotiation schemes: server-driven negotiation, client-driven negotiation, and transparent negotiation (a combination of server-driven and client-driven).

The *server-driven* scheme is used when the server has a choice of representations and the rules for deciding the appropriate form are not easily described to the client. The client request message supplies the server hints for making the choice, such as the data type supported, encoding, and other information. There are two main drawbacks to this approach. First, it is difficult for the server to decide what is best for the user, and second, the list of alternatives specified by the client could impose as much as 1 K per request.

In *client-driven* negotiation, the client selects the appropriate representation from the alternate forms specified in the initial response. The downside of this approach is the need for a second request if the client chooses one of the alternative representations.

The third scheme, *transparent negotiation,* combines both server-driven and client-driven schemes and is applicable to caching environments. Here, the cache is able to perform negotiation on behalf of the destination server by choosing from a list of alternative representations. This takes some of the negotiation load from the server and removes the performance penalty of the second client request once the appropriate response has been cached.

HTTPng

HTTP Next Generation describes a completely different protocol to HTTP 1.x (specifically 1.0 and 1.1) and does not attempt to preserve any of the legacies of these protocols. While HTTP 1.1 and HTTPng add similar features (persistent connections and request/response pipe-lining), HTTPng goes further in improving efficiency and performance.

These improvements can be reduced to the following:

- Persistent connections, like HTTP 1.1, where a single connection is established between client and server to process requests. Unlike HTTP 1.1, each HTTPng connection is actually split up into a number of different channels (virtual sessions)—a control channel for sending and receiving commands, and a channel for each requested object.

- Asynchronous requests and responses allow a client to start a new request without waiting for the response of the previous request, and a server may send back responses in any order and at any time.

- Simplified message formats are used instead of human-readable commands and headers. HTTPng uses a compact and concise representation based on Abstract Syntax Notation (ASN.1).

- Content negotiation assumes that only a small number of object types will be used in practice and that these can be encoded in a compact (bitmap) form. More complex types can be proposed using a name/value pair and the value can be added to the bitmap for subsequent negotiations.

In addition, HTTPng introduces policy-independent security, charging frameworks, and a mechanism for supporting the mandatory display of important information about a requested object such as its author and copyright information. The charging mechanism allows a payment to be initiated in response to a client request and for client and server to negotiate the payment process.

URIs And Related Forms

Before going any further, we'll define what we mean by a URI and its related forms. A URI, or Uniform Resource Identifier, is a generic way of uniquely identifying a resource anywhere over a network. A URI has three subordinate forms:

- Uniform Resource Name (URN) specifies a unique name for a resource within a global name space.

- Universal Resource Characteristic (URC) defines a set of characteristics or properties about the name—one of these being a set of possible locations.

- Universal Resource Locator (URL) specifies a location for a resource.

Unlike a URL, a URN is invariant to a resource's location. It would be quite possible for a resource named by a URN to have multiple locations or to not exist at all. The location independence of URNs offers some hope of solving the frustrating *broken link* problem with URLs. The URL is the only commonly used form of the three. Work is being done on defining a URN scheme, but consensus on a workable approach is not in the near future.

URLs

A URL (as defined in RFC 1738) is a generic specification for locating a resource over a network and tells us how to get to it and where to find it.

For example, the following absolute URL

```
http://www.optimation.co.nz/optimation/seref/feedbback.htm
```

tells us that the file feedback.htm can be accessed via the http protocol on server **www.optimation.co.nz** in the subdirectory optimation/seref. The http component in the example is formally known as a URL scheme. The scheme defines a handler that the client uses to access the resource. Normally the handler implements an Internet protocol such as HTTP, FTP, or Telnet to connect to a server; however, this is not always the case. For example, the **mailto** handler normally causes a Web browser to invoke a mail client that allows the user to send a mail message to the recipient address specified as a **mailto** parameter. Table 1.1 lists some of the more common schemes, but there are many others.

HTTP URLs

In the HTTP scheme, a URL has the following syntax:

```
http://host[:port]/[absolute-path][?search-part]
```

URLs described by this syntax are known as *absolute URLs* because they fully describe how to get to the resource. The following list describes each part of the syntax:

- The host component specifies the network address of the computer that contains the resource and should be a fully qualified domain name (for example, **www.optimation.co.nz**) or an IP address (for example, 202.6.84.18).

- The port is the port number of the server responsible for satisfying the resource request. Each Internet protocol is allocated a unique port number (a *well-known port*) on which a server, implementing the server-side of the protocol, listens for incoming requests. The port component is optional in a URL and if omitted will default to the default port for the scheme (80 for HTTP). Table 1.1 also lists default port numbers for other protocols.

- The absolute-path component is optional and defines the path name of the resource on the host. This is commonly the path name of an HTML file or a CGI script.

Table 1.1 Common URL access schemes.

Scheme	Description	Port
FTP	File Transfer protocol	21
File	Host-specific file names	N/A
HTTP	Hyperlext Transfer Protocol	80
Gopher	The Gopher protocol	70
Irc	Internet Relay Chat	194
mailto	Electronic mail address	N/A
News	USENET news	N/A
NNTP	USENET news using NNTP access	119
TELNET	Reference to interactive sessions	23
WAIS	Wide Area Information Servers	210

- The search-part component is also optional and allows for the inclusion of a query string—most often used for encoding GET requests generated by HTML forms (refer to section *Requests* later in this chapter).

If both the absolute-path and query-string components are left out then the preceding / may also be omitted.

Absolute URLs And Paths

A client sends two kinds of URLs depending on whether the client request is being made to a proxy server. When a proxy server is the destination, the client transmits an absolute URL. This is necessary because a proxy server needs to know the names of all the servers it is forwarding requests to and receiving responses from. When the server is not a proxy (the request is made against the origin server directly), an absolute URL is not used, only the absolute path component of the URL is transmitted.

You can see this behavior for yourself by snooping the network connection between your browser and your in-house proxy server (if you have one) when you select a URL that maps to an in-house resource; for example, /staff/paulm/home.htm. If you set the **No proxies** option of your Web browser (Options|Network|

Preferences:Proxies in Netscape Navigator), the generated request will refer to an absolute path name:

```
GET /staff/paulm/home.htm
```

If **No proxies** is turned off and an in-house proxy server called morgan on port 8080 is specified using Navigator's Manual Proxy Configuration option, then the generated request will refer to an absolute URL:

```
GET http://morgan:8080/staff/paulm/home.htm
```

Throughout this chapter, we will use the term *request URL* to mean either an absolute URL or an absolute path name, depending on whether the request is to a proxy server or an origin server.

Use Snoop To Spy On A Sesssion

*Using a snooping utility such as **tcpdump** or Solaris's **snoop**, you can peek into the conversation between a client and server. These utilities let you see up through all the network layers—from the physical Ethernet layer, through the IP and TCP layers up to the higher level application protocols, such as HTTP. We are not interested in the layers underneath HTTP, so we can strip out that information. The **snoop** utility lets us do this by specifying a byte offset from which it starts displaying the packet contents. For HTTP, the magic offset is 54. We can further restrict our snooping by specifying the name and the port number of the server (in this case, a proxy server on a host called morgan listening on port 8080). Therefore the command we use is: **snoop -x 54 morgan port 8080.***

Relative URLs

When authoring HTML documents, embedded URLs can be specified in an absolute or a relative form. A relative URL (as specified in RFC 1808), sometimes called a partial URL, assumes the host, port, and path name prefix of the document in which the URL appears. For example:

```
<A HREF="feedback.html">SEREF Feedback Form</A>
```

Relative URLs are only seen in the context of an HTML document; they are not part of the HTTP protocol. An HTTP client will always construct the appropriate request URL by prefixing the resource file with the access method, host, port, and the directory path of the surrounding document as required. A Web browser (via a proxy) would expand the relative URL above to:

```
http://www.optimation.co.nz/optimation/seref/feedback.html
```

Relative URLs are handy when authoring a related set of Web documents because you can create a hierarchy of documents without worrying about its final location. Within a relative URL you can use ../ notation to navigate up and down the tree of documents in the same way you would a Unix directory hierarchy. For example:

```
<HREF="../../home.html">Return to Home Page</A>
```

Relative URLs also work correctly when a Web browser accesses the files directly from the file system without connecting to any server.

URL Encoding

A request URL is constructed from a subset of characters drawn from the US-ASCII character set. These characters are basically letters, digits, and a small set of *safe* special characters. A character is safe if it has no special meaning to a server or application processing a request. Each character in turn is fundamentally an 8-bit entity (an octet). All unsafe characters, or any octets, that do not have a value in the US-ASCII character set, must be encoded. The encoding consists of substituting the unsafe character with a % followed by two hexadecimal digits that define the value of the octet.

Specifically, the three situations in which an octet/character in a URL must be encoded are when:

- The octet does not map to a printable US-ASCII character; for example, if the octet has a value of 00–1F and 7F (control characters), and codes 80–FF (not used in US-ASCII).

- The character is one of the following unsafe characters: SP, <, >, ", %, #.

- The characters are reserved for constructing the URL itself, for example: ;, /, ?, :, @, =, and &.

Other characters are deemed unsafe because of possible special interpretation by the server or application that ultimately processes the request are {, }, |, \, ^, ~, [,], and '.

The only characters that do not have to be encoded are alphanumerics, the special characters $, +, !, *, ', (,), and the reserved characters specific to the URL scheme (for HTTP these are /, ;, ?).

Basic Protocol

Fundamentally, HTTP implements a simple message-based, request/response paradigm that allows a client program such as a Web browser to request a resource such as an HTML document from a server (note a resource is often referred to as an *object* in this chapter). Typically this resource is an HTML document.

In a request/response paradigm (illustrated in Figure 1.2), a client sends a single request to the server and the server sends back a single response.

RFC 1945 introduces the term *origin server* to distinguish the server that ultimately satisfies the resource request. Between the client and the origin server, the request

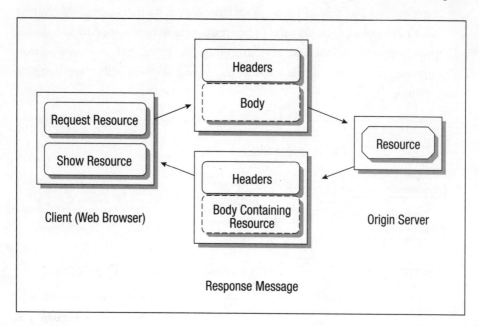

Figure 1.2
The request/response paradigm.

may pass through a chain of intermediary entities including one or more proxies. As shown in Figure 1.3, a proxy server forwards a request in its entirety to the origin server and caches origin server responses so subsequent client requests can be serviced by the proxy instead.

HTTP—A Stateless, Application-Level Protocol

HTTP was initially designed to be lightweight, fast, and *stateless* (although the first two tenets to some extent have been compromised, as the protocol has become more complex). By stateless, we mean that each HTTP request is independent of any previous request, because all information needed to satisfy the request is part of the request message. While inherently stateless, there are ways of maintaining state information between transactions, such as environment variables, files, hidden HTML fields, and HTTP cookies.

HTTP is similar in style to traditional Internet application protocols such as SMTP and NNTP. In HTTP, both clients and servers exchange ASCII messages. The conversation between client and server is in the form of lines of human-readable text terminated by a carriage return and a line feed (CRLF). This makes HTTP easy to understand and debug. Throughout this chapter, we make use of this feature and present examples of the protocol. These examples were obtained by simulating a simple client with Telnet and eavesdropping on the client/server connection using network snooping utilities such as the public domain utility **tcpdump** or Solaris's **snoop**.

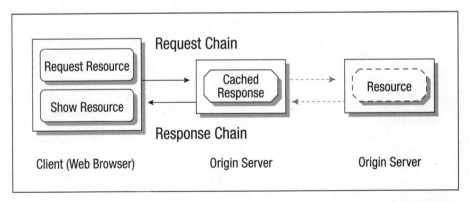

Figure 1.3
Intermediaries between client and server.

TCP As A Transport Protocol

Although HTTP is typically layered over TCP/IP, this is not a prerequisite as long as the underlying protocol provides a reliable, error-free transport. Unfortunately, layering HTTP over TCP may impair HTTP's performance with TCP's inefficiencies.

For example, TCP's three-way handshake on connection establishment requires a client to wait for an acknowledgment before any information can be sent, resulting in a delay of one round-trip time. Also TCP's slow-start behavior means that it takes a while before TCP fully utilizes the bandwidth of the channel. These inefficiencies (exacerbated by HTTP's separate connection per transaction) are particularly noticeable over slow dial-up connections and have begun to be addressed in alternative TCP implementations such as Transaction TCP (T/TCP).

> **Note:** *For more information on T/TCP, refer to RFCs 1644 and 1323. Also, Richard Stevens maintains the T/TCP home page at **www.noao.edu/~rstevens/ttcp.html**.*

HTTP—A Media-Independent, Object-Oriented Protocol

HTTP is capable of dealing with different types of information, from plain text to complex multimedia objects. HTTP messages specify the data type of the object that is transmitted using MIME's notion of a media type. A Web browser uses the data type to invoke the most appropriate viewer for displaying the object.

HTTP is loosely referred to as an object-oriented protocol because it provides a general mechanism for invoking an action (method) against a specified object on a server and a process for introducing new object types and methods.

The Request Life Cycle

HTTP is made up of four distinct phases: connection, request, response, and disconnection, outlined in Table 1.2.

We can easily work through each of the protocol phases ourselves by using Telnet as the client program to establish the connection.

Use Telnet As An HTTP Client

Telnet is an extremely useful tool for studying and debugging application-level Internet protocols such as HTTP and SMTP that have a human-readable ASCII command set. Normally, Telnet connects to a Telnet service listening on port 23, but we can override this and have it connect to a Web server instead. Telnet becomes the client and we can manually type in requests and see the server responses.

Session 1.1 shows an example session where we invoke Telnet from the command line to connect to a computer called morgan and issue a simple GET command (using HTTP 0.9 syntax) to request the author's home page. The computer morgan is running an Apache Web server, which is listening for incoming requests on port 80. Therefore, we'll give that port number as an argument to Telnet.

Session 1.1   Example Telnet session showing an HTTP 0.9 GET request.

```
telnet morgan 80               Connection to host morgan on port 80
Trying 10.0.0.20…              Displayed by telnet
Connected to morgan            Displayed by telnet
Escape character is '^]'.      Displayed by telnet
GET /ose/staff/web/paulm/paulm.htm   Type this line
                               Then a blank line
<!DOCTYPE HTML PUBLIC          HTML document output by the server
  "-//IETF//DTD HTML 3.2//EN">
<HTML>
<HEAD>
<TITLE></TITLE>
<META NAME="GENERATOR" CONTENT="Mozilla/3.0b5aGold (Win95; I) [Netscape]"
</HEAD>
<BODY BACKGROUND="pmbg.jpg">
<TABLE BORDER=1 BGCOLOR="#808080">
<TR>
<TD>
<H1><A NAME="top"></A><FONT COLOR="#800000">Welcome to Paul's Home Page
</FONT></H1>
</TD>
</TR>
</TABLE>
</BODY>
</HTML>
Connection closed by foreign host.   Displayed by telnet when the server
                                     closes the connection
```

Table 1.2 The request life cycle.

Phase	Description
Connection	A client (usually a program such as a Web browser), given the address of a resource in the form of a request URL, establishes a TCP/IP connection to the origin server and port specified in the URL.
Request	Once the server has accepted the connection, the client issues a request message (typically a GET request) specifying the location of the resource on the server and the version of the protocol to use.
Response	The server responds with a request message containing a status code indicating the success or otherwise of the request, headers that further describe the response, and the requested object (usually an HTML document). The object itself is formally known as an entity and consists of two parts—entity headers that describe the object and an entity body that contains the object data.
Disconnection	Once the response message has been sent, the server completes the transaction by disconnecting the TCP/IP session with the client. An important aspect of HTTP is that each request is independent of all other requests.

In accordance with the HTTP 0.9 protocol, the response to the GET request is the requested HTML document itself. There is no additional metainformation sent in the form of status codes or headers.

Notation

Throughout the rest of this chapter, the message formats that make up the HTTP protocol are described, using a simplified form of the BNF rules found in RFC 1945. The rules in this chapter are not designed to be a formal reference—simply a guide to how HTTP messages are constructed. The rules have been reduced and simplified to aid understanding. For an authoritative specification, refer to RFC1945. Refer to Table 1.3 for definitions of protocol syntax.

Messages

Sending and receiving messages is central to HTTP. HTTP defines two different types of messages—a request and a response. The following BNF rule shows that for

Table 1.3 Protocol syntax elements.

Element	Meaning
rule1 | rule2	Indicates two alternative rules.
(rule1 rule2)	Indicates a single element.
*rule	Indicates repctition (for example, 1*element means at least one element).
[rule]	Means that the rule is optional.
#rule	Indicates a list of elements separated by commas (for example, 1#element means at least one element in the list).
Token	A sequence of one or more characters, not including control characters or special characters.
special characters	"(", ")", "<", ">", "@", ",", ";", ":", "\", <">, "/", "[", "]", "?", "=", "{", "}", SP, HT
CRLF	A Carriage Return character (CR) followed by a Line Feed character (LF).
SP	A Space character.
HT	A Horizontal Tab character.

each message type, there are simple and full forms. The simple form from HTTP 0.9 and the full form as defined in HTTP 1.0:

```
                           =  Simple-Request

HTTP-message
                           |  Simple-Response
                           |  Full-Request
                           |  Full-Response
```

Full messages are structured in the same way as Internet mail messages (as defined by RFCs 822 and 1123) and consist of a series of header fields followed by a message body. The header fields further describe the message and the entity encapsulated by it. The message body contains the actual data or entity being transmitted and is typically an HTML document (in the case of a response message) or the contents of an HTML form (in the case of a request message).

Table 1.4   Message header categories.

Header	Description
General	General header fields apply to both request and response messages. They describe aspects of the message rather than the object within it.
Request	Request header fields are part of request messages and provide information about the request and the client sending it.
Response	Response header fields are included with response messages and provide a way for the server to send back additional information.
Entity	Entity header fields allow properties of the object itself to be included in the message.

Message Headers

There are four types of HTTP header fields, listed in Table 1.4.

Although the order in which the header fields appear is not important, it is usual for General header fields to come first, followed by Request or Response header fields, and then Entity fields. Unlike method names, header field names are not case sensitive.

Each message header conforms to the following syntax:

```
                       =  field-name ":" [ field-value ] CRLF
HTTP-header
field-name             =  token
field-value            =  *(field-content | white-space)
field-content          =  <the bytes making up the field-value and
                              consisting of either *TEXT or combinations
                              of tokens, special characters, and quoted-
                              strings>
white space            =  [CRLF] | 1*(SP | HT)
```

General Headers

General headers are applicable to both request and response messages. They contain information about the message itself rather than about the entity encapsulated by it. Currently there are only two general headers: Date and Pragma. Other general headers can only be added by formally extending the protocol.

General headers have the following form:

```
General-Header      =   "Date" ":" HTTP-date
                    |   "Pragma" ":" "no-cache" | extension-pragma
extension-pragma    =   token [ "=" word ]
```

> **Note:** *HTTP 1.1 defines five additional general header fields—Cache-control, Connection, Transfer-encoding, Upgrade, and Via.*

Date Header

The Date header defines the date and time that the message was created in the client or the server. A server should always include a date field in responses. A client need only include a date field if the request message contains an entity body (for example, a POST request).

Three different date/time formats can be used within HTTP headers such as Date (date/time values are also used in the If-Modified-Since request header, and Expires and Last-Modified entity headers). The first and preferred format is based on the format specified in RFC 822 and RFC 1123. The second format still in common use comes from the Usenet standard RFC 1036 and only specifies a two-digit year (less useful as we approach the year 2000). The third format uses ANSI C's asctime() format. While this format should be accepted by clients and servers, it should not be generated by them. These dates must always be represented in GMT (Greenwich Mean Time or Universal time); if a GMT specifier is not present as in the asctime() format, it should be implied.

```
                                 RFC 822, updated by RFC 1123
Sun, 06 Nov 1994 08:49:37 GMT
Sunday, 06-Nov-94 08:49:37 GMT   RFC 1036
Sun Nov  6 08:49:37 1994         ANSI C's asctime() format
```

Throughout this chapter the term HTTP-Date is used to refer to any one of these three date formats.

Pragma Header

The Pragma header is a way of communicating implementation directives through the request chain to the origin server. The only formally defined directive is **no-**

cache, which overrides the cached versions of the object in any intermediary and forces an authoritative response from the origin server. For example:

```
Pragma: no-cache
```

Requests

An HTTP request is either a simple request (HTTP 0.9) or a full request. The format of simple request is just a one-line GET command with a URL argument. In a full request, each request message is made up of a request line followed by zero or more request headers, a blank line to indicate the end of the header information, and an optional entity body (POST operations only). The syntax of a request message is defined as follows:

```
Request            =  Simple-Request | Full-Request

Simple-Request     =  "GET" SP Request-URL CRLF

Full-Request       =  Request-Line
                      *( General-Header | Request-Header | Entity-Header )
                      CRLF
                      [ Entity-Body ]

Request-Line       =  Method SP Request-URL SP HTTP-Version CRLF

Method             =  "GET" | "HEAD" | "POST" | extension-method

extension-method   =  token
```

The request line specifies the request method (such as GET, POST), the request URL, and a string specifying the HTTP version being used. New methods can easily be introduced without requiring formal changes to the protocol. If a server does not support a method, then the client is informed via the appropriate response status code (501 Not implemented).

An HTTP-Version field consists of a major version number followed by a minor version number in the following form:

```
HTTP-Version   = "HTTP" "/" 1*DIGIT "." 1*DIGIT
```

For example: HTTP/1.1 or HTTP/0.9.

Request Headers

A request header allows the client to pass information to the server about the message or the client itself. Each header modifies the meaning of the request in some way. HTTP 1.0 defines five types of request headers:

```
Request-Header        =   "Authorization" ":" credentials
                      |   "From" ":" mailbox
                      |   "If-Modified-Since" ":" HTTP-date
                      |   "Referer" ":" ( absolute-URL | relative-URL )
                      |   "User-Agent" ":" 1*( product | comment )
```

> **Note:** HTTP 1.1 adds 12 additional types: Accept, Accept-Charset, Accept-Encoding, Accept-Language, Host, If-Match, If-None-Match, If-Range, If-Unmodified-Since, Max-Forwards, Proxy-Authorization, Range.

Authorization Header

The Authorization header field is used to authenticate the client request to a server. The header field specifies the authorization credentials required to gain access to the security realm of the resource. Full details of the HTTP authentication mechanism are given in Section "Access Authentication."

From Header

The From header specifies the email address of the user responsible for generating the message. For example:

```
From: paulm@optimation.co.nz
```

If-Modified-Since Header

The If-Modified-Since header is used to construct a conditional GET request where the object is only retrieved if it has been modified since the specified date. For example:

```
If-Modified-Since: Thursday, 08-Aug-96 04:01:54 GMT
```

Referer Header

The Referer header allows the client to specify the address of the object from which the request URL was obtained. This is often useful for logging purposes, for tracing the source of old links, or for returning to a previous page. For example, a CGI script can inspect the Referer field and use this as a general mechanism for generating a link back to a table of contents page. This address can be an absolute or a relative URL. Relative URLs are interpreted as being relative to the request URL. For example:

```
Referer: http://www.optimation.co.nz/optimation/index.htm
```

User-Agent Header

The User-Agent header contains product-specific information about the client that makes the request. Analogous to the Server Response Header, this information takes the form Product/Version. For example, Netscape Navigator Gold Version 3.0 for Windows 95 emits:

```
User-Agent: Mozilla/3.0Gold (Win95; I)
```

CGI programs that dynamically determine the browser type and display content that takes advantage of a browser's special features often use this field.

GET Request Example

In Session 1.2, we eavesdrop on the GET request generated by Netscape Navigator when fetching the author's home page. Notice that the request URL generated by Netscape is an absolute URL. Absolute URLs are sent by the client when talking to a proxy server—even if the proxy server satisfies the request. Also note the use of the If-Modified-Since header, which makes this a conditional GET request.

Session 1.2   Example session showing a Navigator generated GET request.

```
GET http://ow:8080/ose/staff/web/paulm/paulm.htm HTTP/1.0
If-Modified-Since: Thursday, 08-Aug-96 04:01:54 GMT; length = 7305
Proxy-Connection: Keep-Alive
User-Agent: Mozilla/3.0Gold (Win95; I)
Host: ow:8080
Accept: image/gif, image/x-xbitmap, image/jpeg, image/pjpeg, */*
```

The resulting trace shows the inclusion of standard request headers (as defined above) and also some that are not formally part of HTTP 1.0 (from HTTMP 1.1). For example, the Accept header field defines a list of media types that are acceptable responses to the request. The asterisk is used to group media types and subtypes into ranges—thus, */* means all known types and subtypes, and image/* means all subtypes of the type image.

Also from HTTP 1.1 is the Host header, which, if supported by the server, would actually determine the host used to satisfy the request if an absolute URL (containing the host address) was not specified.

Navigator is indicating that it supports the Keep-Alive form of persistent connection sometimes used in HTTP 1.0 by using the Proxy-Connection header. Although the Proxy-Connection header is not defined in HTTP 1.0 or 1.1, it is presumably specific to Netscape servers.

Responses

A server generates response messages as a result of request messages sent to it by a client. Simple responses are only generated in response to HTTP 0.9 requests (or if the server only supports HTTP 0.9). HTTP 0.9 requests are distinguished by their lack of a protocol version field. A simple response is simply the entity itself, normally encoded as HTML, and without any additional status or header information.

> **Note:** Because no status line appears in HTTP 0.9, any server errors must be returned within the body of the HTML message. This means that the client must parse the HTML message to discover which error has occurred.

The rule below depicts the syntax for a full response. A full response is similar in syntax to a full request and consists of a status line followed by zero or more header lines. A blank line indicates the end of the headers and an optional entity body.

```
Response          =  Simple-Response | Full-Response

Simple-Response   =  [ Entity-Body ]

Full-Response     =  Status-Line
                     *( General-Header | Response-Header | Entity-Header )
```

```
                         CRLF
                         [ Entity-Body ]
Status-Line        =     HTTP-Version SP Status-Code SP Reason-Phrase CRLF
```

The status line is always the first line of a response header and contains the protocol version string, a three-digit status code, and a human-readable reason phrase that explains the status code in plain English—each separated by a space. The status code tells the client whether or not the request was successful.

The version string and the status code together are usually sufficient to differentiate a simple HTTP 0.9 response from a full one.

Status Codes

While the status codes are formally defined, the corresponding reason phrases can be written to suit local conditions. An application is not required to understand all the status codes as long as it understands at least the five classes of codes listed in Table 1.5 by inspecting the code's first digit. An application may also arbitrarily extend the range of status codes by introducing new classes or extending the range of existing classes. The actual code values for each category are defined in Table 1.6.

Table 1.5 Response status code categories.

Code	Status Code Type	Meaning
1xx	Informational	Used only for experimental purposes.
2xx	Success	Indicates that the request was received, understood, and accepted by the server.
3xx	Redirection	Indicates that the client must do more work to satisfy the request. In the case of a GET request, this typically means repeating the request again, against one of the alternate URLs specified in the response.
4xx	Client Error	Indicates that the client has generated an error in the server. The client must stop sending data if it receives this class of error.
5xx	Server Error	Indicates that the server has itself generated an error or is unable to satisfy a request. The client must stop sending data if it receives this class of error.

Table 1.6 Response status code values.

Code	Meaning
200	The request was successful and the correct response sent.
201	A new resource has been created by the server (POST).
202	The request has been accepted but processing is not complete—for example, a long-running database operation.
204	The request was successful but there is no content to return.
301	The requested resource has moved to a new permanent URL.
302	The requested resource has moved to a temporary URL.
304	The requested resource has not been modified (conditional GET).
401	An unauthorized request—authentication is required.
403	The request has been understood but the server has denied access to the resource—typically either server or client does not have permission to access the file.
404	The requested resource cannot be found.
500	An internal server error has occurred.
501	The server has not implemented the request method.
502	Bad gateway (invalid response from gateway or upstream server).
503	The server is too busy to handle the request.

Response Headers

The purpose of the response header is to allow the server to return more information than just the status code. New response headers can be created and used informally providing there is agreement between the parties using them, however, it would take a protocol change to formally include new headers. HTTP 1.0 defines only three response header fields as defined below:

```
Response-Header    =  "Location" ":" absolute-URL
                   |  "Server" ":" 1*(product | comment)
                   |  WWW-Authenticate = "WWW-Authenticate" ":" challenge
```

Note: HTTP 1.1 defines a further six response header fields: Age, Proxy-Authenticate, Public, Retry-After, Vary, and Warning.

Location

The Location response header defines the actual location of the requested URL and represents it as an absolute URL. This header is used, for example, when redirecting a Web browser to a new location for the requested resource.

Server

The Server response header contains product and version information about the server that generated the response. This information is of the form product/version. For example:

```
Server: Apache/1.2b3
```

or

```
Server: Netscape-Enterprise/2.0a.
```

WWW-Authenticate

The WWW-Authenticate response header is used to challenge a client when the client makes a request for a protected resource. For example:

```
WWW-authenticate: basic realm="Optimation Staff Pages"
```

This header must be included in **401** (**Unauthorized**) response messages from the server and contains at least one challenge indicating the authentication schemes applicable to the requested URL. In the above example the **basic** authentication scheme is specified. Refer to section "Access Authentication," later in this chapter, for details on HTTP's authentication mechanism.

Entity Headers

Like general headers, entity headers are applicable to either request or response messages. An entity header further describes the entity body or, if no body is present, then the resource specified by the request.

HTTP 1.0 formally defines six entity header fields and the extension-header field, which provides an informal mechanism for defining new entity headers without any need to change the protocol. The syntax of an entity header is defined as follows:

```
Entity-Header    =  "Allow" ":" method-list
                 |  "Content-Type" ":" media-type
                 |  "Content-Length" ":" decimal-number
                 |  "Content-Encoding" ":" "x-gzip" | "x-compress" | token
                 |  "Expires" ":" HTTP-date
                 |  "Last-Modified" ":" HTTP-date
                 |  extension-header
extension-header=  HTTP-header
```

> **Note:** *HTTP 1.1 defines a further six entity header fields: Content-Base, Content-Language, Content-Location, Content-MD5, Content-Range, and Etag.*

Allow

The Allow header informs the client of the methods supported by the resource specified in the request URL. This field might be as follows:

```
Allow: GET, HEAD
```

This is applicable to all requests except for POST, in which the header is ignored if it is supplied. While it is possible for methods not listed in the Allow header to be applied to the resource, this is not good practice. In any event, the server determines the actual methods applicable to a resource. A proxy server must not modify this header based on its own view of which methods apply to a resource—it must pass the header on unmodified so that it can be interpreted by the origin server.

Content-Type

The Content-Type header field specifies the data type of the entity contained within the message or in the case of a HEAD request, the media type of the entity that would have been sent. A Web browser typically inspects this header so that it can invoke the appropriate viewer for displaying the entity to the user.

The media type field has the following form:

```
media-type              =  type "/" subtype *( ";" parameter )
parameter               =  attribute "=" value
attribute               =  token
value                   =  token | quoted-string
```

In this rule, *type* represents a top-level data type such as text, image, audio, and the like. Subtype represents a specific format of that type. For example, the most common media type is:

```
Content-type: text/html
```

This tells the browser that the entity is text formatted as HTML and will usually result in the browser displaying the entity (an HTML document) using the browser's HTML viewer.

The server typically sets the media type in the Content-Type header by looking at the file-extension of the specified resource. For example, the resource feedback.html is identified by the server as an HTML document through its .html file extension resulting in a media type of text/html.

> **Note:** *If the server is unable to determine the type from the file extension, the media type is set to text/plain.*

The media type provides for an optional set of parameters. The most common parameter is **charset**, which allows the character set of the data to be explicitly defined. If the **charset** parameter is not defined for a message of type text, the character set defaults to ISO-8859-1. Any **charset** token can be passed as a parameter, for example:

```
Content-type: text/html; charset=US-ASCII
```

You should only draw **charset** tokens from the set of character sets maintained by the IANA Character Set Registry.

> **Note:** *IANA (Internet Assigned Number Authority) is an Internet organization responsible for the allocation of unique parameters for Internet protocols. For example, IANA manages the registration of new media types, port numbers, protocol numbers. For more information visit IANA at **www.iana.org/iana**.*

IANA, however, does not define a consistent set of tokens for the character sets most likely to be used with HTTP (those specified for use in RFC 1521, US-ASCII, and ISO-8859). Refer to RFC 1945 for the specific character-set tokens.

Further details on media types and their interpretation by Web browsers can be found in the section "Media Types," later in this chapter.

Content-Length

The Content-Length header works in combination with the Content-Type header and specifies the length (in bytes) of the entity embedded in the message, regardless of its media type. For example, the following header field

```
Content-Length: 758
```

should always be specified when the length of the entity can be established prior to transmission of the message. If no length field is provided, the length of response messages can be calculated when the server closes the connection. This obviously can't work for request messages because the client would close the connection before the server could respond. In this case, it will respond with a status code of **400** (bad request).

Content-Encoding

The Content-Encoding header is a modifier to the media type defined by the Content-Type header field. This header specifies an additional operation to be performed by the recipient to decode the entity contained within a message. Normally, this operation will be some form of decompression.

Session 1.3 shows a trace of a session showing a Navigator request for a compressed resource called pmworld.gz.

Session 1.3   Example Navigator session showing a GET request to a compressed resource.

```
GET /ose/staff/web/paulm/pmworld.gz HTTP/1.0
Referer: http://ow:8080/ose/staff/web/paulm/paulm.htm
Connection: Keep-Alive
User-Agent: Mozilla/3.0Gold (Win95;I)
Host: ow:8080
Accept: image/gif, image/x-x, bitmap, image/jpeg, image/pjpeg, */*
```

The server's response to Session 1.3 is as follows:

```
HTTP/1.1 200 OK
Date: Fri, 31 Jan 1997 20:58:37 GMT
```

```
Server: Apache/1.2b3
Connection: Keep-Alive
Keep-Alive: timeout=15, max=5
Content-type: application/x-gzip
Content-Encoding: x-gzip
Last-Modified: Fri, 31 Jan 1997 20:58:37 GMT
ETag: W/"c6c7-196-32f25d5b"
Content-Length: 406
Accept-Ranges: bytes
```

The media type of pmworld.gz is application/x-gzip, meaning that the browser must invoke an application able to cope with the media subtype x-gzip. The Content-Encoding field indicates that the x-gzip encoding scheme has been applied to the entity and that the gzip application should be used to decode the entity. Encoding operations formally supported are listed in Table 1.7.

The Content-Encoding header will accept an arbitrary token as a parameter, allowing other encoding schemes to be specified as needed.

> **Note:** *The ability to use **compress** or **gzip** as encoding specifiers is a historical aberration; in general, the name of the scheme should not be the same as the program used to implement it.*

Expires

The Expires header field affects how resources are cached, and specifies a date and time beyond which the specified resource is considered out of date. This is useful for resources that are being updated regularly, data-producing resources such as CGI scripts, or resources that will disappear after a certain date. Such resources should not be cached after the specified expiration date. Similarly, if the expiration date is the same or earlier than the date in the Date header, the resource must not be cached.

Table 1.7   Content-encoding operations.

Operation	Description
x-compress (or compress)	This is the format used by the compress program normally found with Unix. Compress implements adaptive Lempel-Ziv-Welch coding (LZW).
x-gzip (or gzip)	The format used by GNU's freeware gzip program. gzip also implements a Lempel-Ziv algorithm (LZ77 with 32-bit CRC).

Last-Modified

The Last-Modified header field indicates when the resource was last updated on the server. The way the date is calculated depends on the type of resource. For example, if the resource were a file, the Last-Modified date would be the file's date-of-last-modification as stored by the file system. If the client has a copy of the resource that is older than the Last-Modified date in its cache, the client ignores its local copy and retrieves the updated one. If the specified date is later than response message's creation date (specified in the response's Date header), the Last-Modified date is set to the message creation date.

GET Response Example

In Session 1.4, we look more closely at the response generated by a GET request to an image on the author's home page.

Session 1.4   Example Telnet session showing a GET request to an image file.

```
telnet morgan 80                   telnet to the Web server on morgan
                                       at port 80

Trying 10.0.0.20...                Displayed by telnet
Connected to morgan.               Displayed by telnet
Escape character is '^]'.          Displayed by telnet
GET /ose/staff/web/paulm/
   pmhome.gif HTTP/1.0             We type the HTTP 1.0 GET request
                                       and terminate with a blank line


HTTP/1.1 200 OK                    Response from the server
Date: Sun, 26 Jan 1997 20:50:52 GMT
Server: Apache/1.2b3
Connection: close
Content-type: image/gif
Last-Modified: Mon, 05 Aug 1996 05:40:20 GMT
ETag: "6b74-218-32058944"
Content-Length: 536
Accept-Ranges: bytes

                                   Blank line
...                                The bytes making up the GIF image
                                   are displayed here

Connection closed by foreign host  Displayed by telnet
```

Although we've issued our request as a version 1.0 client, the server has responded that it supports version 1.1. The **200 OK** status code indicates that the server successfully satisfied the request. The Server response header field informs us that the Apache Version 1.2b3 server is being used. We can also see the use of the Content-Type and Content-Length response header fields. These tell us that the object contained in the response is of type image with a subtype of GIF and the length of the GIF image is 536 bytes.

The Accept-Ranges response header field (from HTTP 1.1) informs us that the Apache server accepts byte-range requests—for example, a request in which only a specified portion of the object is retrieved.

Another HTTP 1.1 feature is the Connection general header field, which defines options specific to the connection. In version 1.1, **Connection: close** means that the connection will be closed after the response has completed and is therefore not to be regarded as a persistent connection. Etag (short for Entity Tag), also from HTTP 1.1, defines a tag that can be used as an alternative to HTTP 1.0's Last-Modified entity header field to determine if the entity has changed.

Request Methods

We have already briefly discussed the GET method. Now we'll take a closer look at the methods formally defined by HTTP 1.0: GET, HEAD, and PUSH. The PUT method is also briefly discussed, although this has only recently been formally promoted to HTTP 1.1.

> **Note:** *Method names are case sensitive and that all currently defined methods are in uppercase.*

HTTP 1.1 formally introduces the request methods PUT and DELETE plus new request methods OPTIONS, and TRACE. Additional methods also included are PATCH, LINK, and UNLINK.

GET

The GET method retrieves the object specified by the request URL. When the URL specifies a static resource (typically an HTML document), the contents of the resource are returned as the entity body. In the case of a dynamic resource like a CGI script, the output generated by the resource is returned.

GET can also be used to submit data that has been entered via an HTML form, to a server. In this case, the data is appended to the request URL as a sequence of name/value pairs (refer to "Example POST Session" later in this section). This technique should only be used for small amounts of data.

> **Note:** When the GET request includes an If-Modified-Since request header field, the GET becomes a conditional GET and the object is only returned if it has been modified since the date and time specified in the header.

HEAD

HEAD is identical to the GET method except that no entity body is returned in the response. All other information, including the entity header fields, is returned. This method is often used to validate the existence of a resource without actually retrieving it. There is no such thing as a conditional HEAD. If an If-Modified-Since field is present in the request, it is ignored.

To illustrate, see Session 1.5, which repeats the example in Session 1.4, replacing the GET with a HEAD request.

Session 1.5 Example Telnet session showing a HEAD request.

```
telnet morgan 80                    telnet to the Web server on morgan
                                    at port 80

Trying 10.0.0.20...                 Displayed by telnet
Connected to morgan.                Displayed by telnet
Escape character is '^]'.           Displayed by telnet
HEAD /ose/staff/web/paulm/
   pmhome.gif HTTP/1.0              We type this linefollowed by a
                                    blank line to end the request

HTTP/1.1 200 OK
Date: Mon, 27 Jan 1997 03:56:58 GMT
Server: Apache/1.2b3
Connection: close
Content-type: image/gif
Last-Modified: Mon, 05 Aug 1996 05:40:20 GMT
ETag: "6b74-218-32058944"
Content-Length: 536
```

```
Accept-Ranges: bytes

                                          Blank line
Connection closed by foreign host         Displayed by telnet
```

The same headers have been returned as in Session 1.4, but no entity body has been transmitted.

POST

The POST method allows an entity to be encapsulated in a request and transmitted to the server for further action. Usually, the data transmitted is the contents of a form input by the user. The action performed by the server is defined by the request URL, which in the case of a form is usually a CGI script that accepts the form fields as input and generates an HTML document as output.

> **Note:** POST should be used when you have a large amount of data, possibly from a large form, to send to the server. Using a GET request to transfer a large amount of data may not be possible because most browsers and servers restrict the length of a URL to 1024 bytes.

Session 1.6 defines a user feedback form. The form illustrates the use of the POST method to send information entered by the user to the server for processing by a CGI script. The form requires the user to enter feedback comments, name, company, and email details. Once these fields are entered and the form's submit button is pressed, a POST request is formulated and the entered fields transmitted in the body of the request message.

Session 1.6   An HTML definition of a user feedback form.

```
<FORM method="POST" action="http://www.optimation.co.nz/cgi-bin/
  optimation/feedback.bat">
        <P>What kind of comment would you like to send?</P>
        <PRE>
        <INPUT type=radio name="MessageType" value="Complaint">Complaint
        <INPUT type=radio name="MessageType" value="Problem">Problem
        <INPUT type=radio checked name="MessageType"
          value="Suggestion">Suggestion
        <INPUT type=radio name="MessageType" value="Praise">Praise
          (Required)
        </PRE>
```

```
<P>Enter your comments in the space provided below:</P>
<PRE>
<TEXTAREA name="Comments" rows=5 cols=57></TEXTAREA>(Required)
</PRE>

<P>Tell us how to get in touch with you:</P>
<PRE>
Name     <INPUT type=text size=53 maxlength=256 name="userName">
  (Required)
Company  <INPUT type=text size=53 maxlength=256
  name="companyName"> (Required)
E-mail   <INPUT type=text size=35 maxlength=256 name="userEmail">
  (Required)
Tel      <INPUT type=text size=35 maxlength=256 name="userPhone">
FAX      <INPUT type=text size=35 maxlength=256 name="userFAX">
</PRE>

<INPUT type=submit name="submitButton" value="Submit
  Feedback"><B> or </B>
<INPUT type=reset name="clearButton" value="Clear this Form">
</FORM>
```

In Session 1.7, we snoop the connection between the client and server to view first-hand the format of the request and the corresponding response.

Session 1.7 Example session showing a Navigator-generated POST request.

```
POST http://www.optimation.co.nz/cgi-bin/optimation/feedback.bat HTTP/1.0
Referer: http://www.optimation.co.nz/optimation/seref/support/
  alphafeed.htm
Proxy-Connection: Keep-Alive
User-Agent: Mozilla/3.0Gold (Win95; I)
Host: www.optimation.co.nz
Accept: image/gif, image/x-xbitmap, image/jpeg, image/pjpeg, */*
Content-type: application/x-www-form-urlencoded
Content-length: 203

MessageType=Praise&Comments=Great+framework%0D%0AWhat+comes+next%3F&
userName=Paul+McGlashan&companyName=Optimation+NZ+Ltd&
userEmail=paulm@optimation.co.nz&userPhone=&userFAX=&
submitButton=Submit+Feedback
```

A number of things are worth noting about the POST request. The Content-Type field is set to application/x-www-form-urlencoded (the default media type for requests containing the contents of an HTML form). At the HTML level, the default form encoding can be overridden using the ENCTYPE attribute of the FORM tag.

Content-Length is mandatory in a POST request; it tells the server the size of the entity body that follows. In this case, the entity consists of a one-line query string formatted according to the x-www-form-urlencoded subtype. (The field name and value pairs from the form are delimited by &, spaces are replaced by +, and special characters or nonprintable characters are replaced by the corresponding hexadecimal escape sequences.) In this example, there have been a number of characters escaped. The line feed character in the comments field has been translated into a %0D%0A and the ? in the comments field translated into %3F.

Note that the status code returned by the server is **200** (Request Successful). Had the request required the resource to be created on the server, the code would have been **201** (Resource Created) and the response would have contained further information about the new resource—including its location.

In the example shown in Session 1.8, the server (Netscape Enterprise Server) supports only HTTP 1.0. On receiving the request, the server executes the CGI script feedback.bat specified in the request URL. The script then outputs an HTML document to its standard output and this document is transmitted back to the client as the body of the response message. Note that the Content-Type header field defines the document to be of type text and subtype HTML.

Session 1.8   Netscape Enterprise Server's Response to the POST request.

```
HTTP/1.0 200 OK
Server: Netscape-Enterprise/2.0a
Date: Sat, 01 Feb 1997 08:40:47 GMT
Content-type: text/html

<html>..<head>..<title>
SEREF Registration
</title>
</head>
<body>
<!DOCTYPE HTML PUBLIC "-//IETF//DTD HTML//EN">
<html>
<head>
```

```
<title>SEREF Download Form</title>
<meta name="GENERATOR" content="Microsoft FrontPage 1.1">
</head>
<body bgcolor="#COCOCO" text="#0000FF" link="#808040">
<h1 align=center>SEREF Feedback Form Accepted</h1>
<hr>
<p align=center>Thank you for your feedback</p>
<hr>
<p align=center><font size=2><b>Copyright </b>&#169; <b>1996 Optimation
   New Zealand Ltd.</b></font></p>
<h5 align=center><i>SEREF </i>is a trademark of Optimation New Zealand
   Ltd.</h5>
</body>
</html>
</body>
</html>
```

PUT

The PUT method is very similar to POST. The difference between them is the way the request URL is treated. The URL in a POST request specifies a resource that consumes the enclosed entity, which might be a CGI script that accepts the entity body as input and processes it. In contrast, the URL specified in a PUT request identifies a resource that should be created (if the resource does not already exist) or updated (if the resource does exist). The enclosed entity is the actual data to be placed under the resource.

Media Types

HTTP messages use a MIME-like Content-Type header field to indicate the data type of the entity within a message. This provides an extensible data typing mechanism that allows HTTP to cater to an unlimited range of data types. Supported types must first be registered with IANA. RFC 1590 defines the media type registration process, however, there are many unregistered types and subtypes in common use.

Common Media Types

MIME defines seven top-level types made up of five discrete types and two composite types.

The five discrete types are:

- Application

- Audio

- Image

- Text

- Video

MIME's two composite types are:

- Message

- Multipart

> **Note:** *For a full list of media types visit IANA,* ***ftp://ftp.isi.edu/in-notes/ iana/assignments/media-types***.

While further top-level types may be defined in the future, it is likely that the current set will be sufficient and that the subtype mechanism will handle any new data types. If new top-level types are needed for any reason, they must be prefixed with **x-** in order to highlight their nonstandard status.

Subtypes are treated similarly. New unregistered subtypes are introduced by prefixing the subtype name with **x-**, which distinguishes them as an extended or experimental subtype.

Most of the discrete top-level types are self-explanatory. Others, like application, message, and multipart, require some further explanation.

Application Types

The purpose of the application type is to distinguish application-dependent content. PostScript files are a common example as in:

```
Content-type: application/postscript
```

We have already seen the use of one of the experimental application types (application/x-www-form-urlencoded) used to identify an entity created from the output of an HTML form.

Message Types

An entity labeled as a message type is a message that may have objects embedded within it. For example, the message/http media type defined in RFC 2068 is used in HTTP 1.1's TRACE request header for remote loop-back testing and returns an entity that is the entire request message to the client.

Multipart Types

The multipart type is used to identify compound entities. Compound entities contain multiple parts, in which each part may be a different media type. Traditionally, this type has been used to identify mail messages containing one or more file attachments. Part of the multipart type specification is a boundary string used to delimit each part. Each part subsequently has its own Content-Type and Content-Length fields defining the entity encoded for that part.

The multipart/form-data media type has been formally introduced into HTTP 1.1 to handle the uploading of files to a server from a client. While HTTP 1.0 defines the PUT command for the purposes of uploading files, this has not been widely adopted. Instead an alternative scheme has been defined (see RFC 1867) that uses a form's POST method with an enctype of **multipart/form-data** instead of **x-www-form-urlencoded**.

Instead of the name=value pairs (representing the form's contents) being sent as an encoded string in the body of the request, each pair is represented as a separate MIME body part. Typically the name corresponds to a form field containing the file name of a file to be uploaded. The field name and the file name are specified in a Content-Disposition header. Following this header is the MIME body part consisting of a Content-Type header defining the media type of the file contents followed by a blank line and then the contents of the file. For example:

```
Content-Type: multipart/form-data; boundary=SomethingUnique
—SomethingUnique
Content-Disposition: form-data; name="filename"; filename="mydata.txt"
Content-type: text/plain

Here is the contents of my file called mydata.txt …
—SomethingUnique—
```

File upload is not yet widely supported by the browser vendors. Netscape was the first to provide an implementation, however this differed from RFC 1867 in that it did not require a Content-Type header to describe each body part. In the Netscape implementation, files are simply uploaded in their native format without any encoding. The multipart/mixed media type is often used as the basis for implementing server-side push applications. Netscape has introduced two experimental media types (multipart/x-mixed and multipart/x-mixed-replace) specifically for this purpose. Server-side push is frequently used to implement simple image animations where each animation frame is stored as a separate image body part in the response message.

When the browser receives a response with a multipart/x-mixed-replace media type, it keeps the connection open to keep reading body parts. The browser displays each body part after it is assembled, and each part replaces the one displayed before it. This process continues until an end marker is encountered or the client breaks the connection. (For example, the process will stop if the user hits the browser's stop button.) If the server-side application generates data indefinitely, the client must break the connection to halt the process.

The following hypothetical example would theoretically get the browser to display a spinning line in one character cell:

```
Content-type: multipart/x-mixed-replace; boundary=qwerty

--qwerty
Content-type: text/plain
|
--qwerty
Content-type: text/plain
/
--qwerty
Content-type: text/plain
-
--qwerty
Content-type: text/plain
\
--qwerty
Content-type: text/plain
|
--qwerty--
```

Note that the boundary delimiter is formed by prefixing the boundary string specified in the Content-Type header with two "-" characters. The final boundary delimiter also has two "-" characters appended to it.

Browser Interpretation Of Media Types

Following a request for a resource, the Web browser receives the resulting response message and inspects the Content-Type field to discover the media type of the entity within. The browser uses the media type to perform an action appropriate to the type. For responses containing a text/html entity, it usually displays the HTML document in the browser.

Most browsers provide a mechanism for registering new media types and a corresponding action. Netscape Navigator, for example, provides support for a large number of default media types and actions. In addition, Netscape Navigator allows the user to add media types and actions.

When a user registers a new media type, Navigator provides the following four possible actions:

- Ask User: The browser does not know the type and the user has the option of saving the entity to disk or invoking an application to handle it.

- Browser: The action is to view the entity in the browser window.

- Save to Disk: The user has the option of saving the entity to disk.

- Execute an Application: A registered application is invoked to process the entity.

Browser Plug-ins To Handle Media Types

A browser such as Netscape can also be extended via plug-ins to handle media types in a more seamless fashion. Plug-ins are essentially a library that gets dynamically loaded by the browser when it detects a media type that matches one of the registered plug-ins. The benefit of the using plug-ins over executing an application is that plug-ins operate within the context of the browser, rather than outside as a separate process.

The are two types of plug-ins: *embedded* and *full-page* plug-ins. An embedded plug-in appears inline in the HTML content and, when activated, occupies a portion of the displayed HTML page (possibly to display an image or a movie). A full-page plug-in is activated when a file matching the plug-in's media type is requested. A full-page plug-in typically implements a viewer to display the file and takes over the browser window. Adobe's Acrobat viewer is a good example of a full-page plug-in.

The Relationship Between HTTP And MIME

HTTP draws heavily on MIME for the structure of its headers and encoding of message content. However, because MIME focuses specifically on the needs of Internet mail, HTTP has introduced some differences, listed here:

- MIME requires each entity to be translated into a standard form (canonical form) specific to the entity's media type. HTTP follows this requirement but has different rules for handling the text media type, particularly the use of CR and LF. In HTTP, CRLF, CR, or LF may be used as line break characters within text, whereas in MIME only CRLF can be used.

- In MIME, the Content-Length header applies only to the message/external-body media type and is optional; in HTTP, it should be present whenever it is possible to calculate the length of the entity body.

- HTTP restricts the wide range of date formats acceptable in MIME to just three formats to simplify date handling.

- MIME has no equivalent to HTTP's Content-Encoding header field.

- HTTP does not use MIME's Content-Transfer-Encoding header. Instead, it introduces the Transfer-Encoding header for applying a transformation to an entity. This header is a property of the message rather than the entity within it. Whereas MIME applies Content-Transfer-Encoding to an entity to ensure that it can safely pass through 7-bit environments, HTTP assumes an 8-bit clean environment and instead defines a mechanism for reliably sending large amounts of data by breaking up the message into well-defined chunks.

- HTTP allows multipart body parts to include any header information relevant to the part, whereas MIME restricts these headers to be those prefixed with **Content-**.

HTTP messages can also use the MIME-Version header to indicate that the message is MIME conformant:

```
MIME-Version: 1.0
```

Use of this header is currently optional in HTTP because the header is often used indiscriminately. However, according to RFC 2049, which defines MIME protocol conformance criteria, inclusion of the MIME-Version header is actually mandatory.

Access Authentication

HTTP supports a simple challenge-response mechanism for a server to authenticate client requests. The dialogue between client and server is depicted in Figure 1.4.

When a request is initially made for a protected resource, the server responds with a **401** (Unauthorized Access) response message that contains a www-authenticate response header. The response header contains a challenge that specifies the scheme to use for authenticating the request, the protection realm to which the requested resource belongs, and an optional list of name=value pairs. The realm is fully identified by concatenating the realm value specified in the response with the root URL of the server. Each realm maintained by the server can have its own authentication scheme and associated access database.

```
www-authenticate      =    "www-authenticate" ":" challenge
challenge             =    auth-scheme 1*SP realm *( "," auth-param )
auth-scheme           =    token
auth-param            =    token "=" quoted-string
realm                 =    "realm" "=" realm-value
realm-value           =    quoted-string
```

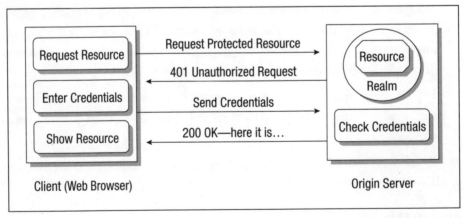

Figure 1.4
The challenge-response dialogue.

Once the client has been challenged with the server's **401** response, the client may respond by sending a new request for the resource containing an Authorization header that specifies the credentials needed to authenticate the request for the realm containing the resource.

```
Authorization          = "Authorization " ":" credentials
credentials            = basic-credentials
                       | ( auth-scheme #auth-param )
```

Once authenticated, the same credentials can be used for subsequent requests. The lifetime of these credentials is dependent on the scheme. The server can deny an authorization request with a **403** (Forbidden) response.

In addition to HTTP's simple challenge-response mechanism, other authentication and security mechanisms can also be applied. These include encryption at the transport layer using SSL (Secure Sockets Layer) or message-based approaches such as S-HTTP [Rescorla, Schiffman].

Basic Authentication Scheme

HTTP defines a basic authentication scheme only. Other schemes can be introduced simply by specifying the scheme name and optional parameters in the **401** challenge message. Any new scheme, of course, would need to be understood by both clients and servers participating in its use.

The basic scheme requires the client credentials for each realm to be in the form of a user name and a password. The syntax for the credentials is:

```
basic-credentials      = "Basic" SP basic-cookie
basic-cookie           = <base64 [5] encoding of userid-password,
                           except not limited to 76 char/line>
userid-password        = [ token ] ":" *TEXT
```

In the following example, we see a client request for a protected resource, paulm.html, and the resulting **401** challenge message from the server. The challenge contains the WWW-Authenticate header:

```
WWW-authenticate: basic realm="Optimation Staff Pages"
```

This indicates that the requested URL is authenticated via the basic scheme and protected by the realm called Optimation Staff Pages. In response to this challenge, the Web browser prompts the user for a name and password for the specified realm. In this example, the name administrator and password **let me in** have been supplied.

The user name and password credentials are encoded using a simple BASE64 transformation (see the next section, "BASE64 Encoding") and formatted into the Authorization header of the new request. In the example shown in Session 1.9, the client credentials are deemed incorrect; the server rejects them with a **401** response.

Session 1.9   Example session showing an invalid challenge and response.

```
GET http://www.optimation.co.nz/optimation/private/paulm.html HTTP/1.0
Proxy-Connection: Keep-Alive
User-Agent: Mozilla/3.0Gold (Win95; I)
Host: www.optimation.co.nz
Accept: image/gif, image/x-xbitmap, image/jpeg, image/pjpeg, */*

HTTP/1.0 401 Unauthorized
Server: Netscape-Enterprise/2.0a
Date: Sun, 02 Feb 1997 09:14:40 GMT
WWW-authenticate: basic realm="Optimation Staff Pages"
Content-type: text/html

<HTML><HEAD><TITLE>Unauthorized</TITLE></HEAD>
<BODY>< H1>Unauthorized</H1>.
Proper authorization is required for this area. Either your browser does
   not perform authorization, or your authorization has failed
</BODY></HTML>

GET http://www.optimation.co.nz/optimation/private/paulm.html HTTP/1.0
Proxy-Connection: Keep-Alive
User-Agent: Mozilla/3.0Gold (Win95; I)
Host: www.optimation.co.nz
Accept: image/gif, image/x-xbitmap, image/jpeg, image/pjpeg, */*
Authorization: Basic YWRtaW5pc3RyYXRvcjpsZXQgbWUgaW4=
HTTP/1.0 401 Unauthorized
Server: Netscape-Enterprise/2.0a
Date: Sun, 02 Feb 1997 09:14:53 GMT
WWW-authenticate: basic realm="Optimation Staff Pages"
Content-type: text/html

<HTML><HEAD><TITLE>Unauthorized</TITLE></HEAD>
<BODY><H1>Unauthorized</H1>.
```

```
Proper authorization is required for this area. Either your browser does
  not perform authorization, or your authorization has failed
</BODY></HTML>
```

Session 1.10 shows a successful authorization request. The correct credentials **paulm** and **secretd00r** have been supplied and the server responds with a **200** (Successful Request) response containing the requested resource.

Session 1.10 Example session showing a valid challenge and response.

```
GET http://www.optimation.co.nz/optimation/private/paulm.html HTTP/1.0
Proxy-Connection: Keep-Alive
User-Agent: Mozilla/3.0Gold (Win95; I)
Host: www.optimation.co.nz
Accept: image/gif, image/x-xbitmap, image/jpeg, image/pjpeg, */*

HTTP/1.0 401 Unauthorized
Server: Netscape-Enterprise/2.0a
Date: Sun, 02 Feb 1997 09:16:13 GMT
WWW-authenticate: basic realm="Optimation Staff Pages"
Content-type: text/html

<HTML><HEAD>
<TITLE>Unauthorized</TITLE></HEAD>.<BODY><H1>Unauthorized</H1>.
Proper authorization is required for this area. Either your browser does
  not perform authorization, or your authorization has failed
</BODY></HTML>

GET http://www.optimation.co.nz/optimation/private/paulm.html HTTP/1.0
Proxy-Connection: Keep-Alive
User-Agent: Mozilla/3.0Gold (Win95; I)
Host: www.optimation.co.nz
Accept: image/gif, image/x-xbitmap, image/jpeg, image/pjpeg, */*
Authorization: Basic cGF1bG06c2VjcmV0ZDAwcg==

HTTP/1.0 200 OK
Server: Netscape-Enterprise/2.0a
Date: Sun, 02 Feb 1997 09:38:31 GMT
Accept-ranges: bytes
Last-modified: Tue, 07 Jan 1997 01:29:06 GMT
Content-type: text/html

...
```

Due to the light level of encoding applied to the client credentials, the basic scheme is not secure and must instead rely on a trusted connection between the client and server. In addition, this scheme provides no security for the entity included in the response, which, by default is transmitted in the clear (with no encryption). While it is common practice for the basic scheme to be used over the Internet today, it should only be used where a low level of security is needed. If higher levels of security are required, use the the basic scheme in conjunction with a secure channel technology such as SSL.

Base64 Encoding

BASE64 (as described in RFC 2045) is a simple way of translating an arbitrary sequence of octets (8-bit entities) into an equivalent string of 6-bit characters. This type of encoding is often used for encoding MIME mail attachments so that binary attachments can be transmitted without their contents being misinterpreted by the systems handling the mail.

HTTP uses the BASE64 encoding to allow for safe encoding of user names and passwords that may contain nonprintable characters. This encoding also serves as an extremely weak encryption mechanism.

BASE64 encoding works by scanning an input character stream from left to right and grouping octets into threes. Each resulting group of 24 bits is then scanned from left to right and split into four lots of 6 bits.

Each 6-bit value is then treated as an index into a look-up table (see Table 1.9), which maps the 6-bit value onto a printable subset of the US-ASCII character set. This subset specifically excludes unsafe characters such as CR, LF, SP, "." and "-". The resulting translated output stream of characters must be broken up into lines not exceeding 76 characters, and any extraneous characters not part of the BASE64 alphabet must be ignored.

At the end of processing, it is possible that there may not be enough octets left over to make up the last 24-bit group. This only occurs when there are one or two octets left over. When one octet is left over, two 6-bit values must be generated. The second value must have four zero bits added to the right to pad it out to six bits. The third and fourth 6-bit values required are set to = padding characters.

Table 1.9   The BASE64 lookup table.

Value	Encoding		Value	Encoding		Value	Encoding		Value	Encoding	
Dec	Oct		Dec	Oct		Dec	Oct		Dec	Oct	
0	0	A	17	21	R	34	42	i	51	63	z
1	1	B	18	22	S	35	43	j	52	64	0
2	2	C	19	23	T	36	44	k	53	65	1
3	3	D	20	24	U	37	45	l	54	66	2
4	4	E	21	25	V	38	46	m	55	67	3
5	5	F	22	26	W	39	47	n	56	70	4
6	6	G	23	27	X	40	50	o	57	71	5
7	7	H	24	30	Y	41	51	p	58	72	6
8	10	I	25	31	Z	42	52	q	59	73	7
9	11	J	26	32	a	43	53	r	60	74	8
10	12	K	27	33	b	44	54	s	61	75	9
11	13	L	28	34	c	45	55	t	62	76	+
12	14	M	29	35	d	46	56	u	63	77	/
13	15	N	30	36	e	47	57	v			
14	16	O	31	37	f	48	60	w	(pad)	=	
15	17	P	32	40	g	49	61	x			
16	20	Q	33	41	h	50	62	y			

Similarly, when two octets are left over, three 6-bit values must be generated. The third value must have two zero bits added to the right to pad it out to six bits. The fourth 6-bit value required is set to the pad character.

As an example, let's look more closely at the authorization credentials, paulm: secretd00r, used in the previous section. Table 1.10 illustrates a simple method of translating the input string by first grouping the input string into groups of three characters. In the second column, we convert each group into its corresponding ASCII value and represent this in binary. This yields a group of 24 bits. In the third column, we regroup each set of 24 bits into four groups of 6-bit values. Finally, in the fourth column, we take each 6-bit value and use the look-up table to map the value onto the corresponding BASE64 character.

Table 1.10   BASE64 translation example.

Input string	Binary equivalent in three 8-bit groups			Binary equivalent in four 6-bit groups				BASE64-mapped output string			
	01110000	01100001	01110101	011100	000110	000101	110101				
Pau	l60	141	165	34	06	05	65	c	G	F	1
	01101100	01101101	00111010	011011	000110	110100	111010				
lm:	154	155	072	33	06	64	72	b	G	0	6
	01110011	01100101	01100011	011100	110110	010101	100011				
Sec	163	145	143	34	66	25	43	c	2	V	j
	01110010	01100101	01110100	011100	100110	010101	110100				
Ret	162	145	164	34	46	25	64	c	m	V	0
	01100100	00110000	00110000	011001	000011	000000	110000				
d00	144	060	060	31	03	00	60	Z	D	A	w
	01110010	011100	100000	PAD	PAD						
R	162			34	40			c	g	=	=

Notice that at the end of the input sequence, we had to do two things:

- Add four zeros to the right-hand side of the last octet so that we end up with an integral number of 6-bit values.

- Add two = characters to pad out the last 24-bit group.

As expected, reading the output string from left to right down the final column yields: cGF1bG06c2VjcmV0ZDAwcg==.

Digest Authentication

HTTP 1.1 defines a Digest Authentication scheme (RFC 2069) that overcomes the limitations of HTTP 1.0's Basic scheme by ensuring that only an encrypted form of the password is ever transmitted. In this scheme, both client and server must have already agreed on user names and passwords using some appropriate mechanism.

Like the Basic scheme, the Digest scheme is based on a challenge/response paradigm. When the client attempts to retrieve a protected resource, the server responds with a challenge that contains an encrypted string (a nonce value) constructed by the server. This string is part of the information that uniquely identifies the client and might contain the client IP address and a time stamp, which determines when the nonce value expires. The server can recalculate the nonce value when a client retries a request to verify that the request comes from the right source. The nonce value is opaque to the client. In other words, the client does not interpret it but just sends it back as part of the authorization information.

In response to a challenge, the client retries the request. This time, the client provides authorization information, which includes a digest concocted by encrypting the user name, password, server-supplied nonce value, the HTTP method, and the address of the requested resource. When the server receives the authorized request, it recalculates the nonce value and its own version of the digest using information provided in the request (user name, method, resource address) along with its copy of the user password. If the nonce value does not match or the server's digest does not match that supplied by the client, the request is rejected.

In this scheme, the password is transmitted as part of the encrypted digest and is never sent in the clear. Also, it is not actually necessary for the server to know the clear-text password because the digest is calculated using an encrypted form of the password only. Actually, encrypting a combination of the user name, protection realm (refer to the section "Basic Authentication Scheme," earlier in this chapter), and password constructs the value needed by the server. The mechanism for distributing this value to the server must have been previously agreed upon and is not covered by the Digest Authentication protocol.

The protocol allows the algorithms used for performing the encryption to be specified as part of the message. These algorithms default to MD5 as described in RFC 1321.

The Digest scheme is not foolproof. While it will stop an eavesdropper from obtaining access to a user's password, it will not prevent replay attacks in which the eavesdropper, pretending to be the client system, captures the authorized request message and sends the request to the server. Attacks based on pretending to be the client system (or spoofing) can be made more difficult by ensuring that the time stamp used in the nonce value is set such that it will have expired by the time the replay is performed.

Summary

We presented a brief history of HTTP, beginning with its origins at CERN, and then looked at how the protocol has evolved from the original HTTP 0.9 through the current version, HTTP 1.0. We then looked briefly at two proposals for improving the performance and scalability of the protocol: HTTP 1.1 (an extension of HTTP 1.0) and a new generation protocol HTTPng, which bucks the traditional approach and starts again.

Most of the chapter has focused on the detail of the HTTP 1.0 protocol, although we have mentioned aspects of the HTTP 1.1 protocol that have begun to creep into common usage. We took advantage of the simplicity and human-readable nature of the protocol and used Telnet to simulate an HTTP client so that we could see first-hand the format of messages generated by the server in response to simple requests. In a similar fashion, we used a network snooping tool to eavesdrop on the connection between a commercial Web browser (Netscape Navigator) and two common Web servers (Netscape Enterprise Server and the Apache server) to better understand how clients and servers interact using HTTP.

In looking at the basic protocol, we highlighted HTTP's major attributes: message based, stateless, transport-layer independent, media independent, and object-oriented. In the process, we highlighted areas where the performance of TCP as a transport layer unduly impacted HTTP's performance, especially over slow dial-up connections.

We looked particularly at HTTP's use of MIME-like media types and how clients and servers interpret these. We also looked at the differences between HTTP and MIME.

Finally, we reviewed HTTP's basic security scheme and discussed the security implications of its use.

Web Server Technology

HIGH PERFORMANCE

CHAPTER

2

The sophistication of Web server technology has rapidly grown to support a much wider range of applications than just the retrieval of simple documents. Multilevel Web-based application architectures are now replacing the traditional two-tier client/server paradigm that grew to prominence in the late 80s and early 90s.

Web Server Technology

The traditional paradigm with its "*fat*," complex client sitting on a powerful networked PC (typically connected to a database server) has not been successful. A major reason for this failure has been the high cost of hardware and software ownership per user (particularly the cost of distributing and updating new software releases to a large population of PCs).

The Web offers an alternative model, which uses a "thin" client (typically a Web browser) to download content and software (for example Java applets or ActiveX components) on demand from a web of distributed servers. While a Web server can serve up static content (prewritten HTML documents) it is also capable of generating content dynamically and in the process mediating access to other application objects and information (database) servers. While it is still possible to build significantly complex client-side applications in a Web-centric world (for example stand-alone Java applications), the balance of complexity is again shifting away from the client back to the server.

Web servers have rapidly grown in complexity as applications are being migrated from the old client/server model to the new. Today's Web servers are a far cry from the first server published by CERN (which for some years provided the benchmark for new Web server development). While the newer Web servers are fundamentally equivalent in their adherence to the HTTP protocol, each has introduced server extension models designed to support more sophisticated server-based application architectures.

Both Netscape and Microsoft provide server extension models implemented via an Application Programming Interface (API). An API provides a more efficient mechanism for extending a server than an approach based on the Common Gateway Interface (CGI). CGI is an extension to HTTP that allows the server to invoke a stand-alone program in response to a client request. The introduction of an API approach has been necessary in order to overcome CGI's inherent performance limitations. Unfortunately, this has caused two significantly different server extension models to proliferate. These separate models present a dilemma for the software developer who needs to support both vendor environments. Chapter X presents one solution to this problem.

Microsoft has published the specification for its API, the Internet Server API (ISAPI was actually developed by Process Software in collaboration with Microsoft), and encouraged other server vendors to implement it. This has been partially successful as vendors such as Spyglass (with their Spyglass server), O'Reilly (WebSite), and Process Software (Purveyor) have adopted ISAPI and implemented it with varying degrees of compatibility in their servers.

> **Note:** A great online ISAPI resource can be found at **www.genusa.com/ isapi/**. This site contains code examples, tutorials, online references and links to the latest ISAPI standard.

The Netscape Server API (NSAPI) is Netscape's own model for server extensions. However, NSAPI is not so easily implemented by other vendors because it is fundamentally interwoven with Netscape's server architecture.

> **Note:** Online resources for NSAPI can be found at **www.developer.netscape. com/library/documentation/index.html**.

From a developer's perspective, this architectural divergence increases as each of the vendors embraces different distributed computing models: Netscape with its allegiance to CORBA (Common Object Request Broker Architecture) and Microsoft with DCOM (Distributed Common Object Model). Netscape has recently embedded a CORBA-compliant ORB (Object Request Broker) in its range of servers, allowing them to serve up application objects (with their own behavior and state) that communicate outside of the HTTP protocol using IIOP (Internet Inter-ORB Protocol). Microsoft servers, in turn, now contain DCOM support.

The number of specialized servers is also increasing rapidly. For example, in addition to its standard Enterprise and FastTrack servers, Netscape now has a family of purpose-built servers including Proxy, Catalogue, Calendar, Merchant, Publishing, and

Community servers. For more details, please refer to Netscape's Web site (**www.netscape.com/comprod/netscape_products.html**).

Similarly, in addition to its Internet Information Server (IIS), Microsoft has introduced its Catapult proxy server and Merchant server for electronic commerce. Refer to **www.microsoft.com/iis**, **www.microsoft.com/proxy**, and **www.microsoft.com/ merchant** for more information on each server.

For information about the most commonly used public domain servers, refer to CERN at **www.w3.org/pub/WWW/Daemon**, NCSA at **hoohoo.ncsa.uiuc.edu**, and Apache at **www.apache.org**.

CERN's server, also known as the W3C HTTPd, is now available through the W3C organization rather than CERN itself. The Apache server has upstaged CERN and NCSA, which were once the most widely used servers. Apache is an outgrowth of the NCSA server development and is now the most widely used of any server in the United States.

The distinguishing feature of the CERN and Apache servers is their support for proxying and caching. A proxy server is typically used behind a firewall to forward requests on behalf of users behind the firewall out to the Internet. A caching server caches recently requested documents and other objects resulting in faster response times to the client. Figure 2.1 illustrates the situation in which two clients have requested the same resource, which happens to have already been cached by the proxy server. Before the proxy satisfies the client request, it performs a "conditional GET" request against the origin server to check that the original resource has not been modified since it was last cached.

While servers may have a specialized function, all of the servers mentioned adhere to the HTTP protocol and each can be extended in various ways.

In this chapter, we'll look at the function of a Web server in more detail and concentrate on the ways in which it can be extended to facilitate development of server-side applications. We'll begin by looking at CGI and FastCGI, a recent CGI derivative from OpenMarket. Then, we'll move on to compare CGI with an in-process API approach to server extensions. Finally, we'll review the two most common server APIs (NSAPI and ISAPI) and the major differences between them.

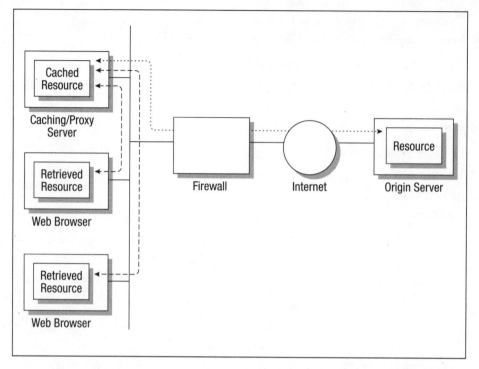

Figure 2.1
A proxy server controlling access to the Web behind a firewall.

Typical Web Server Architecture

A typical Web server architecture supports a request/response paradigm consisting of the following phases:

- Accepting HTTP request messages from a client program (Web browser)

- Locating the resource specified by the URL in the message's request header

- Accessing the resource using the specified request method

- Building an HTTP response message containing status information and the resource itself (the message body)

- Sending a response

- Closing down the client connection

The resource being requested is usually an HTML file, GIF image, or multimedia object (audio, video, and the like). The resource may also be a data-producing object, such as a gateway program that uses data from the request message to request further information from a database (or some other source) before sending it back as the body of a response message.

Gateway programs are usually implemented as Perl scripts or C programs and communicate with the server using CGI. When a server receives a CGI request, it invokes a program to generate the response message. While this approach is simple and easily understood, it becomes inefficient when the server must service a large number of simultaneous requests.

Server Operation

Figure 2.2 shows that the operation of a Web server can be broken into nine distinct steps. A client first establishes a connection with the server and sends an HTTP request message. When the request is received, the server interprets each of the headers in the request message. For protected resources, the server will authenticate the client using an authorization scheme (usually HTTP's basic scheme) and will use header information to access the resource (if necessary, first translating the URL using virtual to physical URL translation rules maintained by the server).

The method specified in the message's request header defines how the resource is to be accessed. Common methods defined by HTTP 1.0 are GET, HEAD, and POST. The request URL informs the server of the resource's location, and may also contain encoded name=value pairs if the GET method has been used to send the contents of an HTML form to the server. Alternatively, if the request is a POST request, the form's name=value pairs are sent in the body of the request message instead.

The server then establishes the type of resource by looking at the form of the request URL. For static, file-based resources, this usually means looking at the file extension and mapping this to a media type that the server uses to fill in the Content-Type response header. This is one of the most important headers because it determines how the client program will interpret the message. For a browser, this would determine which viewer or helper application to invoke.

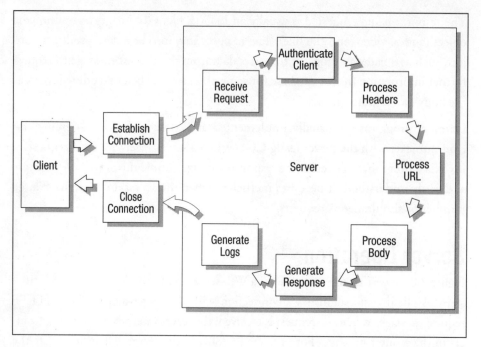

Figure 2.2
The HTTP request lifecycle.

For URLs that refer to a CGI program (either via a .CGI file extension or reference to the cgi-bin subdirectory in the URL), the server invokes the CGI program. In this case, the CGI program is responsible for generating the response message.

The server or CGI program then builds a response message containing:

- A status line indicating success or other status of the request. For example, a successful response would begin with a status line something like: "HTTP/1.0 200 OK".

- General headers describing general properties of the message. A Date is an example.

- Response headers containing information about the response. A Server or WWW-Authenticate header is an example.

- Entity headers describing properties of the resource. A Content-Type header is an example.

Finally, the resource itself (for static resources) or the output of the CGI program is transmitted as the body of the message before closing the client connection.

We will see later in this chapter how it is possible to change the behavior of a server at various points in the life cycle by overriding or augmenting the server's default behavior.

Web Server Implementation

A Web server is usually implemented as one or more standalone processes running on a host computer. Due to the simplicity of the HTTP protocol, this process can be as simple as a shell or Perl script that receives requests on its standard input, interprets them, and generates the appropriate responses on its standard output. The mechanics of connecting the client request to the server can be delegated to the system service daemon **inetd**, which provides a generic mechanism for invoking server processes in response to client connection requests on a specified port.

The complexity and performance demands of today's Web server precludes the script-based implementations of earlier servers, although servers like Plexus (**www.earth.com/ server/doc/plexus.html**) are still used in low volume environments.

For speed, efficiency, and tight integration with system services, servers today are usually implemented using compiled languages such as C or C++. Such implementations, while efficient, require significant porting efforts between different computer platforms. W3C's Jigsaw server is an excellent example of a highly portable server because it has been implemented using Java.

> **Note:** *Java is an object-oriented language invented by Sun Microsystems, Inc. It has cross-platform portability as a fundamental objective. This portability has been achieved by using a Java compiler to translate a Java source program into an equivalent sequence of portable instructions called byte codes, rather than into the native machine code of the computer. Each byte code program is then executed by a Java interpreter (or "virtual machine"). A virtual machine is a program that simulates the operation of a specialized computer in software. You can find lots more information on Java at Sun's Java site **java.sun.com** and **www.gamelan.com** (one of the best collections of Java online resources).*

Normally, however, a Web server runs as a standalone daemon process that looks after establishment of the client connection and related process control. Once created and initialized, the server process listens for HTTP connection requests on TCP port 80. Port 80 is the well-known port for HTTP, although most servers allow a different port to be specified if necessary.

> **Note:** Sometimes the **inetd** network daemon is used to facilitate the connection and spawn a copy of the server process specifically to handle the request, although this is really only suitable for low traffic environments or for debugging.

Web server architectures are optimized for performance in two ways. They allow requests to be spread over multiple copies of the server process and, within each process, allow a server to handle multiple requests concurrently using threads.

The parent server process typically creates a number of child processes when it starts up. Each child process is capable of servicing requests allocated to it by the parent. In turn, each child process creates a number of threads onto which it can schedule requests. Figure 2.3 shows a server configured to run as a parent with three child

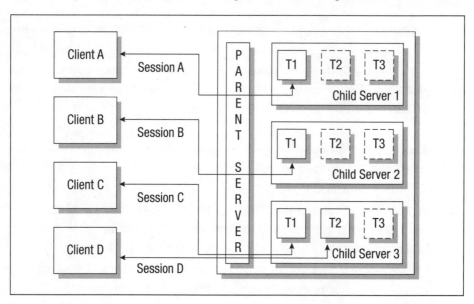

Figure 2.3

Multithreaded, multiserver architecture.

server processes. The parent process dispatches four simultaneous client requests to the available servers. Each server in turn creates a thread to process each request. Note that server 3 has scheduled two concurrent requests onto two separate threads.

The Common Gateway Interface

The CGI is the traditional way of augmenting the functionality of a server. Under this scheme, the server invokes a gateway program (typically a Perl script or a C program) and passes it input data contained in the request message.

The server does this by creating a CGI process (usually by making a copy of itself) and creating input and output pipes between itself and the CGI process (see Figure 2.4). State information about the server, client, and the request is inherited by the CGI process through a set of CGI environment variables set up by the server.

Once established, the CGI process then executes the CGI program specified in the request URL. The program accepts input from the server through a set of environment variables or through its standard input, parses and processes the input data, and generates a response message on its standard output for interpretation by the server before being sent to the client.

Note: *More detail on the CGI 1.1 specification can be found at the NCSA (National Center for Supercomputing Applications) HTTPd Development Team's site at **hoohoo.ncsa.uiuc.edu/cgi/**.*

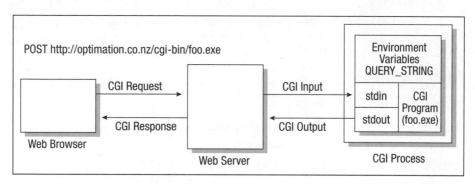

Figure 2.4
The Web server and CGI process.

CGI Environment Variables

The CGI process inherits a set of environment variables from the server. These environment variables describe the state of the server, the client, the request, and possibly input data. See Table 2.1 for a full list.

The environment variables are grouped into five categories:

- General information variables enable a CGI program to determine how to input data from the server. SERVER_PROTOCOL, which is the version of the HTTP protocol implemented by the server, is a general information variable.

- Input information variables contain input data supplied by the server. CONTENT_TYPE, which is the media type that defines how the input data is encoded, is an input information variable.

- Client information variables describe the client program (Web browser). REMOTE_HOST, which is the host name (a fully qualified domain name) of the client computer, is a client information variable.

- Server information variables describe the server. SERVER_PORT, which is the port that the server uses to listen for connection requests, is a server information variable.

- HTTP information variables describe additional properties of the client. These properties come from headers in the request message and information maintained by the server itself. HTTP_USER_AGENT, which is the product name and version of the client program, and HTTP_ACCEPT, which is the list of media types (MIME types) supported by the client program, are HTTP information variables.

Table 2.1   The CGI environment variables.

Environment Variable	Description
AUTH_TYPE	If authentication is being used, this is set to the scheme being used, usually basic.
CONTENT_LENGTH	The size of the input when sent in a POST request. This variable is undefined for GET requests or when there is no input.
CONTENT_TYPE	A media type defining the way in which the data has been encoded. For forms, this is usually application/www-form-urlencoded.

continued

Table 2.1   The CGI environment variables (continued).

Environment Variable	Description
DOCUMENT_ROOT	The top of the server's document tree.
GATEWAY_INTERFACE	The version of the CGI protocol supported by the server. Always set to CGI/1.1.
PATH_INFO	The path following the CGI program name in the request URL.
PATH_TRANSLATED	The path in PATH_INFO translated to a physical path on the server.
QUERY_STRING	The input when sent in a GET request.
REQUEST_METHOD	GET or POST depending on the method used to pass data to the CGI program.
REMOTE_ADDR	The IP address of the client computer.
REMOTE_GROUP	The group the user belongs to, obtained during the authentication process.
REMOTE_HOST	The host name of the client computer.
REMOTE_IDENT	The name of the user using the client computer (client computer must be running an RFC 931-compliant agent e.g., identd).
REMOTE_USER	This is the name of the user obtained during authentication using the basic scheme.
REQUEST_METHOD	GET, HEAD, POST, or an extension method defined by the client.
SCRIPT_NAME	A URL that identifies the CGI script to be invoked.
SERVER_ADMIN	Email address of the server administrator.
SERVER_NAME	The host name of the computer running the server.
SERVER_PORT	The TCP port on which the request was received - usually 80.
SERVER_PROTOCOL	The version of the HTTP protocol being used e.g., HTTP/1.0 or HTTP/1.1.
SERVER_SOFTWARE	The name and version of the server.

Header Variables

A subset of the header variables that are possible. These are constructed directly from headers supplied in the client request message.

Header Variable	Description
HTTP_ACCEPT	The list of media types the client is able to handle.
HTTP_ACCEPT_LANGUAGE	The list of languages the client supports.

continued

Table 2.1 The CGI environment variables (continued).

Header Variable	Description
HTTP_COOKIE	The list of HTTP cookies the client stores.
HTTP_USER_AGENT	Product and version information about the client program.
HTTP_REFERER	The URL of the document that referred you to the current URL.

CGI URLs

A server is able to distinguish between a static resource and a CGI program by one of two methods. The first is based on looking at the file extension of the requested resource. The following is a URL for a CGI script:

```
http://www.optimation.co.nz/optimation/feedback.cgi
```

This approach relies on *cgi* being registered to the server as a media type and allows CGI programs to be placed alongside other files in the server's document tree.

Registering directories that are dedicated to CGI programs with the server is a more common approach. Any URL that references a file in these directories is assumed to be calling a CGI program. CGI programs stored in this way are much easier to secure and maintain. These directories are often named cgi-bin, as in the following:

```
http://www.optimation.co.nz/optimation/cgi-bin/feedback.bat
```

A URL that references a CGI program is interpreted differently from a URL that references a static resource, such as an HTML file. A CGI URL is broken into three parts:

```
[Virtual path][Additional Path Information]?[query string]
```

The following is a URL generated by a form using a GET method to send form data to a CGI program feedback.bat:

```
http://www.optimation.co.nz/optimation/cgi-bin/feedback.bat/
feedback?MessageType=Praise&
Comments=Great+framework%0D%0AWhat+comes+next%3F&
userName=Paul+McGlashan&companyName=Optimation+NZ+Ltd&
userEmail=paulm@optimation.co.nz&userPhone=&userFAX=&
submitButton=Submit+Feedback
```

The virtual path is the URL prefix up to and including the name of the CGI program, for example:

```
http://www.optimation.co.nz/optimation/cgi-bin/feedback.bat
```

The additional path information is the portion of the URL following the virtual path up to the ?. For example: **/feedback.**

The additional path information environment variable, PATH_INFO, provides a way of passing additional information to the CGI program. Typically, it is used in conjunction with the server's virtual to physical path translation feature, which takes the additional path information and maps it to a physical path name relative to the root of your server's document tree.

In our example, the root of our document tree is **/webs/optimation**; therefore, **/feedback** is automatically translated to **/webs/optimation/feedback** and passed to the CGI program using the PATH_TRANSLATED environment variable.

The query string component can be supplied in three different ways:

- Explicitly within an HTML anchor

- The result of data input by the user from an ISINDEX query

- Output from an HTML form (this is the most common method)

CGI Input

Input to a CGI program typically comes from the contents of an HTML form. This data is formatted as a string of name=value pairs, where *name* is the name of a form field and *value* is the value of the field entered by the user. Each pair is separated by & and encoded so that all spaces are substituted by + and other unsafe characters *escaped* by using the notation %## (where ## are two hexadecimal digits representing the ASCII value of the escaped character; ? would be translated to %3F).

CGI programs receive input according to the request method used to send the form data. If the GET request method is used, the server copies the encoded name=value pairs, which is appended to the request URL by the client, into the QUERY_STRING environment variable. The CGI program then parses the QUERY_STRING variable for input. A ? separates the form data from the request URL. However, if the

PUSH method is used, the string transmitted as the body of the request message is placed on the standard input of the CGI program and the CONTENT_LENGTH environment variable is set to the number of bytes in the message body.

Once the CGI program has parsed the input stream (it must decode the encoded query string), it performs its requisite function; perhaps attaching to a remote information source or database to execute a query before generating an appropriate response.

It is also possible to pass input data to the CGI program via the command line. This occurs when an ISINDEX HTML tag is encountered by the client browser (note use of ISINDEX has been superseded by HTML forms).

A Web browser interprets an ISINDEX tag by displaying a search field prompting the user to enter a series of keywords separated by spaces. The query string entered by the user is encoded by substituting each space with a +. The client then appends a ? and the encoded string to the URL specified in the ISINDEX tag.

When a server encounters such a request, in addition to the query string being copied into the QUERY_STRING environment variable, each keyword is parsed out of the query string by the server and mapped to a corresponding command-line argument of the CGI program specified in the URL. The server distinguishes between this type of request and one generated by an HTML form by looking for = in the encoded query string.

CGI Output

The CGI program is responsible for formatting any result data into an HTTP response message, complete with headers and entity body containing the data itself.

The most important headers are the status line and the Content-Type header. If everything went well, the status line should indicate a successful operation via a **200 OK** status code, followed by at least the Content-Type HTTP header (defining the media type of the data).

Other headers present might include:

- *Location*—a new location for the resource to be returned.

- *Content-Length*—the number of data bytes to be output.

- *Expires*—the date after which the data will become unavailable.

- *Content-Encoding*—the decoding method the client should use before displaying or processing the data further.

Once it has generated the headers, the CGI program generates a blank line indicating the end of the headers before outputting the data. The CGI program must ensure that the data is formatted appropriately for the media type defined in the Content-Type header and any subsequent encoding applied as specified by the Content-Encoding header.

When a CGI program sends data back to the server, the server interprets the output stream and performs additional operations if required. For example, if the CGI program did not emit a status header, the server would create one: **200 OK** by default. The server will also interpret headers such as Location, by which it will automatically locate a path name specified in the Location header and, transparently to the client, regenerate a response containing the new resource with all the appropriate headers.

> **Note:** *If an absolute URL is specified instead of a path name in a Location header, the server generates a response with a **302** (Temporarily Moved) status, indicating that the requested resource has moved to the new location. In this case, the client is responsible for navigating to the new URL.*

For efficiency, the server buffers all output from the CGI program so blocks of data, rather than a raw stream of individual bytes, are sent back to the client.

There are situations in which a CGI program may want to bypass the server completely so that it can send data directly to the client; unbuffered server-side push applications work this way. This is achieved by using the server's *Non-parse headers* feature. When this feature is used, the standard output of the client is directly connected to a copy of the socket connection back to the client. In this case, the CGI program must correctly format the entire response message, including all headers. CGI programs that use this feature have a *nph-* prefix in their name.

In-Process Extensions

A number of server vendors have provided proprietary Application Programming Interfaces (APIs), which allow their Web servers to be extended in a more efficient way than with CGI. Using this approach, the logic you would otherwise encode in a CGI program is implemented as a series of application functions (normally in C) and linked into the Web server itself.

Application functions are typically packaged as shared libraries, like a Dynamic Linked Library (DLL) in a Windows environment or a Shared Object (SO) in a Unix environment. Exactly when the server loads the shared library and how the request is mapped to a specific function is dependent on the server.

For example, in a Windows NT environment, both Netscape and Microsoft servers allow you to define DLLs that implement CGI-like services. The server invokes a DLL when a request is made to a resource to which a DLL/function mapping has been defined. The way this mapping is defined and the DLL subsequently invoked differs significantly between Netscape and Microsoft servers.

With Netscape, a configuration file (objects.conf) defines a mapping between the resource and a corresponding service function from a registered DLL. When the server encounters a reference to the resource, it invokes the service function to generate the appropriate response.

Conversely, Microsoft allows you to invoke a DLL in the same way you would a CGI program. The only visible difference is that DLL is the specified file extension. When the server sees the DLL file extension, it loads the DLL (if it is not already loaded) and jumps to the DLL entry point to begin execution. Microsoft calls these extensions Internet Server Applications, or ISA, extensions.

Such extensions to the server are known as *in-process* because the shared library is mapped into the server's address space. This allows the application functions direct access to the server's data structures.

Invoking a program as in CGI or an in-process shared object is only one way of extending the behavior of a server. Both Netscape and Microsoft provide mechanisms for augmenting or overriding the behavior of their servers by allowing you to extend or modify the way the servers implement the various phases of the request lifecycle. Both of these mechanisms are quite different.

Netscape's approach is based on the same model it uses for invoking a DLL to service a CGI-like request. In contrast, Microsoft's introduces the notion of a filter extension, which Microsoft refers to as an ISAPI filter. Using either of these approaches, it is possible, for example, to override and replace the credentials authentication phase of HTTP's basic authentication scheme (refer to the section "Access Authentication" in Chapter 1) with an alternative mechanism.

CGI Vs. In-Process Extensions

CGI is the most widely used method for extending a Web server. This is mainly due to its inherent advantages outlined in the following points:

- *Simplicity*—The mechanism for invoking a program is simple to understand and to implement. The invocation mechanism is analogous to a remote procedure call, with parameters to the program being passed through a simple set of environment variables or through the command line.

- *Safety*—CGI programs run as a separate process, completely isolated from the Web server. This makes it difficult for a buggy CGI program to compromise the internal integrity of the server. CGI programs are also easier to debug because it is possible to trace execution of the CGI process without other applications (such as a Web server) getting in the way.

- *Security*—The server can strictly control access to CGI programs.

- Portability—Applications adhering to the CGI 1.1 specification are portable across almost any Web server. Also, because many programs are written in portable scripting languages such as Perl, they are portable across a wide range of computer platforms.

CGI's disadvantages are as follows:

- *Performance*—CGI does not perform well in environments in which a large number of requests must be handled. For each CGI request, the server must create a new process. The overhead of creating each process and the resources consumed by a potentially large number of concurrently executing CGI programs can soon slow a server machine to a crawl.

- *State*—There is no natural way for different CGI programs to share working data. Because each program is a separate process, it is not possible to use in-memory variables or data structures to pass state information between one program and the next. Instead, you must rely on using external storage techniques. There are client-side techniques such as client cookies and hidden HTML fields; server-side techniques such as temporary files; and URL encoding techniques, in which state information is passed around in the URL itself.

In-process extensions overcome CGI's two main disadvantages, but also introduce some problems of their own. In-process extensions provide for much faster operation than CGI because the process creation and interprocess communication overhead largely disappears. Typically, converting from a CGI to an in-process approach will increase performance up to five times.

Invocation of a program is replaced by the loading of a shared object (DLL or SO). Typically, the shared object is only loaded once. Also, the overhead of loading a shared object is significantly less than creating a completely new process and having it execute a program. Once loaded, the shared object stays within the server's address space and requests against it incur only the overhead of a function call. Some environments, like Windows, may remove shared objects from memory after they have been inactive for a specified time.

In-process extensions also overcome CGI's data sharing restrictions because the application state can be maintained between application functions using in-memory data structures stored in the server's address space. A shared object has complete access to the server's internal data structures. This is immensely powerful, but it is also potentially dangerous. While a server provides APIs and protocols to formalize access to their internals, it also makes it relatively easy for a rogue shared object to crash the server.

CGI implements a simple model based on the HTTP request/response paradigm. This mechanism is tailored specifically to invoke a remote application, pass it data, and obtain a result.

While most server API schemes provide a way of invoking a function or a DLL to satisfy a resource request, they may also provide a way of overriding or augmenting the default behavior of the server itself. This allows much more detailed control over the server than is possible with CGI. Both Netscape and Microsoft servers define different models for doing this.

In Netscape, each phase of the request lifecycle is implemented by invoking a sequence of built-in functions that define the default server behavior. It is possible to redefine all or part of a life cycle phase by substituting these functions with your own (refer to the section "Netscape Plug-in Technology," later in this chapter) or by providing additional functions.

Microsoft provides a similar scheme for augmenting default server behavior through the use of filters. Filters are implemented as DLLs that effectively sit between the client and the server. A filter can respond to a specific set of events that occur as the request life cycle progresses and augment or override default server behavior.

FastCGI

FastCGI is a variant of CGI put forward by OpenMarket Inc. It provides an alternative approach to reducing CGI's process startup and teardown overhead.

*Note: You can find out more about FastCGI at **www.fastcgi.com**.*

FastCGI replaces the CGI process with a daemon process, which, once started, never dies. The logic of the CGI program is placed inside the daemon. When the client initiates a CGI request, the Web server connects to the CGI daemon via a full-duplex pipe if the daemon is on the same machine or via a socket if the daemon is on a different machine. This connection is used for both input to and output from the CGI daemon. The server sends data to the CGI daemon using a simple packet protocol. Then, the daemon de-multiplexes each packet and processes the request. Finally, it sends back output data via the packet protocol and closes the connection. At this point, the daemon does not die, but simply waits around, listening for the next connection request from the server.

In contrast to the way in which a CGI program receives input data (through environment variables, the standard input, or command line), FastCGI uses a simple messaging protocol to package up this same information before sending it over the pipe/socket connection to the CGI daemon. The daemon receives and de-multiplexes each message, then processes its contents according to the message type. For example, messages containing name=value pairs are copied to the corresponding environment variables in the CGI process and messages containing standard input data are unpacked and the data placed on the standard input of the CGI process.

By removing the process creation overhead, the FastCGI approach is significantly faster than CGI, with response times approaching that of retrieving a static resource. In addition to improved performance, other benefits of FastCGI include:

- The ability to distribute CGI applications around a network

- The ability to hide CGI applications behind a firewall

- Independence from any one server architecture or vendor

- Independence from programming languages

- Loosely coupled to the Web server (it operates safely outside the server's address space)

Netscape Plug-in Technology

When a Netscape server receives a request, it parses the request message into a set of server data structures and then processes the request through seven distinct phases:

- The Authenticate Transaction phase is responsible for decoding a client's authentication credentials that are supplied in an Authorize header and converting these into a user name, password, and group.

- The Translate URL phase allows the virtual address component of the request URL to be mapped to an alternative physical location.

- The Check Path phase performs various conversion functions and safety checks on the path component of the request URL, including client authorization, extraction of CGI extra path information, and expansion of ~username notation to the user's home directory.

- The Determine Object Type phase determines the media (MIME) type of the requested resource from the resource's file extension.

- The Perform Service phase generates the server's response message by sending the status line, headers, and entity body. Then, it closes the connection.

- The Update Logs phase logs information about the request in the server logs.

- The Generate Error phase controls how the server responds to an error condition.

Directives stored in a server configuration file implement each phase. This file contains a series of object definitions, each specifying a set of directives to be executed when a resource matching the object definition is requested.

The server steps through the directives for each object and invokes the specified Server Application Function (SAF) for each directive. SAFs are grouped into classes, where a class corresponds to one of the above life cycle phases. A status code returned by the function controls the next phase the server enters.

Each directive has the form:

```
directive fn="function_name" param_name1="value1" ~ param_nameN="valueN"
```

The *directive* matches one of the request lifecycle phases, like **AuthTrans** (Authenticate Transaction); *function* refers to a unique function name from a shared library registered to the server during the server initialization phase; and the remaining *param_name=value* pairs an arbitrary list of parameters to be passed to the function.

Netscape provides standard directives and built-in SAFs to implement the server's default behavior. However, it is possible to override or augment this behavior by substituting the built-in SAFs or adding your own. These user-defined functions are called Server Plug-ins and are written according to the NSAPI specification. Server Plug-ins are registered to the server through a configuration file when the server starts up. Netscape Plug-ins are covered in detail in Chapter 3.

Microsoft ISAPI Filters And ISA Extensions

Microsoft adopts a different model than Netscape, separating out the notion of a service extension for providing CGI-like services from the ability to override various aspects of the request life cycle.

Microsoft defines an Internet Service Application as a DLL (assuming Windows) containing functions that implement a CGI-like service. As we've already explained, an ISA is referenced using the same mechanism as a CGI program.

Further server extension is provided through an ISAPI filter. You can imagine a filter as lying between the client and the server, where it can intercept aspects of the re-

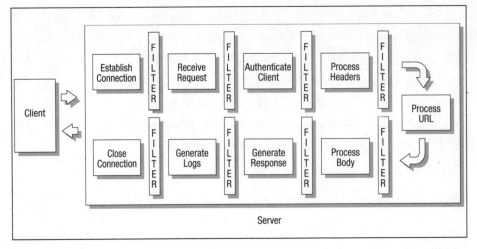

Figure 2.5
The ISAPI filter model.

quest and response, as illustrated in Figure 2.5. A filter is also implemented as a DLL, but it is only invoked when an event occurs for which it has previously registered an interest. The events available to a filter roughly correspond to the phases of Netscape's request life cycle.

ISA Extensions

In the Windows environment, an Internet Service Application is implemented as a DLL. This approach provides a more efficient way of implementing a CGI program because the DLL is loaded directly into the server address space rather than outside it, as a separate process. Here, there is not only the advantage of the vastly reduced overhead of loading the DLL as compared with starting a CGI process, but being part of the server address space gives the ISA complete access to the internal data structures of the server.

An ISA request is specified the same way as a CGI request. The only difference is that the name of the file in the request URL has a DLL extension instead of CGI, BAT, EXE, or PL. This aids in the process of converting CGI programs to ISAs.

> **Note:** With the introduction of ISAPI Version 2.0, ISAs are distinguished with an ISA extension (DLL is still supported).

Each ISA must first be registered to the server via the Windows registry. ISA DLLs are usually loaded on demand by the server when the server receives a request and remain in memory for as long as they are being used. The time an unused DLL stays in memory is configurable in the server. When this time expires, the server can unload the DLL from memory leaving room for others.

While the time required to start an ISA is low compared to CGI, there is still a startup cost. This startup time can be reduced to zero by preloading DLLs when the server first starts.

CGI processes communicate with the server via a set of environment variables (refer back to Table 2.1). In contrast, an ISA uses a server in-memory data-structure called an Extension Control Block (ECB), which provides equivalent ways of referencing the same information contained in the server environment variables.

ISAPI Filters

The Microsoft server architecture is based on an event-driven model. As the server enters each phase of the request life cycle, it generates an event corresponding to the phase. By catching these events, a filter is able to access a request before the server does. This provides a powerful way for extending the server with facilities such as custom encryption and logging.

Each filter must register for the events in which it is interested. Filter DLLs are registered to the server via the Windows registry. When the server loads the DLL, the DLL announces to the server the events it is interested in, along with a priority. The filter is then called each time the server generates an event of interest.

Having more than one filter register for the same event can form chains of filters. The order in which filters are invoked in a chain is determined by the filter's priority, which is announced by the filter when it is loaded. By carefully specifying the priority, it is possible for the filter to augment or completely modify the default action of the server. Each filter is able to determine whether or not to pass control to the next filter in the chain.

Filters can register with the recommended **default** priority, or **low**, **medium**, or **high**. Where two filters have the same priority, the order of invocation is determined by the order they are shown in the registry.

Table 2.2 Events an ISAPI filter may respond to.

Event	Description
Connection to Secure Port	The filter is notified when a client connection request is made to a secure port, like when the client wants to establish a Secure Sockets Layer (SSL) connection.
Connection to Non-Secure Port	The filter is notified when a client connection request is made to a non-secure port, typically port 80.
Reading Raw Data	The filter is notified before the server reads data from the connection giving the filter access to the complete request message, its headers, and any data.
Preprocessing Headers	The filter is notified before the server has preprocessed the headers in the request message.
Translating URL	The server is about to map the virtual URL to a physical URL.
Authenticating Transaction	The server is about to authenticate the client.
Sending Raw Data	The server is about to send the response message back to the client.
Updating Log	The server is about to write information to the server logs.
Closing Connection	The connection to the client is about to be closed.

Note: A filter should only register for an event if it is going to do something with it. Registering for events and then not doing anything with them can significantly slow server performance, particularly when multiple filters are being invoked per event. Similarly, a filter should only assign itself a high priority if it will actually be processing the majority of events.

When a server invokes a filter in response to one of the events in Table 2.2, the filter will determine the type of the event that invoked it and respond accordingly. For example, a filter implementing a specialized encryption method will need to respond to the **Reading Raw Data** event so that it can first decrypt the input stream before processing the decoded headers and data. Similarly, a filter implementing a custom logging scheme will have registered to receive notification of the **Updating Log** event. It is common practice for all filters to respond to **Closing Connection** so that they can deallocate any data structures used during their operation, including the release of any buffers the filter uses for memory management.

Note: ISAPI Filters and Internet Service Applications are covered in detail in Chapter 10.

Summary

With the shift to the new Web-based client/server paradigm, Web servers have had to provide more powerful mechanisms for extending the server to meet specific application requirements.

Traditionally, the functionality of a Web server has been extended using CGI. However, this approach can impose a heavy load on the server because each CGI request requires a new process to be started.

Microsoft IIS and Netscape's range of servers, have introduced in-process extensions to overcome CGI's performance limitations. Netscape uses **Service** functions implemented using the Netscape Server API (NSAPI) and Microsoft uses its Internet Server Applications (ISAs). In-process extensions provide CGI-like behavior but use dynamically loaded shared objects to load applications directly into the server's address space. This significantly improves performance, but also leaves the server open to being compromised by rogue, in-process applications.

FastCGI providesss an alternative implementation of CGI. This goes a long way to solving the performance problems, but does not yield the high performance of an in-process approach.

Conceptually, both NSAPI and ISAPI provide similar ways of adding to or modifying the behavior of the server. Netscape provides a general method of overriding or adding steps in the request life cycle by allowing you to completely define the chain of functions to be executed at each step. Microsoft's ISAPI filters provide a similar mechanism, allowing you to register chains of filter functions, which are triggered by the server as the request is processed.

Netscape
Server API

CHAPTER

3

The Netscape Server API (NSAPI) provides a comprehensive, powerful, in-process method to extend Netscape servers. Developers may use the well-defined programmatic interface of the NSAPI to implement custom server behavior and accomplish a variety of tasks.

Netscape Server API

As you will discover, in-process extension of a Web server uses an operating system's dynamic shared object support (DLLs under Windows NT, shared libraries under Unix). Shared objects can be attached to the server by certain methods and with a defined protocol. This provides a means to alter or augment the behavior of the standard, shipped product without server object or source code.

Netscape provides what could be termed as a suite of various APIs on the server side. Recently, they provided server-side Java applet support via a small Java class library. There is also LiveWire Pro, which uses a combination of server- and client-side JavaScript to construct back-end applications. NSAPI, which Netscape sometimes refers to as the Server Plug-in API (SPAPI), is the third and least understood API.

Netscape created NSAPI to allow third-party software developers to achieve in-process extension via a C linkage API. While NSAPI is at a lower level than other Netscape-supported APIs, it does allow high performance extensions to be constructed. With good design and efficient software construction techniques, a developer may produce server extensions that easily outperform equivalent Java and LiveWire offerings. However, the price paid for improved performance is greater complexity and a more obtuse programming model. This chapter will attempt to remove any mystery that surrounds NSAPI and provide an explanation of the server's internal workings. We will also discuss ways to make software more portable, as well as highlight the differences between writing for Windows NT and Unix platforms.

Before we move on, you should also note that the reference server for the code in this chapter is Enterprise Server version 2.01. The software works under Windows NT Server 4.0, with Service Pack 2 applied, and under Solaris 2.5.

Netscape Server Architecture

We are concerned here with the basic function and behavior of the server, so a detailed description of the administration is beyond the scope of this chapter. The administration server that is provided with the Netscape servers uses HTML and a Web browser (Netscape Navigator is part of the package) for administrative tasks. A separate process (Unix) or service (Windows NT) executes to provide administrative tasks to the browser. This process or service runs on its own port, which is specified at installation time, and is protected from casual browsing by basic HTTP authentication. The administration interface, sometimes referred to as the *server manager* or *server selector*, provides full online help, which is a good source of information if the administration of the server is your concern.

Unix

For the purpose of discussion, we will assume that the server software is installed under a directory called /usr/local/netscape. Any path names mentioned in this section will be relative to this directory and assume a standard installation has been performed.

The basic hierarchy for a single server installation on a machine with a hostname of *beetle* will appear something like that shown in Figure 3.1.

The HTTP server executable (daemon) is called ns-httpd and resides in bin/https. If you examine this directory, you will also see (under Solaris) the ns-httpd.so shared library, which contains a large portion of the HTTP server functionality. There are various other shared libraries, but only libvdk150.so is dynamically referenced by the main HTTP server executable. Verity Inc. manufactures this shared library that implements the search engine that provides the search facilities of Enterprise Server.

The installation program creates a directory called https-beetle, which includes the hostname after the hyphen. In this directory, there are some simple shell scripts, start and stop, which invoke or terminate the server; restart, which sends a kill -HUP to the running HTTP master daemon (this causes it to re-examine and reload the configuration files). In addition, several subdirectories are created, for example, the subdirectory called logs, which houses the error and access logs; and config, which holds vital configuration files such as magnus.conf, obj.conf, and mime.types. We'll discuss these files in greater depth later in the chapter. While routine maintenance

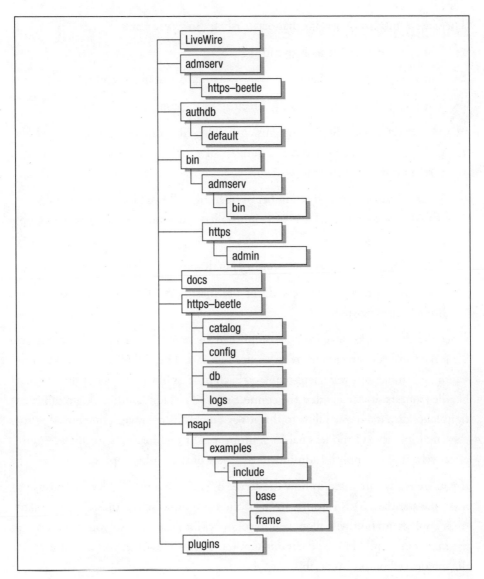

Figure 3.1
Netscape Enterprise Server under Unix, a partial
installation directory hierarchy.

can also be performed via the browser-based administration mentioned above, when developing extensions it is obviously more expedient to perform some of these tasks (especially start, stop, and restart) via the command line.

There are a number of actions that occur when the server starts:

- The server executable ns-httpd loads.

- The server opens the shared libraries ns-httpd.so and libvdk150.so.

- The server changes the working directory to the config subdirectory.

- The server opens the file magnus.conf. This file contains information about which port to listen on and the number of processes to spawn, including the thread limits for each process.

- The server determines the number of open files allowed for a process and what shared objects to load. This is when installed third-party extension's shared objects are loaded.

- The server creates access and error logs, with the date written into the error log.

- The server writes the process ID of the master HTTP daemon into the file https-beetle/logs/pid.

Once the above tasks have been accomplished successfully, the necessary processes are forked and the server is ready to service requests. The child processes take turns handling connections and client requests. Each process has a number of threads that handle requests; it is likely that the connection and request handling logic runs in a tight loop, dispatching requests to threads as quickly as possible. The multiple-process, multiple-thread model enables multiprocessor architectures to operate more effectively. It also simplifies administrators' view of the multiple-process system.

If you are really interested in how the server operates at a low level, consider using *truss*, the standard SVR4 utility, to track the daemon as it executes. The standard truss implementation will allow you to follow child processes, so you can monitor the master and child HTTP daemons simultaneously. However, you must interpret the interleaved output to do this.

Windows NT

For the purpose of our discussion, we will assume that the server software is installed under a directory called C:\Netscape\Server. Any path names mentioned in this section will be relative to this directory and assume a standard installation has been performed.

The basic hierarchy for a single-server installation, on a machine with a hostname of *jaguar,* will appear something like that shown in Figure 3.2.

The HTTP server manager process runs as a service under NT and is called ns-httpd.exe, which resides in bin/https. If you examine this directory, you will see that there is also an executable called httpd.exe, which is the real HTTP server.

Because our example installation is on the host jaguar, the installation program creates a directory called https-jaguar. This directory holds a simple batch file called startsrv.bat that may be used to start the server if it is not already running. Subdirectories here include logs, which houses the error and access logs; and config, which holds vital configuration files such as magnus.conf, obj.conf, and mime.types. (Again, we'll discuss these files in greater depth later in this chapter.) Note that routine maintenance is usually performed via the browser-based administration mentioned above. It obviously can be more expedient to perform some of these tasks (especially start, stop, and restart) manually when developing extensions. Some aspects of server administration that can be performed under Unix via the command line, such as server restart, will not operate under NT. Instead, you will have to use either the server selector (browser-based admin) or the services applet in Control Panel.

A number of tasks are performed to start the server process:

- The server executable ns-httpd is loaded.

- The server creates a number of threads that relate to one or more HTTPd processes. In many NT installations, there will be only one HTTPd process.

- The server retrieves the basic process configuration from magnus.conf. This includes details such as which port the daemon should listen on, whether client name DNS resolution is activated, and so on.

- The server checks for the existence of access and error logs and creates them if necessary.

- The server writes the start date into the error log.

Once the above tasks have been accomplished successfully, all necessary processes are running and the server (which you'll notice is a somewhat general term) is ready to service requests. The HTTPd processes take turns handling connections and client requests. Each process has a number of threads that handle and it is likely that the

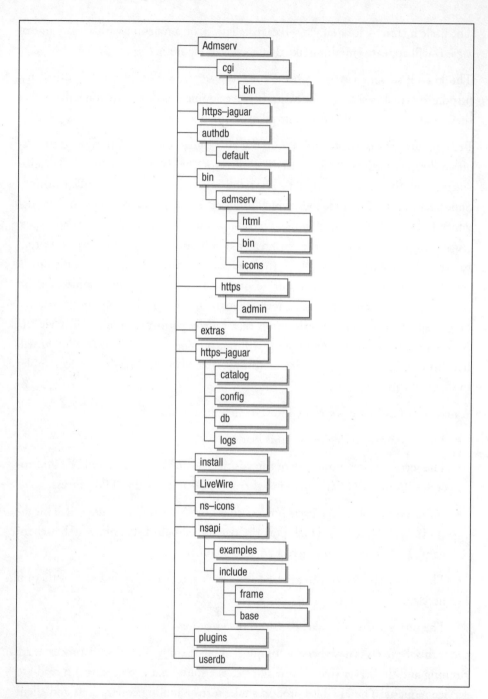

Figure 3.2
Enterprise Server under Windows NT, a partial installation directory hierarchy.

connection and request handling logic runs in a tight loop, dispatching the requests to threads as quickly as possible. The purpose of the multiple-process, multiple-thread model is to enable multiprocessor architectures to operate more effectively (it also simplifies the administrator's view of the multiple process system).

> **Note:** *If you are really interested in how the server operates at a low level, consider using the Spy utility that ships with Visual C++.*

How Requests Are Handled

We will simplify the discussion to follow by considering only HTTP requests. Once the server accepts a connection from a client and the client submits a request to the server, the server performs the appropriate actions. In the case of an encrypted channel (such as with SSL or HTTPS), the server decodes the request first.

The client waits at the end of a TCP/IP socket for a response from the server. Before the server can write that response, it must use the information contained in the configuration file obj.conf to determine what actions to perform against the request. Using this information, the server creates the appropriate response, which may be a denial of access, authorization failure, or other response. In an *out of the box* server, obj.conf holds Netscape-supplied default directives only, which reference the functions implemented by Netscape to provide necessary HTTPd functionality. This file has a well defined and reasonably simple syntax that allows a number of rules to be associated with a number of objects.

An object, in Netscape terms, is what other servers may call a resource. When a request is decoded, it effectively belongs (or is assigned internally) to an object or objects. There may be just one, or multiple relationships for a request. Each object has a number of rules or actions associated with it, and each rule is applied to the request as it is processed. Restated, for each object that the request matches, each directive for each object is applied successively to the request in the order that it appears in the obj.conf file. It is possible for a directive to terminate processing for a request when no further action should be taken or when a request should be aborted. An example of this is authorization; it is definitive identification if a client is authorized via the basic HTTP mechanism, even if there are 10 other directives concerned with authenticating clients. The authenticating directive (whether this is Netscape or a directive developed by you) should return the appropriate value, which indicates what action it has performed and what it desires the server to do upon the directive's return.

Do not be concerned if this sounds complex. There are a number of examples in this section that deal with the interpretation and use of obj.conf.

Request Processing Sequence

In the previous section, we mentioned that certain directives exist that can be applied by the HTTP server to a request as it is processed. Now we'll provide a basic explanation of their application and semantics. The overall view of the sequence is shown in Figure 3.3.

It may help you to think of directives as events, because that is all they really are. This model is invariant across all supported platforms for Netscape.

Authentication

This initial phase is also called Authorization Translation. Netscape HTTP servers support only HTTP basic authentication. This event seems to have been large-

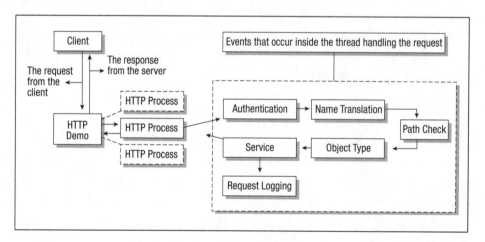

Figure 3.3

Potential progression of request processing.

ly superseded in Enterprise Server by access control lists, but can still be used to implement specialized decryption techniques. There is a natural connection between this event and the Path Check event described below.

Authentication functions are specified in obj.conf with the *AuthTrans* directive.

Name Translation

Name translation involves the mapping of a URL from a virtual path (the resource specified) to a physical path (the real operating system designation for the resource specified).

This phase is often very simple. If the virtual portion of the URL can be directly mapped to a physical path, this phase has no real action to perform. For other object types, such as CGI calls mapped through directories (cgi-bin for example), the name translation function may redirect the processing to another directive. Finally, custom implementations may completely mutate the supplied URL, which depends on individual implementations.

Name translation functions are specified in obj.conf with the *NameTrans* directive.

Path Check

The previous step translates, if successful, a virtual path into a physical one. This event determines if the client is allowed to retrieve (or even write, in the case of a PUT request for example) the operating system object implied by the URL. If the client is allowed to access the object, the request is eligible to pass through the remaining phases. If it is not, an error message will be sent to the client. A typical message is an *object not found* (**404**) type message, but Netscape server administration allows this message to be customized.

The installation process defines some standard path check functions. One such function is a clean URI function, which will clean up any potentially dangerous URI that references parent directories with the .. notation. All requests will pass through this function (unless a developer defines otherwise) by virtue of the sequence we described in the section *Request Processing Sequence*.

If the client supplies any authorization information when requesting a resource under access control, it will probably aid in determining the accessibility of the target resource. It is interesting to note that the resolved physical object does not necessarily have to be an operating system file—it could quite easily be a CGI program, or database connection request.

Path check functions are specified in obj.conf with the *PathCheck* directive.

Object Type

Let's take stock of where we are so far. We have an authenticated client, whose virtual path URL has been mapped to a physical path, and it appears that the client is allowed to retrieve the requested object.

HTTP responses have a MIME type and subtype as one of their properties. The client (typically a Web browser) will use this information to determine the appropriate handling method, for example display or user prompt.

The Netscape server processes those objects known to it via the mime.types configuration file. Otherwise, it forces the type to be text/plain, which most browsers will just display on screen. Not all responses have an obvious MIME type. That is where this directive is of use for the customized MIME type/subtype setting of retrieved documents. This is normally used when the type is potentially dynamic, because a static mapping is best served by an entry in the mime.types file.

Object type functions are specified in obj.conf with the *ObjectType* directive.

Service

Service is the most important event of all. This event signifies the return of the response to the client. All the information provided by the previous steps is potentially used here to transmit the result of the required actions back to the client. Also, at this stage the server inserts HTTP headers for transmission to the client.

Netscape provides a number of utility functions that allow you to write directly to the client as desired. The NSAPI library also includes functions to: map open file descriptors to file buffers (buffered I/O), send the contents of a file buffer to a socket, allocate and deallocate memory and data structures, allow the passing of data between events, and many others. These are described in the Chapter 2.

Service functions are specified in obj.conf with the *Service* directive.

Request Logging

Web servers log access and errors to themselves. To aid in the development of log analysis utilities, there is a Common Log format that most servers use to record these details.

However, for some sites, this may not be enough or may be too restrictive. You may require that the log include more or less information or even record information in a compressed format directly. (Logging each request in a heavily loaded Web server may cause the size of the log to become problematic.) You may even elect to use a file other than the server's normal access log.

The *AddLog* directive allows you to augment, alter, or otherwise control the behavior of the logging action for the server.

Logging functions are specified in obj.conf with the AddLog directive.

Configuration Files

We have briefly mentioned files such as obj.conf, magnus.conf, and mime.types. You will find yourself regularly editing at least one of these files when you develop Netscape server extensions.

> **Note:** *Netscape switched from using the Windows Registry for the Windows NT version 1.1 server (which was called Commerce Server) when Enterprise Server was created. There is now a common configuration file used across all platforms.*

We will take a look first at magnus.conf, then obj.conf, and finally mime.types.

The Server Configuration File: magnus.conf

When the ns-httpd executable (the HTTP daemon) commences execution, it uses the file magnus.conf to extract certain globally applicable server parameters. Each line in magnus.conf holds a key-value pair (Netscape refers to them as *directives*) that describes a particular part of the server configuration. Table 3.1 shows the most important magnus.conf keys, along with their type, default values, and brief semantics.

Table 3.1   Basic magnus.conf directives.

Name	Type	Default	Semantics
ServerName	String	None	The FQDN (fully qualified domain name) of the server.
Port	Unsigned integer	80	The TCP/IP port that the server should listen on. This is an unsigned integer between 0 and 65535.
LoadObjects	String	obj.conf	The absolute or relative path name of the object configuration file.
RootObject	String	None	The object directive that is to be consulted first during request processing.
ErrorLog	String	None	The full path name of the error log file. SYSLOG (all upper case) may be used to redirect to syslog (Unix) or Event log (Windows NT).
PidLog	String	None	Full path name of log file that records the master HTTPd processes' ID.
User	String	User Account at server startup	The account name that the user should run as.
MaxProcs	Unsigned integer	1	The number of processes that should be forked when the server is invoked. Applies to a Unix-based server only.
MinThreads	Unsigned integer	4	Minimum number of threads the server should create.
MaxThreads	Unsigned integer	128	Maximum number of threads that the server should create.
DNS	String	on	DNS is either on or off. This setting controls whether the server resolves a client IP address to a FQDN.
Security	String	off	If on, the server will assume that either SSL3 (Secure Socket Layer) or SSL2 encryption is active. SSL3 is checked first.

There are a number of other directives available for more advanced server use, such as the ability to define and activate SSL and SSL ciphers (for SSL3), access control lists, server certification, HTTP KeepAlive times, and others. Many of these additional facilities cannot be altered by extension software developed using the NSAPI. The server manuals provide a complete list and reference for this type of information.

It is common for magnus.conf to be modified indirectly using the server manager rather than by manually changing the file, although this is not enforced. It is sometimes more expedient during development, assuming you possess appropriate permissions, to make changes by hand and restart the server manually rather than using the server manager. However, any manual modification of this file should adhere to the following rules:

- Regard directives as case sensitive.

- Do not prepend any form of punctuation before introducing a directive.

- Follow a directive name by an equals sign and then its corresponding value.

- Enclose string values that include white space in double quote characters.

- Continue lines by specifying a character . (period) on the preceding line.

- Comments may be introduced by using a # (pound sign)as the first character on a line.

Note that if you do include comments, any editing performed with the server manager will eliminate them. Listing 3.1 shows how a typical magnus.conf appears after installation.

Listing 3.1   A typical magnus.conf configuration file.

```
#ServerRoot /export/EnterpriseServer201a/https-beetle
ServerName beetle.akl.optimation.co.nz
Port 666
LoadObjects obj.conf
RootObject default
ErrorLog /export/EnterpriseServer201a/https-beetle/logs/errors
PidLog /export/EnterpriseServer201a/https-beetle/logs/pid
User nobody
MaxProcs 3
MinThreads 4
MaxThreads 128
```

```
DNS off
Security off
Ciphers +rc4,+rc4export,+rc2,+rc2export,+des,+desede3
SSL3Ciphers +rsa_rc4_128_md5,+rsa_3des_sha,+rsa_des_sha,+rsa_rc4_40_md5,
  +rsa_rc2_40_md5,-rsa_null_md5
ACLFile /export/EnterpriseServer201a/httpacl/generated.https-beetle.acl
```

The Objects Configuration File: obj.conf

For the purpose of NSAPI extension development, this is the most important configuration file that the server consults. There are many options, dependencies, and keywords available for use in obj.conf. The server refers to obj.conf for almost every request that it must process.

In an attempt to manage this complexity, certain directives will be identified as standard directives. Standard obj.conf directives are those options and directives supplied with the Netscape server, whose behavior cannot be augmented by third-party extensions. As each directive's behavior is described, we will mention standard functions supplied by Netscape, which will allow you to decide when to develop or when to use the Netscape's directives. Also note that each directive has certain *associations* (key-value pairs) associated with it. This scheme is used to pass required (or optional) information to the function that implements the directive's behavior, which is sometimes the server itself.

The format of obj.conf has two basic sections: the initialization section and 2 to N sections, which describe certain objects and directives that may be applied to them. Remember that an *object* is an encoded, explicit, or implied reference to some resource that the server can access. References to objects are explicit/implicit in requests that the server receives. For example, when a GET HTTP request is received (see Chapter 1 for a thorough discussion of HTTP Request Types) for a document, the URL or URI that is the argument to GET is required. If there is an obj.conf object that matches this resource in obj.conf, the directives attached to this object are applied successively to the request until either an error or a response is determined. Note that obj.conf supports the notion of a default object, so that there are directives that are always applied to a request in the absence of an object directive set specifically targeted at a resource that is requested.

The Initialization Section

The initialization section of obj.conf specifies additional initialization steps for the server, such as logging, MIME type loading, the setting of serverwide CGI parameters, and others. Netscape describes this behavior as the initialization of server sub systems.

Consider the extract from a typical obj.conf shown in Listing 3.2.

Listing 3.2   An excerpt from obj.conf, which highlights the init section.

```
# Netscape Communications Corporation - obj.conf
# You can edit this file, but comments and formatting changes
# might be lost when the admin server makes changes.
Init fn="flex-init" format.access="%Ses->client.ip% - %Req->\
vars.auth-user% [%SYSDATE%] \"%Req->reqpb.clf-request%\" \
%Req->srvhdrs.clf-status% %Req->srvhdrs.content-length%"
  access="/export/EnterpriseServer201a/https-beetle/logs/access"
Init fn="load-types" mime-types="mime.types"
Init fn="load-modules" funcs="null,checkperms" \
shlib="/EnterpriseServer201a/slibs/highperf.so"

<Object name="default">
NameTrans fn="pfx2dir" from="/ns-icons"
dir="/export/EnterpriseServer201a/ns-icons"
NameTrans fn="document-root" root="/export/EnterpriseServer201a/docs"
PathCheck fn="unix-uri-clean"
PathCheck fn="find-index" index-names="index.html,home.html"
```

The first two Init functions are examples of the standard built-in server functions. The third Init directive, beginning with the string Init fn="load-modules", is the interesting rule from our NSAPI perspective. As we discussed in Chapter 2, Web server extension currently uses a paradigm centered around the attachment of shared objects to a running process (the server). Each Web server must therefore make available a configuration mechanism that allows you to specify what shared objects are to be loaded at runtime and thus attached to the server. With Netscape, this is accomplished by using the *load-modules* association with its attendant parameters.

The general syntax of the load-modules association is shown below

```
Init fn=load-modules funcs=[function names] shlib=[library name]
```

The [*function names*] parameter is a list of function names. Comma characters (,) are used to separate multiple function names. There should be no other embedded punctuation unless it forms part of a function name. The [*library name*] parameter is the full path name of a shared object.

In the example directive in Listing 3.2, we instructed the server to load the shared object (in this case, a Solaris shared library) called /EnterpriseServer201a/slibs/ highperf.so. We also informed the server that there are two exported functions called **null** and **checkperms**.

Shared Object Load Failures

During development, you may experiment with NSAPI. Because of the nature of dynamically loaded objects, it is quite possible that a misconfiguration may occur, which can have dire consequences for the server. The Netscape HTTP daemon will refuse to start if you specify the loading of a shared object that it cannot find. However, it does record such failures in the error log. Here is an example error message from a Solaris-based server:

```
conf_init: line 17: dlopen of
/export/EnterpriseServer201a/nsapi/highperf.so failed
(ld.so.1: ./ns-httpd: fatal:
/export/EnterpriseServer201a/nsapi/highperf.so:
  can't open file: errno=2)
```

The above message was obtained from the errors log that exists in the logs subdirectory of the http-<host name> directory created at installation. A quick look at the error message shows us that we must have supplied an incorrect name. Other errors can be more subtle (especially under Unix), but most are simple to diagnose and fix.

The supply of exported function names to the load-modules association means that the library is searched at load time for such symbols.

The Object Directives Sections

Figure 3.3 depicts the steps that a request will pass through when the server processes it. A requested resource will match one or more object sections in the obj.conf file and each section will contain a number of directives. The server applies each of the matching object section directives to the request in the order they appear in the file.

Therefore, it should come as no surprise to learn that the directives that may be attached to an object section are those that are shown in Figure 3.3 and summarized again in Table 3.2.

As you will have noticed, **Error** is a directive that is not a *true* event but has also been shown in Table 3.2. The **Error** directive is not covered further in this text as it is beyond the scope of this book.

To aid in understanding this request processing, consider another excerpt from the sample obj.conf file, shown in Listing 3.3.

Listing 3.3 An excerpt from obj.conf, which highlights object sections.

```
Netscape Communications Corporation - obj.conf
# You can edit this file, but comments and formatting changes
# might be lost when the admin server makes changes.

Init fn="flex-init" format.access="%Ses->client.ip% - %Req->vars.auth-
user% [%SYSDATE%] \"%Req->reqpb.clf-request%\" %Req->srvhdrs.clf-status%
%Req->srvhdrs.content-length%" access="/export/EnterpriseServer201a/
https-beetle/logs/access"
Init fn="load-types" mime-types="mime.types"
Init fn="load-modules" funcs="null,test_auth"
shlib="/export/EnterpriseServer201a/nsapi/highperf.so"
<Object name="default">
NameTrans fn="pfx2dir" from="/ns-icons"
dir="/export/EnterpriseServer201a/ns-icons"
NameTrans fn="pfx2dir" from="/mc-icons"
dir="/export/EnterpriseServer201a/ns-icons"
NameTrans fn="pfx2dir" from="/cgi-bin"
dir="/export/EnterpriseServer201a/cgi-bin" name="cgi"
NameTrans fn="document-root" root="/export/EnterpriseServer201a/docs"
PathCheck fn="unix-uri-clean"
PathCheck fn="find-pathinfo"
PathCheck fn="find-index" index-names="index.html,home.html"
```

```
PathCheck fn="check-acl" acl-disabled="https-beetle_formgen-READ-
   ACL_allow-7057"
PathCheck fn="check-acl" acl-disabled="https-beetle_formgen-WRITE-
   ACL_deny-7057"
ObjectType fn="type-by-extension"
ObjectType fn="force-type" type="text/plain"
Service fn="imagemap" method="(GET|HEAD)" type="magnus-internal/imagemap"
Service fn="index-common" method="(GET|HEAD)" type="magnus-internal/
   directory"
Service fn="send-file" method="(GET|HEAD)" type="*~magnus-internal/*"
AddLog fn="flex-log" name="access"
</Object>
<Object name="cgi">
ObjectType fn="force-type" type="magnus-internal/cgi"
Service fn="send-cgi"
 </Object>
```

Each Object section is enclosed in *<Object>, </Object>* delimiters. Every line between these delimiters is a directive or a comment. There may be one or many of each of the directives enumerated in Table 3.2.

In our simple configuration, there are two objects defined, *default* and *cgi*. These always have to be present in obj.conf; if absent, the server may break. Also, you will see that the default object section contains four separate **NameTrans** directives, through which a request may pass. Some of the directives in the example are reasonably subtle. Consider this one:

```
NameTrans fn="pfx2dir" from="/cgi-bin"
 dir="/export/EnterpriseServer201a/cgi-bin" name="cgi"
```

Table 3.2 Directives that may be specified in an object section.

Name	Event	Brief Semantics
AuthTrans	Authentication	User authentication
NameTrans	Name Translation	URL path mapping
PathCheck	Path Check	Accessibility of path for client
ObjectType	Object Type	MIME type determination
AddLog	Logging	Customized logging
Error	N/A	Customized error handling

This is a good example of the power of the obj.conf setup that represents a standard server function. Simply put, if the virtual path supplied in the request matches /cgi-bin, the cgi-bin component will be translated to /export/EnterpriseServer201a/cgi-bin and the processing redirected to the directive that has the name **cgi-bin**. In our example, this is the second object section shown. This is a rather neat way of translating CGI target URLs.

> **Note:** *The directives shown in the excerpt are all standard Netscape-supplied functions. The symmetry of this approach is admirable because the Netscape standard functions are just function names that have been exported from a shared object , which is the same method used by developers to extend the server.*

So what really happens when a request is received and processed? Consider an HTTP GET request that asks for the document /marketing/Marketing.html. If you traced the processing of this request, you would see that all of the **NameTrans**, **ObjectType**, **PathCheck**, and **AddLog** directives of the default object in Listing 3.3 are applied as it makes its way closer to the client. Additionally, the service directive *send-file* will be executed to dispatch the contents of the document.

The thrust behind NSAPI also allows you to interpose (or even completely replace) behavior for some or all of these directives with your own custom software.

Before you can do this successfully, we will walk through the protocol and etiquette necessary to create proper NSAPI functions. Because extension software runs in the same address space as the server itself, it's easy to see that a poorly implemented extension will compromise the server's operation. Chapter 6 covers fully each object directive's syntax, semantics, and example software.

Checking A Web Server's Accessibility

How do you know if your Web server is accessible and serving documents? When you are developing, it's sometimes tedious to switch to a Web browser to test. The lazy way to check this is to use the telnet command: telnet <web server host name> <web server port> (for example, telnet marketServer 8080). If you can connect, the Web server is listening. Now try GET / (the server is case sensitive).

You should see the home page of the Web server fly past. If not, it might be time to start checking the server more closely. The best way to do this is to resort to using the server selector, which contains an option to determine if the server is running.

The mime.types File

We mentioned earlier that the Netscape server uses the mime.types file to map document requests to MIME types and subtypes. Netscape provides one standard **ObjectType** directive that is used to perform this mapping, the *type-by-extension* function. Below are the **ObjectType** directives from Listing 3.3:

```
ObjectType fn="type-by-extension"
ObjectType fn="force-type" type="text/plain"
```

The **type-by-extension** function extracts the file extension from the document name supplied, and uses this as a key to search the mime.types file. An excerpt from this file is shown below:

```
#--Netscape Communications Corporation MIME Information
# Do not delete the above line. It is used to identify the file type.

# New Microsoft MIME types
type=application/msword             exts=doc
type=application/vnd.ms-excel       exts=xls,xlw,xla,xlc,xlm,xlt

type=application/octet-stream        exts=bin
type=application/x-javascript         exts=js
type=image/gif                       exts=gif
type=image/jpeg                      exts=jpeg,jpg,jpe
type=image/png                       exts=png

type=text/html                        exts=htm,html
type=text/plain                       exts=txt

type=magnus-internal/imagemap     exts=map
type=magnus-internal/parsed-html  exts=shtml
type=magnus-internal/cgi            exts=cgi,exe,bat
```

Most of these extensions will be familiar to you. If during **Object Type** processing (in a standard setup), a file is requested whose type cannot be determined by **type-by-extension**, the next function invoked will be *force-type*, which forces the MIME type/subtype to be whatever is supplied as the type parameter to it.

Summary

The Netscape family of servers utilizes contemporary architectures that operate similarly across the supported platforms. Heavy use of threads is used as an alternative to the use of processes. This enables superior performance when compared to their process-based relations.

The server takes its configuration from a number of plain ASCII files. The global server configuration is held in magnus.conf. The rules that govern the actions to perform for a request are stored in obj.conf. The MIME translations necessary for successful HTTP processing are defined in mime.types.

Each HTTP request passes through a number of phases before it is considered handled. In order, they are authentication, name translation, path check, object type, service, and logging.

The NSAPI exists to enable developers to augment or even replace the behavior of the server. This is a C-based API that allows the creation of server extensions, which are pieces of software that implement appropriate behavior for one of the request processing phases. NSAPI defines a simple system of integer return codes and data structures that combine to provide a protocol for propagating custom effects. Extension functions are *grafted* on to the server using the shared object support of the native platform.

HIGH PERFORMANCE

NSAPI Extension Function Basics

CHAPTER

4

This chapter describes the basic syntax of NSAPI extension functions, the supporting structures, and some of the available utility functions. In addition, this chapter will explain some of the NSAPI higher level abstractions.

NSAPI Extension Function Basics

Although Netscape offers a very flexible framework for creating server extensions, any extensions that you create must have a specific signature or prototype. Each extension function should have the following syntax:

```
int function_name(pblock *pBlock, Session *pSession, Request *pRequest)
```

Failure to use this exact signature in an exported function intended for server extension will normally cause the server to fail upon startup. It will fail because it will not be able to locate the symbol you have specified in the *fn* association to the *load-modules* directive.

All extension functions, regardless of the directive whose behavior they are designed to alter or augment, will have the same signature. Such a system calls for good naming conventions to be in place, so, in case of error, a quick perusal of the obj.conf file will expose which extension is doing what.

As you can see, the extension functions receive three pointer parameters. They are pointers to **pblock**, **Session**, and **Request** structures. The following sections discuss them in more detail.

NSAPI Include Files

Before we launch into our discussion of *pblocks* and the other parameters, we'll see where their definitions come from and where you can find them in the server installation. In a normal installation, a NSAPI subdirectory exists off of the server root directory. In Figure 4.1, we show an abbreviated listing of the nsapi directory.

As we discuss the techniques of NSAPI extension development in increasing detail, we will refer to header files based upon the name relative to nsapi/include only. This saves a lot of repetition. So if we say, base/pblock.h, you'll know what we mean. We won't list all of the header files now, but introduce them as necessary.

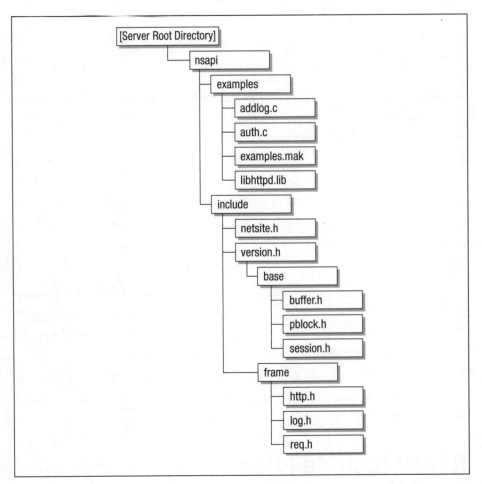

Figure 4.1
The relative position of the NSAPI directory.

Memory Management In NSAPI

All but the most trivial extension functions will require the use of heap allocated memory. NSAPI thus defines certain functions that you should use to manage memory when utilizing the C API.

With release 2.0 of Enterprise Server, the memory management scheme for requests changed subtly. In releases prior to 2.0, memory allocated by NSAPI developers had to be managed by developer code. With 2.0, Netscape decided to use a memory pooling system, that allows the server to optimize its memory management.

The *pool-init* init directive, which may be specified in obj.conf, controls the pool memory system. It is active by default—you probably don't want to disable this feature. If it needs to be disabled, place this initialization directive in obj.conf:

```
Init fn=pool-init disable=true
```

Obviously, the major caveat here is to be consistent. However, if you plan on developing extensions for commercial use, do not assume that a particular setting is in place. Netscape does provide two flavors of memory allocation. One is deemed *permanent* because it allocates memory that has a lifetime greater than that of any one request. The other flavor is *transient* because it allocates memory whose lifetime may be tied to the request in which it is created. The **pool-init** directive always controls the transcience property of NSAPI allocated memory unless the memory is allocated during a call to an initialization function. In such a case, it is always permanent and must be actively managed.

Transient Memory Allocation

Include file: netsite.h

Syntax
```
void * MALLOC(int iSize)
void * REALLOC(void *vPtr, int iSize)
void   FREE(void * vPtr)
```

Return Value

- For **MALLOC** and **REALLOC**, a pointer to void *. A null value is not precluded.

- For **FREE**, there is no return value.

Semantics

The names shown above are manifest constants that wrap server private memory allocation routines. It is not necessary for you to manage memory that is allocated using these functions. The use of **FREE**, therefore, is deprecated.

Permanent Memory Allocation

Include file: netsite.h

Syntax
```
void * PERM_MALLOC(int iSize)
void * PERM_REALLOC(void *vPtr, int iSize)
void   PERM_FREE(void * vPtr)
```

Return Value

- For **PERM_MALLOC** and **PERM_REALLOC**, a pointer to void *. A null value is not precluded.

- For **FREE**, there is no return value.

Semantics

The names shown above are manifest constants that wrap server private memory allocation routines. It is necessary for you to manage memory that is allocated using these functions. The use of these functions is deprecated.

What Is A pblock?

A pblock is a simple system of pointer-based structures that use a linked list to allow for the storage of associations (key/value pairs) and their retrieval based upon the key. Listing 4.1 shows the set of structures that the generically referred to pblock is composed of.

Listing 4.1 The **pb_param**, **pb_entry**, and **pblock** structures.

```
typedef struct {
    char *name,*value;
} pb_param;
struct pb_entry {
    pb_param *param;
    struct pb_entry *next;
};

typedef struct {
    int hsize;
    struct pb_entry **ht;
} pblock;
```

Extension functions commonly use the **pblock** structure to access parameters passed via some association in obj.conf. To explain this, consider the following custom **NameTrans** directive:

```
NameTrans fn="bespokeNameTranslation" tmp=/tmp delete=true
```

The two associations supplied (*tmp* and *delete*) will be placed into the pblock supplied to the *bespokeNameTranslation* function when, or if, it is called during NameTranslation for whatever requests it is defined for. If the values of the associations have been supplied, they may be accessed using the key (to query the pblock pointer passed to the function). Netscape states that the pblock pointer passed to an extension function conceptually references read-only memory. In later sections, you will see the use of read/write pblocks encapsulated in other NSAPI defined structures.

Although there are quite a few pblock functions defined, only a few are actually required during the course of development. It is possible to use pblocks in your own code independently of the pblock parameter that is supplied to your function, but their lack of sophistication and performance tuning limits their utility. With this in mind, the following is a list of the most important functions you will need to manipulate pblocks:

- pblock_find
- pblock_findval
- pblock_nvinsert

- pblock_nninsert

- pblock_remove

pblock_find

Include file: base/pblock.h

Syntax
```
pb_param * pblock_find(char * cpName, pblock * pSuppliedBlock)
```

Return Value

- Returns a pointer to a **pb_param** or a **NULL** pointer.

Semantics
Given a pointer to a key in **cpName**, it searches the supplied pointer to a **pblock** for an association that matches the key. Upon success, the pointer is returned. Both the key and value can then be accessed via the **name** and **value** pointers.

pblock_findval

Include file: base/pblock.h

Syntax
```
char *pblock_findval(char *cpName, pblock *pSuppliedBlock)
```

Return Value

- Returns a pointer to char or a **NULL** pointer.

Semantics
Given a pointer to a key in **cpName**, it searches the supplied pointer to a **pblock** for an association that matches the key. Upon success, the **value** pointer of the associated **param_block** is returned.

pblock_pblock2str

Include file: base/pblock.h

Syntax
```
char *pblock_pblock2str(pblock *pSuppliedBlock, char *cpString)
```

Return Value

- Returns a newly allocated pointer to char. A **NULL** pointer or the pointer to char passed as **cpString**.

Semantics

This function is very useful for debugging purposes. It traverses the associations in **pSuppliedBlock** and writes them into the string **cpString**. The format of the created string is **<key>=<value><space>**. If a null pointer is supplied as the value for **cpString**, this function allocates as much memory as is necessary to hold the string version of **pSuppliedBlock**. If a char pointer is supplied, it must have been allocated from the heap, preferably using the memory allocation routines defined by NSAPI.

pblock_nvinsert/pblock_nninsert

Include file: base/pblock.h

Syntax

```
pb_param *pblock_nvinsert(char *cpName, char *cpValue, pblock
  *pSuppliedBlock)
pb_param *pblock_nninsert(char *cpName, int iValue, pblock *
  pSuppliedBlock)
```

Return Value

- Returns a newly allocated pointer to the **pb_param** inserted into the supplied **pblock**.

Semantics

These functions insert an association into the **pblock** referenced by **pSuppliedBlock**. The first variation inserts two strings, whereas the second inserts a string and an integer value. Copies are taken of passed strings and memory is newly allocated to hold the association. The return value may be captured and used immediately.

pblock_remove

Include file: base/pblock.h

Syntax

```
pb_param * pblock_remove(char * cpName, pblock * pSuppliedBlock)
```

Return Value

- Returns a pointer to a **pb_param** or a **NULL** pointer.

Semantics

Given a pointer to a key in **cpName**, it searches the supplied pointer to a **pblock** for an association that matches the key. Upon success, the pointer is removed from the given **pblock** and returned. Both the key and value can then be accessed via the **name** and **value** pointers.

The Session Structure

The second argument in any NSAPI extension function is a pointer to a *Session* structure, which is defined in base/session.h. Listing 4.2 is a definition of the **Session** structure.

Listing 4.2   The **Session** structure.

```
typedef struct Session {
    /* Client-specific information */
    pblock *client;

    SYS_NETFD csd;
    netbuf *inbuf;
    int csd_open;

    struct in_addr iaddr;
#ifdef MCC_PROXY
    int req_cnt;
#endif
#ifdef MALLOC_POOLS
    pool_handle_t *pool;
#endif /* MALLOC_POOLS */
    void *clauth;       /* ACL client authentication information */
    struct Session *next;
    int fill;
} Session
```

Session is a basic encapsulation of the session that exists between a client and server for the duration of the request that is processed. Most sessions will be HTTP sessions, and will only contain one response. The **Session** structure was designed to act as a repository for those facets of a request that apply globally over the request. One such invariant is obviously the client's IP address.

The nature of the C language **struct** construct exposes to public access certain parts of the **Session** structure that should be private. We discourage use of such structure members due to the potentially volatile nature of their existence in different NSAPI versions.

We know that a client will request something of the server. We also know that the server keeps records of access by its clients. Part of the negotiation involved in creating a TCP/IP socket between a client and server will make the IP address of the client available to the server. The server records this and sometimes the DNS name of the client in the client **pblock** pointer of **Session** (pblock *client). Time for some code. The code snippet shown in Listing 4.3 demonstrates how to access the IP address and DNS name in **Session**.

Listing 4.3   Accessing the IP address and DNS resolved name of a client.

```
int some_extension_function_name(pblock *pBlock,
                                              Session *pSession,
                                              Request *pRequest) {
char *  cpIPAddress, * cpDNSName;
        cpIPAddress = pblock_findval("ip", pSession->client);
        cpDNSName = session_dns(pSession);
return 0;
}
```

There are only two associations present in **client**, those with the keys **ip** and **dns**.

> **Note:** *Notice the use of the **session_dns** function, which must be used to access the implied dns key.*

A server configuration is usually set to not automatically resolve IP addresses to host names, because DNS resolution can be an expensive process if multiple DNS requests are required to achieve name resolution. The use of **session_dns** does this extra processing. It inserts the host name in the session's **client** pblock if the name can be resolved and is not already present. If it is already there, it is returned. Heavy or repeated use of **session_dns** with a varied client population may cause server performance degradation, so use it when prudent.

After the **client** pointer, there are the related structure members shown here:

```
SYS_NETFD csd;
netbuf *inbuf;
int csd_open;
```

The manifest constant **SYS_NETFD** varies between NT and Unix. Under Unix, it is the traditional type of a socket descriptor, an integer. Under NT, it is the Windows Sockets socket descriptor type, **SOCKET**. This value may be passed to some of the functions defined by Netscape to allow the writing of data to the client. If the network connection denoted by **csd** is open, the value of **csd_open** is not equal to zero. The **netbuf** structure referenced by **inbuf** is the inbound data stream from the client, if applicable. The **netbuf** structure is sufficiently involved to warrant a separate section, which we will cover next. Consider all other members of the **Session** structure as *transparent*. Later chapters describe issues related to cross API/cross-platform issues and how they can be truly hidden.

The netbuf Structure

When creating an API that will be available on different platforms, platform-dependent features should be abstracted to a sufficiently high level so that source code portability is not unduly compromised. Netscape has tried to do this with the **netbuf** structure. The **netbuf** structure represents a network connection buffer (an area that may be read and written). It also provides a (operating system) file-oriented version called **filebuffer**, which allows platform-independent file operations. This version is slightly more adventurous because it admits the possibility of using memory mapped files for file buffers. Both **netbuf** and **filebuffer** are defined in the include file base/buffer.h.

In the context of the **Session** structure, the **netbuf** is used as an input character stream connected to the client. If there is any outstanding traffic buffered in the network connection between a client and server, it may be accessed using the **inbuf** pointer and the **netbuf** functions that we now discuss.

netbuf Functions

Include file: base/buffer.h

Syntax

```
int netbuf_getc(netbuf *pBuffer)
int netbuf_next(netbuf *pBuffer, int iAdvance)
int netbuf_grab(netbuf *pBuffer, int iSize)
int netbuf_buf2sd(netbuf *pBuffer, SYS_NETFD iDescriptor, int iLength)
```

Return Value

- **netbuf_getc** returns **IO_ERROR** in case of error.

- **netbuf_next** returns **BUFFER_EOF** at EOF or **BUFFER_ERROR** in case of error.

- **netbuf_grab** returns **IO_EOF** at EOF or **IO_ERROR** in case of error. Otherwise it returns the number of bytes read.

- **netbuf_buf2sd** returns **IO_ERROR** in case of error or the number of bytes sent.

Semantics

Use **netbuf_getc** to read a character from the **netbuf** pointer supplied as an argument. The character (or byte) read is returned as an integer. If there are insufficient bytes in the **netbuf**'s encapsulated internal buffer, a single byte will be read directly from the associated network connection. More buffering could occur because of this.

The **netbuf_next** function attempts to buffer **iAdvance** more bytes into the buffer of **pBuffer** and returns the first one in the manner of **netbuf_getc**.

The function **netbuf_grab** attempts to resize the internal buffer of the given **netbuf** object **pBuffer**. This is a number between 1 and n, in which n is the associated platform's limit for reads on a network connection. The return value is normally the number of bytes read to accommodate the requested size change. The default size for a network buffer is given by the manifest constant **NET_BUFFERSIZE**, which in most cases is 8192 (this constant is defined in base/net.h).

If you wish to send bytes from a network buffer to a network connection, you can use the function **netbuf_buf2sd**. This will attempt to transfer **iLength** bytes from **pBuffer** to **iDescriptor**. Using a value of less than zero for **iLength** sends all available bytes from **pBuffer** to **iDescriptor**. Using a negative **iDescriptor** is equivalent to discarding the bytes from **pBuffer**. This last type of behavior may be useful for crude parsing of input streams.

File Descriptors And File Buffers

In a similar vein to the **netbuf** structure and its abstracted view of network buffers, Netscape applied the same model to the notion of system files and file buffers. The file buffer notion is slightly more adventurous because it admits the possibility of using memory mapped files for file buffers. The **filebuffer** is defined in the include file base/buffer.h.

> **Note:** Memory mapped files are a service provided by operating systems that allow the virtual memory capabilities of the operating system to be used to map a file into memory. When using memory mapped files, a file can be addressed as a (potentially) large character stream, which can be arbitrarily addressed. Memory mapped file access usually results in much faster file manipulation.

You are probably wondering what the **filebuffer** is a buffer on (with respect to the underlying implementation), because the supported Netscape platforms implement operating system file access differently. This is the purpose of another Netscape abstraction, the system file descriptor and its associated services. Functions associated with file descriptors and their manipulation are prototyped in base/file.h.

The next section describes the facilities provided for file manipulation.

File Descriptors And File Manipulation Functions

The set of functions we will describe now operate in terms of Netscape's view of a file descriptor. An excerpt from base/file.h is shown in Listing 4.4.

Listing 4.4   Excerpt from base/file.h that shows the **SYS_FILE** abstraction.

```
typedef int SYS_FILE;
#define SYS_ERROR_FD -1
#define SYS_STDERR STDERR_FILENO
```

```
#elif defined(FILE_WIN32)
#include "sem.h"

typedef struct {
    HANDLE fh;
    char *fname;
    SEMAPHORE flsem;
} file_s;
typedef file_s* SYS_FILE;
```

As you can see, the Unix implementation uses a straight integer description that could also be used, for example, in a call to the standard library functions. The NT version, on the other hand, constructs **SYS_FILE** in terms of a pointer to a structure that includes a WIN32 handle, the file name, and a semaphore (for locking). The method of using a manifest constant is crude but accomplishes the establishment of a portable base of source code (as long as you subscribe to the Netscape world). Because we have the notion of portable file descriptors, Netscape provides some functions that operate on these types.

System Functions To Open Files

Include file: base/file.h

Syntax
```
SYS_FILE system_fopenRO(char *cpPath)
SYS_FILE system_fopenWA(char *cpPath)
SYS_FILE system_fopenRW(char *cpPath)
SYS_FILE system_fopenWT(char *cpPath)
```

Return Value

- 0 if the function failed, a valid **SYS_FILE** otherwise.

Semantics
Each of the variants for **system_fopenXX** will return a valid and open file descriptor if the operation requested succeeds. For some of these operations, a failure does not necessarily mean the nonexistence of a file—there may be an issue of ownership, permissions, and so on. For example:

- **system_fopenRO** opens the file in read-only mode.

- **system_fopenWA** opens the file in append mode (all writes are appended).

- **system_fopenRW** opens the file in read/write mode (random seeks allowed).

- **system_fopenWT** opens the file in write truncate mode (file is truncated if it exists).

> *Note:* Under the Unix implementation, if a file is created as a result of the requested operation, the permissions mask used is 0644.

System Function To Close Files

Include file: base/file.h

Syntax

```
void system_fclose(SYS_FILE rDescriptor)
```

Return Value

- No return value.

Semantics

The file referenced by **rDescriptor**, if it is open and valid, is closed.

System Function To Read And Write Files

Include file: base/file.h

Syntax

```
int system_fread(SYS_FILE rDescriptor,char * cpBuffer, int iSize)
int system_fwrite(SYS_FILE rDescriptor,char *cpBuffer,int iSize)
int system_fwrite_atomic(SYS_FILE rDescriptor, char *cpBuffer, int iSize)
```

Return Value

- **system_fread** returns the number of bytes read, **IO_ERROR** on error or **IO_EOF** when at EOF.

- **system_fwrite** returns the number of bytes written or **IO_ERROR** on error.

- **system_fwrite_atomic** returns the number of bytes written or **IO_ERROR** on error.

Semantics

The **system_fread** function attempts to read **iSize** bytes from **rDescriptor** into the supplied buffer **cpBuffer**. It normally returns the number of bytes read or **IO_EOF**.

The function **system_fwrite** attempts to write **iSize** bytes from **cpBuffer** to the file descriptor **rDescriptor**. It will normally return the number of bytes written. The **system_fwrite_atomic** function also writes data from a byte buffer in a similar fashion to **system_fwrite**, except that it will lock and unlock the file appropriately before writing. In the case of **system_fwrite_atomic**, a write failure can mean an I/O error or a lock acquisition failure.

Changing The Position Of The File Pointer

Include file: base/file.h

Syntax

```
int system_lseek(SYS_FILE rDescriptor, long lOffset, int iWhence)
```

Return Value

- **IO_ERROR** if the reposition failed, otherwise the actual seek value.

Semantics

This function attempts to place the implied file pointer at the position specified by **lOffset** measured relative to the **iWhence** value. Traditionally, **iWhence** assumes the values 0, 1, or 2 for beginning of file, current position, and end of file. This function is a macro in both instances, under Unix it refers to the standard function **lseek**, under NT it references the WIN32 API function **SetFilePointer**.

System Function To Lock Files

Include file: base/file.h

Syntax

```
int system_flock(SYS_FILE rDescriptor)
int system_ulock(SYS_FILE rDescriptor)
```

Return Value

- **system_flock** returns **IO_OK** or **IO_ERROR** on error.

- **system_ulock** returns **IO_OK** or **IO_ERROR** on error.

Semantics

Use **system_flock** to lock the file referenced by **rDescriptor** before performing an operation that should be atomic. Use **system_ulock** to release a previously acquired lock on a file.

File Buffers And Their Manipulation

The set of functions we will describe now operates in terms of Netscape's view of a buffer that wraps and operates upon a file descriptor. An excerpt from base/file.h is shown in Listing 4.5.

Listing 4.5 Excerpt from base/file.h that shows the **filebuffer** abstraction.

```
#ifdef FILE_MMAP
typedef struct {
    SYS_FILE fd;
#ifdef FILE_UNIX_MMAP
    caddr_t fp;
#else /* FILE_WIN32_MMAP */
    HANDLE fdmap;
    char *fp;
#endif /* FILE_UNIX_MMAP */
    int len;
    unsigned char *inbuf;    /* for buffer_grab */
    int cursize;

    int pos;
    char *errmsg;
} filebuffer;
#else
typedef struct {
    SYS_FILE fd;
    int pos, cursize, maxsize;
    unsigned char *inbuf;
    char *errmsg;
} filebuffer;
```

As you can see, the memory mapped implementation is quite different from the ordinary version. So when does Netscape use memory mapped files and when does it not? The answer lies in the file base/systems.h. This header file defines the characteristics of a number of systems in terms of support of certain features that the Netscape server will take advantage of, if present. If you need to know if memory mapping will be used on a particular operating system, look in there. If you are interested in whether a particular Unix variant will, and you can find a **FILE_UNIX_MMAP** manifest constant for it, then it will. Under Windows NT, memory mapping is used.

There are a number of functions that support the opening, closure, and reading of file buffers.

Opening And Closing File Buffers

Include file: base/buffer.h

Syntax
```
filebuffer *filebuf_open(SYS_FILE rDescriptor, int iSize)
void filebuf_close_buffer(filebuffer *pBuffer)
```

Return Value

- **filebuf_open** returns 0 in case of error, or a valid **filebuffer** pointer.

Semantics
If you wish to create a buffer over a file, use the **system_fopenXX** functions to open a file, and then use the **SYS_FILE** descriptor from that operation as an argument to **filebuf_open** to create the buffer. The function **filebuf_close** should be used to release the buffer associated with a file descriptor.

> **Note:** The file descriptor used by the buffer does not have to be closed in a separate step because **filebuf_close** will perform this operation.

Filebuffer Manipulation Functions

Include file: base/buffer.h

Syntax
```
int filebuf_getc(filebuffer *pBuffer)
int filebuf_next(filebuffer *pBuffer, int iAdvance)
int filebuf_grab(filebuffer *pBuffer, int iSize)
int filebuf_buf2sd(filebuffer *pBuffer, SYS_NETFD iDescriptor, int
  iLength)
```

Return Value

- **filebuf_getc** returns **IO_ERROR** in case of error.

- **filebuf_next** returns **BUFFER_EOF** at EOF or **BUFFER_ERROR** in case of error.

- **filebuf_grab** returns **IO_EOF** at EOF or **IO_ERROR** in case of error. Otherwise it returns the number of bytes read.

- **filebuf_buf2sd** returns **IO_ERROR** in case of error or the number of bytes sent.

Semantics

Use **filebuf_getc** to read a character from the **filebuf** pointer supplied as an argument. The character (or byte) read is returned as an integer. If there are insufficient bytes in the **filebuf**'s encapsulated internal buffer, a single byte will be read directly from the associated object, which may cause more buffering to occur.

The function **filebuf_next** attempts to buffer **iAdvance** more bytes into the buffer of **pBuffer** and returns the first one in the manner of **filebuf_getc**.

The function **filebuf_grab** attempts to resize the internal buffer of the given **filebuf** object **pBuffer**. This is a number between 1 and n, in which n is the associated platform's limit for reads on a file object. The return value is normally the number of bytes read to accommodate the requested size change. The default size for a file buffer is given by the manifest constant **FILE_BUFFERSIZE**, which in most cases is 4096 (this constant is defined in base/file.h).

If you wish to send bytes from a file buffer to a network connection, you can use the function **filebuf_buf2sd**. This will attempt to transfer **iLength** bytes from **pBuffer** to **iDescriptor**.

The Request Structure

The third and final parameter passed to an extension function is a pointer to a *Request* structure. This structure represents the request associated with the session (that is passed via the **Session** argument to the extension function) and in most cases will be an HTTP request. As such, there are a number of types of information that will be associated with the request. The abbreviated composition of this data structure is shown in Listing 4.6. We say abbreviated, because all members that should be regarded as transparent have been removed.

Listing 4.6 The Request structure.

```
typedef struct {
    /* Server working variables */
    pblock *vars;
    /* The method, URI, and protocol revision of this request */
    pblock *reqpb;
    /* Protocol specific headers */
    int loadhdrs;
    pblock *headers;
```

```
      /* Server's response headers */
      int senthdrs;
      pblock *srvhdrs;
      /* The object set constructed to fulfill this request */
      httpd_objset *os;
      /* The stat last returned by request_stat_path */
      char *statpath;
      struct stat *finfo;
} Request
```

The following sections describe the semantics of the identified Request members.

Semantics Of Request.vars

This part of the **Request** structure is normally used by the server to hold directive dependent state. What does this really mean? Well, as you have seen, there are a number of steps that each request must pass through before (and for one step, logging, after) its content (in the HTTP sense) can be returned to the client. The purpose of **Request.vars** then, is to make available the variables that are valid at each processing step.

> *Note: Request.vars is a pblock structure, whose semantics and defined NSAPI functions have already been described.*

The following sections cover the information present at each stage. Our example HTTP request is shown here:

```
GET /marketing/Marketing.html HTTP/1.0
```

Authentication

There are no associations present for authorization apart from *ppath* (mentioned next).

Name Translation

The associations present are dependent on the stage of processing that name translation has reached. There are seldom more than these associations defined:

- *ppath*—The corresponding value is a string that represents the URI of the request. For our example, this will be /marketing/Marketing.html. If this key is present in **Request.vars**, name translation has not concluded.

- *path*—The related value is the physical path that the URI has been mapped to. If this key is present, extension functions should regard name translation as having had occurred. In our example, this is /export/EnterpriseServer201a/docs/marketing/Marketing.html.

- *ntrans-base*—If present, the value pointed to by this key will be the root document directory of the web server. In our example, this is /export/EnterpriseServer201a/docs. This key is normally added to **Request.vars** by the directive in obj.conf (placed there at installation time) that looks similar to this:

```
NameTrans fn="document-root" root="/export/EnterpriseServer201a/docs"
```

Path Check

At this stage of processing, we need to check the accessibility of a resource for a particular request. There may, at this juncture, be an authenticated user associated with the request—this having been negotiated with the challenge response mechanism of HTTP 1.0 if it has been enabled for the target resource. So, apart from the *path* and *ntrans-base* keyed associations described above, the following keys may exist:

- *auth-db*—If present, the value referenced by this key will be the full path name of the authorization database that has been used to authenticate the client. An example value may be /export/EnterpriseServer/201a/authdb/default, this indicates that the default authorization database has been used to authenticate the request.

- *auth-user*—If present, the value associated with this key will be the user name that was sent by the client.

- *auth-type*—The value of this key can only be basic if it exists.

Object Type And Service

The standard contents of **Request.vars** will not be different at these stages than at **PathCheck**.

Add Log

The contents of **Request.vars** at this final step are only different from those at **PathCheck** when authentication is occurring. Chapter 1 described how authentication might take place for an HTTP request. It is easy to determine when a resource has been requested that necessitates the authentication of the client, because the key *status* will exist in **Request.srvhdrs** with a value of **401 Unauthorized**. If this exact association is present, the server is refusing the request for the resource. If the key *WWW-Authenticate* exists, the server is also providing the necessary authentication realm information to the client. If this challenge/response mechanism is successful, the request will be honored.

> **Note:** For a request that has not provided the appropriate authorization response for a protected resource, the keys auth-db, auth-user, or auth-type will not exist in **Request.vars**.

Semantics Of Request.reqpb

This part of the **Request** structure contains the client's HTTP request in a parsed and unparsed state. Keep in mind that **Request.reqpb** is a pblock structure. For all stages of a request's processing, there will be these associations present:

- *protocol*—The value of this key is the revision of the HTTP protocol that the client understands. For our example request, the value at this key is HTTP/1.0.
- *uri*—The value of this key is the URI (see Chapter 1) of the request. For our example, this is /marketing/Marketing.html.
- *method*—The type of operation that the client has requested. This may have the values GET, HEAD, POST, PUT, and so on. Trivially, our example is a GET request.
- *clf-request*—The full unparsed version of the client's request as received. Thus, our complete example is GET /marketing/Marketing.html HTTP/1.0.

Semantics Of Request.headers

This pblock structure holds whatever headers the client has sent to the server. As described in Chapter 1, a number of different headers may be sent from the client to the server as part of the request. Again, the associations present in this pblock are invariant with respect to the stage of processing a request has reached. Some of the more common are:

- *host*—If sent by the client, it means that they are aware of software multi-homing, which is a technique for hosting what appear to be multiple sites from the same IP address. Enterprise server supports this technique. The value at this key is therefore the host/port combo that prefixes normal HTTP requests. An example string could be beetle:1667.

- *authorization*—If present, the value referenced will be a fixed keyword with an appended BASE64-encoded string. BASE64 encoding is a means of encoding octets (bytes) in a portable manner. The technique is fully described in RFCs 1521 and 1421. BASE64 was originally designed for the safe encoding of mail for transmission. Safe in this case means not liable to lose information. BASE64 encoding is fully covered in Chapter 6 when we examine means to actually develop an AuthTrans extension. An example value for this key is Basic dQ9ufEI6Z23lhCBZ7, in which *Basic* is a fixed string, and the next string represents the BASE64-encoded user name and password.

- *accept*—Indicates the content types the client can accept image/gif, image/x-xbitmap, image/jpeg, image/pjpeg, and */*.

- *user-agent*—If the client is a Web browser, this header will normally be sent to the server. A value for a user running Netscape 3.0 under Windows NT is Mozilla/3.0 (WinNT; I).

- *connection*—Indicates the status of the connection for HTTP. This may take the literal value Keep-Alive.

Semantics Of Request.srvhdrs

Another member of the ubiquitous pblock family is **Request.srvhdrs**. This structure holds those headers that are part of the server's response to the client request. The style and scope of this response naturally varies as a function of the version of the HTTP protocol that is used.

*Note: The integer **Request.senthdrs** is tightly coupled with **Request.srvhdrs**. If it is equal to 0, then the server headers have not been sent. If equal to 1, then the headers have been sent.*

Authentication, Name Translation, Path Check

There are normally no associations present for these phases. This is quite reasonable as the server has not yet had a real chance to formulate an idea of the required response.

Object Type And Service

As we have discussed, the responsibility of the **ObjectType** event is to discover and ascribe a MIME type to the object that is requested by the client. Ordinarily this would mean that after the **ObjectType** phase has completed, there would be a *content-type* key in the **srvhdrs** pblock, with a value that corresponds to MIME type/ subtype combo. A simple example of this is text/html. Once the **ObjectType** phase has been completed, a content type must have been set.

The **Service** phase sees only the Content-Type key but is responsible for the insertion of whatever headers are deemed useful or necessary for the client.

Add Log

The contents of **Request.srvhdrs** at this final step will vary according to the version of HTTP that is used, whether authentication is commencing negotiation, and whether (and which) entity headers have been inserted as part of the **Service** events activity.

If the request being processed is attempting to access a resource that is access controlled, the initial phase of the authentication will result in certain headers (described in Chapter 1's description of HTTP basic authentication) being returned to the client as part of the challenge/response mechanism employed by HTTP. Typically, when such a request is first processed, the **NameTrans** event will translate the URI into a physical path. Just before the server calls the directives for **PathCheck**, it (the server) will detect that the path inserted into the pblock **Request.vars** is protected by the server's access control system. If it determines that this is the case, it will create the appropriate authorization response for the client to respond to and send them.

Typically, the keys inserted will be similar to the following (values for **WWW-Authenticate** vary according to the protection configured for the resource in question):

```
status="401 Unauthorized"
WWW-authenticate="basic realm="lowrisk"
```

After receiving this response, the client should respond with the original request and an authorization sequence (discussed in Chapter 1). The server will call the **AddLog** function even when the authentication *handshake* is occurring. Requests that require authentication are normally logged with their status of **401**.

The normal actions of the **Service** response include entity headers that are seen by the client and any extension functions that are registered for the **AddLog** event. These headers are simple pblock associations that represent the standard HTTP-style entity headers. Some typical associations include:

- *status*—The status of the request. Normal processing is indicated by **200 OK** whereas **403 Forbidden** indicates that the resource is definitely not allowed to be accessed.

- *last-modified*— If specified, the value at this key will be the HTTP-style date in which the server believes that the resource was last modified. An example value for this is: Sat, 18 Jan 1997 03:44:03 GMT.

- *content-length*—This should normally be present. The value of content-length will be the decimal encoding of the length of the resource entity body (in bytes) to be sent to the client. So, a value of 5120 indicates a 5 K resource.

- *content-type*—This key should always be present. Its value is normally the MIME type of the response that is sent to the client. This is also referred to as the media type in the HTTP specification. If no content type is notified to the client, extra processing may be involved at the client end, as they may resort to inspection of the octet stream as it is read. For this reason alone it is important to include it. An example value for this key is: application/x-zip-compressed.

Miscellaneous Request Members

There is one remaining member of the **Request** structure that has not been discussed.

The stat_path character array, if not null, holds a full path name that results from the NameTrans directives' actions. It is tightly coupled; therefore, the stat structure pointer, which holds information concerning the file, as denoted by stat_path. Implementation of the stat structure may vary from platform to platform. You should consult local include files to determine exactly what is defined; however, stat should be standard across Unix flavors, which leaves only Windows NT different. As a compromise, you can always use the intersection of the standard Unix stat structure and that of Windows NT to ensure maximum portability.

Summary

Each extension function that you create is expected to have the syntax shown here:

```
int function_name(pblock *p, Session *s, Request *r)
```

The pblock C structure is a simple pointer-based set of associations. Each association is comprised of a character string key and value. A number of API functions are implemented to allow for the creation, query, manipulation, and destruction of pblocks.

The Session C structure is the NSAPI encapsulation of the session that exists between client and server for the purpose of information exchange.

The Request C structure is the NSAPI model of a request sent from the client and the server's response to it. The information that may be gleaned from the Request structure varies as a function of time, by virtue of its relationship to the progression of a request's processing.

As part of its overall utility, and in an attempt to provide for cross-platform development, NSAPI defines abstractions for network and file buffers (along with a small but useful API for the manipulation). Also available is server-allocated and controlled-memory management.

Creating A Server Extension

CHAPTER

5

The major problem with most developers' initial attempts at extension development is that a naive design and implementation can compromise the server, either in terms of performance, stability or, in the worst case, both. In the interests of promoting server-friendly extensions; therefore, we now cover some issues that you will have to consider in any significant development. While a few of these issues are presented in the context of our NSAPI discussion, many apply equally well to ISAPI development also. Refer to the appropriate ISAPI chapter for further specific discussions.

Creating A Server Extension

As professional developers, we strive to create well-architected software. This is not possible unless we anticipate and properly execute a design phase. Rather than talking about the many different styles, designs, or idioms that we could employ, we plan to present the fundamental tenets of the design and implementation stage.

Design And Implementation

We realize that there are many developers who would like to use C++ for extension development as well as (or in place of) plain C, so we'll touch on C++ issues when relevant.

> **Note:** Chapters 12,13, and 14 are concerned with an object-oriented cross-API/cross-platform framework and covers many C++ issues.

Performance

Every developer knows that software will always be expected to run faster than it actually does. In the context of a server extension, this is the primary design consideration. An exquisite, flawlessly designed extension or set of cooperating extensions will fail miserably and be rejected if it monopolizes resources such as CPU or memory.

Your extension should treat a request as a hot potato and deal with it as quickly as possible. By association, it also should keep the client session open for as few CPU cycles as possible if it deals directly with the client. Remember that a heavily loaded server will often behave erratically and a saturated server will refuse client connections. This is not desirable if your extension is doing something of importance, such as handling electronic commerce over the Internet.

137

A C implementation should consider the following issues:

- Use of memory
- Use of compiler optimization options
- Locking and atomic operations (covered later in this chapter)
- Avoidance of global resources
- Efficient algorithms

In an ISAPI environment performance is especially important when developing filters. Because any filter you deploy is executed for every request, you must be very careful about which server events your filter registers interest in and the priority at which the filter is called. Refer to Chapter 9 for more details on filter registration and priority.

In addition to the considerations for a C implementation, a C++ implementation should consider the following issues:

- Coalesced methods
- Careful choice of virtual functions
- Efficient copy constructor implementations
- Avoiding the passing of objects by value
- Limiting or banning the use of multiple inheritance
- Avoiding virtual base classes

Depending on which language you choose, apply at least these heuristics to your extension development. No one likes a bloated extension!

Memory Usage

Memory usage is also a performance consideration. Extensions and their use of heap-allocated memory is an important issue. Greedy, repeated, or indiscriminate heap allocations may cause the server to thrash as it attempts to fill your requests.

For C-based NSAPI extensions, the Netscape pool system performs acceptably under load. However, the standard heap management functions of your compiler may be less satisfactory, and some may exhibit pathological behavior under heavy load. Some implementations of **malloc**, for instance, will treat each request for memory individually. In such cases, this will lead to a heavier load on the host operating system, which will often respond poorly. A typical and more efficient scheme involves using a *heap manager*.

Heap managers obviously vary in the techniques they utilize, but here is a typical scheme:

- When a request for N bytes is received, the heap manager examines a pool of memory that it has previously been allocated by the operating system.

- If the current request can be filled from the pool, then the pool's available size will be decremented appropriately and the request serviced.

- If it cannot be serviced, the heap manager will ask for a specific chunk of memory from the operating system and add it to the pool it manages.

The request will then be satisfied from the newly enlarged pool.

A heap manager may request blocks of 32 K, 64 K, 128 K and so on. This is so that multiple requests for small amounts of heap memory will not unduly burden either the server, heap manager, or operating system. There are other issues that must be solved (such as managing heap fragmentation, low cost memory defragmentation, and so on) but most professionally written heap managers work very effectively.

Note: Borland's C and C++ each include an efficient heap manager. Third -party products such as SmartHeap also perform admirably.

We advise that you check out your compiler's philosophy if you don't use the Netscape-provided functions for memory management.

For a C++ implementation, the memory allocation/deallocation global functions **new** and **delete** often may be little more than wrappers around **malloc** and **free**. Thus the preceding discussions may also apply to a C++ implementation. One technique used is to override **new** and **delete** on a class or global level, making them use the Netscape-provided functions. This can be very efficient, because if the **new** implementation uses the nonpermanent **MALLOC** of Netscape, the **delete** implementation does not actually need to do anything. In terms of design heuristics, this technique is frowned upon, because the class or classes (if global **new** is replaced) depends upon a particular type of nonstandard behavior. If you are in a bind and memory is the constraining factor, you may consider using this technique—and justify it later.

ISAPI provides some help with memory management when developing filters via the **AllocMem** callback function provided in the **HTTP_FILTER_CONTEXT** structure. You can use this to allocate memory for a filter and rely on the server freeing it when the request completes. However, for ISA development you must use Win32 SDK (such as **LocalAlloc** or **HeapAlloc**) or compiler-based support (for example, **malloc/free** and **new/delete**) to allocate memory from the heap. More details and techniques for ISAPI-specific memory management are provided in Chapter 10.

Global Resources

If at all possible, you should try to avoid using global resources. Their use often dictates serialized access that may impact extension performance in a multi-threaded environment. For certain implementations, the use of a globally accessibly service may be unavoidable, so the section "Techniques For Ensuring Thread Safety" details some ways and means of ensuring safe and reliable behavior.

Threads And Thread Safety

In our discussions of the Netscape and Microsoft IIS server architectures, we mentioned that requests are dispatched to threads and then processed to completion. For those of you who are fully familiar with threads, thread safety issues, and how to implement thread safety schemes, we suggest you skip this section and review the sections entitled "NSAPI-Provided Locking Mechanisms" and "Locking In ISAPI."

Threads

We are all probably familiar with the concept of a *process* as informally defined by both Unix and Windows NT. A process is a heavyweight object that exists in full view of the operating system kernel and is actively managed by it. When an executable program is loaded, a process is created that is the operating system embodiment of the executable code. Obviously, only a small portion of the program may actually be in memory at any one time, and may be shuttled between places in memory. Most programs will consist of only one process, although certain daemon type software (such as the Netscape server), will spawn multiple processes and control them. Operating system services used or provided for a process include the management of virtual memory, paging, swapping (as a last resort), priority management, allocation of a process ID, relocation in memory, and many others.

Now, this process model is all well and good—but it doesn't scale well. If it is the only means by which work is performed by software, it will result in a *single-threaded* model that is entirely sequential in execution, starting and inexorably proceeding to its conclusion with no side trips. For many types of applications, this is acceptable. However, for applications that need to perform tasks in parallel, the only option with this kind of model is to use multiple processes, which (as we have said) are quite heavy objects to maintain (the implied operating system overhead, context switching, and more). At a certain threshold, the operating system level of service will start to decline as increasingly heavy demands are made upon it, and it will begin to thrash. And merely throwing more hardware at the problem is an inelegant approach.

One solution to this dilemma is the use of threads. A thread is an independent sequence of execution through a defined area of a piece of software, operating within the context of a process. Under Unix, threads are virtually invisible entities that are scheduled to run on *lightweight processes*, which are a sort of subprocess that run within a process. Under Windows NT, threads have a higher visibility than compared to Unix but do not incur much more overhead than their Unix counterparts. The key here is the lightweight nature of a thread, in that it incurs a drastically reduced overhead relative to a process. Both Netscape and IIS servers, for example, will have up to N threads executing and processing requests.

You can think of the server as allocating each received request to a waiting thread. This thread then begins executing the standard or augmented behavior of the server with respect to each request.

So, for example with the Netscape server, an object set will be constructed for the request, a **Session** structure will be created, a **Request** structure will be created, and the object set (which is just a set of extension functions that are applied to the request) will begin to execute. When complete, the thread will be returned to the pool of threads managed by the server until it is needed again.

There are two main models of scheduling threads, *preemptive* and *non-preemptive*. With preemptive thread scheduling, any executing thread can be interrupted according to the operating system's local rules and control transferred to another waiting thread. With non-preemptive scheduling, a thread will retain control until it either dies or relinquishes control. Non-preemptive scheduling is quite primitive and normally requires an application developer to explicitly cede control, which relegates scheduling to an exercise in good manners.

Thread Safety

You have probably heard this phrase thrown around. A piece of code is considered thread safe if it can operate in a multi-threaded environment without injurious effect and with deterministic behavior. Simply, it is concerned with the notions of *deadlock* and *race conditions (synchronicity)*.

Synchronicity is a required property of access to a shared resource (at least from a thread's eye view). A problem arises when multiple threads attempt to access such a resource simultaneously. If this occurs, any sequence of critical state-changing operations should be guaranteed to be *atomic*. Atomic in this case means indivisible, so that no other thread of execution can affect the sequence to result in non-deterministic behavior.

As an example of this, consider what would occur if a simple array of characters were treated as a stack, from which multiple threads were extracting characters. Further, say there was a function in existence that, when called, popped the next character from the stack. Listing 5.1 shows the pro forma code for such a function.

Listing 5.1 Example code that is not suited for use in a multi-threaded environment.

```
char * cpStackOfCharacters;
int iGlobalStackPointer = 0;


int popCharacter() {
    int iReturn = -1;
    if (iGlobalStackPointer >= 0)
        iReturn =
            (int) cpStackOfCharacters[iGlobalStackPointer--];
return iReturn;
}
```

Is the function **popCharacter** guaranteed to be safe in the presence of multiple threads? The answer is a resounding no, because it is not possible to predict when a thread might enter the area of code shown in Listing 5.1. This piece of the function could be considered a *critical region* of code because it directly alters a global (shared) resource and makes a test dependent upon its state. Erratic behavior may result if thread A were to execute the test as follows

```
if (iGlobalStackPointer >= 0)
```

just as a different thread, thread B, executed the next line:

```
(int) cpStackOfCharacters[iGlobalStackPointer--];
```

Consider that thread A tests the variable and finds it is equal to zero, just before thread B decrements the variable. The next action of thread A will be to attempt to access an illegal area of memory because the integer variable is quite likely less than zero. Even if it is not less than zero, erratic behavior will still occur, because both threads A and B will have popped the zeroeth character. Even if you could reduce the critical section of code so that it consisted of one language operation, it will still probably map onto more than one assembly language instruction. Atomicity, then, is not a property that can be dealt with on a *reductio ad absurdum* basis.

Deadlock (sometimes called *deadly embrace*) will occur when threads using synchronization primitives (such as *mutual exclusion locks,* commonly called *mutex*es) may proceed only if they can gain control of a lock that the other holds, and vice versa. When such a condition is true, the system is in deadlock and neither thread can proceed unless an external force is applied.

Techniques For Ensuring Thread Safety

In the presence of multiple threads, there is the need to guarantee that atomic operations can exist if required. This is not to say, however, that such conditions are required. Indeed, the use of atomic operations results in a loss in concurrency and effectiveness of the multi-threaded model. Although this is undeniable, the gains for a well-designed, threaded application are significant. This is perhaps the reason that both Netscape and IIS use threads to the extent that they do.

To guarantee the atomicity of a section of code, it is necessary to *serialize* execution of it. By this we mean that at any one time, only one thread may be active in the section of code. This section of code is sometimes termed a *critical region.*

The first and simplest means of implementing serialization is to use a *mutex* to guard critical regions. A mutex is created by an operating system call (such as **pthread_mutex_init** on POSIX-compliant systems, and **CreateMutex()** under WIN32). Once created, a thread (or even a process) can ask to lock the mutex. If no other thread has the mutex locked, this request will be granted. If it is locked, the requesting thread will block until the lock becomes available There may be many threads waiting on a mutex unlock, so the order in which threads gain a mutex is unpredictable. Listing 5.2 shows the code in Listing 5.1 with pseudomutex code in place. Assume that the mutex variable **rMutex** has previously been created and initialized.

Listing 5.2   Code made safe for use in a multi-threaded environment.

```
char * cpStackOfCharacters;
int iGlobalStackPointer = 0;

int popCharacter() {
int iReturn = -1;
rMutex.lock();
if (iGlobalStackPointer >= 0)
iReturn =
            (int) cpStackOfCharacters[iGlobalStackPointer--];
rMutex.unlock();
return iReturn;
}
```

The shaded code between the **rMutex.lock()** and **rMutex.unlock()** code is the critical region.

Another method of implementing serialization is to use a *readers/writer lock (rwlock)* to guard shared resources. A rwlock has great benefit in scenarios in which there is a distinctly polarized read-only access to the resource. They operate by allowing only one thread to acquire a write lock on the resource, which is only possible when there are no read or write locks in existence. Threads requiring read-only access to the resource also lock the rwlock when they need to access the resource, with the exception that many read locks can be in existence simultaneously. Compared to ordinary mutex locks, which we could describe as having a fairly coarse grain, rwlocks allow you to apply your knowledge of the access patterns related to a resource to your advantage.

A C++ Idiom

A particularly nice way in C++ of dealing with the acquire/release protocol used by simple locks is to hijack the behavior defined for stack-based objects. Basically, this means using a default constructor to acquire a lock, and the destructor to release the lock. Here is a sample fragment of an implementation for such a lock class:

```
class SimpleLock {
private:
CoarseLock rBasicLock;
public:
SimpleLock() { rBasicLock.acquire(); }
~SimpleLock() { rBasicLock.release(); }
};
```

*If you place an auto variable of type **SimpleLock** at the top of a method that needs protection, as shown here*

```
void SomeClass::addElement(SomeClass const & rElement) {
SimpleLock rLock;
rArray[iIndex++] = rElement;
}
```

*the method becomes serialized, assuming that the class **CoarseLock** has the appropriate exclusivity behavior. When **rLock** is constructed, the lock will be acquired. When **rLock** is destroyed, as it goes out of scope, the lock will be released.*

NSAPI-Provided Locking Mechanisms

With release 2.0 of Enterprise Server, Netscape has included some synchronization functions into NSAPI. They are of a coarse grain, and effectively model a mutex type lock.

Include file: base/crit.h

Syntax

```
CRITICAL crit_init();
void crit_enter(CRITICAL vLock);
void crit_exit(CRITICAL vLock);
void crit_terminate(CRITICAL vLock);
```

Return Value

- **crit_init** will return a **CRITICAL** value.

Semantics

The function **crit_init** creates a critical region variable. This is a value of type **CRITICAL** (in fact a void pointer). The variable created can be used to serialize access to areas of code and guarantee safety in the presence of multiple threads.

The function **crit_enter** attempts to lock the **CRITICAL** variable **vLock**. If another thread already has **vLock** locked, the requesting thread will be blocked until the lock owner calls **crit_exit**, which releases the lock previously acquired on **vLock**.

When the critical region variable is no longer required, it should be released using **crit_terminate**.

Listing 5.3 shows the code in Listing 5.1 modified to use the Netscape critical region functions:

Listing 5.3   Code for use with NSAPI functions.

```
char * cpStackOfCharacters;
int iGlobalStackPointer = 0;
CRITICAL vLock;

void initCriticalVariable() {
    vLock = crit_init();
}

int popCharacter() {
    int iReturn = -1;
    crit_enter(vLock);
    if (iGlobalStackPointer >= 0)
        iReturn = (int) cpStackOfCharacters[iGlobalStackPointer--];
```

```
    crit_exit(vLock);
return iReturn;
}
```

Listing 5.3 assumes that the **CRITICAL** variable **vLock** will be the argument passed to a **crit_terminate** function call by a clean-up function not shown.

Locking In ISAPI

Unlike NSAPI, ISAPI does not itself provide any locking mechanisms. You must use locking facilities provided by the operating system. Windows NT provides an excellent range of thread synchronizing objects including: mutex, semaphore, event handlers, and critical sections. These are discussed further in Chapter 10.

Tips For Optimizing Thread Safety

Our motto is: Be safe, but no safer than necessary. A conservative approach to serialization can damage the efficiency of software so that it appears poorly written, slow, and single threaded. Here we offer a few optimization tips:

- Lock for only as long as is necessary. Each statement executed under the protection of a lock is a choke point for multiple threads. Ensure that your code treats the lock as a very precious item.

- Be mindful of deadlock. Trace critical region code and attempt to cover all relevant scenarios. Keep it simple—if you have 10 shared resources governed by the same number of locks, you are asking for trouble if interdependence of locking requirements exists.

- Determine the best locking scheme for your requirements. If you only need a readers/writer lock, then use it. Don't go for the easiest or coarsest lock just to save time—it will rear up and bite you later. Analyze the access patterns for the resource—if it is skewed to the read only end of the spectrum, it is a good candidate for a rwlock.

- Consider if you need the resource to be shared. If it can be allocated on a per thread basis without adversely affecting the stack requirements for a thread or the memory committed to the process, consider using a per thread copy.

Aspects Not To Worry About

After the commandments of the previous sections, here is something you don't have to worry about. Recall the signature of an NSAPI extension function, shown here:

```
int function_name(pblock *pBlock, Session *pSession, Request *pRequest)
```

We have discussed how an extension is executed in a thread and that access to a shared resource in such a function should be aware of multi-threading issues.

When developing NSAPI applications, the good news is that unless you have an exceptionally tortured extension function, the **Session** and **Request** pointers are immune to interference from other threads. Netscape allocates such structures a per request basis and a request will only be actively processed in one thread. So you can write into both these heap-allocated structures with impunity.

In ISAPI, each filter and ISA gets a pointer to its own Filter Context and Extension Control Block respectively. You can operate on these quite independently from requests being handled on other threads.

A problem may arise if you create your own threads that operate within the context of your extension function and try to update these variables simultaneously. The simple strategy is to avoid this behavior if possible.

Deployment In Shared Objects

We described Netscape's process that allows a shared object (a DLL under Windows NT, a shared library under flavors of Unix) to be attached to itself and extension functions to be used to augment the server's operation. Each Netscape-supported Unix platform provides different linker (ld) options to allow the creation of a shared library. Netscape's Web site (**www.netscape.com**) contains, under its technical documentation section, a concise table that lists the appropriate options for each platform.

> **Note:** If applicable, you must compile any source code with whatever compiler options are necessary to generate position-independent code. For example, under Solaris you should use the -PIC option to CC or the -kPIC option to GNU C++. Failure to do this can result in an invalid library.

When developing NSAPI or ISAPI extensions under Windows NT, you must use a compiler that understands libraries in COFF (Common Object File Format). If you use a professional development system such as Visual C++, the application wizard will enable you to create a DLL easily.

For NSAPI, you will also need to include the library libhttpd.lib, which defines the functions described in this book. This library is located in the nsapi/examples directory of a standard Netscape installation. Chapter 3 describes in detail the directory structure of a Netscape server.

> **Note:** *This note concerns NSAPI development. If compiling under Windows NT, you must define the manifest constant* **XP_WIN32**. *If compiling under Unix, define* **XP_UNIX**. *The value of the constant is unimportant. You can use the -D switch on most Unix compilers, the /D with Microsoft Visual C++ or define a constant in the Preprocessor section under the C/C++ tab in the Visual C++ settings for a project. Failure to define this will cause any compilation to fail.*

Debugging Server Extensions

Debugging server extensions is notoriously difficult. Part of the problem is the very model that gives server extensions their flexibility—the shared object.

Shared objects are attached to the server at runtime. When debugging an extension, it is quite likely that you will need to make alterations to the software and then retest it. You won't be able to get the server to reload the shared object unless you stop and then restart the server. Depending on your site administration policy, this could be a minor procedure or a logistical nightmare.

However, assuming you can sort out the administrative side, there is the serious business of meaningfully debugging extensions. We have used two methods successfully, one quite crude and the other slightly more elegant.

The crude method is one that developers have used for years—inserting statements at tactical points in the software and writing out some useful information regarding the current state of the software under test. With the NSAPI, you can use functions such as **log_error** to do this if you don't mind cluttering the server's error log.

Alternatively, if you are using C++, you can consider using a global variable (yes, the global variables we warned you not to use) that is an open **ofstream**. State can then be sent to the stream via the standard insertion operators.

Although that method works, it is invasive. Another means of debugging is to use custom software that runs as a daemon on a server that is accessible to the extension. You can then connect (via sockets or other means) to the daemon and throw information at it in much the same way you talk to an output stream. The advantage of this approach is that the daemon can send this output to any medium.

Things look slightly rosier if you are debugging on an SVR4-compliant Unix platform. Then you can use the *truss* utility we mentioned in Chapter 3, if you want to trace the behavior of the server at a low level. The *truss* utility allows you to attach to a running server and follow child processes. This means that you don't have to wade through masses of debug output to get the information you need.

If you are debugging on Windows NT, you may also use one of the professional debugging packages, such as *Soft*ICE *3.0* by NuMega Technologies. Products such as this can allow you relative ease in tracing the execution flow of multiple threads and processes. Using these tools enable you to drill down as deep as required to monitor the state of your extension as it executes. The URL for NuMega is **www.numega.com**.

Debugging techniques specific to ISAPI filters and ISAs in a Windows NT environment are discussed in Chapter 10.

Summary

When creating extension functions, as with all software, design must be carefully considered. The most important aspects constraining design are performance, memory usage, global resources, and safety in the presence of multiple threads. We favor object-oriented techniques for both analysis, design, and implementation, but structured techniques are just as applicable for procedural language implementations.

In this chapter we have described in depth a number of heuristics that may be applied to the design of extensions as well as common pitfalls and traps. Finally, we considered some techniques for debugging shared objects and some simple means of discerning extension state.

Creating And Deploying NSAPI Extension Functions

CHAPTER

6

This chapter covers all the events for which you can create NSAPI-based extension software. Each event is thoroughly explained, including its semantics, include files used, the typical state of the **Session** and **Request** pointers during processing, acceptable return codes, and configuration. Complete, tested, and annotated extensions are described.

Creating And Deploying NSAPI Extension Functions

An initialization function is one configured to be called by the server as it commences execution and initializes server subsystems and developer-specified extensions.

Initialization Functions

An initialization extension may create a resource that will be used by other extension functions; such a resource will be globally visible. Such a resource may need to be subject to locking if it is potentially volatile.

Signature

Initialization functions have the following prototype:

```
int function_name(pblock * pBlocker, Session * pSession, Request *
    pRequest)
```

Semantics

The initialization function has no required semantics and performs whatever actions the developer has defined.

Include Files

To define the structures that are passed via pointers to the function, you should include the following lines in your source code:

```
#include "base/pblock.h"
#include "base/session.h"
#include "frame/req.h"
```

Important Session Structure Members

The **Session** structure pointer will be NULL upon entry to this class of function.

Important Request Structure Members

The **Request** structure pointer will be NULL upon entry to this class of function.

pblock Variables Defined

There are no standard defined associations in the **pblock** pointer **pBlocker** that is passed. However, it may include associations that you have defined yourself and specified in obj.conf.

Initialization Extension Return Codes

You should be aware of these points regarding return codes:

- All return codes are defined in frame/req.h.

- An initialization function should return **REQ_ABORTED** if a problem occurred during initialization. They may also insert an association into the supplied **pblock pBlocker** that has, as its key, the string **error** with a value of some suitably descriptive error string. This error message will be logged to the server's **errors** file.

- Any other return code indicates success. It is customary to use **REQ_PROCEED** to signal this.

Configuration For This Event

Initialization directives that stand outside of any object are therefore defined separately in obj.conf. Here is an extract from obj.conf that highlights two Init directives that we have added:

```
# Netscape Communications Corporation - obj.conf
# You can edit this file, but comments and formatting changes
# might be lost when the admin server makes changes.

Init fn="load-types" mime-types="mime.types"
Init fn="load-modules" funcs="initLock,serviceRequest" shlib="/var/
   extensions/highperf.so"
Init fn=initLock errorString="Failed to create a CRITICAL for use by
   highperf.so"
<Object name="default">
AuthTrans fn="example_auth"
NameTrans fn="pfx2dir" from="/ns-icons" dir="/export/
   EnterpriseServer201a/ns-icons"
NameTrans fn="pfx2dir" from="/mc-icons" dir="/export/
   EnterpriseServer201a/ns-icons"
```

This is an appropriate example of the configuration required in general for an extension function or functions. When the server processes the Init directives, it will interpret the line

```
Init fn="load-modules" funcs="initLock,serviceRequest"
shlib="/var/extensions/highperf.so"
```

such that it will try to load the shared object specified by **shlib** (/var/extensions/highperf.so) and locate the symbols (exported or publicly visible function names) **initLock** and **serviceRequest**. As we have seen, if it can't perform all of these actions successfully (loading the library and locating the symbols), an error will be logged and the server will not start. But if this stage completes successfully, the directive

```
Init fn=initLock
errorString="Failed to create a CRITICAL for use by highperf.so"
```

will execute next, and the server will call the function **initLock**, which we have already defined as the one located in the /var/extensions/highperf.so shared object. When this function has performed its tasks, whatever they may be, it will return a value as noted in the "Initialization Extension Return Codes" section.

Example Initialization Function

The code we present in Listing 6.1 is a simple function designed to create a **CRITICAL** variable for use in locking a shared resource. It uses the NSAPI-defined functions for creating and destroying a **CRITICAL** variable (which is an opaque pointer to **void**). It also introduces the notion of a function that can be called upon server restart.

Listing 6.1 Initialization function that creates a **CRITICAL** variable.

```
#if defined(__cplusplus)
extern "C" {
#endif

#include "base/pblock.h"
#include "base/session.h"
#include "frame/req.h"
#include "base/crit.h"
#include "base/daemon.h"

CRITICAL vLock = (CRITICAL) NULL;
#if defined(XP_WIN32)
#define EXPORT __declspec(dllexport)
#else
#define EXPORT
#endif

EXPORT void restartLock(void * vParameter);
EXPORT int initLock(pblock *pb, Session *sn, Request *rq)
{
char * cpErrorMessage;
    vLock = crit_init();
    if((CRITICAL NULL) == vLock) {
        cpErrorMessage = pblock_findval("errorString");
        pblock_nvinsert("error",
                  (cpErrorMessage != (char *) NULL) ?
                  cpErrorMessage :
                  "An Error Occurred In initLock()",
                  pb);
     return REQ_ABORTED;
    }
daemon_atrestart(restartLock, NULL);
return REQ_PROCEED;
}

EXPORT void restartLock(void * vParameter)
{
    crit_terminate(vLock);
    vLock = (CRITICAL) NULL;
}
```

```
#if defined(__cplusplus)
}
#endif
```

Now we'll step through the code as defined. First, we encounter an **#if defined**(). This will ensure that name mangling does not occur if the code is compiled with a C++ compiler:

```
#if defined(__cplusplus)
extern "C" {
#endif
```

This is followed by the inclusion of several header files that define the **pblock**, **Session** and **Request** types and the **CRITICAL** constant. These files also define prototypes for critical region functions:

```
#include "base/pblock.h"
#include "base/session.h"
#include "frame/req.h"
#include "base/crit.h"
#include "base/daemon.h"
```

This next line declares a globally visible (even from the perspective of an external function) **CRITICAL** variable, and initializes it to **NULL**. This is our lock that threads can use to lock a critical region of code or serialize access to a shared resource:

```
CRITICAL vLock = (CRITICAL)  NULL;
```

Here we define an appropriate qualifier that will attach to a function to export it from the library. This step enables the server to actually resolve (locate) the symbol (function name) at runtime. This is also when it loads the shared object in which the functions reside. Under Unix, no qualification is required, whereas under Windows NT, a macro to export the name from the DLL is necessary:

```
#if defined(XP_WIN32)
#define EXPORT __declspec(dllexport)
#else
#define EXPORT
#endif
```

Now we'll encounter the declaration of the function **initLock**, which was referenced in the **load-modules** initialization directive. The usual Netscape extension signature is used for this function:

```
EXPORT int initLock(pblock *pBlocker,
                    Session *pSession,
                    Request *pRequest)
{
```

Notice that we qualified the function declaration with **EXPORT**, which we defined earlier. Now we'll define a character pointer for use later (in C++ we could defer definition until the point at which **cpErrorMessage** was needed). We'll also initialize the **CRITICAL** variable using the NSAPI **crit_enter()** function that we have already described:

```
char * cpErrorMessage;
vLock = crit_init();
```

Because we are model code warriors, we'll test the value returned by and then stored in **vLock**:

```
if((CRITICAL) NULL == vLock) {
```

The next statement is slightly trickier. Here, we use a **pblock** manipulation function to ascertain the value (if any) of the association whose key is **errorString**, in the **pblock** that we were supplied when called by the server, **pBlocker**:

```
cpErrorMessage = pblock_findval("errorString");
```

You have probably guessed where the value at this key comes from. Look at the initialization that we placed in obj.conf:

```
Init fn=initLock
errorString="Failed to create a CRITICAL for use by highperf.so"
```

You can see that we specified an association with a key of **errorString**, with the value shown. This is where the association originates. The server parses such associations and includes them in the **pblock** supplied to any extension function. So, if we altered the Init directive to be

```
Init fn=initLock
errorString="Failed to create a CRITICAL for use by highperf.so"
numLocks=2
```

our extension function **initLock** would then be able to access two associations including one with a key of **numLocks**. Okay, diversion over. If the following lines are executed

```
pblock_nvinsert("error",
     (cpErrorMessage != (char *) NULL) ?
     cpErrorMessage :
     "An Error Occurred In initLock()",
     pb);
return REQ_ABORTED;
}
```

we know that the **crit_init** function returned a null **CRITICAL** value. Using the Netscape standard, we then insert an error message into the **pblock**, with a key of **error**. Here, our Init directive is designed to pass an error message to our **initLock** function, which we insert as the value of the **error** association. Notice our test for **cpErrorMessage** as a null pointer. If it is a null pointer, we substitute a nonspecific error message.

This piece of code

```
daemon_atrestart(restartLock, NULL);
return REQ_PROCEED;
}
```

registers a function with the server that will be called if the server is restarted. The function (**restartLock**) is not called when the server terminates. We supply the address of a function with the signature *void (*fn)(void * vParameter)* where the pointer to void parameter *vParameter* is specified by the developer. In our example, we have set this to **NULL**.

The final part of the code declares the restart function that is supplied to **daemon_atrestart**:

```
EXPORT void restartLock(void * vParameter)
{
crit_terminate(vLock);
vLock = (CRITICAL) NULL;
}
```

Because the initialization function will be called after the restart function, we free the **CRITICAL** variable and assign it **NULL**.

Key Features

Here is a summary of the characteristics for this class of function:

- The **Session** and **Request** pointers are always **NULL**.

- The user defines a restart function if appropriate and registers it with **daemon_atrestart**.

- Functions registered with **daemon_atrestart** are not called at server termination.

- If an error occurs, insert an association with a key of **error** and a value of an error message into the **pblock** supplied.

- Return **REQ_PROCEED** for success.

- Return **REQ_ABORTED** on error.

Authentication Functions

An authentication function is designed to augment or replace the authentication that the server may perform on clients. Therefore, such an extension may implement specialized authentication schemes more rigid than those implemented using a Netscape server. You may also create implementations that use stronger encryption for supplied user names and passwords (Netscape only supports BASE64 encoded authentication information per the HTTP 1.0 specification). Such information, if transmitted over an unencrypted link and captured, is trivial to decode.

Signature

Authentication functions have the following prototype:

```
int function_name(pblock * pBlocker,
                        Session * pSession,
                        Request * pRequest)
```

Semantics

The authentication function, required to perform a number of actions, is one of the more complex directives. We'll consider both scenarios in which an authentication extension may be called.

The first scenario is when a client requests a resource for which authentication is required, but offers no authorization information in the request. This one is fairly easy to deal with—we must notify the client that authorization is necessary by setting the status of the server's response to **401 Unauthorized** and setting the WWW-Authenticate header according to the following syntax:

```
Basic <Authentication realm>
```

The <Authentication realm> is a string that may be used by the client to prompt the user for an appropriate user name and password. The realm is considered opaque to the client, but the server may use it as a hint to determine the relevant authentication database.

When most clients see a status of **401** and a **WWW-Authenticate** header they will prompt the user for a name and password, encode whatever is entered, and then resend the request with an *authorization* header that is similar to the following format:

```
Basic dG9ueWI6ZGVlcDA5
```

As Chapter 1 described, the encoded string is a BASE64 encoded string composed of the user name, a colon, and a password.

This brings us to our second scenario, in which authorization information is supplied by the client. An extension function must examine the string presented and, assuming it understands the method of encryption, extract the user name and password. It should then perform the necessary steps to ensure that the credentials presented are valid. The method of validation for your own authentication extensions is made entirely at your discretion.

If the credentials are invalid, the extension may direct the server to respond again with a **401** status (as before), or it can abort the request without changing the default status (which is **500**). Choosing the latter method normally denies the client the chance to respond unless it reissues the request without an authorization header.

If the extension validates the user name and password, it should place the user name in the **Request.vars pblock** under the key *auth-user*, and an association with the key *auth-type* in **Request.vars** with a value that corresponds to the type of authentication performed. In standard HTTP, this is the string basic. If your authentication implementation supports the notion of groups (as Netscapes does), you may insert the resolved group name (which is usually not supplied by the client) into **Request.vars** under the key *auth-group*.

Include Files

To define the structures that are passed via pointers to the function, you should include the following lines in your source code:

```
#include "base/pblock.h"
#include "base/session.h"
#include "frame/req.h"
```

Important Session Structure Members

The **Session** structure pointer contains the information shown in Table 6.1.

Important Request Structure Members

The **Request** structure pointer contains the information shown in Table 6.2.

Table 6.1 Session structure members available.

Means of access	Type	Meaning
pblock_findval("ip", pSession->client)	char *	The IP address of the client.
session_maxdns(pSession)	char *	The FQDN of the client.
pSession->csd	SYS_NETFD	System-dependent file descriptor connected to the client.
pSession->inbuf	netbuf *	Network connection buffer to the client (inbound).
pSession->csd_open	int	If not equal to zero, the connection to the client through csd is open.

Table 6.2 Request structure members available.

Means Of Access	Type	Meaning
pblock_findval("ppath", pRequest->vars)	char *	The partial path of the request.
pblock_findval("protocol", pRequest->reqpb)	char *	The protocol of the request.
pblock_findval("uri", pRequest->reqpb)	char *	The URI of the request.
pblock_findval("method", pRequest->reqpb)	char *	The method of the request.
pblock_findval("clf-request", pRequest->reqpb)	char *	The full request string.
pRequest->loadhdrs	int	Normally 0.
pblock_findval("host", pRequest->headers)	*char **	*The host target of the request.*
pblock_findval("if-modified-since", pRequest->headers)	*char **	*The HTTP date of the document that the client has already cached.*
pblock_findval("accept", pRequest->headers)	char *	The types the client can accept.
pblock_findval("user-agent", pRequest->headers)	*char **	*The client designation.*
pblock_findval("connection", pRequest->headers)	*char **	*The Keep-Alive directive.*
pblock_findval("authorization", pRequest->headers)	*char **	*The authorization sent with the request.*
pRequest->senthdrs	int	Normally 0—no response headers have been sent.
pRequest->servhdrs	pblock *	Usually an empty pblock at this stage.
pRequest->statpath	char *	The last path that was passed to request_stat_path.
pRequest->request_is_cacheable	int	Normally 1. Set to zero if the request is not to be cached.
pRequest->directive_is_cacheable	int	Normally 0. Set to 1 if the directive is to be cached.

Entries in italics may not be sent by some client software implementations.

pblock Variables Defined

There are no standard defined associations in the **pblock** pointer **pBlocker** that is passed. However, it may include associations that you have defined yourself and specified in obj.conf.

Authentication Extension Return Codes

You should be aware of these points regarding return codes:

- All are defined in frame/req.h.

- An authentication function may return **REQ_ABORTED** if a problem occurred during authentication that requires termination of the request.

- A return of **REQ_NOACTION** means that authentication was not successful. The server will normally apply any other matched authentication functions until the client is authenticated or no functions are left to apply.

- A return of **REQ_PROCEED** means that authentication was successful. The server will not apply any other matched authentication functions. The authentication function must have set at least the *auth-user* and *auth-type* (usually *basic*) associations in the **Request.vars** with the decoded values. It may also insert an *auth-group* associate if the authentication extension supports the membership of users in groups, and the authenticated user is a group member.

Configuration For This Event

Authentication directives may be associated with one or many Object sections in obj.conf. Here is an extract from obj.conf that highlights an authentication directive applied to all requests (via its association with the default object):

```
# Netscape Communications Corporation - obj.conf
# You can edit this file, but comments and formatting changes
# might be lost when the admin server makes changes.

Init fn="load-types" mime-types="mime.types"
Init fn="load-modules"
funcs=fullAuthChecker shlib="D:/var/extensions/highperf.dll"

<Object name="default">
```

```
AuthTrans fn="fullAuthChecker"
NameTrans fn="pfx2dir" from="/ns-icons"
 dir="D:/var/docs/ns-icons"
NameTrans fn="pfx2dir" from="/mc-icons"
 dir="D:/var/docs/ns-icons"
```

When the server processes the Init directives, it will interpret the line

```
Init fn="load-modules" funcs="fullAuthChecker"
shlib="D:/var/extensions/highperf.so"
```

such that it will try to load the shared object specified by **shlib** (D:/var/extensions/highperf.DLL) and locate the symbol (exported or publicly visible function names) **fullAuthChecker**. This function will be called for every request that the server processes. When this function has performed its tasks it will return a value as noted in the "Authentication Extension Return Codes" section, earlier in this chapter.

Most installations will not require authentication for every request. To express this in obj.conf, apply the *ppath* qualification to an Object section. Here is an example that states that the **fullAuthChecker** should authenticate for all resources in a special directory under the server's document root PROTECTED:

```
<Object ppath="D:/var/docs/PROTECTED/*">
AuthTrans fn="fullAuthChecker"
```

The server's root document directory here is *D:/var/docs*. As you can see, we had to specify *ppath* as a translated path and not (as you might expect) as a virtual path (the URI). This is at odds with the Netscape documentation, which states that the semantics of **ppath** are those implied by the **NameTrans** event. However, because all directives of a single class may be applied to a request for each *matching* object name, translation should not have occurred before authentication. Therefore, it is a little confusing to have to specify a physical path in the Object section qualifier.

Trivial Authentication Function

The code in Listing 6.2 is a trivial implementation of an authentication function in C. It assumes that the authorization data sent by the client is standard HTTP basic.

Listing 6.2 Trivial authentication implementation.

```
#if defined(__cplusplus)
extern "C" {
#endif

#include "base/pblock.h"
#include "base/session.h"
#include "frame/req.h"
#include "frame/log.h"
#include <string.h>

#if defined(XP_WIN32)
#define EXPORT __declspec(dllexport)
#else
#define EXPORT
#endif


#define MAX_AUTH 256
static
unsigned int containsAuthKey(
                        char * cpAuthString,
                        Request * pRequest);
static unsigned int isValidAuthentication(char * cpAuthString);

int EXPORT
simpleAuthTrans(pblock *pBlocker,
                        Session *pSession,
                        Request *pRequest)
{
char cAuthString[MAX_AUTH];
    return (!containsAuthKey(cAuthString, pRequest) ||
            isValidAuthentication(cAuthString))
            ? REQ_PROCEED : REQ_ABORTED;
}


static
unsigned int containsAuthKey(
                        char *cpString,
                        Request * pRequest)
{
    char * cpClientAuthHeader =
            pblock_findval("authorization", pRequest->headers);
        *cpString = ''\0'';
        if (cpClientAuthHeader)
            strcpy(cpString, cpClientAuthHeader);
```

```
    return strlen(cpString);
}

#define BASIC_AUTH_HEADER "Basic "
unsigned int isValidAuthentication(char * cpAuthString) {
    unsigned int iReturn = 0,
                 iHeaderLength = strlen(BASIC_AUTH_HEADER);
    if (strncmp(BASIC_AUTH_HEADER,
                  cpAuthString, iHeaderLength) == 0)
        iReturn = ((strlen(cpAuthString) - iHeaderLength) % 2) == 0;
return iReturn;
}



#if defined(__cplusplus)
}
#endif
```

Now we'll step through the code again. First, the **#if defined**() that ensures that name mangling will not occur if the code is compiled with a C++ compiler:

```
#if defined(__cplusplus)
extern "C" {
#endif
```

Next we include the NSAPI header files that define **Session**, **Request**, and **pblock**:

```
#include "base/pblock.h"
#include "base/session.h"
#include "frame/req.h"
#include "frame/log.h"
#include <string.h>
```

We now define a manifest constant that allows the function to be exported from a DLL if the extension is compiled under WIN32. No such qualification is necessary under Unix:

```
#if defined(XP_WIN32)
#define EXPORT __declspec(dllexport)
#else
#define EXPORT
#endif
```

Some definitions for the compiler follow:

```
#define MAX_AUTH 256
static
unsigned int containsAuthKey(
                        char * cpAuthString,
                        Request * pRequest);
static unsigned int isValidAuthentication(char * cpAuthString);
```

Now we've reached the entry point for the extension function. This is the function that would be that target *fn* of the **AuthTrans** directive if we deployed this extension:

```
int EXPORT
simpleAuthTrans(pblock *pBlocker,
                        Session *pSession,
                        Request *pRequest)
{
char cAuthString[MAX_AUTH];
    return (!containsAuthKey(cAuthString, pRequest) ||
            isValidAuthentication(cAuthString))
            ? REQ_PROCEED : REQ_ABORTED;
}
```

And a pretty simplistic function it is, too. First we grab some stack in the form of a 256-byte character array. Then we call the function **containsAuthKey**, passing it the character array and the **Request** pointer. If this function returns a non-zero value, the **isValidAuthentication** function will be called. If the result of this proposition is non-zero, **REQ_PROCEED** is returned. If zero, we abort the request (this is a little harsh—but still acceptable).

Use The Stack Where Possible

Use stack-based storage for variables in an extension, because they should be designed to be multi-thread safe. This is, of course, a natural consequence of each thread having its own allocated stack.

So what do these other functions do? The following snippet is the first part of **containsAuthKey**:

```
static
unsigned int containsAuthKey(
                        char *cpString,
                        Request * pRequest)
```

```
{
char * cpClientAuthHeader =
        pblock_findval("authorization", pRequest->headers);
```

The first thing this *static* function does is query the **Request.headers pblock** for an authorization header—the one that *may* have been sent by the client (refer back to Table 6.2). The **pblock_findval** function will return (**char ***) **NULL** if the key is not present.

The caller of this function passes in a character array pointer that will be filled with the authorization string, if present. First, however, we set the return to an empty string (in case there is no authorization header):

```
*cpString = ''\0'';
if (cpClientAuthHeader)
    strcpy(cpString, cpClientAuthHeader);
return strlen(cpString);
}
```

Then, we'll copy the contents of the authorization header into the character array (if it is not null). The return code from this function is the length of the authorization header, which is tested for in **simpleAuthTrans**.

With a non-zero return code from **containsAuthKey**, the function **isValidAuthentication** is called, with a parameter of the authorization string. The following function gives this implementation its trivial flavor, in that it will authenticate the client as long as it sends an authorization string with an even-numbered length:

```
#define BASIC_AUTH_HEADER "Basic "
unsigned int isValidAuthentication(char * cpAuthString) {
unsigned int iReturn = 0, iHeaderLength = strlen(BASIC_AUTH_HEADER);
        if (strncmp(BASIC_AUTH_HEADER,
                        cpAuthString, iHeaderLength) == 0)
            iReturn = ((strlen(cpAuthString) - iHeaderLength) % 2)
                            == 0;
return iReturn;
}
```

Assuming that it has an even-numbered length, the extension function will return **REQ_PROCEED**, which means that the client is authenticated.

Although the function presented does not attempt the decoding of the authorization string, it *does* show how an extension function may be implemented in its most simplistic form.

> **Note:** Communication with the server is, at the lowest level, done with simple data structures and an integer code system.

Complete Authentication Function

The next implementation, shown in Listing 6.3, is significantly more complex than the previous one and illustrates the use of a BASE64 decoder implementation to create a fully operational authorization extension. It is designed to correctly validate basic HTTP credentials and inform the client properly (as per HTTP 1.0) if the validation fails.

Listing 6.3 Full HTTP authentication implementation.

```
extern "C" {
#include "base/pblock.h"
#include "base/session.h"
#include "frame/req.h"
#include "frame/http.h"
#include "frame/log.h"
}

#include "OptString.h"
#include "base64.h"
#include "httpcreds.h"

extern "C" {
#if defined(XP_WIN32)
#define EXPORT __declspec(dllexport)
#else
#define EXPORT
#endif

int EXPORT fullAuthChecker(pblock *pBlocker,
                           Session *pSession,
                           Request *pRequest)
{
```

```
BasicHTTPCredentials rAuthObject(pblock_findval("authorization",
                                pRequest->headers),
                                new Base64Decoder());
int iRetCode = rAuthObject.validate();
    if (!iRetCode) {
        protocol_status(pSession, pRequest,
                        PROTOCOL_UNAUTHORIZED, NULL);
        pblock_nvinsert("WWW-authenticate",
                        "basic realm=\"HighPerformance\"",
                        pRequest->srvhdrs);
    }
    else if (rAuthObject.getUser().length() > 0) {
        pblock_nvinsert("auth-user",
                        (char *)
                        rAuthObject.getUser().c_str(),
                        pRequest->vars);
        pblock_nvinsert("auth-type",
                        "basic", pRequest->vars);
    }
return iRetCode == 0 ? REQ_ABORTED : REQ_PROCEED;
}


}
```

The first part of Listing 6.3 is the usual inclusion of NSAPI header files. The next lines:

```
#include "OptString.h"
#include "base64.h"
#include "httpcreds.h"
```

include a string class called **OptString**, a BASE64 decoder, and an HTTP credentials class, used by our implementation. Because these header files make available the definitions of C++ classes, they are not wrapped in the linkage specification **extern C**. Following this is our standard method of declaring a macro, which defines the appropriate platform-dependent tokens for exporting a symbol from a shared object.

Following the standard declaration of the extension function (**fullAuthChecker**), the first line of the function declares an automatic object of type **BasicHTTPCredentials** (see Listing 6.5 later in this chapter), a class that provides an interface to an HTTP authenticator:

```
BasicHTTPCredentials rAuthObject(pblock_findval("authorization",
                                           pRequest->headers),
                                           new Base64Decoder());
```

To construct the object, we pass in the authorization string that may have been supplied by the client (remember, this can be a null pointer). Note that we could have designed the class to accept the **Request** pointer, but this act would have unnecessarily bound us to NSAPI. The second argument is a heap-allocated **Base64Decoder** object (described in a sidebar, later in this chapter, "A C++ BASE64 Decoder"), that can take the responsibility for decoding a BASE64 encoded sequence. Because our HTTP extension is guaranteed to operate correctly only in the presence of basic HTTP authentication, this is not an issue.

The real action takes place in the following lines. We start by asking **rAuthObject** to validate itself—this returns an integer value of zero if validation fails:

```
int iRetCode = rAuthObject.validate();
```

Next, and very important, we test the return code of the validation. If the validation failed, for whatever reason, we use the **protocol_status** function of NSAPI to set the status of the server's response for this session:

```
if (!iRetCode) {
    protocol_status(pSession, pRequest,
                          PROTOCOL_UNAUTHORIZED, NULL);
```

As you can see, **protocol_status** accepts both the **Session** and **Request** pointers and potentially modifies them (to set the status). The most important parameter is the third one, which is the actual status code to use. Table 6.3 shows the status codes as defined in the include file frame/http.h.

The default status of a session, unless it is otherwise modified, is **PROTOCOL_SERVER_ERROR.**

The last parameter, which we pass as **NULL** in our example, is the reason for the status code if the request fails. By passing it as **NULL**, we instruct the **protocol_status** function to substitute an appropriate value. This is the preferred method.

Our next action is to insert a **WWW-Authenticate** header into the server response headers that will be sent to the client. This will enable a client configured this way to either create or solicit authorization data from the user:

Table 6.3   Predefined session status codes.

Manifest constant	Value
PROTOCOL_OK	200
PROTOCOL_CREATED	201
PROTOCOL_NO_RESPONSE	204
PROTOCOL_PARTIAL_CONTENT	206
PROTOCOL_REDIRECT	302
PROTOCOL_NOT_MODIFIED	304
PROTOCOL_BAD_REQUEST	400
PROTOCOL_UNAUTHORIZED	401
PROTOCOL_FORBIDDEN	403
PROTOCOL_NOT_FOUND	404
PROTOCOL_PROXY_UNAUTHORIZED	407
PROTOCOL_SERVER_ERROR	500
PROTOCOL_NOT_IMPLEMENTED	501

```
pblock_nvinsert("WWW-authenticate",
                "basic realm=\"HighPerformance\"",
                pRequest->srvhdrs);
}
```

In our case, we state that we will accept basic HTTP authentication, and that the realm (which is opaque to the client) has the identification string **HighPerformance**. Note that we could have passed in the realm via the **pblock pBlocker** if we had really wanted to. As we have discussed, this is achieved by passing in a directive to the extension function by using the key=value association syntax. If we assume that the client is a browser, such a challenge may appear as shown in Figure 6.1.

Let's suppose that the user has supplied a user name and password that is an acceptable authorization couplet. This is what the next section of code tests for, because here the authorization is not definitely invalid (**iRetCode** is not equal to zero):

```
else if (rAuthObject.getUser().length() > 0) {
```

Now we'll examine the user name, or rather, the length of it. As you will see, the interface for the **BasicHTTPCredentials** class provides for access to the user name,

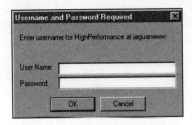

Figure 6.1

Netscape Navigator Authentication dialog box.

password, and group of a decoded authorization string (if all the data is manifest). An authentication extension must insert the user name, authentication type, and, optionally, the user group (if known or valid). This next function call performs these actions:

```
pblock_nvinsert("auth-user",
                (char *) rAuthObject.getUser().c_str(),
                pRequest->vars);
pblock_nvinsert("auth-type", "basic", pRequest->vars);
}
```

The user name must be inserted under the **auth-user** key and the authentication type under **auth-type**. If we were to include a group, we would insert it under an **auth-group** key. Notice that we do not insert a status code, as we did for a failed authorization attempt. Other extension functions will do that—it is typically the job of a Service class function.

Now that we performed the appropriate behavior, we just need to return an integer code to be interpreted by the Object handling engine. We are again quite strict. If authentication failed, we will return **REQ_ABORTED**, which will cause the server to terminate the request. If we have inserted the status code and realm information, this will be sent to the client and appropriate actions will probably take place on the client side. If, on the other hand, we are satisfied with the credentials given, we will return **REQ_PROCEED**, which is interpreted by the server so that it will ignore any remaining **AuthTrans** directives that are in the current requests Object set.

Now we'll move on to illustrate the HTTP authenticating classes. These are worth discussing, because they are written to be portable to ISAPI. They also provide a virtual function hook so that you can provide your own validation as necessary by sub-classing the **BasicHTTPCredentials** class. You also might adjust the design of the **BasicHTTPCredentials** class so that the same utility extension could be achieved by delegation. The code described in this section (available on the CD-ROM enclosed with this book) can be easily plugged into a Netscape server and provide an alternative authentication scheme with minimal effort.

Listing 6.4 shows the **Credentials** abstract class, which provides some limited state and a small interface that includes the pure virtual function **validate**. Concrete sub-classes of **Credentials** must provide an implementation for **validate**. The semantics of this function are such that a return value of zero means that validation failed, and a non-zero value means it succeeded. The exact semantics of what validation actually is are not stated, but in most cases it would probably entail taking the user, password, and/or group names and validating them. Notice that the accessors that set the user name, group name, and so on, have been made **protected**. This is so that unless sub-classes expose these functions, they will be inaccessible to the public.

Listing 6.4   The **Credentials** class.

```
class Credentials {
private:
    OptString rUser;
    OptString rPassword;
    OptString rGroup;
protected:
    void setUser(OptString const & rNewUser)
        { rUser = rNewUser; }
    void setPassword(OptString const & rNewPassword)
        { rPassword = rNewPassword; }
    void setGroup(OptString const & rNewGroup)
        { rGroup = rNewGroup; }
public:
    Credentials() { }
    virtual ~Credentials() { }
    OptString const & getUser() const { return rUser; }
    OptString const & getPassword() const { return rPassword; }
    OptString const & getGroup() const { return rGroup; }
    virtual int validate() = 0;
};
```

Listing 6.5 shows the concrete class **BasicHTTPCredentials**, which provides the necessary interface and encapsulates the code required to perform authentication on a supplied authorization string that is in the basic HTTP style.

Listing 6.5 The **BasicHTTPCredentials** class.

```
class BasicHTTPCredentials : public Credentials {
private:
    Decoder *pDecoder;
    OptString rAuthString;
protected:
    Decoder const * decoder() const { return pDecoder; }
    virtual int isValid() { return 1; }
public:
    BasicHTTPCredentials(char const * pAuthString,
                                   Decoder * pCodec)
        : pDecoder(pCodec), rAuthString(pAuthString) {
                if (rAuthString.length() > 0) {
                    size_t iIndex = rAuthString.find("Basic");
                    if (iIndex == 0)
                        rAuthString = rAuthString.substr(6);
                }
    }
    ~BasicHTTPCredentials() { delete pDecoder; }
    int validate() {
        setUser("");
        setPassword("");
        setGroup("");

        int iReturnCode = pDecoder->decode(rAuthString);
        if (iReturnCode &&
            pDecoder->getDecodedSequence().length() > 0) {
            size_t iIndex = pDecoder->
                                getDecodedSequence().find(":");
            if (iIndex != (size_t) -1) {
                setUser(pDecoder->
                    getDecodedSequence().substr(0, iIndex));
                setPassword(pDecoder->
                    getDecodedSequence().substr(iIndex+1));
                iReturnCode = isValid();
            }
        }
        return iReturnCode;
    }
};
```

This class is a little more interesting than the abstract class that it publicly inherits from, so we'll take some time to step through it. As you can see, it has two private instance variables, one a pointer to a **Decoder**, the other a string (of type **OptString**).

The string holds the encoded authorization string, whereas the **Decoder** pointer points to an object that implements the **Decoder** interface.

This is the constructor code:

```
BasicHTTPCredentials(char const * pAuthString,
                                 Decoder * pCodec)
      : pDecoder(pCodec), rAuthString(pAuthString) {
            if (rAuthString.length() > 0) {
                  size_t iIndex = rAuthString.find("Basic");
                  if (iIndex == 0)
                        rAuthString = rAuthString.substr(6);
            }
      }
```

Apart from initialization, the constructor examines the authorization and strips out the word *Basic* if found in the string. Remember that under HTTP 1.1, authorization strings take the form **Basic {BASE64 encoded credentials}**, so we strip out the unencoded string if applicable. We could consider throwing an exception here if the keyword was not found or if the authorization string was of zero length. But this would complicate matters, and increase overhead, which is still an issue with exception handling in most compilers.

The most important part of our authenticating class is the implementation provided for the pure virtual function, **validate**. In our case, we use the **Decoder** supplied at construction to decode the authentication string we have:

```
int validate() {
      setUser("");
      setPassword("");
      setGroup("");

      int iReturnCode = pDecoder->decode(rAuthString);
```

You will remember that the extension function shown in Listing 6.3 supplied a concrete class called a **Base64Decoder** to achieve this decoding. The **decode** member function of a **Decoder** will return a non-zero value if decoding was successful. In the following piece of code, we test for this value and make sure that the decoding sequence is significant:

```
if (iReturnCode &&
      pDecoder->getDecodedSequence().length() > 0) {
```

Assuming that this test succeeds, we'll proceed to parse the decoded sequence. We expect to see a *{user name}:{password}* string, so we locate the index of the colon:

```
size_t iIndex = pDecoder->
                    getDecodedSequence().find(":");
```

If found, we extract the user name and password and set them using the protected methods of the **Credentials** class:

```
if (iIndex != (size_t) -1) {
    setUser(pDecoder->
        getDecodedSequence().substr(0, iIndex));
    setPassword(pDecoder->
        getDecodedSequence().substr(iIndex+1));
```

Almost done. Next, we'll set the return code for this member function to whatever the virtual member function **isValid** returns. In our implementation it always returns **1**, signaling validity. This is where you can provide your own validation logic, by providing a substantive function:

```
            iReturnCode = isValid();
    }
        }
        return iReturnCode;
    }
```

Of course, there are other ways of doing this. One alternative, which we have already mentioned, is delegation. Another potential method is to let a sub-class override the **validate** method of **BasicHTTPCredentials**, calling the super-class version first and then implementing the validation logic when appropriate. The following is a skeleton implementation for this:

```
int LocalHTTPAuthentication::validate() {
        int iRetCode = BasicHTTPCredentials::validate();
        if (iRetCode) { //** Validate against a local database
```

Key Features

Here is a summary of the characteristic tasks of an authentication class function. It should:

- Return **REQ_NOACTION** to request that the server attempt to apply other authentication directives.

- Return **REQ_PROCEED** for success, after having inserted **auth-user** and **auth-type** keyed associations into **Request.vars** as necessary. This stops the server applying other **AuthTrans** directives.

- Return **REQ_ABORTED** on error. Supply a **WWW-Authenticate** header and set the status of the request as appropriate.

A C++ BASE64 Decoder

*As we mentioned in the authentication extension main text, it is necessary to use a BASE64 decoder to decipher a basic HTTP authorization string sent by a client. The class we provide implements an interface defined simply by an abstract class called **Decoder**. This class is shown in Listing 6.6.*

*As you can see, concrete **Decoder** implementations only have to provide two public member functions: **decode** and an accessor, **getDecodedSequence**. For a BASE64 decoder, the decode phase will extract the string, as described inversely in Chapter 1. We say inversely because a reverse mapping must occur for a string when it is presented in a BASE64 form.*

For each input byte, then, we must map the value of that byte as a character according to the table presented in RFC 1421. An example of this is the character Q, which maps to the integer 16. As we unmap a byte, we must store it somewhere.

After we have accumulated four bytes, we are in a position to decode a portion of the sequence. We do this by regarding the four bytes as a 32-bit group where the real bytes are encoded noncontiguously through the bit stream. The bytes are reconstructed by reading the stream from MSB to LSB, initially skipping two bits, reading six, skipping two, reading two, and so on. If the special pad byte (0x41) is encountered, the decode of the stream completes.

*Listing 6.7 shows the complete BASE64 decoder, implementing both **decode** and **getDecodedSequence**. This listing includes comments to explain the code.*

Listing 6.6 The **Decoder** abstract class.

```
class Decoder {
public:
Decoder() { }
    virtual ~Decoder() { }
    virtual int decode(OptString const & rAuthString) = 0;
    virtual OptString const & getDecodedSequence() const = 0;
};
```

Listing 6.7 The **Base64Decoder** class.

```
class Base64Decoder : public Decoder {
private:
    OptString rDecodedSequence;
    int iChars;
    char cBuffer[4];

// buildSequence accepts an input stream byte and maps it
// according to RFC 1421. If 4 encoded bytes have been accumulated,
// a sequence is ready for decode. Once decoded, 0 encoded bytes
// have been accumulated, but (potentially) 3 extra bytes have been
// appended to rDecodedSequence.
void buildSequence(int iCh) {
    if (iChars == 4) {
        decodeSequence();
        init();
    }
    unsigned int iChar = map(iCh);
    cBuffer[iChars] = iChar;
    iChars++;
}

// Given an index I, returns the byte as encoded in the
// current encoded 4 byte group.
int getByteGroup(int i) {
    static int iMask[] = { 0x3f, 0x0f, 0x03 };
    static int iNextBitsMask[] = { 0x30, 0x3c, 0x3f };
    int iOffset = (i+1) * 2;
    return ((cBuffer[i] & iMask[i]) << iOffset) |
        ((cBuffer[i+1] & iNextBitsMask[i]) >> (6-iOffset));
}

// Member function to decode the current encoded sequence.
// If the pad character is encountered during decode,
// the function terminates precipitously but not abnormally
void decodeSequence() {
```

```
        for (int i=0; i<iChars-1 ; i++) {
            if (cBuffer[i+1] == 0x41)
                break;
            char iChar = getByteGroup(i);
            rDecodedSequence.append(iChar);
        }
    }


// Set the length of the currently known encoded sequence to zero
void init() { iChars = 0; }

// Map the supplied character according to RFC 1421
int map(int iCharacter) {
    if ((iCharacter >= 00'') && (iCharacter <= 99''))
        return iCharacter - å0'' + 0x34;
    if ((iCharacter >= aa'') && (iCharacter <= zz''))
        return iCharacter - åa'' + 0x1A;
    if ((iCharacter >= aA'') && (iCharacter <= zZ''))
        return iCharacter - AA'' ;
    switch (iCharacter) {
        case "=':
            return 0x41 ;
        case "+':
            return 0x3E; //62 ;
        case "/':
            return 0x3F;
        default:
            return -1 ;
    }
}


void setDecodedSequence(OptString const & rSeq)
        { rDecodedSequence = rSeq; }

public:
    Base64Decoder() { init();  }
    ~Base64Decoder() { }
    // Decode the supplied string, which should be in BASE64
    // format for best results !! Returns the length of the decoded
    // sequence, which may be accessed using the accessor
    // member function getDecodedSequence()
    int decode(OptString const & rAuthString) {
        setDecodedSequence("");
        int iStringLength;
            if ((iStringLength=rAuthString.length()) == 0)
                return 0;
```

```
        for (int i=0, j=iStringLength; i<j; i++)
            buildSequence(rAuthString[i]);
        decodeSequence();
        return getDecodedSequence().length() != 0;
}

OptString const & getDecodedSequence() const
                { return rDecodedSequence; }
};
```

Name Translation Functions

A name translation class function in NSAPI may alter the processing that occurs when the server maps a virtual path (implied from the URI of an HTTP request) into a physical path.

Signature

Name translation functions have the following prototype:

```
int function_name(pblock * pBlocker,
                          Session * pSession,
                          Request * pRequest)
```

Semantics

The majority of virtual to physical path translations in Netscape involve little more than prepending the document root to the virtual path. This yields a physical operating system object, which is then (MIME) typed and returned to the client.

However, in some instances you may wish to customize this process. Obviously, if the default rule is not sufficient, then alternative behavior can be supplied using an extension function. A name translation may set or otherwise alter the physical path to whatever is appropriate to actually reference an object.

The **Request.vars pblock** (dereferenced by **pRequest->vars** in the signature shown before) contains an association with a key of **ppath** and a corresponding value of the translated path so far. We say so far, because any number of name translation directives may be applied to a request before the next type of directive (**PathCheck**) is executed. A name translation may modify or replace the value of **ppath** as it requires. Initially, the value of **ppath** will be the URI.

You may also insert a key **name** into **Request.vars**, with a value that represents the string name of another Object section. This object's **NameTrans** directives should be added to the list of those to be applied to the current request. We have yet to see this used in a practical manner.

Include Files

To define the structures that are passed in via pointers to the function, you should include the following lines in your source code:

```
#include "base/pblock.h"
#include "base/session.h"
#include "frame/req.h"
```

Important Session Structure Members

The **Session** structure pointer contains the information shown in Table 6.4.

Important Request Structure Members

The **Request** structure pointer contains the information shown in Table 6.5.

pblock Variables Defined

There are no standard defined associations in the passed-in **pblock** pointer **pBlocker**. However, it may include associations that you have defined and specified in obj.conf.

Table 6.4   Session structure members available.

Means of access	Type	Meaning
pblock_findval("ip", pSession->client)	char *	The IP address of the client.
session_maxdns(pSession)	char *	The FQDN of the client.
pSession->csd	SYS_NETFD	System-dependent file descriptor connected to the client.
pSession->inbuf	netbuf *	Network connection buffer to the client (inbound).
pSession->csd_open	int	If not equal to zero, the connection to the client through csd is open.

Table 6.5   Request structure members available.

Means Of Access	Type	Meaning
pblock_findval("ppath", pRequest->vars)	char *	The partial path of the request.
pblock_findval("protocol", pRequest->reqpb)	char *	The protocol of the request.
pblock_findval("uri", pRequest->reqpb)	char *	The URI of the request.
pblock_findval(method", pRequest->reqpb)	char *	The method of the request.
pblock_findval("clf-request", pRequest->reqpb)	char *	The full request string.
pRequest->loadhdrs	int	Normally 0.
pblock_findval("host", pRequest->headers)	*char **	*The host target of the request.*
pblock_findval("if-modified-since", pRequest->headers)	*char **	*The HTTP date of the document that the client already has cached.*
pblock_findval("accept", pRequest->headers)	char *	The types the client can accept.
pblock_findval("user-agent", pRequest->headers)	*char **	*The client designation.*
pblock_findval("connection", pRequest->headers)	*char **	*The Keep-Alive directive.*
pblock_findval("authorization", pRequest->headers)	*char **	*The authorization sent with the request.*
pRequest->senthdrs	int	Normally 0—no response headers have been sent.
pRequest->servhdrs	pblock *	Usually an empty pblock at this stage.
pRequest->statpath	char *	The last path that was passed to request_stat_path.
pRequest->request_is_cacheable	int	Normally 0. Set to zero if the request is not to be cached.
pRequest->directive_is_cacheable	int	Normally 0. Set to 1 if the directive is to be cached.

Entries in italics may not be sent by some client software implementations.

Name Translation Extension Return Codes

You should be aware of these points regarding return codes:

- All are defined in frame/req.h.

- An extension function may return **REQ_ABORTED** if a problem occurred during name translation that requires the request be terminated.

- A return of **REQ_NOACTION** means that the server should apply any other matched name translation functions. Remember, this may include those added by a custom extension function using the **name** key described in a previous section of this chapter.

- A return of **REQ_PROCEED** means that name translation occurred. The server should not apply any other matched name translation functions. The extension function is normally expected to have altered **ppath** in **pRequest->vars** to be a physical path.

Configuration For This Event

Name translation directives may be associated with one or many Object sections in obj.conf. Here is an extract from obj.conf, which highlights a name translation directive applied to requests with a specific **ppath** target:

```
# Netscape Communications Corporation - obj.conf
# You can edit this file, but comments and formatting changes
# might be lost when the admin server makes changes.

Init fn="load-types" mime-types="mime.types"
Init fn="load-modules" funcs="fullAuthChecker,userNameToPhysical"
  shlib="D:/var/extensions/highperf.dll"

<Object ppath="D:/Netscape/Server/docs/+*">
AuthTrans fn=fullAuthChecker
NameTrans userBase="D:/Netscape/Server/docs/users/"
  fn="userNameToPhysical"
PathCheck userBase="D:/Netscape/Server/docs/users/"
  fn="checkAccessToHomeDirectory" exempt="root"
</Object>
```

When the server processes the Init directives, it will interpret the line:

```
Init fn="load-modules" funcs="fullAuthChecker,userNameToPhysical"
   shlib="D:/var/extensions/highperf.so"
```

such that it will try to load the shared object specified by **shlib** (D:/var/extensions/ highperf.DLL) and locate the symbols (exported or publicly visible function names) **fullAuthChecker** and **userNameToPhysical**.

Notice that we have used the *ppath* qualification available to an Object section.

We assume that the server's root document directory is called *D:/Netscape/Server/ docs*. As you can see, we had to specify **ppath** as a translated path and not (as you might expect) as a virtual path (the URI). If a request is received that has a URI with a + (plus) sign as its first character after the initial slash, the name translation directives in the Object section shown will be applied.

The application of **ppath** to Object sections in this manner has great utility.

Sample Name Translation Function

The code we present in Listing 6.8 is a C-based name translation function that can be used with the **ppath**-qualified Object shown in the configuration section for this extension class. It looks for a + sign followed by a user name in the current value of **ppath**, and, if found, translates it to a physical path that cannot be derived by the default rules of the server.

Listing 6.8   Simple name translation function.

```
#if defined(__cplusplus)
extern "C" {
#endif

#include "base/pblock.h"
#include "base/session.h"
#include "frame/req.h"
#include "frame/log.h"
#include <string.h>

#if defined(XP_WIN32)
#define EXPORT __declspec(dllexport)
#else
#define EXPORT
#endif
```

```c
#define MAX_USER_NAME 512

int EXPORT userNameToPhysical(pblock *pBlocker,
                                          Session *pSession,
                                          Request *pRequest)
{
  char * cpRealDirectory, * cpBaseDirectory =
                      pblock_findval("userBase", pBlocker);
  char * pPartialPath = pblock_findval("ppath", pRequest->vars);
  char * pBase = (pPartialPath == (char *) NULL) ?
          pPartialPath : strchr(pPartialPath, '+');
  int iReturnCode = REQ_NOACTION;
  pb_param * pOldPath;

  if (pBase != (char *) NULL) {
    if (!cpBaseDirectory) {
      log_error(LOG_MISCONFIG, "userNameToPhysical",
              pSession, pRequest,
              "Missing userBase association for %s",
              pPartialPath);
      iReturnCode = REQ_ABORTED;
    }
    else {
      cpRealDirectory = MALLOC(MAX_USER_NAME);
      strcpy(cpRealDirectory, cpBaseDirectory);
      strcat(cpRealDirectory, pBase + 1);
      if (pPartialPath[strlen(pPartialPath) - 1] != '/')
        strcat(cpRealDirectory, "/");
      pOldPath = pblock_remove("ppath", pRequest->vars);
      param_free(pOldPath);
      pblock_nvinsert("ppath",
              cpRealDirectory,
              pRequest->vars);
      iReturnCode = REQ_PROCEED;
    }
  }
  return iReturnCode;
}


#if defined(__cplusplus)
}
#endif
```

For this function, we are going to skip the preliminaries and assume that the inclusion of the NSAPI files and definition of an **EXPORT** macro is now taken as read.

The interesting parts are again at the beginning of the function:

```
char * cpRealDirectory, * cpBaseDirectory =
                  pblock_findval("userBase", pBlocker);
```

Here, we declare two pointers to **char** and initialize them. First we set the value of **cpBaseDirectory** to the **char** pointer returned, by performing a **pblock_findval** on the **pblock pBlocker**. That is the first argument to the extension function—and is the first argument to all extension functions. Now we look for the value associated with a key of **userBase**. But where does the **userBase** association get set up? To answer this, we have to refer back to the configuration section for this function. Here it is again:

```
NameTrans userBase="D:/Netscape/Server/docs/users/"
  fn="userNameToPhysical"
```

Now it's obvious where the key and its value originate. Earlier on, we did mention that this is one way of passing soft-coded values to an extension function. In our case, the **userBase** associated value represents a path name that we should use in our name translation. The benefits of passing in the path this way are obvious.

In accordance with our name translation status, we also look for the current value pointed to be **ppath** in **pRequest->vars**, as in:

```
char * pPartialPath = pblock_findval("ppath", pRequest->vars);
```

Now the next piece of code looks arcane,

```
char * pBase = (pPartialPath == (char *) NULL) ?
                    pPartialPath : strchr(pPartialPath, '+');
```

but it isn't. If we found a value for **ppath**, we check to see if it has a plus symbol in it, storing a reference to the position of the first such symbol located in partial path.

Now we'll attempt to process the values we've gleaned from the structures passed to us. In this snippet

```
if (pBase != (char *) NULL) {
    if (!cpBaseDirectory) {
      log_error(LOG_MISCONFIG, "userNameToPhysical",
              pSession, pRequest,
```

```
        "Missing userBase association for %s",
        pPartialPath);
  iReturnCode = REQ_ABORTED;
}
```

first we ensure that the **ppath** has a + in it by testing that **strchr** worked. If it did, we'll check that the configuration for the extension function is correct. Our design dictates that we must have a **userBase** supplied to us externally, so if we do not find it, we'll log a misconfiguration error to the server's log file using the standard NSAPI function **log_error**. The sidebar in this chapter, "Logging To The Server's Error File," discusses **log_error**. At this stage we'll also set the return code to **REQ_ABORTED**.

Next, we'll grab some memory from the server's pool using the Netscape **MALLOC** function (which in most cases will map to a specialized server memory allocation function):

```
else {
    cpRealDirectory = MALLOC(MAX_USER_NAME);
```

Now we'll copy in the base directory supplied via the **userBase** association, and tack on the portion of the original **ppath** *after* the first + sign. If the last character of these concatenated strings is not a slash (/), we'll add one:

```
strcpy(cpRealDirectory, cpBaseDirectory);
strcat(cpRealDirectory, pBase + 1);
if (pPartialPath[strlen(pPartialPath) - 1] != '/')
  strcat(cpRealDirectory, "/");
```

This implies that the extension function expects to receive a directory name—otherwise the slash trailer would not be necessary. Now, the crucial action of altering the **ppath** in **Request.vars** must occur. First we'll remove the old **ppath** association and free it:

```
pOldPath = pblock_remove("ppath", pRequest->vars);
param_free(pOldPath);
```

An Alternate Means Of Changing Param_Block Values

*Another way of doing this would be to free the value associated with **ppath** (**pOldPath->value** in our example), and insert a new dynamically allocated value as appropriate (**cpRealDirectory** in this case).*

Next we insert the new **ppath** with our derived and massaged value:

```
pblock_nvinsert("ppath",
                cpRealDirectory,
                pRequest->vars);
    iReturnCode = REQ_PROCEED;
}
```

Our last action is to set the appropriate return code. Because we have performed the definitive name translation for this type of request, we return a value of **REQ_PROCEED**.

Key Features

Here is a summary of the characteristic tasks for a name translation function. It may:

- Massage the value of **ppath** in **pRequest->vars** as appropriate to yield the desired physical name.

- Return **REQ_NOACTION** if the server should apply other name translation directives.

- Return **REQ_PROCEED** for success. This stops the server applying other name translation directives. The normal implication here is that the **ppath** parameter block has been meaningfully set by the extension function.

- Return **REQ_ABORTED** on error. This is an unusual action for a name translation function, as the act of translating a URI should not yield any information that would require this.

Logging To The Server's Error File

*The function **log_error** is used to log an error to the error log specified in **magnus.conf**.*

Include file: frame/log.h

Syntax

```
int log_error(int iLevel, char *cpFunction, Session *pSession,
  Request *pRequest,  char *cpFormat, ...)
```

Return Value

Zero if the log entry was made, non-zero otherwise.

Semantics

*The entry made to the error file includes a description of the nature of the error, as indicated by the **iLevel** parameter. The manifest constants **LOG_WARN**, **LOG_MISCONFIG**, **LOG_SECURITY**, **LOG_FAILURE**, **LOG_CATASTROPHE**, and **LOG_INFORM** are defined. The semantics of these values are fairly obvious.*

*The **cpFunction** string represents the name of the function in which the message was generated. The **Session** and **Request** pointers are those that are passed into the extension by the server and may be null.*

*The actual text of the log message is specified by the **cpFormat** parameter, which is a **printf**-like string. The ellipsis denotes the parameters that may be required by the **cpFormat** string.*

Path Check Functions

A path check class function in NSAPI may be used to complement the authentication of a request. Currently all Netscape authentication (at the basic level) is split over two events.

Signature

Path check functions have the following prototype:

```
int function_name(pblock * pBlocker,
                            Session * pSession,
                            Request * pRequest)
```

Semantics

In this class of function, we must determine whether the client is allowed access to the resource named by the physical path created by the name translation phase. The physical path may also be formatted so that it may represent malicious behavior on the part of the request. An example of this is when the URI contains a reference to the parent directories of some path.

If any authorization information was supplied by the client, it will be present in the **pRequest->vars** pblock. See Table 6.7 under the keys **auth-user**, **auth-group**, and **auth-basic**.

So, by whatever means necessary, extension functions of this class determine whether the target resource falls within the domain of the client's authorization. Only a return code is significant.

Include Files

To define the structures that are passed in via pointers to the function, you should include the following lines in your source code:

```
#include "base/pblock.h"
#include "base/session.h"
#include "frame/req.h"
```

Important Session Structure Members

The **Session** structure pointer contains the information shown in Table 6.6.

Table 6.6 Session structure members available.

Means of access	Type	Meaning
pblock_findval("ip", pSession->client)	char *	The IP address of the client.
session_maxdns(pSession)	char *	The FQDN of the client.
pSession->csd	SYS_NETFD	System-dependent file descriptor connected to the client.
pSession->inbuf	netbuf *	Network connection buffer to the client (inbound).
pSession->csd_open	int	If not equal to zero, the connection to the client through csd is open.

Important Request Structure Members

The **Request** structure pointer contains the information shown in Table 6.7.

pblock Variables Defined

There are no standard defined associations in the passed-in **pblock** pointer **pBlocker**. However, it may include associations that you have defined and specified in obj.conf.

Path Check Extension Return Codes

For a **PathCheck** extension function:

- All are defined in frame/req.h.

- Return **REQ_ABORTED** if a problem occurs during operation that requires termination of the request.

- Return **REQ_NOACTION** or **REQ_PROCEED** if the server should apply any other matched path check functions.

Configuration For This Event

Path check directives may be associated with one or many Object sections in obj.conf. The following is an extract from obj.conf that highlights a path check directive, **PathCheck**, applied to requests with a specific **ppath** target. Validating access to a specific part of the server is the usual application for a path check function.

```
<Object ppath="D:/Netscape/Server/docs/+*">
AuthTrans fn=fullAuthChecker
NameTrans userBase="D:/Netscape/Server/docs/users/"
  fn="userNameToPhysical"
PathCheck userBase="D:/Netscape/Server/docs/users/"
  fn="checkAccessToHomeDirectory" exempt="root"
</Object>
```

We have already discussed, earlier in this chapter, how the server locates the functions to load and how they are specified in obj.conf.

We assume that the server's root document directory is called *D:/Netscape/Server/docs*. The **ppath** is again specified as a translated path and not (as you might expect)

Table 6.7 Request structure members available.

Means Of Access	Type	Meaning
pblock_findval("path", pRequest->vars)	char *	The physical path of the request.
pblock_findval("auth-user", pRequest->vars)	*char **	*The authenticated user name.*
pblock_findval("auth-type", pRequest->vars)	*char **	*The authentication type.*
pblock_findval("auth-group", pRequest->vars)	*char **	*The authenticated user group.*
pblock_findval("protocol", pRequest->reqpb)	char *	The protocol of the request.
pblock_findval("uri", pRequest->reqpb)	char *	The URI of the request.
pblock_findval("method", pRequest->reqpb)	char *	The method of the request.
pblock_findval("clf-request", pRequest->reqpb)	char *	The full request string.
pRequest->loadhdrs	int	Normally 0.
pblock_findval("host", pRequest->headers)	*char **	*The host target of the request.*
pblock_findval("if-modified-since", pRequest->headers)	*char **	*The HTTP date of the document that the client already has cached.*
pblock_findval("accept", pRequest->headers)	char *	The types the client can accept.
pblock_findval("user-agent", pRequest->headers)	*char **	*The client designation.*
pblock_findval("connection", pRequest->headers)	*char **	*The Keep-Alive directive.*
pRequest->senthdrs	int	Normally 0—no response headers have been sent.
pRequest->servhdrs	pblock *	Usually an empty pblock at this stage.
pRequest->statpath	char *	The last path that was passed to request_stat_path.
pRequest->request_is_cacheable	int	Normally 0. Set to zero if the request is not to be cached.
pRequest->directive_is_cacheable	int	Normally 0. Set to 1 if the directive is to be cached.

Entries in italics may not be sent by some client software implementations.

as a virtual path (the URI). For every translated path with a plus symbol in its URI, we ask the server to add the function **checkAccessToHomeDirectory** to the set of directives to be processed.

Sample Path Check Function

The code presented in Listing 6.9 is a C-based name translation function that complements our name translation example. It verifies access to a translated home directory by using either the authenticated user name (if given) or the DNS-resolved host name (if possible). The extension function also checks for a key called **exempt** in the **pblock pBlocker**, and, if found, interprets this as a user who is able to view *any* directory.

Listing 6.9   Simple path check function.

```
#if defined(__cplusplus)
extern "C" {
#endif

#include "base/pblock.h"
#include "base/session.h"
#include "frame/req.h"
#include "frame/log.h"
#include "frame/http.h"
#include <string.h>

#if defined(XP_WIN32)
#define EXPORT __declspec(dllexport)
#else
#define EXPORT
#endif

static unsigned int checkIPAddress(Session *, char *);

int EXPORT checkAccessToHomeDirectory(
                            pblock *pBlocker,
                            Session *pSession,
                            Request *pRequest)
{
char * cpSuperUser = pblock_findval("exempt", pBlocker);
int iReturnCode = REQ_ABORTED;
char * cpName = MALLOC(512),
                * cpPortion = MALLOC(256),
```

```
                        * cpBase, * cpSlash;
char * cpSupplied = pblock_findval("auth-user",
                                    pRequest->vars),
       * cpPartialPath =  pblock_findval("path",
                                          pRequest->vars);
        if (cpSupplied)
                strcpy(cpName, cpSupplied);
        if (cpSupplied || checkIPAddress(pSession, cpName)) {
                if (cpSuperUser &&
                    strcmp(cpName, cpSuperUser) == 0)
                        iReturnCode = REQ_PROCEED;
                else {
                        cpBase =
                            pblock_findval("userBase", pBlocker);
                        if (!cpBase) {
                                log_error(LOG_MISCONFIG,
                                        "checkAccessToHdir",
                                        pSession, pRequest,
                                        "Check obj.conf"
                                        "[need userBase]",
                                        pblock_findval("ip",
                                        pSession->client));
                                iReturnCode = REQ_ABORTED;
                                protocol_status(pSession, pRequest,
                                                PROTOCOL_FORBIDDEN,
                                                NULL);
                        }
                        else {
                                strcpy(cpPortion,
                                        cpPartialPath +
                                        strlen(cpBase));
                                cpSlash = strchr(cpPortion, '/');
                                if (cpSlash)
                                        *cpSlash = '\0';
                                iReturnCode =
                                        (strcmp(cpName,cpPortion) == 0)
                                        ? REQ_PROCEED : REQ_ABORTED;
                        }
                }
        }
        return iReturnCode;
}

static unsigned int checkIPAddress(Session * pSession,
                                                char * cpAnswer) {
        char * cpHostName = session_maxdns(pSession);
```

```
        *cpAnswer = '\0';
        if (!cpHostName) {
                log_error(LOG_WARN, "checkIPAddress(pcheck)",
                                    pSession, NULL,
                                    "Help!: Cannot translate %s",
                                    pblock_findval("ip",
                                                        pSession->client));
                return 0;
        }
        strcpy(cpAnswer, cpHostName);
        return strlen(cpAnswer);
}


#if defined(__cplusplus)
}
#endif
```

Again, we'll skip the preliminaries and assume that the inclusion of the NSAPI files and definition of an **EXPORT** macro is now taken as read.

The interesting parts are at the beginning of the function:

```
char * cpSuperUser = pblock_findval("exempt", pBlocker);
int iReturnCode = REQ_ABORTED;
char * cpName = MALLOC(512),
                * cpPortion = MALLOC(256),
                * cpBase, * cpSlash;
char * cpSupplied = pblock_findval("auth-user",
                                    pRequest->vars),
        * cpPartialPath = pblock_findval("path",
                                        pRequest->vars);
```

Here, we'll look for our "exempt" from restriction user, by looking for the **exempt** key in **pBlocker**. Next we set a default return code of **REQ_ABORTED**, grab some memory, and try and locate the physical path and the authenticated user name (if any).

Now we'll copy the supplied authentication name and test against a proposition:

```
if (cpSupplied)
                strcpy(cpName, cpSupplied);
        if (cpSupplied || checkIPAddress(pSession, cpName)) {
```

Here we'll check to see if the client has authenticated itself or, if not, determine if we can ascertain the remote host name, storing the answer in **cpName**. If we can find a non-null string by either of these means, we'll try to interpret it as a name that can be used to determine if the request should be granted.

Now we'll compare the "exempt" user (if supplied) against the name we are using for the client remote user name

```
if (cpSuperUser &&
        strcmp(cpName, cpSuperUser) == 0)
        iReturnCode = REQ_PROCEED;
        else {
```

and set a success return code if this is true.

At this juncture, we have a symbolic name that identifies the remote user and we also know that they are not the superuser, so we need to further qualify them before letting the request through. First, we'll check to make sure that the configuration is correct. For this extension, the configuration must include the designation of the directory name that will precede the translated name, and this should be passed in via the **userBase** association in the **pblock** pointer passed to all extension functions:

```
cpBase = pblock_findval("userBase", pBlocker);
if (!cpBase) {
        log_error(LOG_MISCONFIG,
                        "checkAccessToHdir",
                        pSession, pRequest,
                        "Check obj.conf"
                        "[need userBase]",
                        pblock_findval("ip",
                        pSession->client));
        iReturnCode = REQ_ABORTED;
        protocol_status(pSession, pRequest,
                                        PROTOCOL_FORBIDDEN,
                                        NULL);
```

Notice here that we explicitly set the status of the request to forbidden if there is a misconfiguration.

We can now validate the client's symbolic name against the *base* name of the physical path of the request:

```
strcpy(cpPortion,
        cpPartialPath + strlen(cpBase));
cpSlash = strchr(cpPortion, '/');
 if (cpSlash)
    *cpSlash = '\0';
iReturnCode = (strcmp(cpName,cpPortion) == 0)
                    ? REQ_PROCEED : REQ_ABORTED;
```

We can also set a return code of either **REQ_PROCEED** or **REQ_ABORTED** if our criterion is not met. Note that instead of **REQ_ABORTED** we *could* have used **REQ_NOACTION** to signal that other directives should be applied. However, this is not considered appropriate for this example because the URI is in a very specific format.

For example, if we authenticate as user Tony and attempt to access the URI /+root, we will receive a server error message. If we don't send any authorization information to the server, the only URI we could access would be of the form /+{Host}, in which {Host} is the DNS-resolved host name of our client.

As a final note, the **checkIPAddress** function uses the Netscape **session_maxdns** function (taking an argument of the **Session** structure pointer passed to any extension function) to determine the client's host name.

Key Features

Here is a summary of the characteristic tasks of a path check function. It should:

- Return **REQ_NOACTION** if the server should apply other path check directives.

- Return **REQ_PROCEED** for success. This will not stop the server applying other path check directives.

- Return **REQ_ABORTED** on error. This is an unusual action but may be acceptable for stringent path check functions.

Object Type Functions

An object type class function in NSAPI may be used to specify the content type of a request when it may not otherwise be reasonably determined.

Signature

Object type functions have the standard extension prototype:

```
int function_name(pblock * pBlocker,
                            Session * pSession,
                            Request * pRequest)
```

Semantics

In this class of function, we must decide, if it has not been already decided, what the content type of the resource referenced by the request is. This is (for the sake of argument) the appropriate MIME type.

Ordinarily, the content type of a non-CGI request is discovered by the built-in Netscape function **type-by-extension**. This uses a simple resource (file) extension mapping technique and consults the server configuration file mime.types for the appropriate mappings. If this look-up fails, then another built-in function (**force-type**) will set the content type to (normally) text/plain.

When implementing a function of this class, you must check that the content type has not already been set, to avoid doing extra work or overriding a previous directive's computational effort. Also, consider using a static mapping if the MIME type extension relationship is easily discernible and nonvolatile. You may do this by using the mime.types file.

Customarily, the association **content-type** (with its value as the response's MIME type) will be present in the **pblock pRequest->srvhdrs** when object type functions have completed processing for a request.

Include Files

To define the structures that are passed in via pointers to the function, you should include the following lines in your source code:

```
#include "base/pblock.h"
#include "base/session.h"
#include "frame/req.h"
```

Important Session Structure Members

The **Session** structure pointer contains the information shown in Table 6.8.

Important Request Structure Members

The **Reqest** structure pointer contains the information shown in Table 6.9.

pblock Variables Defined

There are no standard defined associations in the passed **pblock** pointer. However, it may include associations that you have defined yourself and specified in obj.conf.

Object Type Extension Return Codes

For this class of extension:

- All are defined in frame/req.h.

- Return **REQ_ABORTED** if a problem occurred during operation that requires the request be terminated. This is a very unusual step.

- Return **REQ_NOACTION** or **REQ_PROCEED** if the server should apply any other matched object type functions.

Table 6.8   Session structure members available.

Means of access	Type	Meaning
pblock_findval("ip", pSession->client)	char *	The IP address of the client.
session_maxdns(pSession)	char *	The FQDN of the client.
pSession->csd	SYS_NETFD	System-dependent file descriptor connected to the client.
pSession->inbuf	netbuf *	Network connection buffer to the client (inbound).
pSession->csd_open	int	If not equal to zero, the connection to the client through csd is open.

Table 6.9 Request structure members available.

Means Of Access	Type	Meaning
pblock_findval("path", pRequest->vars)	char *	The physical path of the request.
pblock_findval("auth-user", pRequest->vars)	*char **	*The authenticated user name.*
pblock_findval("auth-type", pRequest->vars)	*char **	*The authentication type.*
pblock_findval("auth-group", pRequest->vars)	*char **	*The authenticated user group.*
pblock_findval("protocol", pRequest->reqpb)	char *	The protocol of the request.
pblock_findval("uri", pRequest->reqpb)	char *	The URI of the request.
pblock_findval(method", pRequest->reqpb)	char *	The method of the request.
pblock_findval("clf-request", pRequest->reqpb)	char *	The full request string.
pRequest->loadhdrs	int	Normally 0.
pblock_findval("host", pRequest->headers)	*char **	*The host target of the request.*
pblock_findval("if-modified-since", pRequest->headers)	*char **	*The HTTP date of the document that the client already has cached.*
pblock_findval("accept", pRequest->headers)	char *	The types the client can accept.
pblock_findval("user-agent", pRequest->headers)	*char **	*The client designation.*
pblock_findval("connection", pRequest->headers)	*char **	*The Keep-Alive directive.*
pRequest->senthdrs	int	Normally 0—no response headers have been sent.
pblock_findval("content-type", pRequest->srvhdrs)	*char **	*The response content type.*
pRequest->statpath	char *	The last path that was passed to request_stat_path.
pRequest->request_is_cacheable	int	Normally 0. Set to zero if the request is not to be cached.
pRequest->directive_is_cacheable	int	Normally 0. Set to 1 if the directive is to be cached.

Entries in italics may not be sent by some client software implementations or may not yet be present.

Configuration For This Event

Object type directives may be associated with one or many Object sections in obj.conf. Here is a larger extract from obj.conf, which highlights an object type directive **ObjectType** applied to all requests. Note that we placed it first in the directive list and thus before the Netscape processing is applied:

```
<Object name="default">
NameTrans fn="livewireNameTrans" name="LiveWire"
NameTrans from="/ns-icons" fn="pfx2dir"
  dir="C:/Netscape/Server/ns-icons"
NameTrans from="/mc-icons" fn="pfx2dir"
  dir="C:/Netscape/Server/ns-icons"
NameTrans fn="pfx2dir" from="/cgi-bin"
  dir="d:/Netscape/Server/cgi-bin" name="cgi"
NameTrans root="D:/Netscape/Server/docs" fn="document-root"
PathCheck fn="nt-uri-clean"
PathCheck fn="find-pathinfo"
PathCheck index-names="index.html,home.html" fn="find-index"
ObjectType fn="dbmObjectType" ext=".pages"
ObjectType fn="type-by-extension"
ObjectType fn="force-type" type="text/plain"
```

We discussed in Chapter 3 how the server locates the functions to load and how they are specified in obj.conf.

As is obvious from the configuration extract, this extension function (**dbmObjectType**) also accepts a parameter that will be passed in via the **pBlocker** parameter available to an extension function.

Sample Object Type Function

The code presented in Listing 6.10 is a very simple C-based object type function that implements a fixed content-type mapping. The mapping occurs for requests that resolve to a physical resource with the file name extension specified with an **ext** key in the **pblock pBlocker**. This use of an **object-type** function suggests that a *Service* request will be able to handle the mapping it imposes. Merely changing the content type for a (potentially) untranslated resource type does not achieve very much.

Listing 6.10   Simple object type function.

```
#if defined(__cplusplus)
extern "C" {
#endif

#include "base/pblock.h"
#include "base/session.h"
#include "frame/req.h"
#include "frame/log.h"
#include <base/util.h>
#include <string.h>

#if defined(XP_WIN32)
#define EXPORT __declspec(dllexport)
#else
#define EXPORT
#endif

int EXPORT dbmObjectType(pblock *pBlocker,
                         Session *pSession,
                         Request *pRequest)
{
char * cpExtension = pblock_findval("ext", pBlocker);
char * cpFullPath = pblock_findval("path", pRequest->vars);
char * cpBrowser;

if(pblock_findval("content-type", pRequest->srvhdrs)
                                  || !cpFullPath)
    return REQ_NOACTION;

if(!cpExtension) {
    log_error(LOG_MISCONFIG, "dbmObjectType",
              pSession, pRequest, "Must specify an extension");
    return REQ_NOACTION;
}

if (util_strcasecmp(cpFullPath + strlen(cpFullPath)
                         - strlen(cpExtension), cpExtension) != 0)
    return REQ_NOACTION;

if(request_header("user-agent", &cpBrowser,
                  pSession, pRequest) != REQ_PROCEED)
    return REQ_NOACTION;

if (!util_is_mozilla(cpBrowser, "2", "0"))
    return REQ_NOACTION;
```

```
pblock_nvinsert("content-type", "text/html",
                    pRequest->srvhdrs);
return REQ_PROCEED;
}

#if defined(__cplusplus)
}
#endif
```

We won't enumerate each action of this function. Rather, we'll list the circumstances it tests for. It will return **REQ_NOACTION** on encountering the following scenarios:

- The **content-type** association is present in **pRequest->srvhdrs**.

- The function is misconfigured (in this case, no **ext** association present in **pBlocker**).

- The extension specified via **ext** is not the extension of the physical path (this is determined using the Netscape function **util_strcasecmp**).

- The client did not supply a **user-agent** header in the request.

- The **user-agent** header does not indicate that the client is at least Netscape Navigator version 2.0.

If none of the listed conditions occurs, then we force the **content-type** to be **text/html**, by the following function call:

```
pblock_nvinsert("content-type", "text/html",
                    pRequest->srvhdrs);
```

Key Features

Remember that if the **content-type** keyed association has been set, you should not normally apply your implementation. To ensure you always get first option on the content type, insert your object type directive as the first one in the default Object section. Any object type function should adhere to the following protocol:

- Return **REQ_NOACTION** if the server should apply other object type directives.

- Return **REQ_PROCEED** for success. This will not stop the server applying other object type directives.

Service Class Functions

A service class function in NSAPI is used to return a response to the request of a client. As such, a service class function acts in a similar manner to a CGI executable, in that it writes the appropriate information back to the client. However, a NSAPI service function can outperform an equivalent CGI program by anything up to a magnitude, and runs (as other extensions) in the same process as the server, avoiding the overhead of the CGI model.

Signature

Service functions have the standard extension prototype:

```
int function_name(pblock * pBlocker,
                              Session * pSession,
                              Request * pRequest)
```

Semantics

In most cases, the service class function results in an operating system object being memory mapped, and the appropriate HTTP headers dispatched to the client followed by the contents of the object.

The important aspect here is the temporal order of these events, which is reflected in the structure of most service class implementations, which usually:

1. Set the status of the response.

2. Use the NSAPI function **protocol_start_response** to start the response to the client.

3. Perform custom actions, writing as appropriate to the client via NSAPI functions.

4. Return an appropriate request code to the server.

For ordinary requests, there is not much else that needs to be done.

Matters become slightly more complicated when there is data associated with a request that has to be processed. Although data in this sense could mean literally anything, we will only use the interpretation implied by the HTTP protocol. This means our discussion will be limited to processing information that is presented as an encoded sequence of associations (key=value pairs). Such data typically results from the submission of an HTML form to the server.

Get Requests

Chapter 1 extensively covers the GET and POST request types, which are by far the most prevalent. Let's hearken back to Chapter 1's discussion of GET usage: GET can also be used to submit data to a server that has been entered via an HTML form, although this technique should only be used for small amounts of data. In this case the data is appended to the request URL as a sequence of name=value pairs.

Thus, GET is normally used for idempotent exchanges (one that results in no lasting change of state in the observable world). Netscape, upon encountering data in the correct initial format attached to the request, will place that data in the **pRequest ->reqpb** pblock with a key of **query**.

To access data presented in this manner, you would need to issue this function call:

```
pblock_findval("query", pRequest->reqpb)
```

If such a query is present, this function returns a **char *** pointer to it or the null pointer if it is absent.

Post Requests

Now let's consider Chapter 1's discussion of POST requests: POST is normally used when there is a large amount of data to be transmitted to the server, for example, a large form. In such situations, using a GET request to transfer a large amount of data is not possible because most browsers and servers restrict the length of a URL to 1024 bytes.

The delivery method of NSAPI is quite different for this type of request, though there is little need for this to be so. The NSAPI view is that the determination of what actions need to occur to fetch the client-supplied data will be left to the extension function to handle. This is because the data will not be directly available without some kind of further interaction with the client—or at least the client socket.

Luckily, you are not totally on your own. As Chapter 1 points out, a POST request should always have a content length sent as one of its headers. As it happens, if we can ascertain this value, this should be the number of bytes waiting to be read from the client. If the **content-length** header has been sent by the client, its **char *** value can be found by the following function call

```
pblock_findval("content-length", pRequest->headers)
```

or even indirectly, like this:

```
char *cpLength;
::request_header("content-length", &cpLength,
                      pSession, pRequest);
```

The second method, though somewhat indirect, is considered faster.

If you refer back to the section entitled "The netbuf Structure," in Chapter 4, there is a complete description concerning the Netscape abstraction of network buffers via the **netbuf** structure. We discuss the functions available for use, including **netbuf_getc**, **netbuf_next**, **netbuf_grab**, and **netbuf_buf2sd**. The simple database extension shown later in the section "A Database-Driven Service Extension," illustrates the structure of a class designed to discover client-supplied data using these functions or the simpler **query** association method described for GET requests. Any extensions that you write must be prepared to accept data via both means.

Finally, we should mention that the data fetched in this manner will normally be expected to have the form as illustrated in Chapter 1, including all the special delimiter and character processing that is part of the HTTP 1.0 specification. An example is shown here:

```
Praise&Comments=Great+framework%0D%0AWhat+comes+next%3F
&userName=Paul+McGlashan&companyName=Optimation+NZ+Ltd&
userEmail=paulm@optimation.co.nz&userPhone=&userFX=&
submitButton=Submit+Feedback
```

Include Files

To define the structures that are passed in via pointers to the function, you should include the following lines in your source code:

```
#include "base/pblock.h"
#include "base/session.h"
#include "frame/req.h"
```

You will also need to include this file, which specifies the prototype for the **protocol_start_response** function:

```
#include "frame/http.h"
```

Technically speaking, the include file you should use is protocol.h, which defines the protocol via a manifest constant. For HTTP, this constant is **MC_HTTPD**. So a properly NSAPI-compliant version is shown here:

```
#define MC_HTTPD
#include "frame/protocol.h"
```

> **Note:** The function **protocol_start_response** is in reality a manifest constant that maps onto the function **http_start_response** for HTTP.

Important Session Structure Members

The **Request** structure pointer contains the information shown in Table 6.10.

Table 6.10   Session structure members available.

Means of access	Type	Meaning
pblock_findval("ip", pSession->client)	char *	The IP address of the client.
session_maxdns(pSession)	char *	The FQDN of the client.
pSession->csd	SYS_NETFD	System dependent file descriptor connected to the client.
pSession->inbuf	netbuf *	Network-connection buffer to the client (inbound).
pSession->csd_open	int	If not equal to zero, the connection to the client through csd is open.

Table 6.11 Request structure members available.

Means Of Access	Type	Meaning
pblock_findval("path", pRequest->vars)	char *	The physical path of the request.
pblock findval("auth-user", pRequest->vars)	*char **	*The authenticated user name.*
pblock_findval("auth-type", pRequest->vars)	*char **	*The authentication type.*
pblock_findval("auth-group", pRequest->vars)	*char **	*The authenticated user group.*
pblock_findval("protocol", pRequest->reqpb)	char *	The protocol of the request.
pblock_findval("uri", pRequest->reqpb)	char *	The URI of the request.
pblock_findval("method",pRequest->reqpb)	char *	The method of the request.
pblock_findval("clf-request", pRequest->reqpb)	char *	The full request string.
pRequest->loadhdrs	int	Normally 0.
pblock_findval("host", pRequest->headers)	*char **	*The host target of the request.*
pblock_findval("if-modified-since", pRequest->headers)	*char **	*The HTTP date of the document that the client already has cached.*
pblock_findval("accept", pRequest->headers)	char *	The types the client can accept.
pblock_findval("user-agent", pRequest->headers)	*char **	*The client designation.*
pblock_findval("connection", pRequest->headers)	*char **	*The Keep-Alive directive.*
pblock_findval("content-length", pRequest->headers)	*char **	*The content length of the data sent by the client.*
pRequest->senthdrs	int	Normally 0—no response headers have been sent.
pblock_findval("content-type", pRequest->srvhdrs)	*char **	*The response content type.*
pRequest->statpath	char *	The last path that was passed to request_stat_path.
pRequest->request_is_cacheable	int	Normally 0. Set to zero if the request is not to be cached.
pRequest->directive_is_cacheable	int	Normally 0. Set to 1 if the directive is to be cached.

Entries in italics may not be sent by some client software implementations or may not yet be present.

Important Request Structure Members

The Session structure pointer contains the information shown in Table 6.11.

pblock Variables Defined

There are no standard defined associations in the passed **pblock** pointer **pBlocker**. However, it may include associations that you have defined and specified in obj.conf.

Service Extension Return Codes

The following points apply:

- All are defined in frame/req.h.

- A service class extension may return **REQ_ABORTED** if a problem occurred during request servicing that requires the request be terminated.

- A return of **REQ_NOACTION** means that the server should apply any other matched service functions.

- A return of **REQ_PROCEED** means that the server should not apply other matched service functions, as the response was successfully sent to the client.

Configuration For This Event

Service directives may be associated with one or many Object sections in obj.conf. Here is an extract from obj.conf that highlights a Service directive, **Service,** applied to a specific request identified by a **ppath**:

```
<Object ppath="D:/Netscape/Server/docs/memorystatus">
Service fn="showMemoryStatus" method="(GET|HEAD)"
</Object>
```

We have already discussed in Chapter 3 how the server locates the functions to load and how they are specified in obj.conf.

From the configuration extract, the service class extension function (**showMemoryStatus**) should be called for all requests of either GET or HEAD type. This qualification by type is a built-in switching function provided by the

NSAPI implementation. Our service extension would not be called if we made the following erroneous entry in obj.conf:

```
Service fn="showMemoryStatus"
```

A Noninteractive Service Extension

The code presented in Listing 6.11 is a simple C-based service function that operates only under platforms that support the WIN32 API. It sends the client a brief report of the statistics returned by calling the **GlobalMemoryStatus** WIN32 API function.

Although brief, it illustrates all the required behavior of a service extension with the exception of reading client-supplied data, which is covered in the subsequent example.

Listing 6.11   The memory status service function.

```c
#if !defined(XP_WIN32)
#error "Sorry, this extension can only be compiled for WIN32"
#endif

#if defined(__cplusplus)
extern "C" {
#endif

#define MCC_HTTPD
#include "base/pblock.h"
#include "base/session.h"
#include "frame/req.h"
#include "frame/log.h"
#include <base/util.h>
#include "frame/protocol.h"
#include "frame/conf.h"
#include <string.h>
#include <windows.h>

#define EXPORT __declspec(dllexport)


static int dumpStatus(Session *);
static int writeToClient(Session *, char const * cpString);
static int writeStatistic(Session *,
                          char const * cpString,
                          double dStat);
```

```
int EXPORT showMemoryStatus(pblock *pBlocker,
                            Session *pSession,
                            Request *pRequest)
{
    char cMessage[256];
    pblock_remove("content-type", pRequest->srvhdrs);
    pblock_nvinsert("content-type", "text/html",
                    pRequest->srvhdrs);
    protocol_status(pSession, pRequest, PROTOCOL_OK, NULL);

    if(protocol_start_response(pSession, pRequest)
                    == REQ_NOACTION)
        return REQ_PROCEED;

    sprintf(cMessage,"<CENTER><H1>HTTP Server Memory Status</h1>"
                     "<h2>[%s on port %d]</h2>",
                     MAGNUS_VERSION_STRING,
                     conf_getglobals()->Vport);
    if (!writeToClient(pSession, cMessage))
        return REQ_EXIT;
    if (!dumpStatus(pSession))
        return REQ_ABORTED;
    return REQ_PROCEED;
}

static int writeToClient(Session * pSession,
                                      char const * cpString)
{
    return net_write(pSession->csd, (char*) cpString,
                     strlen(cpString)) != IO_ERROR;
}

static int dumpStatus(Session * pSession) {
MEMORYSTATUS rStatus;
        rStatus.dwLength = sizeof(MEMORYSTATUS);
        GlobalMemoryStatus(&rStatus);
        // percent of memory in use
        writeStatistic(pSession, "Memory load",
                       (double) rStatus.dwMemoryLoad / 1024);
        // bytes of physical memory
        writeStatistic(pSession, "Physical Memory",
                       (double) rStatus.dwTotalPhys  / 1024);
        // free physical memory bytes
        writeStatistic(pSession, "Free Physical Memory",
                       (double) rStatus.dwAvailPhys  / 1024);
```

```
        // bytes of paging file
        writeStatistic(pSession, "Page file",
                       (double) rStatus.dwTotalPageFile  / 1024);
        // free bytes of paging file
        writeStatistic(pSession, "Paging file free",
                       (double) rStatus.dwAvailPageFile  / 1024);
        // user bytes of address space
        writeStatistic(pSession, "Total virtual",
                       (double) rStatus.dwTotalVirtual  / 1024);
        // free user bytes
        writeStatistic(pSession, "Free user",
                       (double) rStatus.dwAvailVirtual  / 1024);
return 1;
}

#define MAX_MESSAGE 1024

static int writeStatistic(Session * pSession,
                          char const * cpStatName,
                          double dStatValue) {
    char cMessage[MAX_MESSAGE];
    sprintf(cMessage, "<b>%s</b> == %.02f<br>",
                      cpStatName, dStatValue);
    return writeToClient(pSession, cMessage);
}

#if defined(__cplusplus)
}
#endif
```

After the usual preamble of header files and constant definitions, we encounter the forward prototypes of three functions that perform the majority of the work in this example:

```
static int dumpStatus(Session *);
static int writeToClient(Session *, char const * cpString);
static int writeStatistic(Session *,
                          char const * cpString,
                          double dStat);
```

Next we see what is by now a familiar sight, the definition of the NSAPI extension function, and the first few lines of the function itself:

```
int EXPORT showMemoryStatus(pblock *pBlocker,
                            Session *pSession,
                            Request *pRequest)
{
    char cMessage[256];
    pblock_remove("content-type", pRequest->srvhdrs);
    pblock_nvinsert("content-type", "text/html",
                    pRequest->srvhdrs);
```

Our extension function is designed to be used as per the event configuration that we showed before and repeat in the following excerpt:

```
<Object ppath="D:/Netscape/Server/docs/memorystatus">
Service fn="showMemoryStatus" method="(GET|HEAD)"
</Object>
```

This should explain the need to massage the content type. If you think back to the way the object sections are processed, the default object-typing sections will have been performed prior to the service function that is executed. This means that, because the URI contains no extension by which a mapping could be inferred, the type will have been forced to be **text/plain** by the built-in Netscape function **force-type**. So, we'll remove the old content type and insert a **text/html** value (because we will be returning an HTML format document).

Note that we could have saved implementation space by using the **force-type** function ourselves, as here:

```
<Object ppath="D:/Netscape/Server/docs/memorystatus">
ObjectType fn="force-type" type="text/html"
Service fn="showMemoryStatus" method="(GET|HEAD)"
</Object>
```

This illustrates a fundamental tenet of extension programming: Never do more work than is necessary.

As per the steps we described as necessary for a service class function, we set the status of our response to **OK**

```
protocol_status(pSession, pRequest, PROTOCOL_OK, NULL);
```

and instruct the server to start the response to the client:

```
if(protocol_start_response(pSession, pRequest)
              == REQ_NOACTION)
    return REQ_PROCEED;
```

The test for **REQ_NOACTION** is important, because if this value is returned from **protocol_start_response**, the caller (as in the service function) should not send a response, but instead, should return immediately.

Having gotten this far, we are in a position to send something to the client. We do this by creating a simple HTML marked-up string with a heading, the version number of server, and the port on which it listens:

```
sprintf(cMessage,"<CENTER><H1>HTTP Server Memory Status</h1>"
                    "<h2>[%s on port %d]</h2>",
                    MAGNUS_VERSION_STRING,
                    conf_getglobals()->Vport);
    if (!writeToClient(pSession, cMessage))
        return REQ_EXIT;
```

If the **writeToClient** function fails, we immediately signal a critical error, by returning **REQ_EXIT**. As you have probably surmised, the **writeToClient** function sends a string to the client referenced by the **pSession** structure pointer. The **net_write** function, which **writeToClient** wraps, is discussed in the sidebar, "Writing Data To The Client," in this chapter. Our penultimate step is to call the **dumpStatus** extension function, which calls the **GlobalMemoryStatus** WIN32 API function, and write some HTML-formatted memory statistics to the client. Our return code is **REQ_PROCEED**, signaling that we have sent a response and that the server should consider the request answered.

Figure 6.2 illustrates a typical result of calling a **memoryStatus** function. Note the URL that is used.

Writing Data To The Client

*The function **net_write** is used to send a number of bytes to the client.*

Include file: base/net.h

Syntax
```
int net_write( SYS_NETFD rDescriptor, char *cpBuffer, int iSize)
```

Return Value
*The number of bytes written from **cpBuffer**, which should normally match **iSize**. In case of error, the manifest constant **IO_ERROR** is returned.*

Semantics

*The abstracted network descriptor **rDescriptor** is usually referenced by **Session.csd** (the connection to a client known to the server). The **cpBuffer** variable should not be null, and is best limited to no more than 32 K. Actively check for the **IO_ERROR** return code.*

A Database-Driven Service Extension

The code presented in Listing 6.12 is a straight-forward C++ service class extension that implements simple database searching (using the popular *Berkeley DB* public domain database package). To execute a database search, the user fills out an HTML form with a search criterion, and submits it via GET or POST (and by clicking on the OK or Submit button, usually). The extension will read the input data from the client, parse the data into a usable form, and search the database externally supplied

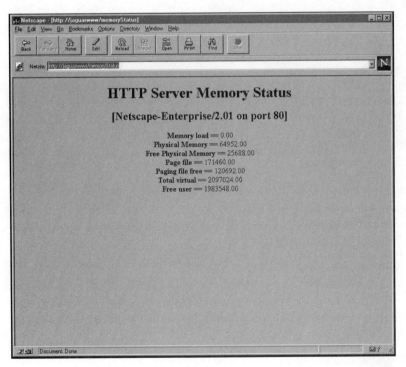

Figure 6.2

Screen shot from a memory status request.

via a **pblock** parameter. At the termination of the search, the client receives an HTML document that contains the search results or a diagnostic message.

Though possible, this extension does not implement or demonstrate features such as database connection caching, multiplexing, or sharing.

> **Note:** As a quick aside, you may be wondering just why we chose the Berkeley package. The answer is simple. For Enterprise Server 2.01, Netscape decided to convert the user and group files created via user/group maintenance from NDBM to DB format. So you can (and we have) used the classes described next to build your own means of (read-only recommended) access to these files.

To learn more about the DB package, you should visit the Berkeley DB Package Home page **mongoose.bostic.com/db/index.html**.

Listing 6.12   The Berkeley DB service extension.

```
extern "C" {
#include "base/pblock.h"
#include "base/session.h"
#include "frame/req.h"
#include "frame/log.h"
#include <base/util.h>
#include "frame/http.h"
#include <string.h>
#include <fcntl.h>
#include <ndbm.h>
#include <errno.h>
#include <unistd.h>
#include <string.h>
#include <fcntl.h>
#include <sys/stat.h>
#include "BerkeleyDB/db.1.85/PORT/include/db.h"
}

#define EXPORT

#include "OptString.h"
```

```
class EncodedFormParser {
private:
    OptString rString;
    int fetchQuery(Request * pRequest) {
        char * cpString;
        if (!(cpString = pblock_findval("query",
                                            pRequest->reqpb)))
            return 0;
        rString = cpString;
        return rString.length();
    }
    int fetchQuery(Session * pSession, Request * pRequest) {
        char *cpLength;
        ::request_header("content-length", &cpLength,
                    pSession, pRequest);

        if (!strlen(cpLength))
            return 0;

        int iLeft = ::atoi(cpLength);

        if (iLeft <= 0)
            return 0;

        rString = "";
        while (iLeft) {
            int iChar = netbuf_getc(pSession->inbuf);
            if(iChar == IO_ERROR || iChar == IO_EOF)
                break;
            rString.append(iChar);
            iLeft--;
        }
     return rString.length();
    }
public:
    EncodedFormParser(Session * pSession, Request * pRequest) {
        if (!fetchQuery(pRequest))
            fetchQuery(pSession, pRequest);
    }
    ~EncodedFormParser() { }
    OptString & rawString()  { return rString; }
    class Iterator {
    private:
        EncodedFormParser  & rStream;
        OptString rKey, rValue;
        int iCount;
```

```
          size_t iLastPos, iNextEquals;
          void clean(OptString & rStr) {
                  rStr.replace('+', ' ');
          }
      public:
          Iterator(EncodedFormParser & rEnclosing) :
                  rStream(rEnclosing), iCount(0), iLastPos(0),
                  iNextEquals(0) { }
          ~Iterator() { }
          int next() {
              if (rStream.rawString().length() == 0)
                  return 0;
              rKey = rValue = "";
              if (iLastPos < rStream.rawString().length()
                   && iNextEquals != NPOS) {
                  iNextEquals =
                          rStream.rawString().index("=", iLastPos);
                  if (iNextEquals != NPOS) {
                      size_t iNextAmpersand =
                              rStream.rawString().
                                  index("&", iNextEquals + 1);
                      rKey = rStream.rawString().
                              substr(iLastPos,
                              iNextEquals-iLastPos);
                      clean(rKey);
                      iNextAmpersand = (iNextAmpersand == NPOS) ?
                                  rStream.rawString().length() -1:
                                      iNextAmpersand-1;
                      rValue=rStream.rawString().
                                  substr(iNextEquals+1,
                                          iNextAmpersand - iNextEquals);
                      clean(rValue);
                      iLastPos = iNextAmpersand + 2;
                  }
              }
              return rKey.length() != 0;
          }
          OptString const & currentValue() { return rValue; }
          OptString const & currentKey() { return rKey; }
      };

      Iterator begin() { return Iterator(*this); }


};
```

```cpp
class EXPORT DBMReader;
class EXPORT DBMWriter;

class EXPORT DBMDatabase {
private:
    OptString rFileName;
    void * pSource;
protected:
    void setSource(void * pPrim) { pSource = pPrim; }
public:
    DBMDatabase(OptString const & rName) :
            rFileName(rName), pSource(0) { }
    virtual ~DBMDatabase() { }
    OptString const & getName() const { return rFileName; }
    void setName(OptString const & rName) { rFileName = rName; }
    void * getPrimitive() { return pSource; }
    virtual int open(int iMode = O_RDONLY) = 0;
    virtual int close() = 0;
    virtual DBMReader * getReader() = 0;
    virtual DBMWriter * getWriter() = 0;
};


class EXPORT DBMRoot {
private:
    DBMDatabase * pDatabase;
protected:
    DBMDatabase * getDatabase() { return pDatabase; }
public:
    DBMRoot(DBMDatabase * pSource) : pDatabase(pSource) { }
    virtual ~DBMRoot() { }
};

class EXPORT DBMReader : public DBMRoot {
public:
    DBMReader(DBMDatabase * pSource) : DBMRoot(pSource) {}
    ~DBMReader() { }
    virtual int hasKey(OptString const & rKey) = 0;
    virtual OptString getValueAtKey(OptString const & rKey) = 0;
    virtual OptString first() = 0;
    virtual OptString next() = 0;
};
```

```
class EXPORT DBMWriter : public DBMRoot {
public:
    DBMWriter(DBMDatabase * pSource) : DBMRoot(pSource) {}
    ~DBMWriter() { }
    virtual int addKeyAndValue(OptString const & rKey,
                               OptString const & rValue) = 0;
    virtual int removeKeyAndValue(OptString const & rKey) = 0;
};

class EXPORT BDBMReader : public DBMReader {
private:
    DBT rLastFetch;
    DB * pBerk;
    int fetchDatum(OptString const & rKey) {
        DBT rSearch = { (char*) (rKey.c_str()), rKey.length() };
        int iCode = pBerk->get(pBerk, &rSearch, &rLastFetch, NULL);
        return iCode;
    }
public:
    BDBMReader(DBMDatabase * pSource) : DBMReader(pSource) {
        pBerk = (DB*) (getDatabase()->getPrimitive());
    }
    ~BDBMReader() { }
    virtual int hasKey(OptString const & rKey) {
        return fetchDatum(rKey) == 0;
    }
    virtual OptString getValueAtKey(OptString const & rKey) {
        return fetchDatum(rKey) == 0 ?
                OptString((char*) rLastFetch.data,
                rLastFetch.size)
                : OptString();
    }
    virtual OptString first() {
        DBT rKey, rData;
          pBerk->seq(pBerk, &rKey, &rData, R_FIRST);
        return OptString((char*) rKey.data, rKey.size);
    }
    virtual OptString next() {
        DBT rKey, rData;
          pBerk->seq(pBerk, &rKey, &rData, R_NEXT);
        return OptString((char*) rKey.data, rKey.size);
    }
};
```

```cpp
class EXPORT BDBMDatabase : public DBMDatabase {
private:
    DB * pDBM;
    int iOpen;
    int iType;
public:
    BDBMDatabase(OptString const & rName,
                         int iDbType = DB_BTREE)
        : DBMDatabase(rName), pDBM((DB*) NULL),
            iOpen(0), iType(iDbType) { }
    ~BDBMDatabase() { }
    virtual int open(int iMode = O_RDONLY) {
        pDBM = ::dbopen((char *) getName().c_str(),
                    iMode, S_IRUSR | S_IWUSR, iType , NULL);
        setSource(pDBM);
        return (iOpen = pDBM != NULL);
    }
    virtual int close() {
        if (pDBM != NULL) {
            pDBM->close(pDBM);
            iOpen = 0;
            setSource(pDBM = (DB*) NULL);
        }
        return 1;
    }
    virtual DBMReader * getReader() {
        return new BDBMReader(this);
    }
    virtual DBMWriter * getWriter() {
        return (DBMWriter *) NULL;
    }
    int isOpen() const { return iOpen; }
};


/**
 * <Object name=default>
 * PathCheck fn="findSimpleKey" database="/tmp/what.pag"
 */
extern "C" {
static int writeToClient(Session * pSession, char const * cpString);
int doSearch(EncodedFormParser & rParser,
            char * cpDatabase,
            Session * pSession);
```

```
int EXPORT findSimpleKey(pblock *pBlocker,
                         Session *pSession,
                         Request *pRequest)
{
    protocol_status(pSession, pRequest, PROTOCOL_OK, NULL);

    if(protocol_start_response(pSession, pRequest) == REQ_NOACTION)
        return REQ_PROCEED;

    if (!writeToClient(pSession, "<H1>Results Of Search</h1>")) {
            log_error(LOG_WARN, "fsk", NULL, NULL,
            "Couldn't write to client");
            return REQ_EXIT;
    }
    EncodedFormParser rParser(pSession, pRequest);
    char * cpDatabase = pblock_findval("database", pBlocker);
    if (!cpDatabase) {
        writeToClient(pSession,
        "Config error; No database defined for search");
        return REQ_ABORTED;
    }
    if (rParser.rawString().length() == 0) {
        writeToClient(pSession, "You didn't supply a search");
        return REQ_ABORTED;
    }
    writeToClient(pSession, "<h2>Searching now.....</h2><hr>");
    writeToClient(pSession,
                     !doSearch(rParser, cpDatabase, pSession) ?
                     "<br><b>Searches Failed...." :
                     "<br><hr><em>Success !!");
    return REQ_PROCEED;
}

/**
 * Expect Name, Name
 */

int doSearch(EncodedFormParser & rParser,
             char * cpDatabaseName,
             Session * pSession) {
    BDBMDatabase rDatabase(cpDatabaseName);
    if (!rDatabase.open()) {
        writeToClient(pSession,
                         "<h2>Could not open database<h2>");
```

```
            log_error(LOG_WARN, "fsk", NULL, NULL,
                    "Error %d occurred for %s",
                    errno, cpDatabaseName);
            return 0;
        }
        EncodedFormParser::Iterator rIterator = rParser.begin();
        int iLocated = 0, iKeys = 0;
        DBMReader * pReader = rDatabase.getReader();
        while (rIterator.next()) {
            OptString rKey = rIterator.currentKey();
            if (rKey == "FIND") {
                OptString rValue = rIterator.currentValue();
                OptString rMessage(iKeys > 0 ? "<br>" : "");
                rMessage.append("<b>Key: ").append(rValue);
                if (!pReader->hasKey(rValue))
                    rMessage.append("</b> wasn't found");
                else {
                    rMessage.append("</b> found, value ").
                        append(pReader->getValueAtKey(rValue));
                    iLocated++;
                }
                writeToClient(pSession, rMessage.c_str());
                iKeys++;
            }
        }
        delete pReader;
        rDatabase.close();
        return iLocated;
}

static int writeToClient(Session * pSession,
                                    char const * cpString)
{
    return net_write(pSession->csd,
                        (char*) cpString,
                        strlen(cpString)) != IO_ERROR;
}

}
```

Again, because you are familiar with the preamble of an extension function, we are just going to highlight the one include file you may not be familiar with, in this line:

```
#include "BerkeleyDB/db.1.85/PORT/include/db.h"
```

You have probably guessed what is in it by now—the definitions of Berkeley DB functionality. The first declaration we encounter is that of class **EncodedFormParser**, which we'll now describe.

The EncodedFormParser Class

We know that for this extension and potentially for many others, we will be required to parse a data input stream in the form prescribed by HTTP 1.0. So, the responsibility of the **EncodedFormParser** class is to parse some data source and make an iterator available over the decoded contents.

Before we continue, we would like to point out that this class has a noticeable deficiency in that it is tightly coupled to the **Session** and **Request** structures of Netscape. This would hamper porting efforts and maintainability. An alternative (and superior) approach is presented in Chapters 12 and 13, where we discuss a C++ framework that directly addresses the issue of portability across different APIs. It would be possible in this example to hide the access to the **query**, **content-length** request headers as well as create a suitably descriptive abstract interface to the **netbuf** structure and its associated functions. The increase in complexity would, however, tend to shift the focus from NSAPI on to the finer nuances of object-oriented practice, which we defer to Chapters 11 onwards.

Consider also that, instead of making available an iterator over the keys and values of the input stream, we could have used another type of object (such as a Dictionary) to allow direct and random keyed access, and passed that out to (object) clients of **EncodedFormParser**. In fact, this is how Chapter 13 demonstrates query access. Our aim here is to provide diverse examples of achieving results. Another advantage of that type of scheme is that the parsing of the client data stream only has to be done once.

So let's begin to dissect the class. The constructor demonstrates the binding problem we have mentioned, accepting a **Session** and **Request** pointer that is then used internally:

```
EncodedFormParser(Session * pSession, Request * pRequest) {
        if (!fetchQuery(pRequest))
            fetchQuery(pSession, pRequest);
}
```

Basically, if we can't fetch a query string from the **Request.reqpb pblock** (a GET request), we switch our attention to the POST style of request where we need to access members from both **Session** and **Request**. We could test for the request method directly, by interrogating the **method** key in **Request.reqpb**, like this:

```
pblock_findval("method", pRequest->reqpb)
```

This will return the string GET, POST, and so on.

So let's examine the **fetchQuery member** function declared privately in **EncodedFormParser**:

```
int fetchQuery(Request * pRequest) {
        char * cpString;
        if (!(cpString = pblock_findval("query",
                                        pRequest->reqpb)))
            return 0;
        rString = cpString;
        return rString.length();
    }
```

It is just as simple as you would expect. We'll grab and test the value of the **query** key in **pRequest->reqpb**. If it is null, this means that that client either sent no data with the request or it has been POSTed. Otherwise, we'll copy the string into a private instance variable, called **rString**. We return the length of the result of the string we found.

The alternative course of action in our constructor is to call the other **fetchQuery** function that will look for POST data. Here are the first few lines of the function:

```
int fetchQuery(Session * pSession, Request * pRequest) {
        char *cpLength;
        ::request_header("content-length", &cpLength,
                pSession, pRequest);

        if (!strlen(cpLength))
            return 0;

        int iLeft = ::atoi(cpLength);

        if (iLeft <= 0)
            return 0;
```

Our first action is to see if the client supplied a **content-length** header, by using the **request_header** NSAPI function to bind to it. If there is no such header, the value pointed to by **cpLength** will be zero; otherwise we use the standard C library function **atoi** to convert the string to an integer. If it's greater than zero, there should be data waiting at the client end.

If we drop through to the next part of the code, then we have a non-zero content length, which we'll try to read using the **netbuf_getc** functions described earlier:

```
        rString = "";
        while (iLeft) {
        int iChar = netbuf_getc(pSession->inbuf);
        if(iChar == IO_ERROR || iChar == IO_EOF)
            break;
        rString.append(iChar);
        iLeft--;
    }
 return rString.length();
}
```

Note that we are not reading literally a character at a time from the network connection, because at least the NSAPI function will be buffering the data as it is read (not to mention the operating system, network interface, and so on).

We test after each character that the return code does not signal that an error has occurred. As we iterate, we append each character to our internal string, **rString**.

The EncodedFormParser::Iterator Class

We mentioned in the previous section that the **EncodedFormParser** class makes available the keys and associated values of the collected client data stream via an iterator. An iterator is a reasonably standard object-oriented idiom for allowing multiple independent access to some kind of collection.

The iterator of **EncodedFormParser** is modeled as a *nested class*. This draws on a practice adopted by the implementers of the Standard Template Library, who discarded the other, more common method, a separate class that contains some constant reference to the target collection. When a client of an **EncodedFormParser** instance sends a **begin** message to it, the result is of type **EncodedFormParser::Iterator** and is an iterator positioned just before the first key and value. Keys and values are held and accessed as simple strings, using our **OptString** string class.

To iterate over the discovered keys of the client stream, the message **next** is sent repeatedly to the iterator. If the method call returns non-zero, then another key is available and may be accessed using the **currentKey** and **currentValue** member functions.

Iterators are pretty simple beasts. The **EncodedFormParser::Iterator** is more unusual in that it assumes the responsibility for parsing the data stream into keys and values. We have adopted this design because it is conceptually simpler and emphasizes decoding the HTTP-encoded stream. Remember that we mentioned that the parsing could have been done up front and placed in some kind of Dictionary container. The iterator would then have been reduced to a role of simply allowing sequential access to a set of associations stored in a (yet another) container. This is a somewhat cleaner scheme, but introduces another class and its attendant interface (which detracts from our intent), which is to describe a way of parsing the stream.

The parsing for the stream is done in the **next** call. The beginning is described now:

```
int next() {
          if (rStream.rawString().length() == 0)
               return 0;
```

Our first action tests to make sure that there is a string to parse, and then tests to see if we have reached the end of the input string:

```
rKey = rValue = "";
if (iLastPos < rStream.rawString().length()
                    && iNextEquals != NPOS) {
```

Iterator keeps as instance variables the position in the string it has parsed up to and where the next equal (=) symbol occurs. Next we look for the next = sign by using the **index** member function of class **OptString**, which returns the position in the target string (the data stream) of the supplied character relative to the start position given (if any):

```
iNextEquals = rStream.rawString().index("=", iLastPos);
```

If the **index** method did not return **NPOS**, which is a manifest constant for ([**size_t**] **-1**), then an = must have been found. Remember, we are looking for key=value pairs separated by ampersands, so we must be able to find an equal sign at least. If there is only one key, we won't see an ampersand:

```
if (iNextEquals != NPOS) {
```

Now we'll scan forward for an ampersand separator:

```
size_t iNextAmpersand =
           rStream.rawString().index("&", iNextEquals + 1);
```

Next, we'll gather the key from wherever we started our parsing up to just before the equal sign. We discovered:

```
rKey = rStream.rawString().
           substr(iLastPos, iNextEquals-iLastPos);
```

When we get the data stream from the request, it may be encoded as per the HTTP 1.0 specification. So, the next method call is very important:

```
clean(rKey);
```

We must be prepared to decode this. The **clean** member function partially implements this cleansing by replacing any + characters encountered in the supplied string with a space. Because it neglects hexadecimal sequence parsing—among other things, this is not a full implementation.

Now we'll determine how much of the string after the = sign we need to cut to create the value associated with the key. If there is no ampersand to be seen, we take the rest of the string—otherwise we take all the characters just prior to the ampersand, like this:

```
iNextAmpersand = (iNextAmpersand == NPOS) ?
           rStream.rawString().length() -1:
             iNextAmpersand-1;
rValue=rStream.rawString().
           substr(iNextEquals+1,
                    iNextAmpersand - iNextEquals);
```

Finally, we clean up the value, and set our internal record of where we are in the input string to immediately after the ampersand:

```
        clean(rValue);
        iLastPos = iNextAmpersand + 2;
    }
}
```

Our return value is the length of the key we discovered.

The Database Classes

Because there are a number of variations on a theme for public domain type packages, we decided to design and implement this part of the extension more carefully.

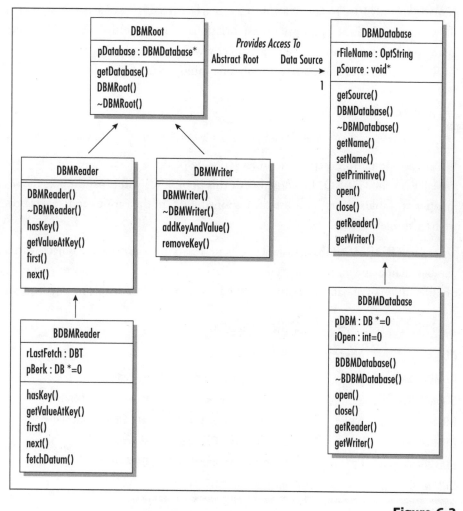

Figure 6.3

UML notation class diagram of the simple database classes.

We aim to show how the construction of an object-oriented Web server extension is worthwhile but polarized towards the design phase in terms of effort. We have only made these classes as complete as they need to be for our purposes.

An overall view of the design is depicted in Figure 6.3 using the UML 1.0 notation.

We describe these classes briefly in Table 6.12.

We have noted the existence of the **DBMWriter** class but have not provided an implementation.

The rationale underpinning design in this manner is fairly obvious. With this design in place, we only have to talk to an abstract interface to a DBM type database, which allows us to substitute appropriate instantiations at runtime if desired. Thus, the main body of the extension is reusable directly with older style DBM, NDBM, and GDBM packages (to name a few) if only one minor change is made.

Thread Safety

It is important to note that the DBM style packages are not MT safe, so be careful!

We are not going to describe the inner working of these classes directly (they are available on the CD-ROM enclosed with this book). We will expand upon the semantics of Table 6.12 to illustrate the responsibilities of the various concrete classes we have implemented.

To create a **BDBMDatabase** instance, it is necessary to construct the object with a database name and an optional type. The Berkeley DB package supports a number of different types of database (Btree, Hashed, RecNo), so it's possible to construct an

Table 6.12 Classes in the DBM abstraction.

Class	Abstract	Semantics
DBMDatabase	Yes	Defines protocol for a DBM abstraction.
BDBMDatabase	No	Implements Berkeley DB database coarse behavior.
DBMRoot	Yes	Root class, holds pointer to some DBM abstraction.
DBMReader	Yes	Interface for a DB reader.
BDBMReader	No	Concrete implementation for Berkeley DB.
DBMWriter	Yes	Interface for a DB writer.

object with a type identifier that matches that of the target database. The default for **BDBMDatabase** is **DB_BTREE**.

Once you have an initialized instance, you may send it the message **open** with an optional mode in the same style as in the standard include file fcntl.h. The default for the mode argument is **O_RDONLY**. You can always ask a database instance if it is open by sending it the message **isOpen**. This returns a value that is not equal to zero if the object believes the database is open.

To read from or search in the database, it is necessary to ask the database instance for a reader by using the **getReader**() member function. This will return a pointer to a **DBMReader**, which is our abstract interface to a DBM-style database reader. The caller is responsible for releasing the memory after finishing with the reader. (Another alternative is to use a reference counting system with a concrete class wrapping the polymorphic class pointer, but this technique is beyond the scope of this chapter.)

The **BDBMReader** concrete implementation of a **DBMReader** is worth discussing in more detail. It implements all the pure virtual functions defined in **DBMReader**, and shows how a simple C-style API may be wrapped into an object-oriented interface. Interestingly, we could have made another abstraction for the reader type, because it also offers iterator-type behavior in its **first** and **next** features. However, we have taken a pragmatic approach again, in that the abstraction offered is sufficiently designed such that it is usable.

To illustrate the C wrapping, consider the following extract from **BDBMReader**:

```
int fetchDatum(OptString const & rKey) {
    DBT rSearch = { (char*) (rKey.c_str()), rKey.length() };
    int iCode = pBerk->get(pBerk, &rSearch, &rLastFetch, NULL);
    return iCode;
}
```

This shows the implementation of the *private* member function **fetchDatum**. Given a search key in its **rKey** reference to a string, it is this function's job to access the C API **get** function of the **DB** type, first having converted the search key into a form that DB understands (a simple structure is used). It also caches the search result in an internal instance variable so that it doesn't unduly compromise the performance of other functions that directly use the search result of a database query.

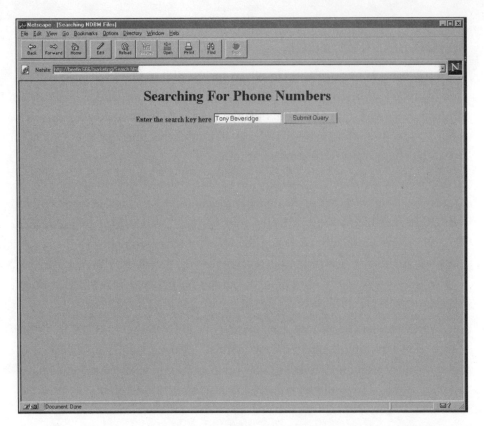

Figure 6.4

Simple HTML search form displayed in Netscape Navigator.

The Service Extension Function

To recap, the purpose of this extension is to read some encoded form input from a client, parse it, and search a Berkeley DB-style database. Once the search has completed, an HTML document describing the results should be returned to the client.

For the purposes of test and demonstration, Listing 6.13 is the HTML source of the form we used.

Listing 6.13 Simple HTML search form.

```
<HTML>
<TITLE>Searching NDBM Files</TITLE>
<BODY>
<CENTER>
<H1>Searching For Phone Numbers</H1>
```

```
<FORM METHOD=POST ACTION=http://beetle:666/marketing/NDBMsearch>
<b>Enter the search key here</b>
<INPUT TYPE=Text NAME=FIND>
<INPUT TYPE=SUBMIT NAME=Search>
</FORM>
</BODY>
</HTML>
```

Figure 6.4 shows how it appears in Netscape Navigator 3.0.

In a similar vein, here we show the configuration used:

```
<Object ppath="/export/E201a/docs/marketing/BDBMsearch">
ObjectType fn="force-type" type="text/html"
Service fn=findSimpleKey database="/ Marketing/addressBook.btree"
          method=(GET|HEAD|POST)
</Object>
```

As you can see from the **Service** directive, we pass in the name of the Btree DB database to our extension. We also use the built-in Netscape function **force-type** to force the content type of our response to be HTML.

Now that we are configured, the server has been either started or restarted, and our extension function awaits activation on a particular **ppath**. We'll walk you through the body of the function **findSimpleKey** to show you exactly what it does.

The top of the function is what we have come to expect for Service class extensions, in which we set the status (**protocol_status**) and start the response (**protocol_start_response**):

```
int EXPORT findSimpleKey(pblock *pBlocker,
                         Session *pSession,
                         Request *pRequest)
{
    protocol_status(pSession, pRequest, PROTOCOL_OK, NULL);

    if(protocol_start_response(pSession, pRequest) == REQ_NOACTION)
        return REQ_PROCEED;
```

After this, we send the beginning of the HTML document to the client, using our own function **writeToClient**, shown here, which is just a wrapper for **net_write**:

```
if (!writeToClient(pSession, "<H1>Results Of Search</h1>")) {
        log_error(LOG_WARN, "fsk", NULL, NULL,
        "Couldn't write to client");
        return REQ_EXIT;
}
```

Here is the interesting part. The next declaration constructs an **EncodedFormParser** object with our **Session** and **Request** pointers. If your refer back to the discussion of this class you will note that the data stream will be read from the client now, by the appropriate means (POST or GET):

```
EncodedFormParser rParser(pSession, pRequest);
```

One of the configuration requirements for this function, the database name to be searched, is passed in via the pblock argument **pBlocker**. We'll use the trusty, if somewhat crude, **pblock_findval** function to try and fetch this value:

```
char * cpDatabase = pblock_findval("database", pBlocker);
if (!cpDatabase) {
    writeToClient(pSession,
    "Config error; No database defined for search");
    return REQ_ABORTED;
}
```

If the value is not there, we'll write an error message to the client and signal an abort request to the server. We could also have written an error of type **LOG_MISCONFIG** to the server's error log using **log_error**. After this step we query what length of data the client sent:

```
if (rParser.rawString().length() == 0) {
    writeToClient(pSession, "You didn't supply a search");
    return REQ_ABORTED;
}
writeToClient(pSession, "<h2>Searching now.....</h2><hr>");
```

If it has zero length, it will write another message and abort the request.

The next step is slightly more complex. We'll call the **doSearch** function (described next) and, depending upon the return code of that function, tack on a success or failure message to the response that has been sent to the client:

```
writeToClient(pSession,
              !doSearch(rParser, cpDatabase, pSession) ?
              "<br><b>Searches Failed...." :
              "<br><hr><em>Success !!");
return REQ_PROCEED;
}
```

Our last step is to return **REQ_PROCEED** so that the server knows we have serviced this request.

The actual search functionality of this extension is placed in a static function called **doSearch**, which accepts arguments of a reference to the **EncodedFormParser** (a character pointer to the database name and the **Session** pointer):

```
int doSearch(EncodedFormParser & rParser,
             char * cpDatabaseName,
             Session * pSession) {
```

Its initial action is to try to construct a **BDBMDatabase** object with the database name **cpDatabaseName**:

```
BDBMDatabase rDatabase(cpDatabaseName);
```

The implied type of the database is that of Btree, because we supplied no argument to override the default argument of **BDBMDatabase**. Now we'll try to open the database:

```
if (!rDatabase.open()) {
    writeToClient(pSession,
                       "<h2>Could not open database<h2>");
    log_error(LOG_WARN, "fsk", NULL, NULL,
            "Error %d occurred for %s",
            errno, cpDatabaseName);
    return 0;
}
```

If this doesn't work, write an error message to the client and return a code for failure.

Now we'll perform the actual search. First we'll get an iterator over the keys and values of the known input stream, by calling the member function **begin** on the **EncodedFormParser** object:

```
EncodedFormParser::Iterator rIterator = rParser.begin();
int iLocated = 0, iKeys = 0;
```

Next, we'll ask the database to create a **DBMReader** object for us to search with:

```
DBMReader * pReader = rDatabase.getReader();
```

And finally, we step sequentially through the iterator looking for any values associated with a key of **FIND**:

```
while (rIterator.next()) {
    OptString rKey = rIterator.currentKey();
    if (rKey == "FIND") {
        OptString rValue = rIterator.currentValue();
        OptString rMessage(iKeys > 0 ? "<br>" : "");
        rMessage.append("<b>Key: ").append(rValue);
        if (!pReader->hasKey(rValue))
            rMessage.append("</b> wasn't found");
        else {
            rMessage.append("</b> found, value ").
                append(pReader->getValueAtKey(rValue));
            iLocated++;
        }
        writeToClient(pSession, rMessage.c_str());
        iKeys++;
    }
}
```

For each **FIND** key that we encounter, we'll write its value to the client and use the **DBMReader** object **pReader** to query the database for the existence of this value as in the open database. If it is found, we'll write its value to the client, otherwise we'll write a string saying that we couldn't find it.

Our final tasks after iteration is complete are to delete the **pReader**, close the database, and return the number of searches whose result was success:

```
delete pReader;
rDatabase.close();
return iLocated;
}
```

To show the response of this extension to a successful search performed via a browser, please see Figure 6.5. This concludes our discussion of this extension function type.

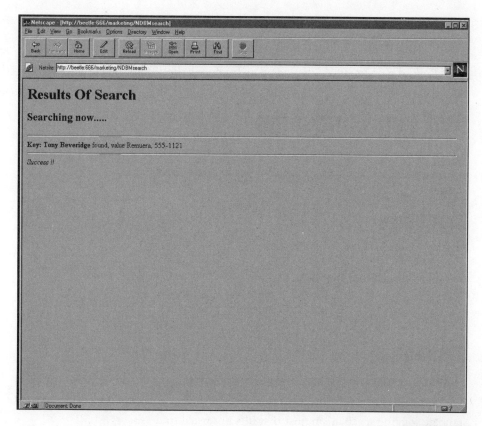

Figure 6.5

Simple search results seen in Netscape Navigator.

Key Features

Here is a summary of the characteristic tasks of a service class function:

- Sets the status of the server's response using the **protocol_set_status** NSAPI function.

- Starts the server's response using the **protocol_start_response** NSAPI function.

- Returns **REQ_NOACTION** if the server should apply other Service directives.

- Returns **REQ_PROCEED** for success. This stops the server applying other Service directives.

- Returns **REQ_EXIT** to signal a catastrophic error.

- Returns **REQ_ABORTED** to signal a fatal error.

- If processing data from a client input stream, be cognizant of the fact that GET or POST results in different behavior.

- Think of performance—Service class functions should not be tardy.

Add Log Functions

An add log class function in NSAPI is ordinarily used to log extra or alternative information about a request that the server has processed.

Signature

Add log functions have the standard extension prototype:

```
int function_name(pblock * pBlocker,
                        Session * pSession,
                        Request * pRequest)
```

Semantics

This function does not, as one might expect, serve to alter the standard information that is sent to the server's log. That does not mean that you can't replace the server's standard logging mechanism, just that it is not usual to do so.

Why is this? Basically, there are many scripts, programs, and such that are available for analyzing an HTTP server's log file as long as it is in the *Common Log Format*. Altering your server's log file, if even by just a field swap, will break virtually all of these tools. So our advice is simple: If you are going to log request information, use a separate file. If you have your own log analysis tools and don't mind some change, then it is entirely up to you.

When an add log function is called, all of the request headers, server headers, and so on are available to it, so there is a regular smorgasbord of choice.

Include Files

To define the structures that are passed in via pointers to the function, you should include the following lines in your source code:

```
#include "base/pblock.h"
#include "base/session.h"
#include "frame/req.h"
```

Important Session Structure Members

The **Session** structure pointer contains the information shown in Table 6.13.

Important Request Structure Members

The **Request** structure pointer contains the information shown in Table 6.14.

pblock Variables Defined

There are no standard defined associations in the passed **pblock** pointer **pBlocker**. However, it may include associations that you have defined and specified in obj.conf.

Add Log Extension Return Codes

These points apply:

- All are defined in frame/req.h.

- A return of **REQ_NOACTION** or **REQ_PROCEED** means that the server should apply any other matched add log functions.

Table 6.13   Session structure members available.

Means of access	Type	Meaning
pblock_findval("ip", pSession->client)	char *	The IP address of the client.
session_maxdns(pSession)	char *	The FQDN of the client.
pSession->csd	SYS_NETFD	System-dependent file descriptor connected to the client.
pSession->inbuf	netbuf *	Network connection buffer to the client (inbound).
pSession->csd_open	int	If not equal to zero, the connection to the client through csd is open.

Table 6.14   Request structure members available.

Means Of Access	Type	Meaning
pblock_findval("path", pRequest->vars)	char *	The physical path of the request.
pblock_findval("auth-user", pRequest->vars)	*char **	*The authenticated user name.*
pblock_findval("auth-type", pRequest->vars)	*char **	*The authentication type.*
pblock_findval("auth-group", pRequest->vars)	*char **	*The authenticated user group.*
pblock_findval("protocol", pRequest->reqpb)	char *	The protocol of the request.
pblock_findval("uri", pRequest->reqpb)	char *	The URI of the request.
pblock_findval("method." pRequest->reqpb)	char *	The method of the request.
pblock_findval("clf-request", pRequest->reqpb)	char *	The full request string.
pRequest-> loadhdrs	int	Normally 0.
pblock_findval("host", pRequest->headers)	*char **	*The host target of the request.*
pblock_findval("if-modified-since", pRequest->headers)	*char **	*The HTTP date of the document that the client already has cached.*
pblock_findval("accept", pRequest->headers)	char *	The types the client can accept.
pblock_findval("user-agent", pRequest->headers)	*char **	*The client designation.*
pblock_findval("connection", pRequest->headers)	*char **	*The Keep-Alive directive.*
pRequest->senthdrs	int	Normally 1—the response headers have been sent.
pblock_findval("content-type", pRequest->srvhdrs)	*char **	*The response content type.*
pRequest->statpath	char *	The last path that was passed to request_stat_path.
pRequest->request_is_cacheable	int	Normally 0. Set to zero if the request is not to be cached.
pRequest->directive_is_cacheable	int	Normally 0. Set to 1 if the directive is to be cached.

Entries in italics may not be sent by some client software implementations.

Configuration For This Event

Add log directives may be associated with one or many Object sections in obj.conf. Here is an extract from obj.conf that highlights an object-type directive, **AddLog**, applied to all requests:

```
<Object name="default">
AddLog fn="flex-log" name="access"
AddLog fn="specialLog"
```

We have already discussed in Chapter 3 how the server locates the functions to load and how they are specified in obj.conf.

Here we have defined an **AddLog** class-extension function called **specialLog**.

Sample AddLog Function

The code presented in Listing 6.14 is a very simple C-based **AddLog** function that records custom information in a file named by the **log-file** key in the **pblock pBlocker**. The use of an **AddLog** function in this manner suggests that it is responsible for creating and maintaining the **log-file**.

Listing 6.14   Simple **AddLog** class function.

```
#if defined(__cplusplus)
extern "C" {
#endif

#include "base/pblock.h"
#include "base/session.h"
#include "frame/req.h"
#include "base/daemon.h"

static SYS_FILE theLog = SYS_ERROR_FD;

#if defined(XP_WIN32)
#define EXPORT __declspec(dllexport)
#else
#define EXPORT
#endif
```

```
EXPORT void gotRestart(void * vParameter) {
    if (theLog != SYS_ERROR_FD) {
        system_fclose(theLog);
        theLog = SYS_ERROR_FD;
    }
}


EXPORT int initLog(pblock *pBlocker,
                   Session *pSession,
                   Request *pRequest)
{
    char *cpFile = pblock_findval("log-file", pBlocker);

    if(!cpFile ||
       (theLog = system_fopenWA(cpFile)) == SYS_ERROR_FD) {
        pblock_nvinsert("error",
                         "initLog: no file name/bad permissions",
                         pBlocker);
        return REQ_ABORTED;
    }
    daemon_atrestart(gotRestart, NULL);
    return REQ_PROCEED;
}


EXPORT int specialLog(pblock *pBlocker,
                            Session *pSession,
                            Request *pRequest)
{
char * cpMethod = pblock_findval("method", pRequest->reqpb);
char * cpURI = pblock_findval("uri", pRequest->reqpb);
char * cpMime = pblock_findval("content-type", pRequest->srvhdrs);
char * cpLength = pblock_findval("content-length", pRequest->srvhdrs);
char * cpAgent = pblock_findval("user-agent", pRequest->headers);
char * cpBuffer;
    cpBuffer = MALLOC(strlen(cpAgent) +
                       strlen(cpLength) +
                       strlen(cpMime) +
                       strlen(cpURI) +
                       strlen(cpMethod) + 5);
    sprintf(cpBuffer, "%s %s %s %s %s\n",
             cpMethod, cpURI,
             cpMime, cpLength,
             cpAgent);
    system_fwrite_atomic(theLog, cpBuffer, strlen(cpBuffer));
return REQ_PROCEED;
}
```

```
#if defined(__cplusplus)
}
#endif
```

If you have examined the Netscape NSAPI example code, you will probably see similarities between the AddLog example they present and the example we present here. Primarily, the reason for this is that most examples of an **AddLog** function have very little utility besides managing a file (which is best done by an initialization-style function) and write information to it. Hence, there is a basic and standard pattern of behavior for most extensions of this class.

In our example, there are two log file management functions. One is **initLog**, which is responsible for extracting the **log-file** value from the **pblock pBlocker**, and creating it in write *append* mode. The other is called **gotRestart**, which is responsible for closing the file upon server restart (because the **initLog** function will be called next and will open **log-file**).

To create the log file successfully, we would need to add this **Init** directive to obj.conf:

```
Init fn=initLog log-file="/ex/Nsc/https-gorgon/logs/spec.log"
```

We'll assume that this has also been preceded by a **load-modules** directive to load the shared object where **initLog**, and others, reside.

Our extension **specialLog**, performs some very simple actions for each request that it sees. First, it locates the values for the *method, user-agent, uri* of the request, and the *content-type* and *content-length* of the response. Then it uses the NSAPI memory-management routines to allocate some memory that can hold all of these strings concatenated, plus a line feed character. It then copies all these values into the newly allocated memory, and uses the atomic write function in NSAPI to write all the details as one line. (However, the final two lines are broken into two lines each, due to the size restrictions of this book.)

Thus, typical lines in our log file would look like this:

```
GET /PROTECTED/ text/html 277 Mozilla/3.0 (WinNT; I)
GET /Java/Demo/LedClock.html text/html 1932 Mozilla/3.0 (WinNT; I)
GET /Java/Demo/Packages/Java/Optimation/Utils/Led.class application/
  octet-stream 455 Mozilla/3.0 (WinNT; I)
GET /Java/Demo/Packages/Java/Optimation/Utils/LedGroup.class application/
  octet-stream 307 Mozilla/3.0 (WinNT; I)
```

Key Features

Here is a summary of the characteristic tasks of an AddLog function:

- Does not alter the ordinary processing for the server log files.

- Returns **REQ_NOACTION** or **REQ_PROCEED**. This will not stop the server applying other AddLog directives.

Remember to manage custom log file opening and closing properly.

Summary

This chapter has shown how extension functions can be constructed for the Netscape Server API. We have demonstrated how behavior that typically falls into the area of server initialization can allow developers to create global resources. We hope that you will apply the heuristics mentioned in Chapter 5 before implementing such functionality.

For each class of extension function that may be written, we described the syntax of the shared object entry point, the necessary include files, and general semantics attached to the particular phase discussed. We also enumerated the most important **Request** and **Session** structure members that are available.

Because each event is controlled by certain directives in obj.conf, we described how this configuration is effected for each extension type.

NSAPI extension development is a relatively simple business and, with the sample code provided on the CD-ROM enclosed with this book, we hope that you will be able to quickly develop software for deployment.

HIGH PERFORMANCE

Microsoft IIS
And ISAPI

CHAPTER

7

The next four chapters pick up where Chapter 2 left off and provide a more detailed look at Microsoft's Internet Information Server (IIS) architecture and configuration. We'll focus particularly on how IIS can be extended with Internet Server Applications (ISAs) and Internet Server API (ISAPI) filters.

Microsoft IIS And ISAPI

ISAPI filters and ISAs, loosely referred to as ISAPI, form a pivotal part of Microsoft's ActiveX server framework that includes technologies such as Active Server Pages (ASP), Exchange and database connectors, COM/DCOM, message, and transaction processors. This framework provides a powerful architecture for developing next-generation client/server systems.

In this chapter we'll introduce IIS as one of the many services available within Windows NT. We'll then dissect IIS into its component parts and look at how IIS works and is managed. We'll introduce ISAPI as a key integration technology for IIS and explain specifically how ISAs and ISAPI filters are used to extend IIS functionality.

Windows NT Services

IIS is implemented as a Windows NT service. In Windows NT, a service is a program (typically a background process) that runs independently of any logged-in user. Common services include the following:

- *Net Logon*—Handles client logon requests and performs user authentication.

- *DNS Server*—Handles the resolution of Internet domain names. For example, **www.microsoft.com** to a corresponding IP address.

- *Remote Procedure Call (RPC) Service*—Handles client RPC requests and maps them to preregistered RPC servers.

In practice, a service program may implement more than one service—each service running on a separate thread. Services are managed by the Service Control Manager (SCM). This is an RPC server (allowing it to receive management requests from networked clients), which is responsible for tasks such as maintaining a database of installed services, starting/stopping services, and communicating control requests to running services.

A front end to the SCM is provided by Control Panel's Services applet. From this application you can view the services database and control the operation of each service. The Services window shows the service name, its status (for example, Started), and the startup method (Manual or Automatic). For each service you can Start, Stop, or Pause the service and change its startup method.

IIS Architecture

Figure 7.1 shows that IIS actually consists of three core services:

- WWW Publishing Service
- FTP Publishing Service
- Gopher Publishing Service

We are only concerned with the WWW service here and will not discuss Gopher and FTP further.

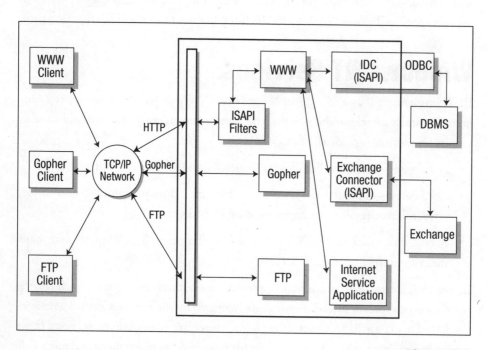

Figure 7.1

IIS Components.

Each of these three services is implemented inside a single task called inetinfo. If you invoke the Task Manager (taskmgr) and select the Processes tab you can see inetinfo running in the background.

This program and related components' help files and administration files are installed in C:\WINNT\system32\inetsrv. The inetinfo task is actually a wrapper application that listens for IIS service requests (FTP, Gopher, or WWW) on their respective ports (remember the well-known port for HTTP is 80) and then loads the appropriate service DLL to handle the request. In addition to implementing these services inetinfo also implements IIS's shared thread pool, cache, logging, and SNMP services.

IIS is designed to handle a large number of incoming requests efficiently. Rather than dispatching each client request to its own thread, which would soon cause IIS to run out of pool threads, inetinfo implements a *worker-thread* model (as opposed to a *client-per-thread* model). This allows a large number of client connections to be multiplexed over a smaller number of threads.

Normally all three IIS services are started automatically. However, as we'll see later in Chapter 10, it is often necessary to run a service manually when debugging server extensions.

In addition to these core services IIS implements *connectors* to other services. Two connectors shown in Figure 7.1 are the Internet Database Connector (IDC) and the Exchange Connector. The IDC is implemented as an ISAPI DLL and provides a simple interface for Web applications to ODBC-compliant database servers such as Microsoft SQL Server. These connectors are examples of how IIS can be extended using ISAPI.

ISAPI actually provides two extension schemes: ISAs and filters. Both are implemented as DLLs. An ISA provides a more efficient alternative to writing a CGI program. You can create your own ISAs, which can be loaded on demand in response to a client request.

ISAPI filters are similar to ISAs in that they are also implemented as DLLs and loaded into the address space of ISS. However, rather than being loaded on demand, they are loaded when IIS initially starts. ISAPI filters provide a way of intercepting events within IIS and overriding or augmenting the default server behavior. Unlike ISAs, which implement a single request, a filter will be activated for all requests no matter where they come from.

IIS Configuration

Although you can use the Services applet from the Control Panel IIS to start and stop IIS services, IIS actually provides its own service manager \WINNT\system32\inetsrv\inetmgr.exe. This application focuses on the three IIS services only and provides a more convenient way of starting and stopping services. In addition to managing an IIS instance on the local system, inetmgr also manages a collection of IIS servers running on other Windows NT machines on a connected network.

In addition to starting and stopping IIS services, inetmgr allows you to change server properties. For example, for the WWW service you can change the following:

- The port the server listens for HTTP requests (normally 80).

- The method for authenticating client requests (Anonymous, Basic, or Windows NT Challenge/Response).

- The server's home directory from which relative URL names are rooted.

- The directories the server has access to, their permissions (read and execute), and corresponding virtual directory names (aliases).

- The default page to be displayed when you first connect to IIS (default.htm).

- The server's logging properties (for example, to log to a file or to an ODBC-compliant database). For file logging, you can change the location and format of the server log files (for example, the use of CERN format).

Figure 7.2 is an example of an inetmgr session that shows the **Service** properties of the WWW Service for the local server (named "ntserver").

IIS Authentication

IIS provides the following three ways of authenticating a client request for a resource:

- Anonymous login

- Basic authentication

- Windows NT Challenge/Response authentication

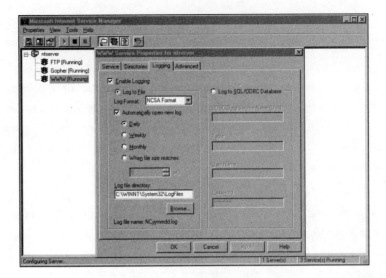

Figure 7.2

An inetmgr session.

You can see these settings when you select the Service tab of the Service Properties dialog box (see Figure 7.3).

Anonymous login, the default setting, allows a request for a resource to be unchallenged by the server. The server uses the User name and Password supplied in the Anonymous Login properties to transparently authenticate the request. This assumes

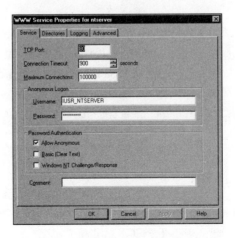

Figure 7.3

IIS authentication schemes.

that the server has granted the anonymous user with appropriate permissions to access these resources. By default, IIS creates an anonymous user name IUSR_*ComputerHostname* with a randomly chosen password.

When a client accesses a resource to which the anonymous user does not have access, the server responds with an Authentication message that indicates to the client which authentication schemes are supported. Depending on the configuration options, these may include Basic and/or Windows NT Challenge/Response authentication.

When a client is told that a Basic authentication scheme is supported, it will then prompt the user for a user name and password. This is then passed back to the server in order to grant access to the resource. This scheme is insecure because the name and password are only encoded using Base64 and essentially pass over the network as clear text. Nevertheless, this form of security is widely used for providing a low level of protection to resources. The Basic Authentication scheme is discussed in detail in Chapter 1.

When a server indicates that it supports the Windows NT Challenge/Response scheme (often referred to as NTLM authentication) and the client supports this, then the client *automatically* sends back the Windows user name and encrypted password. If the Windows' credentials supplied by the client fail, the user is then prompted for an alternative user name and password. This scheme only works with Internet Explorer (2.0 and above).

> **Note:** If you configure the server for both Basic and NTLM schemes, both schemes will be indicated to the client. It is up to the client to select which scheme to use. Normally, a client will use the first scheme listed. With IIS 2.0 and above, NTLM is listed before Basic. In IIS 1.0, the order was reversed. If you don't select any scheme, all access to resources through the server will be blocked.

ISAs

Internet Server Applications (ISAs), also known as ISAPI Extensions, provide an efficient replacement technology for CGI applications.

How An ISA Works

Under Windows, an ISA is implemented as a DLL. When a client makes an ISA request, for example to: http://ntserver/Scripts/Samples/isasample0.dll, the IIS server loads the DLL into its address space.

Once the DLL has loaded, the control is passed to it through predefined entry points exposed by the DLL. There are two mandatory entry points: **GetExtensionVersion** and **HttpExtensionProc** (and an optional entry point **TerminateExtension**).

> **Note:** You can use Windows NT's dumpbin.exe utility to display the exported entry points of a DLL. For example, from an MS-DOS prompt type: **dumpbin helloworld.dll/exports**.

Figure 7.4 shows the flow of control between the server and the ISA.

There are two ways of calling a function in a DLL:

- *Loadtime dynamic linking*—The application directly calls a function in the DLL. This requires that the application be *statically* linked in advance with the DLL's import library to resolve the address of the function.

- *Runtime dynamic linking*—A DLL is loaded by the application at runtime using the Windows **LoadLibrary** function and the address of the function obtained using the companion **GetProcAddress** function.

IIS uses runtime dynamic linking to access functions within an ISA DLL.

The **DllMain** entry point is automatically executed when the DLL is loaded the first time and again when it is unloaded. **DllMain** is optional—if you don't supply this function, the system will define one for you. **DllMain** is one place where ISA initialization and termination functions can be performed. Alternatively, you can also use **GetExtensionVersion** and **TerminateExtension**.

Control is passed to **GetExtensionVersion** each time your extension DLL is loaded and **DllMain** has executed. **GetExtensionVersion** is used to set the version and description of the filter and possibly to allocate global resources for the extension.

Each time the ISA is called (including the first time the DLL is loaded), control is passed to **HttpExtensionProc**, which is then responsible for completely implementing the extension—you can regard this function as the **main**() function of the ISA.

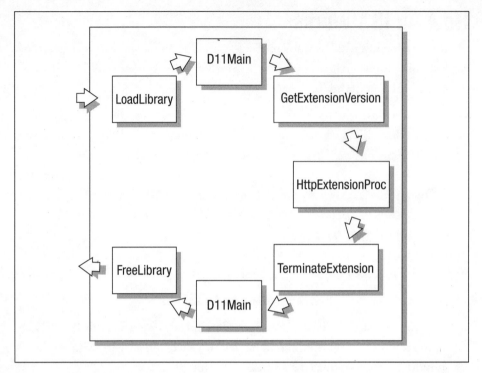

Figure 7.4
Control flow between IIS and an ISA.

When the server terminates or you have requested that the extension DLL be unloaded after each request, IIS explicitly calls **TerminateExtension** just before it unloads the library using **FreeLibrary**. **FreeLibrary** triggers the execution of **DllMain** once again. You can use **TerminateExtension** or **DllMain** to clean up global resources used in your the extension.

> **Note:** *You can force IIS to load and unload your ISA on every request. This is very useful for debugging an extension. See the section "Debugging Techniques For ISAs And Filters" in Chapter 10 for more details.*

How ISAs Integrate With IIS

So far we've looked at how IIS loads a DLL into memory and passes control to the DLL so it can implement the ISA request. Now we'll look at how request and response information is passed between IIS and the ISA.

You will probably be familiar with how this is done with a CGI application (see the next section); however, because we're dealing with an in-process approach here, the CGI model of environment variables and standard input and output for server-to-application communication is not appropriate. Consequently, we'll require access to the internal data structures of IIS.

The ISA specification defines a server memory area that is called **EXTENSION_CONTROL_BLOCK** (also informally known as an *ECB*) for exchanging information between the server and the ISA. The server generates a separate ECB for each client request. When it receives a request, the server parses a subset of commonly used information from the request message and places this into easily accessed variables within the ECB.

A pointer to the ECB is passed to **HttpExtensionProc**, which uses the ECB contents to implement the request.

Table 7.1 provides a subset of this information along with the name of the CGI variable the ECB member variable corresponds to.

These variables are specifically stored in the ECB for your convenience. All other variables such as **AUTH_TYPE**, **REMOTE_USER**, **REMOTE_HOST**, and **SERVER_NAME** must be retrieved using a special ECB-supplied callback function **GetServerVariable**.

The ECB provides a family of useful callback functions for interrogating the request and generating a response. Table 7.2 briefly describes these functions.

We take a more detailed look at the structure of the ECB in the "What Is An ECB?" section of Chapter 8.

ISA As A Replacement For CGI

ISAs are a high-performance alternative to CGI applications. We have already seen that an ISA is a DLL, which is automatically loaded by IIS in response to an ISA request. An ISA request has been designed to be pretty much the same as a CGI request. This makes converting from a CGI to an ISA approach that much easier. The only visible syntactic difference is that the file extension is usually DLL instead of EXE (executable application) or PL (Perl script). For example, **http://ntserver/ samples/isasample1/isasample1.dll**.

Table 7.1 Commonly used ECB members and their CGI counterparts.

ECB Member Variable	Equivalent CGI Variable	What It Means
lpszMethod	REQUEST_METHOD	Method used in the request, for example **GET** or **POST**.
lpszQueryString	QUERY_STRING	The query string data following the "?" in the HTTP **GET** request.
lpszPathInfo	PATH_INFO	The extra path information following the CGI program name in the request URL.
lpszPathTranslated	PATH_TRANSLATED	A translated version of **PATH_INFO** after any physical-to-virtual mapping has been performed.
cbTotalBytes	CONTENT_LENGTH	The length of the request message body in bytes.
lpszContentType	CONTENT_TYPE	The media type of the request.

Table 7.2 ECB-supplied callback functions.

ECB Callback Function	What It Does
GetServerVariable	Fetches information about the client, server, or the request itself.
ReadClient	Reads the body of the client request message.
WriteClient	Sends a response message back to the client.
ServerSupportFunction	Performs one of a number of auxiliary functions, for example, modifying appending additional headers to the response message.

> **Note:** The latest version of the ISAPI specification also provides for an ISA extension as an alternative to DLL.

The obvious advantage of an ISA over a CGI program is performance. Because the DLL is loaded directly into the address space of IIS, the overhead of loading an ISA in comparison to a CGI program is much reduced. With CGI, the server must spawn a separate process in which to execute the CGI application. The overhead of creating the process context and then starting the application can be significant on a busy site, especially if the application has been written in an interpreted language like Perl, which requires the Perl interpreter (a large program in itself) to be loaded before the script actually runs.

Once an ISA DLL has been loaded into the server, it normally stays there until the server terminates or the server explicitly unloads the DLL. This means that normally the overhead of loading the DLL is only incurred once. Subsequent requests are mapped directly to the in-memory copy of the DLL.

This behavior contrasts with CGI in which the application is started for every request. Moreover, it is possible for multiple-extension DLLs to be resident within the server at any one time.

It is also possible for more than one client request to be executing an ISA at any one time. For this reason it is extremely important for ISAs to be *thread safe*. Chapters 5 and 10 discuss thread safety issues in more detail.

While ISAs allow you to write high-performance server extensions there is a slight downside. Because the ISA DLL runs within the context of the server, the DLL must be extremely safety conscious. It is not hard for a memory exception caused by an ISA to crash the server. In Chapter 10 we'll discuss some techniques for reducing the risk of creating a badly behaved ISA.

Another important difference between an ISA and a CGI program is the way in which information is passed to and from the server. CGI defines a list of environment variables that contain information about the request, the client, and the server. For example, a CGI application invoked via a **GET** method extracts the request data from the **QUERY_STRING** environment variable. (A full list of CGI environment variables is provided in Chapter 2).

In contrast, an ISA accesses the same information through the ECB. Inside the ECB the server stores information the ISA needs to process the request. This includes all the information a CGI application would normally have access to through environment variables, plus specialized callback functions such as **ReadClient** and **WriteClient** for reading/writing raw data directly from/to the client, and **GetServerVariable** for extracting additional information from the request.

Figure 7.5 shows the relationship between the server, an ISA, and a CGI program.

In CGI, a **POST** request to a CGI application causes the server to present the request data on the standard input of the application. The application is then

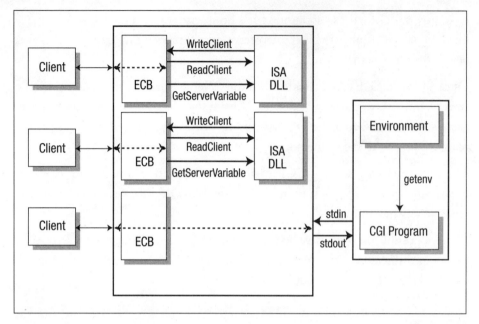

Figure 7.5

Server communication between an ISA and CGI program.

responsible for reading this data from its standard input and interpreting it. This is handled differently in an ISA; the ISA must use the server-supplied function **ReadClient** to read the body of a request message.

Generating a response is handled in a similar fashion. In CGI, you would generate a response by writing a complete response (including all headers) to the standard output of your application for the server to transparently pass back to the client. An ISA would use ECB-provided functions **ServerSupportFunction** and **WriteClient** to generate response headers and body respectively.

ISA Configuration

We have already introduced the Internet Service Manager inetmgr, however there are a couple of server properties that directly affect the running of an ISA. We'll look at these now.

Directory Registration

The directory that contains the ISA must be registered using inetmgr, before the server can execute an ISA. You can then use the Directories tab of the Service Properties for your server to add the physical directory path and a corresponding virtual directory name. Once added, the access property of the directory must be set to Execute. If you set this property to Read-only then the server will open your ISA and send it to you as a binary file rather than executing it.

Registry Access

When an ISA executes it does so in the context of the anonymous user IUSR_*ComputerName* or the user name supplied as part of the client authentication process as described earlier. However, the user profile and registry settings that IIS makes available to the ISA are those of the *default user*. You need to be careful that your ISA does not rely on registry settings for a particular user because these will not be accessible.

ISAPI Filters

An ISAPI filter is a powerful mechanism for augmenting or overriding the default behavior of IIS. With filters, you can implement custom logging, authentication and encryption schemes, implement sophisticated URL mapping, and much more.

A filter is a different beast from an ISA. An ISA is written to handle a specific request and is referenced directly in the request URL; a filter, once installed into IIS, responds to all client requests. Without explicitly looking at the request URL (assuming it is available at that point in the request cycle), a filter doesn't know where a request comes from or how it is manufactured (for example, CGI, ISA, static HTML, and others)—the filter is simply a cog in the IIS machine.

How A Filter Works

Filters are implemented as event handlers, which are called by IIS at defined points in the life cycle of an HTTP request. At each point in the life cycle, IIS generates an event to which filters that have registered to receive notification of the event are called.

Like an ISA, a filter is a Win32 DLL, which is loaded by IIS when it starts up. IIS knows which filters to load by inspecting a special IIS registry parameter. The full path name of each filter DLL must be explicitly defined to IIS through this registry parameter. Once loaded, the filter stays within the address space of the server until the server terminates.

Like an ISA, an ISAPI filter DLL must expose two filter-specific function entry points—**GetFilterVersion** and **HttpFilterProc**. Don't confuse these with the ISA equivalents: **GetExtensionVersion** and **HttpExtensionProc**.

GetFilterVersion, like its extension counterpart, is called first when the DLL is initially loaded and typically sets the filter version number and description attributes.

More important, this is where the filter specifies the events it wants to be notified of and the priority the filter should have with respect to other filters that have also registered to receive this notification.

The order in which filters of the same type are invoked is determined by the priority assigned to the filter when it was registered. Table 7.3 lists the four priority levels.

When there is more than one filter of the same type with the same priority level, the order in which they are called is determined by their order in the registry.

HttpFilterProc is where the real work of the filter is implemented. This function is only called when events for which it has registered occur. This may be some time after **GetFilterVersion** has been called.

As with extensions, the **DllMain** entry point is automatically called when the filter is first loaded, when it is unloaded and is a good place to perform global filter initialization, and clean-up.

Table 7.3 Filter priority levels.

Priority	Description
SF_NOTIFY_ORDER_LOW	Load the filter at low priority.
SF_NOTIFY_ORDER_DEFAULT	Load the filter using the default priority. This is the recommended value.
SF_NOTIFY_ORDER_MEDIUM	Load the filter at medium priority.
SF_NOTIFY_ORDER_HIGH	Load the filter at high priority.

Request Processing Sequence

Once a filter has registered with IIS, IIS knows exactly which events a filter can respond to and when it should be called in relation to other filters of the same type.

As IIS processes an HTTP request it generates a predefined set of event notifications in a particular order. Table 7.4 defines these notifications and the order in which they occur.

This level of granularity allows your filters to completely redefine the way in which IIS responds to HTTP requests. For example you might register filters to respond to:

- *SF_NOTIFY_READ_RAW_DATA*—When the filter expects to receive data that has been encrypted using a custom encryption scheme. The filter has access to the entire message in a buffer accessed through an event-specific data structure. The filter decrypts the entire message to yield the original data.

Table 7.4   ISAPI events.

Event Notification	Description
SF_NOTIFY_SECURE_PORT	The server has just received a client connection request to a secure port.
SF_NOTIFY_NONSECURE_PORT	The server has just received a client connection request to a non-secure port.
SF_NOTIFY_READ_RAW_DATA	The server has read data from the client and is about to process it.
SF_NOTIFY_PREPROC_HEADERS	The server is about to preprocess the headers in the request message.
SF_NOTIFY_AUTHENTICATION	The server is about to authenticate the client user.
SF_NOTIFY_ACCESS_DENIED	The server is about to respond with a **401 Access Denied** message.
SF_NOTIFY_URL_MAP	The server is about to map the logical URL to a physical path.
SF_NOTIFY_SEND_RAW_DATA	The server is about to send the response message back to the client.
SF_NOTIFY_LOG	The server is about to write information to the server logs.
SF_NOTIFY_END_OF_NET_SESSION	The connection to the client is about to be closed.

- *SF_NOTIFY_PREPROC_HEADERS*—When you need to implement *cookies*. Cookies are a mechanism based on special headers **Set-Cookie** and **Cookie** for storing server state information inside the client browser (for example, a shopping basket). Or perhaps to collect statistics of the different media types requested by inspecting a request's **Content-Type** header.

- *SF_NOTIFY_AUTHENTICATION*—When you need to implement a custom authentication scheme that looks up a customer name and password entered by the user in a special database, validates them, and then maps them to a known Windows NT user name and password.

- *SF_NOTIFY_ACCESS_DENIED*—When you want a custom message to be displayed when, after user authentication fails, access to a resource is denied.

- *SF_NOTIFY_URL_MAP*—When you want to implement a custom URL mapping scheme that inspects the requested URL and changes references to obsolete directories to a new directory path. Or to implement a scheme that scans for URLs of a particular type and performs some other URL-specific action (such as statistics collection or subsequent transformation of the referenced document in some way).

- *SF_NOTIFY_SEND_RAW_DATA*—When you want to implement a scheme in which, for particular URLs, you scan pages before they are sent back to the client looking for your own custom macro references and expanding them before the page is sent back to the client.

- *SF_NOTIFY_LOG*—When you want to implement a custom logging scheme that records additional information in the server log files. Or perhaps records statistics about URLs that match certain criteria.

Once a filter has performed its task, the filter influences what happens next using the return code it hands back to IIS. For example, a filter that has successfully handled an event notification would be expected to return **SF_STATUS_REQ_HANDLED_NOTIFICATION**. This particular return value also tells the server that no other handler should respond to the notification. Similarly, if a filter detects an error it should return **SF_STATUS_REQ_ERROR**, which would cause the server to pass on an error indication back to the client.

Communication With IIS

In contrast to an ISA, which obtains all its information about a request via an ECB, a filter is passed information about the request in two separate server memory areas that are given as parameters to **HttpFilterProc**.

The first memory area, **HTTP_FILTER_CONTEXT**, provides only a small amount of information about the current request as member variables, which includes whether the event is over a secure port (as in an SSL connection). It also provides a user-pointer you can use for maintaining state information for the lifetime of the request. All other information must be retrieved using callback functions supplied within **HTTP_FILTER_CONTEXT**. In addition to obtaining more detailed request information, callback functions are also provided to aid in building a response message. For example, the **WriteClient** callback allows you to send raw data back to the client, and **GetServerVariable** allows you to retrieve information about the client, the server, or the request itself. These callback functions are defined fully in Chapter 8.

IIS uses the second memory area to pass notification-specific information to the filter. The structure of this information is different for each notification type.

For example, when a filter receives an **SF_NOTIFY_ACCESS_DENIED** notification, the server passes the event-specific data in the form of the **HTTP_FILTER_ACCESS_DENIED** structure. This particular structure includes information such as the requesting URL, the physical path of the resource, and a code that defines the reason for the access failure.

Filter Configuration

Before you can use a filter, you must first register the DLL in the registry. Use regedit or regedt32 to update the key HKEY_LOCAL_MACHINE/CSYSTEM/CurrentControlSet/Services/W3SVC/Parameters/Filter DLLs.

Figure 7.6 shows a regedit session open at the appropriate place.

The Filter DLLs entry is able to take a list of DLLs separated by commas. Remember that the order in which the DLLs are listed is important. When DLLs have registered to receive notification of the same event at the same priority level, IIS calls the filters in the order their names appear in the Filter DLLs list.

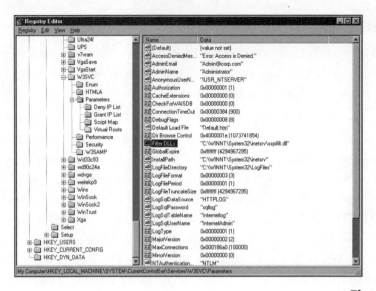

Figure 7.6

Example regedit session for registering filter DLLs.

Access Permissions

All ISAPI filters run in the original context of the IIS service. Because all services by default run with the access permissions of the System user of the local computer, this means that your filter can access just about anything on the system (but has no access to network resources). While the System and Administrator users share the same powers, unlike the Administrator, the System user is internal to Windows NT—it does not show up in the User Manager (usrmgr.exe), cannot be added to groups, and cannot have any rights assigned to it.

Summary

In this chapter we have looked in detail at the architecture of IIS and how ISAs can be used as a more efficient way of implementing CGI applications. We have also seen how ISAPI filters work and how they can be used to change the default way IIS processes HTTP requests.

Now that we've whet your appetite, you're probably itching to create something. From here you have two choices: You can go to Chapters 8 and 9 for more detailed reference information on ISAs and ISAPI filters respectively, or go to Chapter 10 to start doing something practical. We recommend going to Chapter 10 first and referring back to Chapters 8 and 9 as needed.

ISA Application Basics

CHAPTER

8

In this chapter we'll look at the fundamentals of building an ISA application. We'll work our way through the details of the ISA registration process and then discuss the syntax and semantics of each ISA function and data structure. This chapter adopts more of a reference approach, so if you're itching to create something, I suggest that you work through Chapter 10's tutorial and other examples first, and refer back to this chapter as necessary.

ISA Application Basics

An ISA, in contrast to an ISAPI filter, is not registered in advance through the registry. ISAs are loaded on demand by the server as client requests referring to the ISA are received. The ISA registers itself on the first request when the server loads it by a call to the **GetExtensionVersion** entry point.

DLL Entry Points For ISAs

Each ISA DLL must export two function entry points, **GetExtensionVersion** and **HttpExtensionProc**. If either of these entry points is not defined, the DLL will fail to load. A third, optional, entry point **TerminateExtension** was defined in ISAPI Version 2.0 and made available in IIS Version 3.0.

GetExtensionVersion

Signature
```
BOOL WINAPI GetExtensionVersion (HSE_VERSION_INFO *pVer);
```

Semantics
GetExtensionVersion is called once when the ISA DLL containing it is first loaded to register your extension with the server. It is passed a pointer **pVer** to an **HSE_VERSION_INFO** structure (see section "The **HSE_VERSION_INFO** Structure"). In this function, you set the version number of the extension and a brief description of what the extension does by setting variables in **HSE_VERSION_INFO**.

This function is also a good place to allocate and initialize any global data needed by the extension. Note that **GetExtensionVersion** is called within a system context

271

allowing it to access the registry without impersonating a user. This, then, is a good place to read any registry parameters needed by the extension.

It is important to remember that any global data you allocate here will exist for as long as the DLL is loaded in the server. You can use **TerminateExtension** or **DllMain** to deallocate global resources.

Return Codes

TRUE

This is the normal return value and tells IIS to go on and execute **HttpExtensionProc**.

FALSE

You would use this value only if you detected some error during initialization of data needed for the ISA. Returning this value will cause IIS not to call **HttpExtensionProc**.

The HSE_VERSION_INFO Structure

```
typedef struct   _HSE_VERSION_INFO {
    DWORD  dwExtensionVersion;
    CHAR   lpszExtensionDesc[HSE_MAX_EXT_DLL_NAME_LEN];
} HSE_VERSION_INFO, *LPHSE_VERSION_INFO;
```

Member Variables

dwExtensionVersion

The version number of the extension.

lpszExtensionDesc

A descriptive name for the extension.

Example

Here is a typical implementation for this function. Note that we use **strncpy** to ensure that our description doesn't exceed **HSE_MAX_EXT_DLL_NAME_LEN**.

```
#define EXTN_VERSION MAKELONG(HSE_VERSION_MINOR, HSE_VERSION_MAJOR)
#define EXTN_DESCRIPTION "Hello World Extension"

BOOL WINAPI GetExtensionVersion(HSE_VERSION_INFO *pVer)
{
```

```
pVer->dwExtensionVersion = EXTN_VERSION;
strncpy(pVer->lpszExtensionDesc, EXTN_DESCRIPTION,
                            HSE_MAX_EXT_DLL_NAME_LEN);

return TRUE;
}
```

HttpExtensionProc

Signature
```
BOOL WINAPI HttpExtensionProc(LPEXTENSION_CONTROL_BLOCK *pECB);
```

Semantics
Once the ISA DLL has been loaded into memory and **GetExtensionVersion** has executed, the server invokes the **HttpExtensionProc** function. In this function, you actually implement your specific ISA functionality. After the first invocation, assuming that the DLL is cached by the server (the normal mode of operation), only **HttpExtensionProc** (and not **GetExtensionVersion**) will be called for each subsequent ISA request.

When **HttpExtensionProc** is called by the server, it is passed pointer **pECB** to a server-allocated **EXTENSION_CONTROL_BLOCK** (informally, an ECB). Each request is allocated its own ECB so there are no ECB-specific contention or sharing issues to worry about for multi-threaded requests. As we've already discussed, an ECB contains important information about the request along with server-supplied callback functions for interrogating the request and assisting in generating a response.

Return Codes
HSE_STATUS_SUCCESS is the return code you would normally use to indicate successful completion of your application. Here are the four possible return codes possible for **HttpExtensionProc**.

HSE_STATUS_SUCCESS
Your application has successfully completed its processing, so the server can now disconnect with the client.

HSE_STATUS_SUCCESS_AND_KEEP_CONN

Your application has successfully completed its processing but the server should keep the connection open and wait for the next HTTP request. For this to work, the client and server must both support persistent connections. These are negotiated using the **Connection: Keep-Alive** header. Also, the application must supply a **Content-Length** header so that the client can determine the length of the response (otherwise it can only do this when the server closes the session).

HSE_STATUS_PENDING

Your application has not completed processing but will inform the server when it is finished. (Also refer to **HSE_REQ_DONE_WITH_SESSION** in the "**ServerSupportFunction**" section).

HSE_STATUS_ERROR

Your application has encountered an error while it was processing the request. The server should disconnect the client session.

The EXTENSION_CONTROL_BLOCK Structure

The ECB provides a single point of reference for all information about a request including server-provided callback functions for operating on it. For your convenience, the ECB contains commonly needed information about the request such as the **QUERY_STRING, PATH_INFO, CONTENT_LENGTH**, and so on in specific ECB member variables. These variables are similar to the CGI environment variables. Where there is no member variable containing the information you want—for example **REMOTE_USER, SERVER_NAME**—you must use one of the ECB-supplied callback functions, like **GetServerVariable**.

The C type definition for the ECB is provided in Listing 8.1. A detailed description of each member variable is given in the section "What Is An ECB?"

Listing 8.1   The C type definition for the ECB.

```
typedef struct _EXTENSION_CONTROL_BLOCK {
    DWORD    cbSize;
    DWORD    dwVersion;
    HCONN    ConnID;
    DWORD    dwHttpStatusCode;
    CHAR     lpszLogData[HSE_LOG_BUFFER_LEN;

    LPSTR    lpszMethod;
    LPSTR    lpszQueryString;
```

```
LPSTR       lpszPathInfo;
LPSTR       lpszPathTranslated;

DWORD       cbTotalBytes;
DWORD       cbAvailable;
LPBYTE      lpbData;

LPSTR       lpszContentType;

BOOL (WINAPI * GetServerVariable) ( HCONN      hConn,
                                    LPSTR      lpszVariableName,
                                    LPVOID     lpvBuffer,
                                    LPDWORD    lpdwSize );

BOOL (WINAPI * WriteClient) ( HCONN      ConnID,
                              LPVOID     Buffer,
                              LPDWORD    lpdwBytes,
                              DWORD      dwReserved );

BOOL (WINAPI * ReadClient) ( HCONN      ConnID,
                             LPVOID     lpvBuffer,
                             LPDWORD    lpdwSize );

BOOL (WINAPI * ServerSupportFunction)( HCONN      hConn,
                                       DWORD      dwHSERRequest,
                                       LPVOID     lpvBuffer,
                                       LPDWORD    lpdwSize,
                                       LPDWORD    lpdwDataType );

} EXTENSION_CONTROL_BLOCK, *LPEXTENSION_CONTROL_BLOCK;
```

TerminateExtension

Signature

```
BOOL WINAPI TerminateExtension(DWORD dwFlags);
```

Semantics

This function is new in ISAPI Version 2.0 and is only supported in IIS Version 3.0 and newer. **TerminateExtension** is called by the server just before the extension is unloaded by the server. It provides an elegant mechanism for cleaning up threads and deallocating any global resources allocated by **GetExtensionVersion**. Before this function was available, it was common to use **DllMain** to deallocate resources.

TerminateExtension is passed **dwFlags**, a bit field made up of the following values:

HSE_TERM_ADVISORY_UNLOAD
The server sets this value to let the application advise the server whether it should unload the DLL. **TerminateExtension** should return TRUE if the server can unload the application, otherwise it returns FALSE.

HSE_TERM_MUST_UNLOAD
The server sets this value when it is about to unload the application—the application cannot refuse.

```
#define HSE_TERM_ADVISORY_UNLOAD    0x00000001
#define HSE_TERM_MUST_UNLOAD        0x00000002
```

Return Codes
TRUE
If HSE_TERM_ADVISORY_UNLOAD has been in **dwFlags** then allow the server to unload the extension DLL.
FALSE
If HSE_TERM_ADVISORY_UNLOAD has been in **dwFlags** then inform the server not to unload the extension DLL.

Example Using DllMain
```
BOOL WINAPI DllMain(HINSTANCE hinstDLL, DWORD dvReason, LPVOID lpv)
{
    switch (dvReason) {
        case DLL_PROCESS_DETACH:
            /* Deallocate extension resources here */
            break;
    }
    return TRUE;
}
```

Example Using TerminateExtension
```
BOOL WINAPI TerminateExtension(DWORD dvReason)
{
    /* Deallocate extension resources here */

    return TRUE; /* Always allow the server to unload */
}
```

What Is An ECB?

The ECB is the data structure provided by the server for communicating information about the current request to your ISA. Each of the members of the structure is shown in Table 8.1. Where the member variable corresponds to a CGI environment variable, the name of the variable is also provided.

GetServerVariable

Signature

```
BOOL (WINAPI * GetServerVariable) ( HCONN      hConn,
                                    LPSTR      lpszVariableName,
                                    LPVOID     lpvBuffer,
                                    LPDWORD    lpdwSize );
```

Table 8.1   ECB member variables.

ECB Member	In/Out	Equivalent CGI Variable	What It Contains
cbSize	In	n/a	The size in bytes of the ECB.
dwVersion	In	n/a	The version number of the ISAPI specification implemented by the server.
ConnID	In	n/a	A server-allocated context identifier. This ID must be supplied in the ECB callback functions discussed below so that the server can apply the callback to the correct ECB. You must not modify this value.
dwHttpStatusCode	In/Out	n/a	Normally, this field will contain HSE_STATUS_SUCCESS when the extension returns. Otherwise it should be one of the other valid codes defined for HTTPEXTENSIONPROC.

continued

Table 8.1 ECB member variables (continued).

ECB Member	In/Out	Equivalent CGI Variable	What It Contains
lpszLogData	Out	n/a	A NULL-terminated string that will be entered into the server log when the request has completed. You should use this to indicate some description of what the ISA did or any error condition that arose.
lpszMethod	In	REQUEST_METHOD	The HTTP request method—usually **GET** or **POST**.
lpszQueryString	In	QUERY_STRING	A NULL-terminated string containing the query portion of a **GET** request (i.e., everything following the ?).
lpszPathInfo	In	PATH_INFO	The extra path information following the ISA name in the request URL.
lpszPathTranslated	In	PATH_TRANSLATED	The physical version of **PATH_INFO** once virtual-to-physical translation has occurred.
cbTotalBytes	In	CONTENT_LENGTH	The size in bytes of the body of the HTTP request.
cbAvailable	In	n/a	The number of bytes already read into the buffer pointed to by **lpbData**. This means that you will need to use the **ReadClient** callback to read the remaining **cTotalBytes-cbAvailable** bytes.
lpbData	In	n/a	The buffer containing the **cbAvailable** bytes already read by the server. IIS will buffer the first 48 K of client data. Thereafter you must use **ReadClient** to retrieve the rest.
lpszContentType	In	CONTENT_TYPE	The media type of the data in the client request.

continued

Table 8.1   ECB member variables (continued).

ECB Member	In/Out	Equivalent CGI Variable	What It Contains
GetServerVariable	In	n/a	A server-provided callback function for extracting additional information from the request.
WriteClient	In	n/a	A server-provided callback function for writing raw data back to the client.
ReadClient	In	n/a	A server-provided callback function for reading raw data from the client.
ServerSupportFunction	In	n/a	A server-provided callback function that implements auxiliary functions such as writing response header information.

Parameters

The parameters of the **GetServerVariable** are described in Table 8.2.

Table 8.2   The parameters of the **GetServerVariable**.

Parameter	In/Out	What It Is
hConn	In	The connection handle that identifies the client connection the callback is being applied to. This value usually comes from the **ConnID** member of an ECB.
lpszVariableName	In	The name of the variable you require, for example **AUTH_TYPE**, **REMOTE_USER**, and so on.
lpvBuffer	Out	A pointer to a buffer you must supply that will receive the value of the variable you specified.
lpdwSize	In/Out	A pointer to a variable that holds the maximum size of the buffer you provided in **lpvBuffer**. When **GetServerVariable** returns, the variable will contain the number of bytes the server copied into **lpvBuffer**, including the NULL terminating byte.

Semantics

You can use **GetServerVariable** to find out more information about the request, the client, or the server. Those of you familiar with CGI will be used to retrieving this information in the form of CGI variables such as **AUTH_TYPE**, **REMOTE_HOST**, **SERVER_NAME**; and HTTP header variables such as **HTTP_ACCEPT** and **HTTP_USER_AGENT**.

In Chapter 2, Table 2.1 provided a generic list of CGI variable names. However, for completeness, we provide the same information in Table 8.3, tailored to the IIS environment.

Table 8.3   List of possible **lpszVariableNames**.

Variable Name	Description
AUTH_TYPE	Type authentication scheme used. Possible values returned are the empty string if no scheme is being used, "basic" for basic authentication, or "NTLM" for NT's challenge/response scheme. Other values are possible because the range of possible authentication scheme names is unlimited.
CONTENT_LENGTH	The number of bytes to be received from the client in a **POST** request.
CONTENT_TYPE	The media type defining the way in which the data has been encoded. For forms, this is usually **application/www-form-urlencoded**.
PATH_INFO	The extra path information between the ISA program name and the query string in the request URL.
PATH_TRANSLATED	The path in **PATH_INFO** translated to a physical path on the server.
QUERY_STRING	The information following the "?" in the URL of a **GET** request.
REQUEST_METHOD	**GET** or **POST** depending on the method used to pass data to the ISA.
REMOTE_ADDR	The IP address of the client computer.
REMOTE_HOST	The host name of the client computer.
REMOTE_USER	This is the name of the user supplied by the client to be authenticated by the server. This is empty if the user is anonymous.
SCRIPT_NAME	A URL that identifies the ISA to be invoked.

continued

Table 8.3   List of possible **lpszVariableNames** (continued).

Variable Name	Description
SERVER_NAME	The host name or IP address of the computer running the server.
SERVER_PORT	The TCP port on which the request was received—usually 80.
SERVER_PORT_SECURE	A string containing either "1" or "0" indicating whether or not the request is being made over a secure port.
SERVER_PROTOCOL	The version of the HTTP protocol being used e.g., HTTP/1.0 or HTTP/1.1.
SERVER_SOFTWARE	The name and version of the Web server handling the ISA request.
ALL_HTTP	All remaining HTTP headers that have not already been parsed into one of the fields defined in this table. The value returned is a NULL-terminated string containing HTTP headers separated by a line feed character.
HTTP_ACCEPT	The list of media types the client is able to handle. Where multiple "Accept" headers have been included in the request, these are reduced to a single list with values separated by commas. For example: accept: */*;q=0.1 accept: text/html accept: image/gif is shortened to: */*;q=0.1, text/html, image/gif
HTTP_USER_AGENT	Product and version information about the client program.
HTTP_REFERER	The URL of the document that referred you to the current URL.
URL	The base portion of the request URL.

Return Codes

TRUE

The function was successful.

FALSE

The function was not successful. In this case you can use **GetLastError** to determine the cause of the error. See "Applicable Error Codes" for possible error values.

Applicable Error Codes

ERROR_INVALID_PARAMETER

The connection handle you supplied in **hConn** is bad.

ERROR_INVALID_INDEX

The name of the variable in **lpszVariableName** is invalid or not supported.

ERROR_INSUFFICIENT_BUFFER

The buffer size provided in **lpdwSize** is too small. **lpdwSize** bytes are returned.

ERROR_MORE_DATA

The buffer size you provided in **lpdwSize** is too small. Only part of the data has been returned—the total size of the data is unknown.

ERROR_NO_DATA

The data you have requested is not available.

Example

```
DWORD WINAPI HttpExtensionProc(EXTENSION_CONTROL_BLOCK *pECB)
{
    CHAR Buff[MAX_BUFF_SIZE];
    DWORD dwLen = MAX_BUFF_SIZE;

    pECB->GetServerVariable(pECB->ConnID, "HTTP_USER_AGENT", Buff,
                            &dwLen);

    /* Do something with the value returned here ... */

    return HSE_STATUS_SUCCESS;
}
```

ReadClient

Signature

```
BOOL (WINAPI * ReadClient) ( HCONN    ConnID,
                             LPVOID   lpvBuffer,
                             LPDWORD  lpdwSize );
```

Parameters

Table 8.4 describes the parameters of the **ReadClient** callback function.

Table 8.4   The parameters of **ReadClient**.

Parameter	In/Out	What It Is
ConnID	In	The connection handle that identifies the client connection the callback is being applied to. This value usually comes from the **ConnID** member of an ECB.
lpvBuffer	Out	A pointer to a buffer you must supply, which will receive the client data.
lpdwSize	In/Out	A pointer to a variable containing the maximum size of the buffer you provided in **lpvBuffer**. When **ReadClient** returns, the variable will contain the number of bytes the server copied into **lpvBuffer**, including the NULL terminating byte.

Semantics

ReadClient is typically used to read the body of a client's **POST** request. It performs a raw read from the server's socket connection to the client. If more than **lpdwSize** bytes are immediately available from the client, it will copy these bytes into **lpvBuffer** and return. You are responsible for keeping track of how much data you've read and how much is still to be read. You should use ECB members **cbTotalBytes** and **cbAvailable** for this purpose. **ReadClient** will block until data is available from the client. If the connection with the client is closed due, for example, to a connection timeout then **ReadClient** will return TRUE but with **lpdwSize** set to zero.

Return Codes

TRUE
The function was successful (or if the connection is closed while waiting for client data).

FALSE
The function was not successful. In this case you can use **GetLastError** to determine the cause of the error.

Example

```
DWORD WINAPI HttpExtensionProc(EXTENSION_CONTROL_BLOCK *pECB)
{
    DWORD dwBytesToRead;
    CHAR *lpszBuff;
```

```
/* Allocate some space to hold the form data sent in the body of the
   POST request */
lpszBuff = (CHAR *)LocalAlloc(LPTR, pECB->cbTotalBytes);

/* zero out memory */
memset(lpszBuff, '\0', pECB->cbTotalBytes);

/* Copy data already stored by the server */
strncpy(lpszBuff, pECB->lpbData, pECB->cbAvailable );

/* Grab any remaining data from the client and append to what we
   already have */
if ((dwBytesToRead=pECB->cbTotalBytes - pECB->cbAvailable) > 0)
   pECB->ReadClient(pECB->ConnID, (LPVOID)(lpszBuff +
                    pECB->cbAvailable), &dwBytesToRead);

/* Do something with the data here ... /

LocalFree(lpszBuff);

return HSE_STATUS_SUCCESS;
}
```

WriteClient

Signature

```
BOOL (WINAPI * WriteClient) ( HCONN      ConnID,
                              LPVOID     lpvBuffer,
                              LPDWORD    lpdwBytes,
                              DWORD      dwReserved );
```

Parameters

The parameters of **WriteClient** are defined in Table 8.5.

Semantics

WriteClient allows you to write raw data over the socket connection back to the client. Depending on your application, you can write headers and data *including binary data* such as images and audio. Typically you would use **WriteClient** to send an HTML document back to the client. While you can also use it to write back header information, this is normally done with **ServerSupportFunction**—see the "ServerSupportFunction" section coming up.

Table 8.5 The parameters of **WriteClient**.

Parameter	In/Out	What It Is
ConnID	In	The connection handle that identifies the client connection the callback is being applied to. This value usually comes from the **ConnID** member of an ECB.
lpvBuffer	In	A pointer to a buffer you must supply, which contains the data to be written to the client.
lpdwBytes	In/Out	A pointer to a variable containing the number of bytes in **lpvBuffer** to be written to the client. When the function returns, this variable contains the actual number of bytes transmitted. (For synchronous writes only. For asynchronous writes this value has no meaning.)
dwReserved	In	Reserved for future use—set this to 0.

As with **ReadClient**, you must pass in a valid connection handle (obtained from the ECB), which identifies the connection back to the client. Currently, **WriteClient** operates synchronously. This means it performs the write in the calling thread and waits for the data to be transmitted back to the client before returning to your application.

Synchronous writes are fine where only small amounts of data are being transmitted to a small number of clients. However, in large, busy sites that handle millions of requests, server threads start becoming a scarce resource. A way of solving this problem is to allow writes to occur asynchronously.

ISAPI Version 2.0 allows you to perform asynchronous writes to the client where the write operation is placed on an asynchronous thread queue allowing the function to return immediately. This frees the thread from being blocked while waiting for outstanding I/O to complete. Your application is now free to continue processing in the background or to return with an **HSE_STATUS_PENDING** return code. The latter case will mean your thread is returned to the server's thread pool for use by another request.

When the asynchronous write operation finally completes, a special callback function you previously registered using **ServerSupportFunction** is called allowing you to complete your application processing. It is up to your application to tell the server when it has finished with the request by using **ServerSupportFunction** with the **HSE_DONE_WITH_SESSION** request value.

Return Codes

TRUE

The function was successful (or if the connection is closed while waiting for client data).

FALSE

The function was not successful. In this case you can use **GetLastError** to determine the cause of the error.

Example

```
DWORD WINAPI HttpExtensionProc(EXTENSION_CONTROL_BLOCK *pECB)
{
    CHAR Buff[MAX_BUFF_SIZE];
    DWORD dwBytes;

    /* Send HTTP header to client using
       pECB->ServerSupportFunction () ...  */

    /* Send Body of request to client */

    strncpy(Buff, "Hello World\r\n", MAX_BUFF_SIZE);
    dwBytes = strlen(Buff);

    pECB->WriteClient(pECB->ConnID, (LPVOID)Buff, &dwBytes, 0);

    return HSE_STATUS_SUCCESS;
}
```

ServerSupportFunction

Signature

```
BOOL (WINAPI * ServerSupportFunction)( HCONN      hConn,
                                       DWORD      dwHSERRequest,
                                       LPVOID     lpvBuffer,
                                       LPDWORD    lpdwSize,
                                       LPDWORD    lpdwDataType );
```

Parameters

Table 8.6 lists the parameters for **ServerSupportFunction**.

Table 8.6   The parameters of **ServerSupportFunction**.

Parameter	In/Out	What It Is
hConn	In	The connection handle that identifies the client connection the callback is being applied to. This value usually comes from the **ConnID** member of an ECB.
dwHSERRequest	In	The request function to perform. See Table 8.7 for a list of valid request values.
lpvBuffer	In	A pointer to a buffer you must supply that contains the primary argument needed for the support function specified in **dwHSERRequest**.
lpdwSize	In	A pointer to a variable containing the number of bytes contained in **lpvBuffer**.
lpdwDataType	In	A pointer to the secondary argument needed for the support function.

Semantics

ServerSupportFunction provides ISAPI with an extensible mechanism for adding auxiliary callback functions not explicitly defined in the ECB. A common use of this function is to add (or modify) HTTP headers to the response message before it is written to the client, or to redirect a client request to another URL either on the same server or on a different server.

Like the other ECB callback functions, **ServerSupportFunction** is passed a valid client connection handle **hConn**. The second parameter, **dwHSERRequest**, defines which auxiliary function **ServerSupportFunction** should perform. **lpvBuffer** will normally contain the argument to be operated on and **lpdwSize** the dimension of this buffer. After the operation has completed, **lpdwSize** will contain the actual number of bytes copied into the buffer.

> *Note: ServerSupportFunction only supports textual data. It cannot handle binary data in the way WriteClient can.*

Currently **dwHSERRequest** can have one of five possible values. The operation of each of these special requests is defined in Table 8.7. Some simple examples follow that illustrate their operation.

Note: ISAPI Version 2.0 supports two new ServerSupportFunction operations. These are **HSE_REQ_IO_OPERATION** and **HSE_REQ_TRANSMIT_FILE**. As we alluded to earlier, **HSE_REQ_IO_OPERATION** provides support for asynchronous I/O operations, and allows you to register your own callback function that will be called when your queued **WriteClient** operation has completed. **HSE_REQ_TRANSMIT_FILE** allows your application to send a file back to the client asynchronously and lets you register a callback so you can be notified when the file has been sent. For more information on these special operations, refer to Microsoft's ISAPI Programmer's Reference.

Table 8.7   **ServerSupportFunction** Request Types.

Request Value	What It Means
HSE_REQ_SEND_URL_REDIRECT_RESP	This causes a **302 URL Redirect** message to be sent to the client. No further action is required following this operation. When the client receives this message it should automatically make a new request to the specified URL.
	lpvBuffer should contain the new URL with terminating NULL.
	lpdwSize on entry should contain the dimension of **lpvBuffer**. On exit it will contain the number of bytes (including the NULL) copied into the buffer.
	lpdwDataType is not used.
HSE_REQ_SEND_URL	The contents of the URL specified in **lpvBuffer** are sent back to the client as if the client had initiated the request. The URL must point to a resource on the server and should not contain the scheme or host components i.e., it should begin with a "/".
	No further action is required following this operation.
	lpvBuffer should contain the NULL-terminated URL.
HSE_REQ_SEND_URL	**lpdwSize** on entry should contain the dimension of **lpvBuffer**. On exit it will contain the number of bytes (including the NULL) copied into the buffer.
	lpdwDataType is not used.

continued

Table 8.7   ServerSupportFunction Request Types (continued).

Request Value	What It Means
HSE_REQ_SEND_RESPONSE_HEADER	This operation sends a complete set of HTTP response headers to the client. Automatically included are the following headers:

- The status line, for example "HTTP/1.0 200 OK"
- Date, for example "Date: Mon, 27 Jan 1997 03:56:58 GMT"
- Server, for example "Server: Microsoft-IIS/3.0"

Your application may append further headers such as **Content-Type** and **Content-Length** followed by an extra "\r\n" to indicate the end of the headers and the beginning of the data (if there is one) portion of the response.

lpvBuffer contains an optional NULL-terminated status string, for example **401 Access Denied**. If the value of **lpvBuffer** is NULL then a "**200 OK**" response will be automatically generated for you.

lpdwSize on entry should contain the dimension of **lpvBuffer**. On exit it will contain the number of bytes (including the NULL) copied into the buffer.

lpdwDataType contains your additional header information terminated by a NULL.

| HSE_REQ_MAP_URL_TO_PATH | This operation is specific to Microsoft and is used to perform logica-to-physical URL mapping. |

lpvBuffer should initially contain the logical URL and, after the operation completes, the physical path.

lpdwSize on entry should contain the dimension of **lpvBuffer**. On exit it will contain the number of bytes (including the NULL) copied into the buffer.

lpdwDataType is not used.

continued

Table 8.7   ServerSupportFunction Request Types (continued).

Request Value	What It Means
HSE_REQ_DONE_WITH_SESSION	This operation causes the server to close the connection to the client. You might use this operation after control had been returned to your application following notification of completion of an asynchronous **WriteClient** operation.
	lpvBuffer should contain a DWORD indicating the status code of the request, for example, **200**.
	lpdwSize and **lpdwDatatype** are not used.

Return Codes

TRUE

The function was successful.

FALSE

The function was not successful. In this case you can use **GetLastError** to determine the cause of the error.

HSE_REQ_SEND_URL

In this simple example, the current URL in your browser will be automatically redirected by the server to **lpNewURL**. Note that **lpNewURL** must refer to a resource on the same system as the server.

In the example, the HTML file in **lpNewURL** is a standard part of the IIS installation and is found in C:\InetPub\wwwroot\samples\sampsite\default.htm (or the URL http://ntserver/samples/sampsite/default.htm, where *ntserver* is the hostname of the server). **lpNewURL** has been defined relative to the home directory of the server—C:\InetPub\wwwroot.

> *Note: You can view (and modify) the server's home directory using IIS's inetmgr by selecting your running Web service in inetmgr's window, bringing up the Properties for the service and selecting the Directories tab. Your server's current home directory should be the first entry displayed in the list of directories.*

```
DWORD WINAPI HttpExtensionProc(EXTENSION_CONTROL_BLOCK *pECB)
{
    CHAR      NewURL[MAX_BUFF_SIZE];
    DWORD     dwBytes = MAX_BUFF_SIZE;

    strncpy(NewURL, "/samples/sampsite/default.htm", MAX_BUFF_SIZE);

    pECB->ServerSupportFunction(pECB->ConnID, HSE_REQ_SEND_URL,
                            NewURL, &dwBytes, (LPDWORD)NULL);

    return HSE_STATUS_SUCCESS;
}
```

HSE_REQ_SEND_URL_REDIRECT_RESP

In the last example, the target URL had to be relative to the root directory of the local server. To redirect to a URL on another server, you can use the **HSE_REQ_SEND_URL_REDIRECT_RESP** operation. Here you need to specify a fully qualified URL, like http://www.microsoft.com.

```
DWORD WINAPI HttpExtensionProc(EXTENSION_CONTROL_BLOCK *pECB)
{
    CHAR      NewURL[MAX_BUFF_SIZE];
    DWORD     dwBytes = MAX_BUFF_SIZE;

    strncpy(NewURL, "http://www.microsoft.com", MAX_BUFF_SIZE);

    pECB->ServerSupportFunction(pECB->ConnID,
                            HSE_REQ_SEND_URL_REDIRECT_RESP,
                            NewURL, &dwBytes, (LPDWORD)NULL);

    return HSE_STATUS_SUCCESS;
}
```

HSE_REQ_SEND_RESPONSE_HEADER

In this simple example, we fill in the missing bit of our **WriteClient** example and add a **Content-Type** header to the outgoing message using **ServerSupportFunction**.

```
DWORD WINAPI HttpExtensionProc(EXTENSION_CONTROL_BLOCK *pECB)
{
    CHAR      Buff[MAX_BUFF_SIZE];
    DWORD     dwBytes;

    /* Send HTTP header to client. Note the extra \r\n to denote the end
       of the head information in the response message */
```

```
strncpy(Buff, "Content-Type: text/plain\r\n\r\n", MAX_BUFF_SIZE);
dwBytes = strlen(Buff);
pECB->ServerSupportFunction(pECB->ConnID,
                            HSE_REQ_SEND_RESPONSE_HEADER,
                            NULL, &dwBytes, (LPDWORD)Buff);

/* Send Body of request to client */

strncpy(Buff, "Hello World\r\n", MAX_BUFF_SIZE);
dwBytes = strlen(Buff);

pECB->WriteClient(pECB->ConnID, (LPVOID)Buff, &dwBytes, 0);

return HSE_STATUS_SUCCESS;
}
```

Summary

In this chapter we have looked in detail at how the ISA registration process works
and the specific ISAPI functions you use for implementing ISAs. If you've read this
far then we suggest that you jump to Chapter 10 and try your hand at the tutorial.
More experienced CGI developers may like to look at the other examples in Chapter
10, which illustrate **GET** and **POST** processing of forms, the manipulation of CGI-
like server variables, and URL mapping.

ISAPI Filter Basics

CHAPTER

9

In Chapter 7 we provided an overview of how ISAPI filters worked and their relationship to the server. In this chapter we'll focus more on the details of registering a filter, its communication with the server, and the specific events about which a filter can be notified. We'll take an in-depth look at when each event occurs and the data that the server provides with each event notification. The syntax and semantics of each ISAPI function and data structure are explained in detail. While the treatment here is reference-oriented, brief examples are provided to illustrate how you might use each of the event types. For a more practical introduction, go to Chapter 10, which takes a tutorial approach, and refer back to this chapter as needed.

ISAPI Filter Basics

A filter DLL must be registered with the server before it can be used. This is done by updating the **Filter DLLs** registry entry for **W3SVC** with the full path name of your DLL as outlined in Chapter 7. Your DLL must also expose two function entry points: **GetFilterVersion** and **HttpFilterProc**.

When the server starts up, it loads each DLL defined in its **Filter DLLs** registry parameter. The server uses **LoadLibrary** to load the DLL into memory, which automatically invokes the DLL's **DllMain** function. **DllMain** can be used to perform global resource allocation and deallocation.

Requesting Event Notification

Once the DLL is loaded into memory, the server calls **GetFilterVersion**. Your **GetFilterVersion** function is passed a pointer to an **HTTP_FILTER_VERSION** structure, in which you do the following:

- Set and check the filter version number.

- Set a description for your filter.

- Tell the server which events the filter should be notified of and the priority the server should use when it actually calls the filter.

Once registered, a filter can receive notifications for the events it has registered interest in. Each time one of these events occurs, the server calls the second entry point **HttpFilterProc**, which is responsible for doing the filter processing. Your **HttpFilterProc** function is passed a pointer to an **HTTP_FILTER_CONTEXT** structure, which contains generic information from the server for the event, followed by an indication of the type of event notification, and finally a pointer to an event-specific structure containing data specific to the event.

Deciding On A Filter Priority

As we have seen in Chapter 7, you can assign a priority that the server uses to determine when to call the filter—in the chain of filters—for that particular event type.

> **Note:** The priority defaults to **SF_NOTIFY_ORDER_DEFAULT** (actually the same as **SF_NOTIFY_ORDER_LOW**) if you don't assign a priority.

There are four filter priority levels (see Table 9.3, later in this chapter). Normally, you would assign the default priority of **SF_NOTIFY_ORDER_DEFAULT** to your filter.

You should be cautious when determining your filter priority. Remember that your filter will be called every time the events for which you have registered occur. You should only specify a higher priority if your filter is going to process the majority of events it will be notified about.

If you want your filter to be called first, assign it a priority of **SF_NOTIFY_ORDER_HIGH**. If there are other filters in this event chain that may also have set their priority to **SF_NOTIFY_ORDER_HIGH**, make sure your filter appears first in the **Filter DLLs** registry entry for the server to ensure it will be called first.

Similarly, if you want your filter to have the lowest priority, have **GetFilterVersion** set the priority to **SF_NOTIFY_ORDER_LOW** and make sure your filter is the last in the **Filter DLLs** list.

DLL Entry Points For ISAPI Filters

In this section we describe in detail the **GetFilterVersion** and **HttpFilterProc** functions.

GetFilterVersion

Signature
```
BOOL WINAPI GetFilterVersion( PHTTP_FILTER_VERSION pVer );
```

Parameter

The parameter the server passes to this function is described in Table 9.1.

Semantics

GetFilterVersion is called once by the server when it first loads the filter DLL. This function is important because it is here that you tell the server which events you want your filter to receive notification of.

GetFilterVersion is passed a pointer to an **HTTP_FILTER_VERSION** structure (see Table 9.1) in which you define:

- The version of ISAPI that is used to implement your filter (**HTTP_FILTER_REVISION**).

- A short textual description of your filter. Be sure to make this reasonably descriptive because this text can be viewed during filter debugging and administration.

- A combination of flags OR'd together, which specify the events the filter is interested in, and the priority at which the server will call the filter when more than one filter has registered for notification of the same event. See Table 9.2.

> **Note:** The notification flags **SF_NOTIFY_SECURE_PORT** and **SF_NOTIFY_NONSECURE_PORT** don't actually trigger a notification themselves, but just inform the server that you want to receive notifications for requests on secure and non-secure ports respectively. By default the server responds to both types of connections.

Event notification and priority flags are OR'd together. The priority flags are shown Table 9.3.

Table 9.1 Parameter to the **GetFilterProc** function.

Parameter	In/Out	What It Is
pVer	In	A pointer to the **HTTP_FILTER_VERSION** structure.

Table 9.2 Filter event notification flags.

Event Notification Flag	When The Event Occurs
SF_NOTIFY_SECURE_PORT	The server has just received a client connection request to a secure port.
SF_NOTIFY_NONSECURE_PORT	The server has just received a client connection request to a non-secure port.
SF_NOTIFY_READ_RAW_DATA	The server has read data from the client and is about to process it.
SF_NOTIFY_PREPROC_HEADERS	The server is about to preprocess the headers in the request message.
SF_NOTIFY_AUTHENTICATION	The server is about to authenticate the client user.
SF_NOTIFY_ACCESS_DENIED	The server is about to respond with a **401 Access Denied** message.
SF_NOTIFY_URL_MAP	The server is about to map the logical URL to a physical path.
SF_NOTIFY_SEND_RAW_DATA	The server is about to send the response message back to the client.
SF_NOTIFY_LOG	The server is about to write information to the server logs.
SF_NOTIFY_END_OF_NET_SESSION	The connection to the client is about to be closed.

Table 9.3 Filter priority levels.

Priority	Description
SF_NOTIFY_ORDER_LOW	Load the filter at low priority.
SF_NOTIFY_ORDER_DEFAULT	Load the filter using the default priority. This is the recommended value.
SF_NOTIFY_ORDER_MEDIUM	Load the filter at medium priority.
SF_NOTIFY_ORDER_HIGH	Load the filter at high priority.

Return Codes
TRUE

The filter has been properly loaded. Assuming nothing went wrong in **GetFilterVersion**, this is the normal return value.

FALSE

The filter is to be unloaded and will not receive any event notifications. You would use this if you encountered an error during filter initialization.

HTTP_FILTER_VERSION Structure

A pointer to **HTTP_FILTER_VERSION** is passed to **GetFilterVersion** when the filter is loaded. The C type definition for this structure is as follows:

```
typedef struct _HTTP_FILTER_VERSION
{
    DWORD  dwServerFilterVersion;
    DWORD  dwFilterVersion;
    CHAR   lpszFilterDesc[SF_MAX_FILTER_DESC_LEN];
    DWORD  dwFlags;
} HTTP_FILTER_VERSION, *PHTTP_FILTER_VERSION;
```

Table 9.4 describes each **HTTP_FILTER_ VERSION** member.

Example GetFilterVersion Function

A typical example of a **GetFilterVersion** function is shown in Listing 9.1.

Table 9.4   The **HTTP_FILTER_VERSION** members.

HTTP_FILTER_VERSION Member	In/Out	What It Contains
dwServerFilterVersion	In	The version of the ISAPI specification used by the server. You can use this to compare your filter's version number in **dwFilterVersion** to that of the server's to ensure that the two are compatible.
dwFilterVersion	Out	The version of the ISAPI specification used by the filter. You can use **HTTP_FILTER_REVISION** from httpfilt.h for this value.
lpszFilterDesc	Out	A pointer to a buffer containing a NULL-terminated description of the filter.
dwFlags	Out	A combination of **SF_NOTIFY_*** flags that specifies which events the filter is to be notified about.

Listing 9.1 The **GetFilterVersion** function.

```
BOOL WINAPI GetFilterVersion(HTTP_FILTER_VERSION *pVersion)
{
    /* Set ISAPI version */
    pVersion->dwFilterVersion = HTTP_FILTER_REVISION;

    /* Provide a short description of the filter */
    strncpy(pVersion->lpszFilterDesc, FILTER_DESCRIPTION,
                SF_MAX_FILTER_DESC_LEN);

    /* Set the event we want to be notified about and the priority
       at which the filter should be called */
    pVersion->dwFlags = (SF_NOTIFY_ACCESS_DENIED |
                                        SF_NOTIFY_LOG |
                                        SF_NOTIFY_END_OF_NET_SESSION |
                                        SF_NOTIFY_ORDER_DEFAULT);

    /* Indicate successful initialization */
    return TRUE;
}
```

HttpFilterProc

Signature

```
DWORD WINAPI HttpFilterProc( PHTTP_FILTER_CONTEXT pfc,
                             DWORD notificationType,
                             LPVOID pvNotification);
```

Parameters

The parameters passed to the **HttpFilterProc** function by the server are listed in Table 9.5.

Table 9.5 Parameters passed to **HttpFilterProc**.

Parameter	In/Out	What It Is
pfc	In	A pointer to an **HTTP_FILTER_CONTEXT** structure that provides context information for the lifetime of the HTTP request.
notificationType	In	The type of event being processed. Valid values for these are the **SF_NOTIFY_*** flags in Table 9.2 previously.
pvNotification	In/Out	A structure containing data specific to the event notification.

Semantics

Each time an event occurs for which the filter has registered, **HttpFilterProc** is called by the server. This is where you define the processing for each event you've registered interest in. The function is passed three parameters. The first, **pfc**, is a pointer to an **HTTP_FILTER_CONTEXT** structure. This structure provides context information about the current request for the filter and filter-specific callback functions for obtaining more information about the request and for generating a response.

You can use the **pfc->pFilterContext** member as a place for storing a pointer to your own data area for sharing request-specific context information between event notifications implemented by the same filter. You would specifically deallocate this data area by implementing a **SF_NOTIFY_END_OF_NET_SESSION** event handler.

The second parameter, **notificationType**, contains one of the **SF_NOTIFY_*** values as defined in Table 9.2. A filter can register for more than one event, so it is typical for **HttpFilterProc** to switch on the **notificationType** to invoke the appropriate event-specific handler.

The third parameter, **pvNotification**, points to a notification-specific structure defined in Table 9.6.

We discuss each of these structures in detail in the "Events" section later in this chapter.

Return Codes

The value returned by **HttpFilterProc** should be one of the return codes defined in Table 9.7.

Table 9.6   Filter notification type.

Notification Type	Data Structure
SF_NOTIFY_ACCESS_DENIED	HTTP_FILTER_ACCESS_DENIED
SF_NOTIFY_AUTHENTICATION	HTTP_FILTER_AUTHENT
SF_NOTIFY_LOG	HTTP_FILTER_LOG
SF_NOTIFY_PREPROC_HEADERS	HTTP_FILTER_PREPROC_HEADERS
SF_NOTIFY_READ_RAW_DATA	HTTP_FILTER_RAW_DATA
SF_NOTIFY_WRITE_RAW_DATA	HTTP_FILTER_RAW_DATA
SF_NOTIFY_URL_MAP	HTTP_FILTER_URL_MAP

Table 9.7 Values returned by **HttpFilterProc**.

Return Code	When To Use It
SF_STATUS_REQ_FINISHED	The filter has handled the HTTP request. The server should disconnect the session with the client.
SF_STATUS_REQ_FINISHED_KEEP_CONN	The filter has handled the request and you want the server to keep the session open (if this option was negotiated with the client).
SF_STATUS_REQ_NEXT_NOTIFICATION	The next filter in the notification chain should be called.
SF_STATUS_REQ_HANDLED_NOTIFICATION	The filter has handled the notification and no other event handler is called for this type of notification.
SF_STATUS_REQ_ERROR	The filter generates an error. The server will call the Windows **GetLastError** function and indicate the error to the client.
SF_STATUS_REQ_READ_NEXT	The filter is an opaque stream filter and session parameters are being negotiated. This should only be used for raw read notification.

Example HttpFilterProc Function

Listing 9.2 is a simple example of an **HttpFilterProc** function. Notice how we switch on **dwNotificationType** to work out which event we are being called to handle and how we then cast **pvData** to the corresponding event-specific data structure. Each of our specific event handler functions would normally return either **SF_STATUS_REQ_HANDLED_NOTIFICATION** or **SF_STATUS_REQ_FINISHED** if it was able to successfully handle the notification or **SF_STATUS_ERROR** if some problem occurred.

Listing 9.2 An example **HttpFilterProc** function.

```
DWORD WINAPI HttpFilterProc(HTTP_FILTER_CONTEXT *pFC,
                            DWORD dwNotificationType,
                            VOID *pvData)
{
    DWORD dwRet;
```

```
    switch (dwNotificationType) {
        case SF_NOTIFY_ACCESS_DENIED:
            /* Handle the event */
            dwRet = HandleEvent_AccessDenied(pFC,
                          (PHTTP_FILTER_ACCESS_DENIED)pvData);
            break;
        case SF_NOTIFY_LOG:
            /* Handle the event */
            dwRet = HandleEvent_Log(pFC, (PHTTP_FILTER_LOG)pvData);
            break;
        case SF_NOTIFY_END_OF_NET_SESSION:
            /* Handle the event */
            dwRet = HandleEvent_EndOfNetSession(pFC, pvData);
            break;
        default:
            /* Instruct server to call next filter in the chain for this
               event type */
            dwRet = SF_STATUS_REQ_NEXT_NOTIFICATION;
            break;
    }

    return dwRet;
}
```

HTTP_FILTER_CONTEXT Structure

A pointer to an **HTTP_FILTER_CONTEXT** structure is passed to **HttpFilterProc** each time it is called. This structure holds information about the context of the current HTTP request and can be used to store filter-wide data for the duration of the request.

The C type definition for **HTTP_FILTER_CONTEXT** is shown in Listing 9.3, followed by a table defining each of the structure members.

> **Note:** The callback function members **GetServerVariable**, **WriteClient**, and **ServerSupportFunction** have the same semantics as the those defined for an ISA's ECB, except that a pointer to an **HTTP_FILTER_CONTEXT** is passed to them instead of the **ConnID** from the ECB.

Listing 9.3   The C type definition for **HTTP_FILTER_CONTEXT**.

```
typedef struct _HTTP_FILTER_CONTEXT
{
```

```
DWORD     cbSize;
DWORD     Revision;
PVOID     ServerContext;
DWORD     ulReserved;
BOOL      fIsSecurePort;
PVOID     pFilterContext;

BOOL (WINAPI * GetServerVariable) (
    struct _HTTP_FILTER_CONTEXT * pfc,
        LPSTR       lpszVariableName,
        LPVOID      lpvBuffer,
        LPDWORD lpdwSize
    );

BOOL (WINAPI * AddResponseHeaders) (
    struct _HTTP_FILTER_CONTEXT * pfc,
        LPSTR       lpszHeaders,
        DWORD       dwReserved
    );

BOOL (WINAPI * WriteClient)  (
    struct _HTTP_FILTER_CONTEXT * pfc,
        LPVOID    lpvBuffer,
        LPDWORD lpdwBytes,
        DWORD     dwReserved
    );

VOID * (WINAPI * AllocMem) (
    struct _HTTP_FILTER_CONTEXT * pfc,
        DWORD       cbSize,
        DWORD       dwReserved
    );

BOOL (WINAPI * ServerSupportFunction) (
    struct _HTTP_FILTER_CONTEXT * pfc,
        enum SF_REQ_TYPE   sfReq,
        PVOID              pData,
        DWORD              ul1,
        DWORD              ul2
    );

} HTTP_FILTER_CONTEXT, *PHTTP_FILTER_CONTEXT;
```

*Note: The function request values used by **ServerSupportFunction** are different for filters—these values are explained in Table 9.8.*

Table 9.8   The **HTTP_FILTER_CONTEXT** members.

HTTP_FILTER_CONTEXT

Member	In/Out	What It Contains
cbSize	In	The size in bytes of the **HTTP_FILTER_CONTEXT** structure.
Revision	In	The revision level of the structure. This will be less than or equal to the version of the ISAPI specification defined by **HTTP_FILTER_VERSION**.
ServerContext	In	Reserved for use by the server.
ulReserved	In	Reserved for use by the server.
fIsSecurePort	In	This is set to TRUE if the event is occurring over a secure port.
pFilterContext	In/Out	A user-defined pointer to any context information the filter wants to associate with the request.
GetServerVariable	In	A pointer to a server-provided callback function for retrieving more information about the request.
AddResponseHeaders	In	A server-supplied callback function for appending header information to a response message.
WriteClient	In	A server-supplied callback function for sending raw data back to the client.
AllocMem	In	A server-provided callback function for allocating memory. When the request is completed, the server will automatically free any memory allocated with this function.
ServerSupportFunction	In	A server-provided callback function, which provides additional filter callback functions.

GetServerVariable

```
SignatureBOOL (WINAPI * GetServerVariable) (
     struct _HTTP_FILTER_CONTEXT * pfc,
        LPSTR   lpszVariableName,
        LPVOID  lpvBuffer,
        LPDWORD lpdwSize
     );
```

Parameters

The parameters you must pass to the **GetServerVariable** callback are defined in Table 9.9.

Semantics

The **GetServerVariable** function is used to extract additional information about the request in the form of server variables. For a complete list of possible variable names, please refer to Table 8.2 in Chapter 8.

Return Codes

TRUE

The function was successful.

FALSE

The function was not successful. In this case you can use **GetLastError** to determine the cause of the error. See the Table 9.10 for possible error values.

Applicable Error Codes

If an error occurs, **GetServerVariable** provides additional information about the reason for the error by setting one of the Windows error codes from Table 9.10.

Example GetServerVariable Function

We'll show how to retrieve the value of the HTTP **Server:** header using the **HTTP_SERVER_NAME** variable in Listing 9.4.

Table 9.9 Parameters passed to **GetServerVariable**.

Parameter	In/Out	What It Is
pfc	In	The **pfc** passed to **HttpFilterProc**.
lpszVariableName	In	The name of the server variable to retrieve, for example **HTTP_SERVER_NAME**.
lpvBuffer	In	A buffer in which the value of the variable is returned.
lpdwSize	In/Out	The size of **lpvBuffer** and on return, the number of bytes transferred into the **lpvBuffer** including a NULL byte.

Table 9.10 Windows error codes set by **GetServerVariable**.

Error Code	What It Means
ERROR_INVALID_PARAMETER	The filter context pointer **pfc** is bad.
ERROR_INVALID_INDEX	The name of the variable in **lpszVariableName** is invalid or not supported.
ERROR_INSUFFICIENT_BUFFER	The buffer size provided in **lpdwSize** is too small. The **lpdwSize** bytes are returned.
ERROR_MORE_DATA	The buffer size you provided in **lpdwSize** is too small. Only part of the data has been returned—the total size of the data is unknown.
ERROR_NO_DATA	The data you have requested is not available.

Listing 9.4 An example of retrieving the HTTP **Server:** header.

```
CHAR Buffer[MAX_BUFF_SIZE];
DWORD  dwBuffSize = MAX_BUFF_SIZE;

if ( pfc->GetServerVariable(pfc,"HTTP_SERVER_NAME", Buffer,
                                        &dwBuffSize ) ) {

    /* Process variable value returned in Buffer ... */

}
else {
    /* An error occurred so use GetLastError to discover specific error
       */

    /* Only return an error status if the error was something serious */
    if (GetLastError() != ERROR_INVALID_INDEX )
        return SF_STATUS_REQ_ERROR;
}
```

AddResponseHeaders

Signature

```
BOOL (WINAPI * AddResponseHeaders) (
        struct _HTTP_FILTER_CONTEXT * pfc,
        LPSTR       lpszHeaders,
        DWORD       dwReserved
    );
```

Table 9.11 Parameters passed to **AddResponseHeaders**.

Parameter	In/Out	What It Is
pfc	In	The **pfc** passed to **HttpFilterProc**.
lpszHeaders	In	A pointer to a buffer containing the headers to be added. Note that only text can be inserted here—no binary data.
dwReserved	In	Reserved for future server use. This must be set to zero.

Parameters

The parameters you must pass to this function are defined in Table 9.11.

Semantics

This function is most often used in conjunction with **WriteClient** to generate a response to a client. You would normally use this function to add **Content-Type** and **Content-Length** headers to your response.

Return Codes

TRUE

The function was successful.

FALSE

The function was not successful. In this case you can use **GetLastError** to determine the cause of the error.

Example AddResponseHeaders Function

Listing 9.5 is a simple example illustrating the use of **AddResponseHeaders**.

> *Note: We're actually appending two headers. The last header we'll append is the **Content-Length** header, so we'll also append an extra "\r\n" to indicate the end of the headers in the response message.*

Listing 9.5 An example of the use of **AddResponseHeaders**.

```
if ( pfc->AddResponseHeaders( pfc,
    "Content-Type: text/html\r\nContent-Length: 257\r\n\r\n",
    NULL))
```

```
    /* Go on to send the header ...*/
}
else {
    /* An error occurred. Perform error processing here ... */
}
```

WriteClient

Signature

```
BOOL (WINAPI * WriteClient) (
      struct _HTTP_FILTER_CONTEXT * pfc,
          LPVOID    plvBuffer,
          LPDWORD   lpdwBytes,
          DWORD     dwReserved
      );
```

Parameters

The parameters you must pass to **WriteClient** are defined in Table 9.12.

Semantics

WriteClient is used to write raw data back to the client. The client connection is part of the **HTTP_FILTER_CONTEXT** structure. A pointer to this structure is passed as the first parameter **pfc**. **WriteClient** is usually used in conjunction with **AddResponseHeader** to send a response message to the client. Copy the data you want to send as the body of the response into a buffer and pass a pointer **lpvBuffer** to it as the second parameter to **WriteClient**.

Table 9.12   The parameters you must pass to **WriteClient**.

Parameter	In/Out	What It Is
pfc	In	The **pfc** passed to **HttpFilterProc**.
lpvBuffer	In	A buffer containing the data to send back to the client.
lpdwBytes	In/Out	The number of bytes to send from the buffer and on return, the number of bytes actually sent.
dwReserved	In	Reserved for future use.

In contrast to **AddResponseHeader**, which can only deal with text data, you can use **WriteClient** to send binary data because you tell it exactly how many bytes to send from the buffer using **lpdwBytes** rather than relying on a terminating NULL character. When the call completes, **lpdwBytes** contains the number of bytes actually sent to the client. These before and after values should normally be the same; if they're not, an error has occurred and **WriteClient** will return FALSE. When this happens, you can use **GetLastError** to find out the cause of the error.

> Note: If **lpvBuffer** contains a NULL-terminated string then **lpdwBytes** should contain the length of the string.

Return Codes

TRUE

The function was successful.

FALSE

The function was not successful. In this case you can use **GetLastError** to determine the cause of the error.

Example WriteClient Function

Listing 9.6 is an example that simply sends an unsolicited response back to the client—"Hello World" embedded in an HTML document.

Listing 9.6 An example of an unsolicited response sent back to the client.

```
CHAR   Buffer[MAX_BUFF_SIZE+1];
DWORD dwBytesWritten;
DWORD dwError = 0;

strncpy(Buffer,
           "<HTML><BODY><H1>Hello World</H1></BODY></HTML>",
           MAX_BUFF_SIZE);
dwBytesWritten = strlen(Buffer);

if ( pfc->WriteClient( pfc, (LPVOID)&Buffer,
                            (LPDWORD)&dwBytesWritten, NULL)) {
    /* Continue processing here ... */
}
else
    dwError = GetLastError();
```

ServerSupportFunction

Signature
```
BOOL (WINAPI * ServerSupportFunction) (
        struct _HTTP_FILTER_CONTEXT * pfc,
            enum SF_REQ_TYPE    sfReq,
            PVOID               pData,
            DWORD               ul1,
            DWORD               ul2
        );
```

Parameters
The parameters required by **ServerSupportFunction** are defined in Table 9.13.

Semantics
ServerSupportFunction provides a general interface to auxiliary functions for manipulating a request or a response. It is the mechanism that ISAPI provides for introducing filter methods without needing to alter the structure of **HTTP_FILTER_CONTEXT**.

Currently, there are only three additional functions provided (see Table 9.14). The second parameter, **sfReq**, identifies the type of function to be performed and **pData**, **ul1**, and **ul2** are used to pass function-specific parameters.

Table 9.13   ServerSupportFunction parameters.

Parameter	In/Out	What It Is
pfc	In	The **pfc** passed to **HttpFilterProc**.
sfReq	In	A value indicating the function to be performed. The values **sfReq** can have are: **SF_REQ_SEND_RESPONSE_HEADER**, **SF_REQ_ADD_HEADERS_ON_DENIAL**, and **SF_REQ_SET_NEXT_READ_SIZE**.
pData, ul1, and ul2	In	Defined by the value of **sfReq**.

Return Codes

TRUE

The function was successful.

FALSE

The function was not successful. In this case you can use **GetLastError** to determine the cause of the error.

Example ServerSupportFunction

In this simple example (see Listing 9.7) we'll use **ServerSupportFunction** to set the response header to **401 Access Denied** when an **SF_NOTIFY_ACCESS_DENIED** notification occurs.

> **Note:** We have passed a NULL as the last parameter, which will tell **ServerSupportFunction** to send an extra "\r\n".

Listing 9.7   An example of using **ServerSupportFunction**.

```
DWORD WINAPI HttpFilterProc(HTTP_FILTER_CONTEXT *pFC,
                            DWORD dwNotificationType,
                            VOID *pvData)
{
      DWORD dwRet;

      switch (dwNotificationType) {
          case SF_NOTIFY_ACCESS_DENIED:
              /* Handle the event */
              dwRet = HandleEvent_AccessDenied(pFC,
                              (PHTTP_FILTER_ACCESS_DENIED)pvData);
              break;
          default:
              /* Instruct server to call next filter in the chain for
                 this event type */
              dwRet = SF_STATUS_REQ_NEXT_NOTIFICATION;
              break;
      }

      return dwRet;
}

DWORD HandleEvent_AccessDenied(HTTP_FILTER_CONTEXT *pFC,
                               PHTTP_FILTER_ACCESS_DENIED pAccessData)
```

```
{
        CHAR    lpStatusLine = "401 Access Denied\r\n";
        DWORD   dwRet;

        if ( pFC->ServerSupportFunction(pFC,
                SF_REQ_SEND_RESPONSE_HEADER,
                lpStatusLine, 0, (DWORD)NULL)) {

        /* Handle the rest of the event here ...  */

        dwRet = SF_STATUS_REQ_FINISHED;
    }
    else {
        /* Handle error here ...  */

        dwRet = SF_STATUS_REQ_ERROR;
    }
        return dwRet;
}
```

AllocMem

Syntax

```
VOID * (WINAPI * AllocMem) (
        struct _HTTP_FILTER_CONTEXT * pfc,
        DWORD       cbSize,
        DWORD       dwReserved
    );
```

Parameters

Table 9.15 defines the parameters expected by **AllocMem**.

Semantics

AllocMem is a server-provided function for allocating memory for use by a filter during the lifetime of a request. Memory that is allocated using **AllocMem** is guaranteed to be automatically freed by the server when the request terminates.

While **AllocMem** is useful, you should be careful how you use it because you're shifting the responsibility for allocation and deallocation onto the server. It could be better for your filter to explicitly manage its own memory depending on the com-

Table 9.14   ServerSupportFunction functions.

Function Value	What It Does/Parameters Required
SF_REQ_SEND_RESPONSE_HEADER	This allows you to send a complete response header back to the client. The header includes the status, server version, message time stamp, and media type. You are then able to add further headers such as **Content-Type** and **Content-Length**. Parameters: • *pData*—A pointer to a NULL-terminated string containing an optional status string, for example, **401 Access Denied**. If you return NULL then a default **200 OK** status string is given. • *ul1*—A pointer to a NULL-terminated string containing optional headers to be appended to the header, or NULL in which case the header will be terminated with a "\r\n" indicating the end of the header.
SF_REQ_ADD_HEADERS_ON_DENIAL	If the server denies the HTTP request then the headers specified by this function will be added to the response. This allows a custom authentication filter to append **WWW-Authenticate** headers, which define the supported authentication schemes without having to filter every request. Parameters: • *pData*—A pointer to a NULL-terminated string containing one or more headers and a terminating "\r\n".
SF_REQ_SET_NEXT_READ_SIZE	Used by raw data filters that return **SF_STATUS_READ_NEXT**. Parameters: • *ul2*—The size in bytes of the next read.

plexity of your filter. (For example, by allocating chunks of memory out of a separate heap and freeing the memory at the end of the request in a handler for the **SF_NOTIFY_END_OF_NET_SESSION** notification.)

Table 9.15   The parameters expected by **AllocMem**.

Parameter	In/Out	What It Is
pfc	In	The **pfc** passed to **HttpFilterProc**.
cbSize	In	The amount of memory (in bytes) to allocate.
dwReserved	In	Reserved for future use.

*Note: Blocks of memory allocated by **AllocMem** cannot be managed by Windows SDK or compiler runtime support functions.*

Return Values

The return values are either a pointer to a block of memory of the requested size or NULL if the request could not be satisfied.

Example AllocMem Function

Listing 9.8 is an example of how to use the **AllocMem** callback function.

Listing 9.8   How to use the **AllocMem** callback function.

```
LPSTR lpszBuffer;

/* Allocate memory */
lpszBuffer = (LPSTR *)pfc->AllocMem(pfc, 1024, (DWORD)NULL);
if (lpszBuffer != NULL) {
/* Don't rely on the block being zero'd out */
memset(lpszBuffer,'\0', sizeof(lpszBuffer));
}
else {
    /* Handle error ...  */
}
```

Events

Once you have registered to receive event notifications in **GetFilterVersion**, the server will execute your **GetFilterProc** function each time an event you have registered for occurs. For example, if you have registered to receive notification of client requests to a secure port, **GetFilterProc** will be executed each time this event occurs.

When the server invokes **GetFilterProc** it passes to it the context of the request in an **HTTP_FILTER_CONTEXT** and an event-specific data structure containing event-specific information.

In this section we'll work our way through each possible event, looking at when it occurs and the event-specific data available to your filter. For each event we'll also provide a simple example. More complex examples can be found in the Chapter 10.

Secure Port—SF_NOTIFY_SECURE_PORT

IIS allows client requests to be made over a secure or a non-secure port.

A connection to a secure port is made whenever a client connects using the *https* protocol. The https protocol implements the Secure Sockets Layer (SSL) protocol, which provides a strongly encrypted channel between the client and server and theoretically prevents any eavesdropping of the session.

> **Note:** If you do not specify **SF_NOTIFY_SECURE_PORT** or **SF_NOTIFY_NONSECURE_PORT** then the server will default to both flags and your filter will be called for both connection types.

There is no event-specific data structure associated with this event because the filter does not get explicitly notified when the connection occurs. The flags just inform the server that your filter should be called for these connection types. To determine if a secure or non-secure connection has been made test the **fIsSecurePort** member of **HTTP_FILTER_CONTEXT**.

Example Of SF_NOTIFY_SECURE_PORT

In Listing 9.9 we indicate to the server that we want to receive notifications from requests over both secure and non-secure ports.

Listing 9.9 An example of setting connection type flags.

```
BOOL WINAPI GetFilterVersion(HTTP_FILTER_VERSION *pVersion)
{
    /* Set ISAPI version */
    pVersion->dwFilterVersion = HTTP_FILTER_REVISION;
```

```
/* Provide a short description of the filter */
strncpy(pVersion->lpszFilterDesc, FILTER_DESCRIPTION,
        SF_MAX_FILTER_DESC_LEN);

/* Set the event we want to be notified about and the priority
   at which the filter should be called */
pVersion->dwFlags = (SF_NOTIFY_SECURE_PORT |
                     SF_NOTIFY_NONSECURE_PORT |
                     ... Other notification flags as required ...
                     SF_NOTIFY_ORDER_DEFAULT);

/* Indicate successful initialization */
return TRUE;
}
```

Non-Secure Port— SF_NOTIFY_NONSECURE_PORT

Most HTTP connections are non-secure. A connection to a non-secure port means that the connection is not encrypted and the HTTP session occurs *in the clear.* Such connections are potentially open to abuse by eavesdroppers who use network snooping software such as **snoop** or **tcpdump** under Unix or Microsoft's **Network Monitor** to capture user sessions looking for interesting information. Worse still, the use of *man-in-the-middle, session replay,* and other *spoofing* techniques to generate requests that pretend to come from you.

Encrypted channels (using https) should obviously be used when you are requesting confidential resources or the user is transmitting private information such as credit card and bank account details.

Event—Access Denied

The server generates an **SF_NOTIFY_ACCESS_DENIED** notification whenever it is about to send back a **401 Access Denied** response to the client. This occurs after a server has analyzed the security credentials of the client and they turn out to be invalid—for example when the user has supplied an incorrect user name or password.

A response message containing a **401 Access Denied** status line will also include a **WWW-Authenticate** header, which will include at least one of the authentication schemes supported by the server. Typically this is the Basic scheme (we discussed this scheme in detail in Chapter 1).

Catching this event allows you to display an alternative message to the user.

Notification Structure—HTTP_FILTER_ACCESS_DENIED

A pointer to an **HTTP_FILTER_ACCESS_DENIED** structure is passed as the third parameter to **GetFilterProc** when **SF_NOTIFY_ACCESS_DENIED** occurs. Here is the C type definition for the structure:

```
typedef struct _HTTP_FILTER_ACCESS_DENIED
{
const CHAR * pszURL;
const CHAR * pszPhysicalPath;
DWORD        dwReason;
} HTTP_FILTER_ACCESS_DENIED, *PHTTP_FILTER_ACCESS_DENIED;
```

The members of this structure are in Table 9.16.

You can use **dwReason** to analyze the reason for the failure and to return a tailored message. The possible values for **dwReason** are in Table 9.17

> **Note:** The values **SF_DENIED_BY_CONFIG** and **SF_DENIED_LOGON** can occur together if the server configuration did not allow the user to log on.

Example Of SF_NOTIFY_ACCESS_DENIED

This simple example (see Listing 9.10) passively intercepts the notification and writes the client-supplied user name and password (if they exist) to our debug monitor. In

Table 9.16   The **HTTP_FILTER_ACCESS_DENIED** members.

HTTP_FILTER_ACCESS_DENIED

Member	In/Out	What It Contains
pszURL	In	The URL being requested.
pszPhysicalPath	In	The physical path of the resource being requested.
dwReason	In	A bit-field of **SF_DENIED** flags that give the reason for the denial.

Table 9.17 The **dwReason** values.

Reason Code	Value	Description.
SF_DENIED_LOGON	0x00000001	The logon failed.
SF_DENIED_RESOURCE	0x00000002	The user was not authorized to access this resource.
SF_DENIED_FILTER	0x00000004	The user was denied access by a filter.
SF_DENIED_APPLICATION	0x00000008	The user was denied access by an ISA.
SF_DENIED_BY_CONFIG	0x00010000	The server configuration prevented access.

reality you would formulate a complete **401 Access Denied** response back to the client using the **ServerSupportFunction** callback to construct the header and **WriteClient** to send back a security message to be displayed by the client.

Listing 9.10 An example of an **SF_NOTIFY_ACCESS_DENIED** filter.

```
BOOL WINAPI GetFilterVersion(HTTP_FILTER_VERSION *pVersion)
{
    /* Set version */
    pVersion->dwFilterVersion = HTTP_FILTER_REVISION;

    /* Provide a short description of the filter */
    strncpy(pVersion->lpszFilterDesc,
               "Simple Access Denied Filter",
               SF_MAX_FILTER_DESC_LEN);

    /* Set the event we want to be notified about and the notification
       priority */
    pVersion->dwFlags = (SF_NOTIFY_SECURE_PORT |
                          SF_NOTIFY_NONSECURE_PORT |
                          SF_NOTIFY_ACCESS_DENIED |
                          SF_NOTIFY_ORDER_DEFAULT);

    return TRUE;
}

DWORD WINAPI HttpFilterProc(HTTP_FILTER_CONTEXT *pFC,
                             DWORD dwNotificationType,
                             VOID *pvData)
{
    DWORD dwRet = SF_STATUS_REQ_NEXT_NOTIFICATION;
```

```
        switch (dwNotificationType) {
            case SF_NOTIFY_ACCESS_DENIED:
                dwRet = HandleEvent_AccessDenied(pFC,
                                (PHTTP_FILTER_ACCESS_DENIED)pvData);
                break;
        }
        return dwRet;
}


DWORD HandleEvent_AccessDenied(HTTP_FILTER_CONTEXT *pFC,
                                PHTTP_FILTER_ACCESS_DENIED pAccessData)
{
    DWORD    dwRet = SF_STATUS_REQ_NEXT_NOTIFICATION;
    LPSTR    lpszReason = "Unknown";

    /* Figure out why it was denied */
    switch (pAccessData->dwReason) {
        case SF_DENIED_LOGON:
                lpszReason = "the Logon Failed";
            break;
        case SF_DENIED_RESOURCE:
                lpszReason = "you are not authorized to access this
                                resource";
            break;
        case SF_DENIED_FILTER:
                lpszReason = "the Filter denied access";
            break;
        case SF_DENIED_APPLICATION:
                lpszReason = "the ISA denied access";
            break;
        case SF_DENIED_BY_CONFIG:
                lpszReason = "the server configuration denied access";
            break;
        case (SF_DENIED_BY_CONFIG|SF_DENIED_LOGON):
                lpszReason = "the server configuration denied logon";
            break;
    }

    /* Display some information about the denial */
    Debug((DEST, "AccessDenied: Access denied to URL = %s, path = %s",
        pAccessData->pszURL, pAccessData->pszPhysicalPath));
    Debug((DEST, "AccessDenied: The reason is that %s", lpszReason));

    return dwRet;
}
```

Read Raw Data— SF_NOTIFY_READ_RAW_DATA

This event occurs whenever the server has read data from the client and is about to process it. Catching this event lets you see the raw data before the server does and allows you to do anything you like with it.

The data contains the *complete* request message—both headers and any data. Any changes you make to the request data passed to you will affect the behavior of the remaining events—for example, if you change one of the headers in the message then this will affect what the server does when it processes the header information.

Overriding this event is particularly useful for doing things like implementing your own encryption or compression schemes.

Notification Structure—HTTP_FILTER_RAW_DATA

When your filter receives an **SF_NOTIFY_READ_RAW_DATA** notification, your **HttpFilterProc** is passed a pointer to the following structure:

```
typedef struct _HTTP_FILTER_RAW_DATA
{
    PVOID       pvInData;
    DWORD       cbInData;
    DWORD       cbInBuffer;
    DWORD       dwReserved;
} HTTP_FILTER_RAW_DATA, *PHTTP_FILTER_RAW_DATA;
```

The members of this structure are in Table 9.18.

> **Note:** *This same structure is also used for* **SF_NOTIFY_SEND_RAW_DATA** *notifications.*

Example Of SF_NOTIFY_READ_RAW_DATA

This is another simple example that passively reads the first **BUFF_MAX** bytes of the raw data sent from the client and displays in a debug window (see Listing 9.11). Remember that with this notification you get access to the complete request.

Table 9.18 The **HTTP_FILTER_RAW_DATA** members.

HTTP_FILTER_ RAW_DATA

Member	In/Out	What It Contains
pvInData	In	A pointer to a buffer used to receive the client data.
cbInData	In	The number of bytes in the buffer at **pvInData**.
cbInBuffer	In	The maximum size of the buffer at **pvInData**.
dwReserved	In	Reserved for future use.

Listing 9.11 An example of an **SF_NOTIFY_ READ_RAW_DATA** filter.

```
BOOL WINAPI GetFilterVersion(HTTP_FILTER_VERSION *pVersion)
{
    /* Set version */
    pVersion->dwFilterVersion = HTTP_FILTER_REVISION;

    /* Provide a short description of the filter */
    strncpy(pVersion->lpszFilterDesc,
                "Simple Read Raw Data Filter",
                SF_MAX_FILTER_DESC_LEN);

    /* Set the event we want to be notified about and the notification
       priority */
    pVersion->dwFlags = (SF_NOTIFY_SECURE_PORT |
                        SF_NOTIFY_NONSECURE_PORT |
                        SF_NOTIFY_READ_RAW_DATA |
                        SF_NOTIFY_ORDER_DEFAULT);

    return TRUE;
}

DWORD WINAPI HttpFilterProc(HTTP_FILTER_CONTEXT *pFC,
                        DWORD dwNotificationType,
                        VOID *pvData)
{
    DWORD dwRet = SF_STATUS_REQ_NEXT_NOTIFICATION;

    switch (dwNotificationType) {
        case SF_NOTIFY_READ_RAW_DATA:
            dwRet = HandleEvent_ReadRawData(pFC,
                            (PHTTP_FILTER_RAW_DATA)pvData);
```

```
            break;
        }
    return dwRet;
}

DWORD HandleEvent_ReadRawData(HTTP_FILTER_CONTEXT *pFC,
                             PHTTP_FILTER_RAW_DATA pReadData)
{
    DWORD   dwRet = SF_STATUS_REQ_NEXT_NOTIFICATION;
    DWORD   dwBytes;
    LPSTR   lpszBuffer;

    /* Capture no more than BUFF_MAX characters of the raw request */
    lpszBuffer = pFC->AllocMem(pFC, BUFF_MAX+1, 0);
    dwBytes = min(BUFF_MAX, pReadData->cbInData);

    memcpy(lpszBuffer, pReadData->pvInData, dwBytes);
    lpszBuffer[dwBytes]='\0';

    Debug((DEST, "ReadRawData: Request[1-%d]=%s", dwBytes, lpszBuffer));
    return dwRet;
}
```

Preprocess Headers— SF_NOTIFY_PREPROC_HEADERS

An **SF_NOTIFY_PREPROC_HEADERS** event notification occurs just after the server has preprocessed the headers in the request message but before the server has interpreted any of them. This notification is useful for getting or setting the value of specific headers before a request is processed by the server. You can also append additional headers.

Notification Structure—HTTP_FILTER_PREPROC_HEADERS

When an **SF_NOTIFY_PREPROC_HEADERS** notification occurs, your **HttpFilterProc** function is passed a pointer to the notification structure defined in Listing 9.12. This structure contains no header information itself but supplies three callback functions for performing the header get, set, and append operations. Each of the callbacks returns TRUE if the operation succeeded, FALSE otherwise.

Listing 9.12 HttpFilterProc function is passed a pointer to the notification structure.

```
typedef struct _HTTP_FILTER_PREPROC_HEADERS
{
    BOOL (WINAPI * GetHeader) (
        struct _HTTP_FILTER_CONTEXT * pfc,
        LPSTR                 lpszName,
        LPVOID                lpvBuffer,
        LPDWORD               lpdwSize
        );
    BOOL (WINAPI * SetHeader) (
        struct _HTTP_FILTER_CONTEXT * pfc,
        LPSTR                 lpszName,
        LPSTR                 lpszValue
        );
    BOOL (WINAPI * AddHeader) (
        struct _HTTP_FILTER_CONTEXT * pfc,
        LPSTR                 lpszName,
        LPSTR                 lpszValue
        );
    DWORD dwReserved;
} HTTP_FILTER_PREPROC_HEADERS, *PHTTP_FILTER_PREPROC_HEADERS;
```

The members of this structure are in Table 9.19.

GetHeader

The parameters you must pass to **GetHeader** are shown in Table 9.20.

Table 9.19 The **HTTP_FILTER_ PREPROC_HEADERS** members.

HTTP_FILTER_ PREPROC_HEADERS

Member	In/Out	What It Contains
GetHeader	In	A server-provided callback function for obtaining the value of a header.
SetHeader	In	A server-provided callback function for setting the value of or deleting a header.
AddHeader	In	A server-provided callback function for appending a new header.
dwReserved	In	Reserved for future use.

Table 9.20 The parameters for **GetHeader**.

GetHeader Parameters	In/Out	What It Contains
pfc	In	A pointer to the filter context structure for the request as passed to **HttpFilterProc**.
lpszName	In	A pointer to a buffer containing the name of the header to retrieve.
lpvBuffer	In	A pointer to a buffer where the value of the header specified in **lpszName** will be placed.
lpdwSizeofBuffer	In/Out	On entry, the size of the buffer **lpvBuffer** and after the call, the number of bytes copied into **lpvBuffer**—including the NULL terminator.

*Note: The header names specified at **lpszName** should include the trailing ":", for example **Content-Type:**. This function also recognizes the special names: "method", "url", and "version" to retrieve the corresponding components of the request line.*

Remember from Chapter 1, a request line has the following structure:

```
method url version
```

In this example

```
GET /samples/images/powered.gif HTTP/1.0
```

the method is "GET", the URL is "/samples/images/powered.gif" and the version string "HTTP/1.0".

SetHeader

The parameters you should pass to the **SetHeader** function are defined in Table 9.21.

AddHeader

The parameters needed by **AddHeader** are given in Table 9.22.

Table 9.21   The parameters for **SetHeader**.

SetHeader Parameters	In/Out	What It Contains
pfc	In	A pointer to the filter context structure for the request as passed to **HttpFilterProc**.
lpszName	In	A pointer to a buffer containing the name of the header to change or delete.
lpszValue	In	A pointer to a buffer containing the value to set the header to, or NULL to delete the header.

Table 9.22   The parameters for **AddHeader**.

AddHeader Parameters	In/Out	What It Contains
pfc	In	A pointer to the filter context structure for the request as passed to **HttpFilterProc**.
lpszName	In	A pointer to a buffer containing the name of the header to add.
lpszValue	In	A pointer to a buffer containing the value to set the header to.

Example Of SF_NOTIFY_PREPROC_HEADERS

In this simple example (see Listing 9.13) we'll passively extract the "Cookie:" header sent by the client and display its contents in the debug window. Remember that a cookie header will be sent in a client request if it has cookies that are applicable to the request—for example, if the server has previous issued a "Set-Cookie:" for the requested URL.

Listing 9.13   An example **SF_NOTIFY_PREPROC_HEADERS** filter.

```
BOOL WINAPI GetFilterVersion(HTTP_FILTER_VERSION *pVersion)
{
    /* Set version */
    pVersion->dwFilterVersion = HTTP_FILTER_REVISION;

    /* Provide a short description of the filter */
    strncpy(pVersion->lpszFilterDesc,
            "Simple PreProcHeaders Filter",
            SF_MAX_FILTER_DESC_LEN);
```

```
    /* Set the event we want to be notified about and the notification
       priority */
    pVersion->dwFlags = (SF_NOTIFY_SECURE_PORT |
                         SF_NOTIFY_NONSECURE_PORT |
                         SF_NOTIFY_PREPROC_HEADERS |
                         SF_NOTIFY_ORDER_DEFAULT);


    return TRUE;
}


DWORD WINAPI HttpFilterProc(HTTP_FILTER_CONTEXT *pFC,
                            DWORD dwNotificationType,
                            VOID *pvData)
{
    DWORD dwRet = SF_STATUS_REQ_NEXT_NOTIFICATION;

    switch (dwNotificationType) {
        case SF_NOTIFY_PREPROC_HEADERS:
            dwRet = HandleEvent_PreProcHeaders(pFC,
                            (PHTTP_FILTER_PREPROC_HEADERS)pvData);
            break;
    }
    return dwRet;
}


DWORD HandleEvent_PreProcHeaders(HTTP_FILTER_CONTEXT *pFC,
               PHTTP_FILTER_PREPROC_HEADERS pPreProcData)
{
    DWORD   dwRet = SF_STATUS_REQ_NEXT_NOTIFICATION;
    CHAR    HeaderBuff[BUFF_MAX+1];
    DWORD   dwBytes = BUFF_MAX+1;

    /* Display User-Agent header */

    pPreProcData->GetHeader(pFC, "Cookie:", HeaderBuff, &dwBytes);

    Debug((DEST, "PreProcHeaders: Cookie = %s", HeaderBuff));

    return dwRet;
}
```

Authentication—SF_NOTIFY_AUTHENTICATION

An **SF_NOTIFY_AUTHENTICATION** notification is generated just prior to the server authenticating the client request. This allows you to substitute your own authentication scheme.

When this event occurs, your **HttpFilterProc** function is passed a pointer to an **HTTP_FILTER_AUTHENT** structure, which contains the user name and password to be used to authenticate the client request.

Notification Structure—HTTP_FILTER_AUTHENT

The notification structure for this event is defined by the following C type definition:

```
typedef struct _HTTP_FILTER_AUTHENT
{
    CHAR * pszUser;
    DWORD  cbUserBuff;
    CHAR * pszPassword;
    DWORD  cbPasswordBuff;
} HTTP_FILTER_AUTHENT, *PHTTP_FILTER_AUTHENT;
```

The members of this structure are defined in Table 9.23.

One of our filter examples in Chapter 10 will show how we can map the user name and password provided by the user onto a new set of credentials. This technique is useful, for example, when you want to map a potentially large number of registered users onto a smaller number of Windows NT users. The Windows NT credentials are then used to validate the original request.

Table 9.23   The HTTP_FILTER_ AUTHENT members.

HTTP_FILTER_ AUTHENT

Member	In/Out	What It Contains
pszUser	In/Out	A NULL-terminated buffer containing the name of the user for the request. An empty buffer, such as "" indicates an anonymous user.
cbUserBuff	In	The number of bytes in the buffer **pszUser**. This is guaranteed to be at least **SF_MAX_USERNAME**.
pszPassword	In/Out	A NULL-terminated buffer containing the password for the request.
cbPasswordBuff	In	The number of bytes in the buffer **pszPassword**. This is guaranteed to be at least **SF_MAX_PASSWORD**.

Example Of SF_NOTIFY_AUTHENTICATION

Listing 9.14 extracts the user name and password from the "Authenticate:" header, which is sent by the client, and displays them in the debug window.

> **Note:** *For a request that does not contain or require any credentials,* ***pAuthData->pszUser*** *will point to the empty string "".*

Listing 9.14 An example authentication filter.

```
BOOL WINAPI GetFilterVersion(HTTP_FILTER_VERSION *pVersion)
{
    /* Set version */
    pVersion->dwFilterVersion = HTTP_FILTER_REVISION;

    /* Provide a short description of the filter */
    strncpy(pVersion->lpszFilterDesc, "Simple Authentication Filter",
            SF_MAX_FILTER_DESC_LEN);

    /* Set the event we want to be notified about and the notification
       priority */
    pVersion->dwFlags = (SF_NOTIFY_SECURE_PORT |
                         SF_NOTIFY_NONSECURE_PORT |
                         SF_NOTIFY_AUTHENTICATION |
                         SF_NOTIFY_ORDER_DEFAULT);

    return TRUE;
}


DWORD WINAPI HttpFilterProc(HTTP_FILTER_CONTEXT *pFC,
                            DWORD dwNotificationType,
                            VOID *pvData)
{
    DWORD dwRet = SF_STATUS_REQ_NEXT_NOTIFICATION;

    switch (dwNotificationType) {
        case SF_NOTIFY_AUTHENTICATION:
            dwRet = HandleEvent_Authentication(pFC,
                        (PHTTP_FILTER_AUTHENT)pvData);
            break;
    }
    return dwRet;
}
DWORD HandleEvent_Authentication(HTTP_FILTER_CONTEXT *pFC,
                                 PHTTP_FILTER_AUTHENT pAuthData)
```

CHAPTER 9

```
{
    DWORD    dwRet = SF_STATUS_REQ_NEXT_NOTIFICATION;

    /* Display the user name and password */
    Debug((DEST, "Authentication: user = %s, password = %s",
            pAuthData->pszUser, pAuthData->pszPassword));

    return dwRet;
}
```

URL Mapping—SF_NOTIFY_URL_MAP

The **SF_NOTIFY_URL_MAP** notification occurs just before the server is about to map the request URL to a physical path. Your **HttpFilterProc** is passed a pointer to an **HTTP_FILTER_URL_MAP** structure, which contains both the request URL and the corresponding physical path.

Catching this notification allows you to change the logical-to-physical mapping to anything you want. This event is also typically used to analyze the request URL and to perform some action depending on the URL value.

Notification Structure—HTTP_FILTER_URL_MAP

The notification structure for this event is defined by the following C type definition:

```
typedef struct _HTTP_FILTER_URL_MAP
{
    const CHAR *    pszURL;
    CHAR *          pszPhysicalPath;
    DWORD           cbPathBuff;
} HTTP_FILTER_URL_MAP, *PHTTP_FILTER_URL_MAP;
```

The members of this structure are in Table 9.24.

Example Of SF_NOTIFY_URL_MAP

The example in Listing 9.15 extracts the URL and physical path it will be mapped to, and displays them in the debug window.

330

Table 9.24 The **HTTP_FILTER_URL_MAP** members.

HTTP_FILTER_URL_MAP

Member	In/Out	What It Contains
pszURL	In	A buffer containing the NULL-terminated request URL.
pszPhysicalPath	In/Out	A buffer containing the NULL-terminated physical path to which **pszURL** is to be mapped to.
cbPathBuff	In	The number of bytes in the buffer **pszPhysicalPath**.

Listing 9.15 An example of an **SF_NOTIFY_URL_MAP** filter.

```
BOOL WINAPI GetFilterVersion(HTTP_FILTER_VERSION *pVersion)
{
    /* Set version */
    pVersion->dwFilterVersion = HTTP_FILTER_REVISION;

    /* Provide a short description of the filter */
    strncpy(pVersion->lpszFilterDesc, "Simple UrlMap Filter",
                SF_MAX_FILTER_DESC_LEN);

  /* Set the event we want to be notified about and the notification
     priority */
    pVersion->dwFlags = (SF_NOTIFY_SECURE_PORT |
                         SF_NOTIFY_NONSECURE_PORT |
                         SF_NOTIFY_URL_MAP |
                         SF_NOTIFY_ORDER_DEFAULT);

    return TRUE;
}


DWORD WINAPI HttpFilterProc(HTTP_FILTER_CONTEXT *pFC,
                        DWORD dwNotificationType, VOID *pvData)
{
    DWORD dwRet = SF_STATUS_REQ_NEXT_NOTIFICATION;

    switch (dwNotificationType) {
        case SF_NOTIFY_URL_MAP:
            dwRet = HandleEvent_Authentication(pFC,
                                        (PHTTP_FILTER_URL_MAP)pvData);
            break;
    }
    return dwRet;
}
```

```
DWORD HandleEvent_UrlMap(HTTP_FILTER_CONTEXT *pFC,
                         PHTTP_FILTER_URL_MAP pUrlData)
{
    DWORD   dwRet = SF_STATUS_REQ_NEXT_NOTIFICATION;

    Debug((DEST, "UrlMap: URL = %s, Physical path = %s",
           pUrlData->pszURL, pUrlData->pszPhysicalPath));
    return dwRet;
}
```

Sending Raw Data— SF_NOTIFY_SEND_RAW_DATA

Note that **SF_NOTIFY_SEND_RAW_DATA** is complementary to **SF_NOTIFY_READ_RAW_DATA**. This notification is sent when the server is about to send a response message back to the client. Intercepting this event allows you to perform all sorts of interesting output processing on a message before it gets back to the client.

In reality, this event occurs at least twice per response. The first time it occurs is when the server sends back the response headers. How often you are notified of this event after the header has been sent depends on how the response to the client has been generated. For example, an ISA using a **WriteClient** call will cause a notification each time a call is made. Your filter code must be designed to cope with this behavior.

Like **SF_NOTIFY_READ_RAW_DATA**, your **HttpFilterProc** is passed a pointer to an **HTTP_FILTER_RAW_DATA** structure, which contains the response data.

Notification Structure—HTTP_FILTER_RAW_DATA

The notification structure for this event is defined by the following C type definition:

```
typedef struct _HTTP_FILTER_RAW_DATA
{
    PVOID        pvInData;
    DWORD        cbInData;
    DWORD        cbInBuffer;
    DWORD        dwReserved;
} HTTP_FILTER_RAW_DATA, *PHTTP_FILTER_RAW_DATA;
```

Table 9.25 The **HTTP_FILTER_ RAW_DATA** members.

HTTP_FILTER_ RAW_DATA

Member	In/Out	What It Contains
pvInData	In	A pointer to a buffer containing the response message.
cbInData	In	The number of bytes in the buffer **pvInData**.
cbInBuffer	In	The maximum size of the buffer **pvInData**.
dwReserved	In	Reserved for future use.

The members of this structure are in Table 9.25.

Example Of SF_NOTIFY_SEND_RAW_DATA

Here we'll simply capture the first **BUFF_LEN** bytes of the response to be sent back by the server and display it in the debug window (see Listing 9.16). This notification is called at least twice: once when the server sends the response header and again when it sends the body of the response. Depending on how the body of the response is generated (for example, by an ISA using the **WriteClient** callback of the ECB), then a filter can potentially receive many **SF_NOTIFY_SEND_RAW_DATA** notifications within a single request.

Listing 9.16 An example of **SF_NOTIFY_SEND_RAW_DATA**.

```
BOOL WINAPI GetFilterVersion(HTTP_FILTER_VERSION *pVersion)
{
    /* Set version */
    pVersion->dwFilterVersion = HTTP_FILTER_REVISION;

    /* Provide a short description of the filter */
    strncpy(pVersion->lpszFilterDesc, "Simple SendRawData Filter",
            SF_MAX_FILTER_DESC_LEN);

    /* Set the event we want to be notified about and the notification
       priority */
    pVersion->dwFlags = (SF_NOTIFY_SECURE_PORT |
                         SF_NOTIFY_NONSECURE_PORT |
                         SF_NOTIFY_SEND_RAW_DATA |
                         SF_NOTIFY_ORDER_DEFAULT);

    return TRUE;
}
```

```
DWORD WINAPI HttpFilterProc(HTTP_FILTER_CONTEXT *pFC,
            DWORD dwNotificationType, VOID *pvData)
{
    DWORD dwRet = SF_STATUS_REQ_NEXT_NOTIFICATION;

    switch (dwNotificationType) {
        case SF_NOTIFY_URL_MAP:
            dwRet = HandleEvent_SendRawData(pFC,
                            (PHTTP_FILTER_RAW_DATA)pvData);
            break;
    }
    return dwRet;
}
DWORD HandleEvent_SendRawData(HTTP_FILTER_CONTEXT *pFC,
                            PHTTP_FILTER_RAW_DATA pSendData)
{
    DWORD   dwRet = SF_STATUS_REQ_NEXT_NOTIFICATION;
    DWORD   dwBytes;
    LPSTR   lpszBuffer;

    /* Capture no more than BUFF_MAX characters of the raw response */
    lpszBuffer = pFC->AllocMem(pFC, BUFF_MAX+1, 0);
    dwBytes = min(BUFF_MAX, pSendData->cbInData);

    memcpy(lpszBuffer, pSendData->pvInData, dwBytes);
    lpszBuffer[dwBytes]='\0';

    Debug((DEST, "SendRawData: Response[1-%d]=%s", dwBytes, lpszBuffer));

    return dwRet;
}
```

Logging—SF_NOTIFY_LOG

The **SF_NOTIFY_LOG** notification occurs just before the server writes information about the request to the server's request log. Your **HttpFilterProc** is passed a pointer to an **HTTP_FILTER_LOG** structure, which is filled with useful information about the request. By default, the server writes a log record containing this information to the log destination you selected, using inetmgr.

Catching this notification allows you to completely change the server's logging scheme by substituting your own. For example, rather than writing to a log file or to an ODBC data source, you could send log records to your own secure logging server behind a firewall. You can also use this notification to insert additional information into the server logs, by substituting pointers in **HTTP_FILTER_LOG** with pointers to buffers containing the original information plus your own extended information.

Notification Structure—HTTP_FILTER_LOG

The notification structure for this event is defined by the following C type definition:

```
typedef struct _HTTP_FILTER_LOG
{
    const CHAR * pszClientHostName;
    const CHAR * pszClientUserName;
    const CHAR * pszServerName;
    const CHAR * pszOperation;
    const CHAR * pszTarget;
    const CHAR * pszParameters;
    DWORD  dwHttpStatus;
    DWORD  dwWin32Status;
} HTTP_FILTER_LOG, *PHTTP_FILTER_LOG;
```

The members of this structure are in Table 9.26.

Table 9.26   The **HTTP_FILTER_LOG** members.

HTTP_FILTER_LOG

Member	In/Out	What It Contains
pszClientHostName	In/Out	The host name of the client.
pszClientUserName	In/Out	The user name of the client.
pszServerName	In/Out	The name of the server the client is connected to.
pszOperation	In/Out	The request method, for example, **GET** or **POST**.
pszTarget	In/Out	The request URL.
pszParameters	In/Out	The parameters passed to the request method, for example, the query string component of a **GET** request.
dwHttpStatus	In/Out	The HTTP status sent back in the first line of the response header.
dwWin32Status	In/Out	A Win32 error code.

Example Of SF_NOTIFY_LOG

Here (see Listing 9.17) we'll simply display the IP address of the client in the debug window. All the log information is returned as NULL-terminated strings, making it easy to manipulate them.

LIsting 9.17   An example of a filter using **SF_NOTIFY_LOG** filter.

```
BOOL WINAPI GetFilterVersion(HTTP_FILTER_VERSION *pVersion)
{
    /* Set version */
    pVersion->dwFilterVersion = HTTP_FILTER_REVISION;

    /* Provide a short description of the filter */
    strncpy(pVersion->lpszFilterDesc, "Simple Logging Filter",
               SF_MAX_FILTER_DESC_LEN);

  /* Set the event we want to be notified about and the notification
     priority */
    pVersion->dwFlags = (SF_NOTIFY_SECURE_PORT |
                         SF_NOTIFY_NONSECURE_PORT |
                         SF_NOTIFY_LOG   |
                         SF_NOTIFY_ORDER_DEFAULT);

    return TRUE;
}

DWORD WINAPI HttpFilterProc(HTTP_FILTER_CONTEXT *pFC,
            DWORD dwNotificationType, VOID *pvData)
{
    DWORD dwRet = SF_STATUS_REQ_NEXT_NOTIFICATION;

    switch (dwNotificationType) {
        case SF_NOTIFY_LOG:
            dwRet = HandleEvent_Log(pFC, (PHTTP_FILTER_LOG)pvData);
            break;
    }
    return dwRet;
}

DWORD HandleEvent_Log(HTTP_FILTER_CONTEXT *pFC,
                                          PHTTP_FILTER_LOG pLogData)
{
    DWORD   dwRet = SF_STATUS_REQ_NEXT_NOTIFICATION;
```

```
    /* Display client IP address */
    Debug((DEST, "Log: Client IP address = %s",
            pLogData->pszClientHostName));

    return dwRet;
}
```

End Of Session— SF_NOTIFY_END_OF_NET_SESSION

The **SF_NOTIFY_END_OF_NET_SESSION** is not very exciting, but it is important. There is no event-specific data structure associated with this notification.

SF_NOTIFY_END_OF_NET_SESSION is generated when the server is about to terminate the session with the client. Remember, in HTTP, it is the server that shuts down the connection, not the client. This notification is important because a handler for it would be used to deallocate any resources that had been set up for the request. For example, deallocating your own filter buffer pool, or freeing memory referenced by the **pFilterContext** member of **HTTP_FILTER_CONTEXT**.

If you have used **AllocMem** to allocate memory during the request, the server takes care of releasing it automatically once this event has occurred.

Example Of SF_NOTIFY_END_OF_NET_SESSION

A filter would not usually respond to this notification in isolation. For completeness, however, Listing 9.18 is a simple skeleton example.

Listing 9.18   An example of a filter using SF_NOTIFY_END_OF_NET_SESSION.

```
BOOL WINAPI GetFilterVersion(HTTP_FILTER_VERSION *pVersion)
{
    /* Set version */
    pVersion->dwFilterVersion = HTTP_FILTER_REVISION;

    /* Provide a short description of the filter */
    strncpy(pVersion->lpszFilterDesc, "Simple  Example Filter",
            SF_MAX_FILTER_DESC_LEN);

  /* Set the event we want to be notified about and the notification
     priority */
```

```
        pVersion->dwFlags = (SF_NOTIFY_SECURE_PORT |
                             SF_NOTIFY_NONSECURE_PORT |
                             ....
                             SF_NOTIFY_END_OF_NET_SESSION |
                             SF_NOTIFY_ORDER_DEFAULT);

    return TRUE;
}

DWORD WINAPI HttpFilterProc(HTTP_FILTER_CONTEXT *pFC,
                            DWORD dwNotificationType, VOID *pvData)
{
    DWORD dwRet = SF_STATUS_REQ_NEXT_NOTIFICATION;

    switch (dwNotificationType) {
/* Other notification handlers here */
        case .
            break;
        case SF_NOTIFY_END_OF_NET_SESSION:
            dwRet = HandleEvent_EndOfNetSession(pFC);
            break;
    }
    return dwRet;
}

DWORD HandleEvent_EndOfNetSession(HTTP_FILTER_CONTEXT *pFC)
{
    DWORD    dwRet = SF_STATUS_REQ_NEXT_NOTIFICATION;

    Debug((DEST, "EndOfNetSession event"));

    /* Deallocate resources allocated by this filter for this request
       ... . */

    return dwRet;
}
```

Summary

In this chapter, we have taken a fairly formal look at what makes ISAPI filters tick. We have followed through the process of registering a filter DLL in the registry, exposing the **GetFilterVersion** and **HttpFilterProc** entry points, and using

GetFilterVersion to register interest in the events the filter is to be notified about and to set the priority at which the filter should be called. We then looked in detail at the context information the server passes to **HttpFilterProc** in the form of a generic **HTTP_FILTER_CONTEXT** plus a structure specific to each event. Finally, we enumerated each type of event, when it occurs, and the data the server makes available with it.

The next chapter, Chapter 10, takes a much more practical view of filters. It also takes you through a step-by-step tutorial of building and debugging a filter. A number of interesting examples are also worked through.

Creating And Deploying ISAs And ISAPI Filters

CHAPTER

10

In this chapter we'll get our hands dirty, building several real ISAs and ISAPI filters. We take you step by step through the process of building and debugging both ISA and filter DLLs in Microsoft Visual C++. Then we'll look at how we can apply this technology to solve a number of interesting back-end programming problems. We also present some development tips for making your life easier when you are developing, and provide some wisdom on how to debug ISAs and filters using a range of techniques.

Creating And Deploying ISAs And ISAPI Filters

In Chapter 6, our NSAPI examples used a mix of C and C++, but in this chapter our examples will be implemented in C only. Although Microsoft has provided a light C++ wrapper for ISAPI as part of its Microsoft Foundation Classes, we have deliberately chosen to ignore it so that you can see the underlying ISAPI implementation in all its gory detail. Furthermore, our examples throw portability to the wind and assume a Microsoft Windows environment—making frequent use of Microsoft-specific type names and runtime support functions from the Win32 SDK.

In this chapter we'll use a tutorial approach and spend more time on the detail of building and debugging ISAs and filters than we do in Chapter 6. We have this luxury because, unlike NSAPI, which must pander to Windows and multiple Unix development environments, we only have one environment to explain.

All the examples presented here can be found on the CD-ROM enclosed with this book under separate project directories. In general, we provide 95 percent of the source code listings for these examples within the book. Source code not listed is restricted to lower-level utility functions from our support library libiisutils.lib. Both the binary and source versions of the library are also on the CD-ROM.

Creating And Deploying An ISA

In this section we'll start with a tutorial and move on to some more complex examples. Specifically, you'll find examples on how to:

- Interrogate server variables within a request

- Perform automatic URL redirection

- Process form information encoded in a GET and a PUT request

- Maintain and access a back-end database

You'll also find some helpful suggestions on how to convert CGI applications to ISAs.

If you are a novice developer or have not implemented an ISA before, we strongly recommend that you work through the tutorial before you go any further.

Building An ISA—A Step-By-Step Tutorial

We'll begin by creating an ISA implementation of the archetypal and much loved program "Hello World." We will use this simple example to walk through all the steps required to create an ISA written in C using Microsoft Visual C++. The sample program is small enough for you to enter it in verbatim. So if you haven't built an ISA before or are new to Visual C++, we suggest you actually perform each step to get a good feel for the process.

Be aware that ISAPI is a 32-bit interface and IIS is a 32-bit application. Therefore, the extension DLLs you create must also be 32 bit. You cannot and should not call 16-bit DLLs from your extension, because the Universal Thunk support provided by Win32s in a Windows 3.x environment, which allows a Win32 DLL to call a 16-bit DLL, is not available under Windows NT. Even if you could, you should not because Win32 facilities such as thread synchronization objects are not present in a Win16 environment.

Any extension (ISA or filter) you create must also be *thread safe*, meaning that it must use synchronization objects such as Critical Sections or Mutexes to protect resources that could be accessed by multiple concurrent threads of execution running through the extension. Chapter 5 discusses thread safety issues in general and later on in this chapter we'll look at issues specifically in an ISAPI/Windows environment.

Development Environment

We are assuming you have a suitable computer with the following Microsoft development environment installed:

- Windows NT V4.0

- Developer Studio - Visual C++ V4.2

- Internet Information Server 3.0

- Internet Explorer 3.0

While you can get away with something smaller, we've found the minimum workable hardware configuration for this development environment is an Intel Pentium 166-based PC with 32 MB RAM and plenty of disk space, at least 2 GB. (Or maybe I'm just getting impatient in my old age!)

We also assume that you are running IIS on the same machine you are developing on—this makes your life as a developer a whole lot simpler—especially when it comes to debugging.

We have simply used the installation defaults when it comes to installation directory locations. For example, Developer Studio is located in c:\Msdev, and IIS in c:\Winnt\system32\inetsrv. Our machine has the default name of ntserver—yours is probably something more imaginative, but just be aware that in our examples, URLs pointing to resources on the local machine will be prefixed with http://ntserver/.

By default, the root of the IIS content tree is c:\InetPub. It contains root directories for each of the IIS services—FTP, Gopher, and WWW—ftproot, gophrroot, and wwwroot respectively, plus a scripts directory containing admin, tools, and sample subdirectories.

We use the default IIS directory structure for storing our example DLLs and any supporting files because the server is already configured to access these directories. For example, our ISA DLLs (and, later on, ISAPI filter DLLs) are stored in c:\InetPub\scripts\samples. Supporting HTML files are kept in a sample-specific sub-directory within c:\InetPub\wwwroot\samples.

Similarly, we use the default Developer Studio directory c:\Msdev\projects for storing our sample projects.

Create A New Project

Start up Developer Studio and create a new Project Workspace using the File|New option. In the New Project Workspace dialog box, select the *DLL* Workspace type because we are creating an ISA DLL. Then choose a name for your Workspace—we (intuitively) called ours isasample1 (you might call yours HelloWorld). If you chose isasample1 as your Workspace name, the project directory that Developer Studio creates will be c:\Msdev\projects\isasample1.

The standard project settings should work for this example. At a minimum you should make the following conditions true:

- General: Microsoft Foundation Classes set to Not Using MFC

- C Preprocessor: WIN32 *is* defined

- Link: default libraries are *not* ignored

Define DLL Entry points

Before we do anything else, we should specify the functions to be exported by our ISA DLL. This can be done later, but we suggest doing it now because it's something people always forget to do.

Because we're creating an ISA DLL we must explicitly define the DLL entry points **GetExtensionVersion** and **HttpExtensionProc**. As we've previously discussed, these two functions are called by IIS after it has loaded the DLL into memory. The server uses the Win32 SDK function **GetProcAddress** to find the address of the functions within the DLL by name.

If you do not specify the DLL interface as we describe in this step, when the server attempts to execute your DLL, the server will complain. If you referred to the DLL via your browser, you will see an error message back from the server that will look something like this:

```
HTTP/1.0 500 Server Error (The specified procedure could not be found)
```

Usually you have two ways to define the exported function interface of a DLL—the old way via a DEF file, or the usual method for 32-bit applications using the **__declspec(dllexport)** storage class modifier. For example:

```
__declspec(dllexport) BOOL WINAPI GetExtensionVersion(HSE_VERSION_INFO
  *pVersion)
```

> **Note:** *In this case, the prototypes of these functions are predefined by the Win32 SDK and do not use a __**declspec(dllexport)** modifier. This means we must use a DEF file to list the functions exported by the DLL.*

To create the DEF file in Developer Studio, create a new text file called isasample1.def using File|New and insert it into the project using Insert|Files Into Project. In Developer Studio's **FileView** you should now see the DEF file. Go into the DEF file and enter the following:

```
EXPORTS
GetExtensionVersion
HttpExtensionProc
```

Later, when you build your DLL, the linker will generate the DLL along with EXP and LIB files, which contain information about the exported and imported functions.

> **Note:** *ISA DLLs are not statically linked with IIS and therefore the EXP and LIB files are not used. Instead, IIS uses runtime dynamic linking and the* **LoadLibrary** *Win32 SDK function to load the DLLs into memory on demand.*

Include Files And Other Preliminary Definitions

Now create a new *text* file using the File|New menu option and save the file as isasample1.c. Then insert the file into the project using Insert|Files Into Project.

Okay, *now* we can enter some real code. In Listing 10.1 we begin with some preliminary work.

Listing 10.1   Code for isasample1.c—Hello World.

```
/************************************************************************
* Name:            isasample1.c
* Description:     An ISA DLL which is loaded by ISS in response to the
                     URL
*                  http://ntserver/scripts/samples/isasample1.dll
*                  The ISA simply returns an HTML document saying Hello
                     World.
```

```
 * DLL Location:    c:\InetPub\scripts\samples\isasample1.dll
 *****************************************************************/
#define WIN32_LEAN_AN_MEAN
#include <httpext.h>
#include <stdio.h>

#define EXTN_VERSION MAKELONG(HSE_VERSION_MINOR, HSE_VERSION_MAJOR)
#define MAX_BUFF_SIZE    256
/*****************************************************************/
```

ISA applications need to include the file httpext.h. Because ISAPI is now just part of the Win32 SDK, you can find this file in c:\Msdev\include. The compiler knows about this path so you don't need to do anything special other than include the line:

```
#include <httpext.h>
```

The include file httpext.h also includes the windows.h, which is a large file, so you can save yourself a bit of compilation time by defining the symbol **WIN32_LEAN_AND_MEAN**, which excludes some of the less commonly used definitions and reduces the size of the file. Because we use the **sprintf** function from the standard C library within our application, we must also include stdio.h.

> **Note:** The **sprintf** function (though often maligned by purists) is extremely useful for formatting text responses to be sent back to the client. We will use it often throughout this chapter.

Each ISA must be registered with a version number. This is actually a 32-bit integer consisting of two concatenated 16-bit values—the minor version and major version numbers, which together define the version of ISAPI implemented by the server. The **EXTN_VERSION** definition shows how to create a version number using the **MAKELONG** macro. IIS 3.0 currently implements Version 2.0 of the specification.

The definition **MAX_BUFF_SIZE** is a convenient constant for defining ad hoc storage. We will use it frequently throughout our examples to define both stack-based and dynamically allocated scratch memory.

Define GetExtensionVersion

The next step is to define the **GetExtensionVersion** function. This function is exported by the DLL and is called once when the DLL is loaded by the server to pick up the version number of ISAPI used to implement the extension and a brief description of what the extension does. This information is passed back to the server via the **HSE_VERSION_INFO** structure pointed to by **pVersion**. You should use **HSE_MAX_EXT_DLL_NAME_LEN** to restrict the size of the description.

```
BOOL WINAPI GetExtensionVersion(HSE_VERSION_INFO *pVersion)
{
        pVersion->dwExtensionVersion = EXTN_VERSION;
        strncpy(pVersion->lpszExtensionDesc, "Hello World Extension",
                HSE_MAX_EXT_DLL_NAME_LEN);


        return TRUE;
}
```

Define HttpExtensionProc

The second entry point to the DLL is **HttpExtensionProc**. This function is called for every request and is where the real work of the extension is done. Once the server has called your **GetExtensionProc** it then calls **HttpExtensionProc** and passes it an extension-specific data structure **EXTENSION_CONTROL_BLOCK** (informally referred to as ECB).

You will remember from Chapter 8 that the ECB is the structure the server uses to pass you context information about the request, including:

- Commonly used server variables such as **QUERY_STRING**, **PATH_INFO**, and **PATH_TRANSLATED**

- Built-in callback functions such as **ReadClient**, **WriteClient**, **GetServerVariable**, and **ServerSupportFunction**, which you can use for manipulating the request, creating a response, and managing the session between client and server

This function is effectively the main function for the ISA where you begin execution of your application.

```
DWORD WINAPI HttpExtensionProc(EXTENSION_CONTROL_BLOCK *pECB)
{
        DWORD       dwBytes;
        CHAR        HeaderBuff[MAX_BUFF_SIZE];
```

```
LPSTR    BodyBuff = "<HTML><BODY><H1><B>Hello World</B></H1>"
                                     "</BODY></HTML>";

/* Create the header and send it back to the client */
sprintf(HeaderBuff,
        "Content-Type: text/html\r\nContent-Length:%s\r\n\r\n",
        strlen(BodyBuff));
dwBytes = strlen(HeaderBuff);
pECB->ServerSupportFunction(pECB->ConnID,
  HSE_REQ_SEND_RESPONSE_HEADER,

                                         NULL,
                                         &dwBytes,
                               (LPDWORD)HeaderBuff);

/* Now send the body of the message */
dwBytes=strlen(BodyBuff);
pECB->WriteClient(pECB->ConnID, (LPVOID)BodyBuff, &dwBytes, 0);

return HSE_STATUS_SUCCESS;
}
```

Our "Hello World" program illustrates the usage of two important ISAPI functions, **ServerSupportFunction** and **WriteClient**. Remember that the purpose of this ISA is to write back a "Hello World" response to the client browser. To do this, we must formulate a valid HTTP message consisting of headers, a blank line indicating the end of the headers, and finally the body of the message itself—in this case, an HTML document encapsulating the immortal words.

As we described in Chapter 8, **ServerSupportFunction** provides useful supporting functions for generating a response and for managing the server session. In this example, we use its **HSE_REQ_SEND_RESPONSE_HEADER** aspect to send back a fully formed header to the client. By specifying NULL as the third parameter, the function will generate a **200 OK** response code in the response status line.

We'll use the last parameter to pass our own headers to be appended to the default headers generated by the server. In this example, **HeaderBuff** contains both a **Content-Type** and **Content-Length** header; these are not part of the default headers generated by the server.

> **Note:** *It is important to notice that we've appended an extra "\r\n", to indicate the end of the header section of the message. This is often overlooked. If you omit it, you probably won't see any response displayed in the browser, or you'll get some sort of error message saying that the file could not be found.*
>
> *Also, note that if we had set the last parameter to NULL (which indicates there are no additional headers), the server would generate the extra "\r\n" for us.*

The variable **dwBytes** is passed into the function *by reference* (we've passed the address of **dwBytes** using **&dwBytes**). Going into the function, you should set **dwBytes** to be the number of bytes to be sent to the client from **HeaderBuff**—usually this number will be **strlen**(**HeaderBuff**). When the function completes, the server will have updated **dwBytes** to reflect the number of bytes it actually sent to the client. If the two values are different, this means something has gone wrong with the session and should be treated as an error.

Having sent back a header, we'll now send the body of the message using **WriteClient**. Our HTML response is concisely encoded in **BodyBuff**. The semantics of **dwBytes** are the same as **ServerSupportFunction**, so we set it to the length of **BodyBuff** prior to the function call.

The last obligation of **HttpExtensionProc** is to return a status code to the server. If all goes well, this should be **HSE_STATUS_SUCCESS**. However, if we encountered some irrecoverable error condition within our application code, such as running out of memory, then we would return **HSE_STATUS_ERROR** instead.

Build And Install The DLL

Now that the coding part is complete, build your DLL using Build|Build isasample1.dll. With any luck, your program should compile without any errors or warnings.

By default, Developer Studio assumes a debugging configuration (see Build|Set Default Configuration), consequently, your DLL is generated in the Debug subdirectory of the project directory (such as c:\Msdev\projects\isasample1\Debug\isasample1.dll). Use the NT Explorer to copy the DLL from the Debug directory to the c:\InetPub\scripts\samples directory.

If you want to put your DLL into a different directory, then you must use inetmgr (the Internet Service Manager program—see Chapter 7) to register the directory, define a suitable alias, and set the directory's executable attribute.

If you are doing lots of development work, it may be worth it to add your project directory to the list of paths IIS can access. For example, registering the directory c:\Msdev\projects\isasample1\Debug with an alias of /sample1 will allow you to use the logical URL http://ntserver/sample1/isasample1.dll instead (which saves you a bit of typing).

Note, however, that to do this you must ensure that the DLL is loaded and unloaded by the server on every request. You do this by setting the following registry key to 0:

HKEY_LOCAL_MACHINE\SYSTEM\CurrentControlSet\Services\W3SVC\Parameters\CacheExtensions

You should do this anyway to facilitate debugging of your ISA. We'll talk more about debugging later in this chapter.

> **Note:** If you don't set your new directory to be executable and set only the read attribute, IIS will return the contents of the DLL to your browser rather than executing it.

Run The Application

Now you're ready to test your creation!

If you haven't previously stopped it, IIS should be running. It is normally started automatically by the system (you can check if it is running using inetmgr).

If IIS is active, start up your favorite Web browser—we use Internet Explorer (hey it's free!) and in the one-line Address box, type in the URL of your ISA. If you've stuck with our DLL and directory naming structure, then you can enter: http://ntserver/scripts/samples/isasample1.dll.

Pressing Enter on the keyboard should cause the browser to connect to the server and issue a request for the DLL. The server will interpret the request by loading and executing the ISA. The ISA is responsible for generating the response message. So you should see "Hello World" displayed in bold in your browser.

If you've actually taken the time to implement this tutorial and have run it successfully, then congratulations—you are now an honorary member of the Hello World society.

Key Points

So let's quickly recap on the important points we've touched on in this tutorial:

- Export the DLL entry points **GetExtensionVersion** and **HttpExtensionProc**.

- Remember to append an extra "\r\n" to the user-defined headers when you use the **HSE_REQ_SEND_RESPONSE_HEADER** support function.

- Make sure IIS's *execute* attribute is set on the directory in which you install your ISA. In this example, because we are installing our ISA in a directory the server already knows about, we didn't need to explicitly do this step.

- Make sure your ISA is thread safe.

- Do not attempt to call any 16-bit DLLs or libraries from your ISA.

Useful Notes For CGI Conversion

ISAs have been designed to provide an easy migration path from CGI applications. We don't suggest you go out and immediately convert all your existing apps. However, you may well have CGI apps that perform poorly and could do with being reimplemented as ISAs.

From a client application perspective, such a conversion would have a fairly minimal impact because the form of a URL for an ISA reference is almost identical to that of a CGI reference. The difference is simply in the file extension. A CGI program is an executable binary program or script. An ISA is a DLL. For example, a CGI script with the URL http://ntserver/scripts/samples/sample.pl (Perl) would convert to an ISA reference that looks like http://ntserver/scripts/samples/sample.dll. You would need to edit any HTML documents and HTML-generating applications that referenced CGI URLs and modify the file extension.

A CGI program expects to obtain information from the server about the current request through server-supplied environment variables (see Table 7.1 in Chapter 7, and Table 8.2 in Chapter 8), which it extracts from its environment using **getenv**. While an ISA has access to the same information from the server, it must use the **GetServerVariable** callback function that the server provides in the ECB to obtain the variable values.

Also, a CGI program expects to receive input from POST requests from the standard input. There is no such thing as standard I/O for an ISA because it is a DLL and not an application. Therefore, an ISA must use the ECB's **ReadClient** callback function to read raw data directly from the client connection.

Similarly, where a CGI program expects to write its response back to its standard output, an ISA must use the **WriteClient** ECB callback function to send its response back to the client. In a CGI program you must formulate a complete response message including all necessary headers before writing the response to the standard output.

An ISA must also assemble a response message, however, it can make use of the **HSE_REQ_SEND_RESPONSE_HEADER** option of the **ServerSupportFunction** callback function supplied in the ECB to make this job a little easier. This function will generate a complete response (including **Server:** and **Date:** headers) and lets you drop in values for the status code (for example, **401 Access Denied**), and any other headers you may want to append such as **Content-Type** and **Content-Length**. If, however, you want to have absolute control over the entire header, you can generate your own from scratch and use the **WriteClient** callback to send it and any message body.

URL redirection through use of the **Location** header is commonly used in CGI applications. An ISA wanting to do the same thing is able to use the **HSE_REQ_SEND_URL** and **HSE_REQ_SEND_URL_REDIRECT_RESP** forms of the **ServerSupportFunction** callback to do this. **HSE_REQ_SEND_URL** is used to redirect requests to resources on the same computer as the server while the other form is used where the resource is remote. Our URL Redirection example later in this chapter illustrates this.

Architecturally, a CGI application and an ISA are very similar. The two major differences are:

- The way server variables are communicated by the server

- The way in which input and output are handled

It is actually not too hard to wrap an ISA inside an executable and have it appear to be a CGI application. Just connect the ISA's **ReadClient** and **WriteClient** interface to the standard input and output of the wrapper, and connect the ISA's notion of an ECB to the wrapper's environment and provide replacements for the ECB callback functions. Such a program is actually available on the Microsoft Developer Network

Library CD (see MSTOOLS\samples\win32\winnt\isapi\CGIWRAP). This program has two possible uses—debugging an ISA from a console window and running an ISA where it may not be possible to have the ISA loaded into the server.

In general, CGI applications do not have to worry about being thread safe. In an ISA environment, however, thread safety is all-important. In any conversion process, you must look at all the unsafe areas of your application. This means analyzing the need for global data. Where possible, you should always use stack-based memory allocation, however, where this is not possible and you need to allocate memory from the heap, you must use an appropriate synchronization mechanism to serialize any operations that update this data where it's shared by more than one thread. Refer to section "Tips For Easier And Safer Development," later in this chapter for further discussion on this.

Retrieving Server Variables

In this example, we'll demonstrate the use of the **GetServerVariable** callback function provided in the ECB to retrieve a whole range of server variables and return them in a formatted HTML document to the client.

Working our way through Listing 10.1, we first define the mandatory windows.h and httpext.h include files. We also need stdio.h for **sprintf** support. We have used some modules from our support library—**debug** to provide tracing during the execution of the ISA, and **http** and **html** modules, which provide a lightweight wrapper for HTTP and HTML message processing.

> **Note:** The **html** module implements an HTML page as a double-linked list. This implementation is a bit of overkill because all that's really necessary is to use the **WriteClient** callback to send HTML-formatted strings back to the client. However, because we want to use these routines for both ISA and filter applications, it seemed useful at the time to abstract away the dependency on an ISA or a filter context. Not doing so would have resulted in creating two HTML libraries—one for ISAs and one for filters. Abstracting the notion of a page means we can extend the **html** module over time and reuse this for both types of applications.

*Nevertheless, we must still provide an ISA-specific function for writing the page back to the client. This function, **HtmlPage_ExtnWrite(pECB, pPage)**, works its way down **pPage** and uses **pECB->WriteClient** to send each piece of HTML to the client. (The same applies for filters; we must provide **HtmlPage_FiltWrite(pFC, pPage)**, which performs the same function but uses **pFC->WriteClient** to do the actual write to the client.)*

*Refer to the CD-ROM enclosed with this book for source code for the **html** and **http** modules.*

Now that we have defined the include files we then go on to provide definitions for the version number and the description of the ISA. Finally, we have the prototype of a function **ServerVariables_Enumerate** (shown in Listing 10.2), which will actually enumerate the list of variables and construct the resulting HTML page in the process.

Listing 10.2 Code for isasample2.c—displaying the contents of server variables.

```
/***************************************************************************
* Name:          isasample2.c
* Description:   an ISA DLL that is loaded by ISS in response to the URL
*                http://ntserver/scripts/samples/isasample2.dll
*                The ISA uses GetServerVariable to display common
*                   information
*                about the client and server.
* DLL Location: c:\inetpub\scripts\samples\extnsample2.dll
***************************************************************************/

#define WIN32_LEAN_AN_MEAN
#include <windows.h>
#include <httpext.h>
#include <stdio.h>

/* Imported Library Modules */
#include <debug.h>
#include <http.h>
#include <html.h>

/* Defines */
#define EXTN_VERSION MAKELONG(HSE_VERSION_MINOR, HSE_VERSION_MAJOR)
#define EXTN_DESCRIPTION "Server Variable Extension"
#define MAX_VAR_LEN 20
```

```
/* Private Prototypes */
VOID ServerVariables_Enumerate(EXTENSION_CONTROL_BLOCK *pECB,
                                            HtmlPage *pPage);


/************************************************************************/
```

GetExtensionVersion is as we'd expect—all it does is set the version and descriptions we have defined and returns TRUE, indicating that the server should continue to process the ISA.

```
BOOL WINAPI GetExtensionVersion(HSE_VERSION_INFO *pVersion)
{
    pVersion->dwExtensionVersion = EXTN_VERSION;
    strncpy(pVersion->lpszExtensionDesc, EXTN_DESCRIPTION,
              HSE_MAX_EXT_DLL_NAME_LEN);

    Debug((DEST, pVersion->lpszExtensionDesc));

    return TRUE;
}
```

HttpExtensionProc first of all creates a **200 OK** HTTP header and appends a **Content-Type** header field that tells the client to expect an HTML document next. We use **HtmlPage_New** to create a handle to a new HTML page called **pPage** and **HtmlPage_Start** to append the page preamble, including a title of "Server Variables". We then use **HtmlPage_Append** to add a level-1 bold heading "Server Variables" to the page before invoking **ServerVariables_Enumerate** to generate the body of the HTML. Once **ServerVariables_Enumerate** completes, **HtmlPage_End** appends the end of document HTML tags to the page and then **HtmlPage_ExtnWrite** sends the completed page back to the client. Finally, **HtmlPage_Delete** cleans up the memory used by the **pPage**.

```
DWORD WINAPI HttpExtensionProc(EXTENSION_CONTROL_BLOCK *pECB)
{
    HtmlPage *pPage;

    HttpHeader_ExtnWrite(pECB, NULL, "Content-Type: text/html\r\n");
    pPage = HtmlPage_New();
    HtmlPage_Start(pPage, "Server Variables");
    HtmlPage_Append(pPage, "<H1><B>Server Variables</B>
                       </H1>\r\n<HR>\r\n");
```

```
        ServerVariables_Enumerate(pECB, pPage);
        HtmlPage_End(pPage);
        HtmlPage_ExtnWrite(pECB, pPage);
        HtmlPage_Delete(pPage);

        return HSE_STATUS_SUCCESS;
}


/*********************************************************************/
```

ServerVariables_Enumerate iterates through a list of variable names to be retrieved. It uses **GetServerVariable** provided within the ECB to retrieve the corresponding value for each variable and creates a right-justified text line containing the following information, which is then appended to the HTML page **pPage**.

```
VOID ServerVariables_Enumerate(EXTENSION_CONTROL_BLOCK *pECB,
                                                HtmlPage *pPage)
{
    CHAR    Buff[MAX_BUFF_SIZE*10]; /* A bit of guess on the output
                                        buffer size */
    DWORD   dwLen;

    typedef struct {
        LPSTR   lpszVarName;
        CHAR    VarValue[MAX_BUFF_SIZE];
    } Variable;

    Variable *pVar;

    Variable Vars[] =
    {
        {"AUTH_TYPE", {0}},
        {"CONTENT_LENGTH", {0}},
        {"CONTENT_TYPE", {0}},
        {"PATH_INFO", {0}},
        {"PATH_TRANSLATED", {0}},
        {"QUERY_STRING", {0}},
        {"REMOTE_ADDR", {0}},
        {"REMOTE_HOST", {0}},
        {"REMOTE_USER", {0}},
        {"UNMAPPED_REMOTE_USER", {0}},
        {"REQUEST_METHOD", {0}},
        {"SCRIPT_NAME", {0}},
        {"SERVER_NAME", {0}},
        {"SERVER_PORT", {0}},
```

```
            {"SERVER_PORT_SECURE", {0}},
            {"SERVER_PROTOCOL", {0}},
            {"SERVER_SOFTWARE", {0}},
            {"ALL_HTTP", {0}},
            {"HTTP_ACCEPT", {0}},
            {"HTTP_USER_AGENT", {0}},
            {"URL", {0}},
            {"", {0}}
    };

    CHAR      Spaces[MAX_VAR_LEN+1];

    HtmlPage_Append(pPage, "<pre>\r\n");
    for (pVar=Vars; *pVar->lpszVarName != '\0'; pVar++) {
        memset(Spaces, ' ', MAX_VAR_LEN);
        Spaces[MAX_VAR_LEN-strlen(pVar->lpszVarName)]='\0';
        dwLen=MAX_BUFF_SIZE;
        pECB->GetServerVariable(pECB->ConnID, pVar->lpszVarName,
                                                  pVar->VarValue,
                                                  &dwLen);

        sprintf(Buff, "%s%s: %s\r\n", Spaces, pVar->lpszVarName,
                                            pVar->VarValue);
        HtmlPage_Append(pPage, Buff);
    }
    HtmlPage_Append(pPage, "</pre>\r\n");
}
```

Figure 10.1 shows the result of the request http://ntserver/scripts/samples/ isasample2.dll in Internet Explorer.

URL Redirection

Our next example implements a simple "site chooser" application to illustrate how an ISA can perform URL redirection. If you're not familiar with this concept, this is where we can have the server transparently (to the user) redirect the client request.

This operation doesn't require any intervention by the client. Rather, the server generates a **302 Moved Temporarily** response containing the new target URL. When the client receives this, it formulates a new GET request to the specified URL.

We use the **ServerSupportFunction** callback in the ECB to perform the redirection function. **ServerSupportFunction** provides two options for doing the redirection.

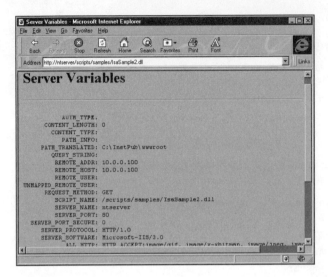

Figure 10.1

The isasample2.dll request.

HSE_REQ_SEND_URL is used where the redirected URL is local to the server and **HSE_REQ_SEND_URL_REDIRECT_RESP** is used where the redirected URL is remote from the server. In the latter case, you must make sure that your URLs are fully qualified, in that they must have an **http://** prefix.

Here is the form for our "site chooser" page:

```
<html>
<head>
<title>URL Redirector</title>
</head>
<body>
<h1 align=left>Site Favourites</h1>
<hr>
<form action="http://ntserver/scripts/samples/isasample3.dll">
<select name="choice">
<option selected value="http://ntserver/scripts/samples/
isasample1.dll">Home
<option value="http://www.microsoft.com">Microsoft
<option value="http://www.netscape.com">Netscape
</select>
<input type="submit" value="Choose a site">
</form>
<hr>
```

```
</body>
</html>
```

Notice that among the options the user can select, the default value references a resource on the local machine and the others are obviously remote.

When the user makes a choice and clicks on the submit button, the browser generates a GET request to our ISA http://ntserver/scripts/samples/isasample3.dll, passing to it the selected choice in the query string appended to the URL.

Our ISA breaks out the new URL from the query string by using our own support function **HttpQueryString_GetParamValue** and it uses the **HSE_REQ_SEND_URL_REDIRECT_RESP** operation provided by **ServerSupportFunction** to issue the **302 Moved Temporarily** response. Listing 10.3 below shows how this is done.

Listing 10.3   The isasample3.c code—URL redirection.

```
/*************************************************************************
 * Name:          isasample3.c
 * Description:   an ISA DLL that is loaded by ISS in response to the URL
 *                http://ntserver/scripts/samples/isasample3.dll?
 *                  to perform
 *                URL redirection to a target site chosen from a
 *                  selection form.
 * Function:      Can be called via a GET or POST method from
 isasample3.htm
 * DLL Location: c:\inetpub\scripts\samples\isasample3.dll
 * HTML Location:c:\inetpub\wwwroot\samples\isasample3\isasample3.htm
 *************************************************************************/

#define WIN32_LEAN_AN_MEAN
#include <windows.h>
#include <httpext.h>
#include <stdio.h>

/* Imported Library Modules */
#include <debug.h>
#include <mem.h>
#include <http.h>

/* Defines */
#define EXTN_VERSION MAKELONG(HSE_VERSION_MINOR, HSE_VERSION_MAJOR)
#define EXTN_DESCRIPTION "Favorite Site Chooser Extension"
```

```
/**********************************************************************/

BOOL WINAPI GetExtensionVersion(HSE_VERSION_INFO *pVersion)
{
    pVersion->dwExtensionVersion = EXTN_VERSION;
    strncpy(pVersion->lpszExtensionDesc, EXTN_DESCRIPTION,
                HSE_MAX_EXT_DLL_NAME_LEN);

    Debug((DEST, pVersion->lpszExtensionDesc));

    return TRUE;
}


DWORD WINAPI HttpExtensionProc(EXTENSION_CONTROL_BLOCK *pECB)
{
    LPSTR   lpszTargetURL;
    DWORD   dwBytes;
    DWORD   dwRet = HSE_STATUS_SUCCESS;

    if (0 == strcmp(pECB->lpszMethod, "get") ||
        0 == strcmp(pECB->lpszMethod, "GET")) {
        lpszTargetURL = HttpQueryString_GetParamValue(
                    pECB->lpszQueryString, "choice");
        if (lpszTargetURL) {
            dwBytes = strlen(lpszTargetURL);
            pECB->ServerSupportFunction(pECB->ConnID,
                            HSE_REQ_SEND_URL_REDIRECT_RESP,
                            lpszTargetURL, &dwBytes, (LPDWORD)NULL);
        }
        Mem_Free(lpszTargetURL);
    }
    else
        dwRet = HSE_STATUS_ERROR;

    return dwRet;
}
```

Our example doesn't bother to check the result of **ServerSupportFunction**—it should though, and if there was an error, it should generate an appropriate HTML response indicating the failure to the client. We'll leave that for you to add.

Note that if you want to send back a **301 Moved Permanently** header, you'll need it to construct the header yourself. You can use **ServerSupportFunction**'s **HSE_REQ_SEND_RESPONSE_HEADER** to make this job a little easier, because it will construct most of the header and allow you to drop in the **301 Moved Perma-nently** status code and append the **Location:** header before sending it back to the client. Otherwise, you must construct the complete header from scratch and use **WriteClient** to send it.

Processing A Registration Form With GET Or POST Requests

Registering user or customer name and address information via an HTML form is a common garden-variety HTML/CGI application. In this example, we'll implement a simple HTML form that accepts customer name, address, phone, and email details. Instead of writing a CGI script to process the form, we'll create an ISA to do the same job.

GET Request

Here is the HTML for the registration form created by Microsoft FrontPage. This document can be found on the CD-ROM enclosed with this book, in the project directory for this example. Its name is isasample4.htm.

```
<!DOCTYPE HTML PUBLIC "-//IETF//DTD HTML//EN">
<html>
<head>
<title>register</title>
<meta name="GENERATOR" content="Microsoft FrontPage 1.1">
</head>
<body>
<h1 align=left>Registration Form</h1>
<hr>
<pre>Please enter your registration details below:</pre>
<form action="http://ntserver/scripts/samples/isasample4.dll"
method="GET">
<pre>Name   <input type=text size=40 maxlength=256 name="name"> (Required)
</pre>
<pre>Address  <input type=text size=40 maxlength=256 name="address">
(Required)</pre>
<pre>Phone   <input type=text size=20 maxlength=256 name="phone">
(optional)</pre>
<pre>Email   <input type=text size=20 maxlength=256 name="email">
(Required)</pre>
<div align=left>
```

```
<pre><input type=submit name="submitBtn" value="Submit"><input type=reset
                                    name="resetBtn"
value="Reset"></pre>
</div>
<pre><hr></pre>
</form>
</body>
</html>
```

Note that the **action** attribute for the **form** tag specifies the URL of the ISA to be called when the customer hits the **submitBtn** and the **method** attribute requires that the browser must formulate a GET request when it sends the form to the server.

> **Note:** We've stored the form of this example in the directory
> c:\InetPub\wwwroot\samples\isasample4\isasample4.htm so that it can be
> referred to by the URL http://ntserver/samples/isasample4/isasample4.htm.

Let's say the user enters information into the form as depicted in Figure 10.2.

When the customer clicks on the Submit button, the browser generates the following request (we have not included the request headers that follow):

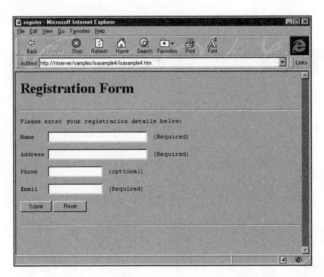

Figure 10.2

A customer registration form.

```
GET /scripts/samples/isasample4.dll?name=Paul&address=PO+Box+106
    104+Auckland&phone=0064-9-3097918&email=paulm@optimation.co.nz HTTP/1.0
```

Notice how the form data has been appended to the request URL. We call this piece of the URL the query string. In a CGI application, you would access this part of the URL using the **QUERY_STRING** server variable. In an ISA, we use the **lpszQueryString** member of the ECB to access this same information.

The query string has been URL encoded—spaces have been substituted with '+' characters, and field name and value pair for each field are delimited by a '&' character. The ISA must parse the query string and break out the name/value pairs before it can process them.

POST Request

If we replaced the form's method attribute with "POST", the browser would generate a POST request with the URL-encoded form data in the request body rather than following the URL in the request header.

POST is actually the recommended method for sending form data, as the body of a POST request can hold arbitrarily large amounts of data. **GET** should only be used for very small forms.

The POST request might look something like this:

```
POST /scripts/samples/isasample4.dll
Proxy-Connection: Keep-Alive
User-Agent: Mozilla/2.0 (compatible; MSIE 3.01; Windows NT)
Host: ntserver
Accept: image/gif, image/x-xbitmap, image/jpeg, image/pjpeg, */*
Content-type: application/x-www-form-urlencoded
Content-length: 91

name=Paul&address=PO+Box+106-104+
    Auckland&phone=0064-9-3097918&email=paulm@optimation.co.nz
```

In a CGI application, we would read the body of the request from the standard input. However, in an ISA, we must use the **ReadClient** callback supplied in the ECB for the request.

Apart from the different methods of retrieving the query string, the remainder of the form processing for the two request methods is identical.

A Server-Side Model Of A Form

To make life easier (and to make this example a little more interesting), our ISA maintains its own model of the form called **RegistrationForm**. This is implemented as an array of **FormField** as follows:

```
FormField RegistrationForm[] = {
      /* Name      Value  Description                 Required  Valid*/
      {"name",     NULL,  "Name of Customer",            TRUE,    TRUE},
      {"address",  NULL,  "Address of Customer",         TRUE,    TRUE},
      {"phone",    NULL,  "Phone Number of Customer",    FALSE,   TRUE},
      {"email",    NULL,  "Email Address of Customer",   TRUE,    TRUE},
      {"",         NULL,  NULL,                          FALSE,   TRUE}
   };
```

This model provides a convenient mechanism for scanning information in the form and for binding other details to each form field.

For each **FormField**, the **RegistrationForm** maintains information in addition to the field name and value such as a long description, an indication of whether the field is a required field, plus a "valid" flag, which will be flipped to FALSE if no field with this name exists in the request. The value and valid entries are populated as the field name/value pairs are parsed out of the query string.

Implementation

Let's take a look at the actual implementation by working our way through Listing 10.4.

Listing 10.4   Code for isasample4.c—Customer Registration Form.

```
/***********************************************************************
* Name:          isasample4.c
* Description:   an ISA DLL that is loaded by ISS in response to the URL
*                http://ntserver/scripts/samples/extnsample1.dll?
* Function:      Can be called via a GET or POST method from
*                   extnsample4.htm that
*                implements a registration form. The ISA accepts the
*                   form fields,
*                processes them and generates a success or error HTML
*                   response depending
*                on the validity of the information.
* DLL Location: c:\inetpub\scripts\samples\isasample4.dll
* HTML Location:c:\inetpub\wwwroot\samples\isasample4\isasample4.htm
***********************************************************************/
```

```
#define WIN32_LEAN_AN_MEAN
#include <windows.h>
#include <httpext.h>
#include <stdio.h>

/* Imported Library Modules */
#include <debug.h>
#include <mem.h>
#include <http.h>
#include <html.h>
#include <form.h>

/* Defines */
#define EXTN_VERSION MAKELONG(HSE_VERSION_MINOR, HSE_VERSION_MAJOR)
#define EXTN_DESCRIPTION "Registration Extension"

/* Private Prototypes */
BOOL RegistrationForm_Request(EXTENSION_CONTROL_BLOCK *pECB,
                                                      FormField
                                                      *pForm);
BOOL RegistrationForm_GetRequest(EXTENSION_CONTROL_BLOCK *pECB,
                                                         FormField
                                                         *pForm);
BOOL RegistrationForm_PostRequest(EXTENSION_CONTROL_BLOCK *pECB,
                                                          FormField
                                                          *pForm);
VOID RegistrationForm_OKResponse(EXTENSION_CONTROL_BLOCK *pECB,
                                                         FormField
                                                         *pForm);
VOID RegistrationForm_ErrorResponse(EXTENSION_CONTROL_BLOCK *pECB,
                                                            FormField
                                                            *pForm);


/************************************************************************/
```

We've seen most of this stuff before. The only things we should mention are the inclusion of our **http**, **html**, and **form** modules from our support library. The form module manages the **RegistrationForm** structure we discussed earlier.

Apart from that, we have prototypes for each of the form handling functions we will implement below. Looking at these you can pretty much intuit how the overall processing flow will occur.

```
BOOL WINAPI GetExtensionVersion(HSE_VERSION_INFO *pVersion)
{
  pVersion->dwExtensionVersion = EXTN_VERSION;
  strncpy(pVersion->lpszExtensionDesc, EXTN_DESCRIPTION,
                              HSE_MAX_EXT_DLL_NAME_LEN);

  Debug((DEST, pVersion->lpszExtensionDesc));

  return TRUE;
}
```

GetExtensionVersion is as we would expect—so no need to comment further here.

```
DWORD WINAPI HttpExtensionProc(EXTENSION_CONTROL_BLOCK *pECB)
{
    /*  Define the form data structure. The value fields are filled in
        by Form_Init() by parsing values out of the QUERY_STRING (for a
        GET) and
        the request body (for a POST). */
    FormField RegistrationForm[] = {
        /* Name      Value    Description                 Required Valid*/
        {"name",    NULL,    "Name of Customer",          TRUE,    TRUE},
        {"address", NULL,    "Address of Customer",       TRUE,    TRUE},
        {"phone",   NULL,    "Phone Number of Customer",  FALSE,   TRUE},
        {"email",   NULL,    "Email Address of Customer", TRUE,    TRUE},
        {"",        NULL,    NULL,                        FALSE,   TRUE}
    };

    /* Process Request and generate an OK or an error response */
    if (RegistrationForm_Request(pECB, RegistrationForm))
        RegistrationForm_OKResponse(pECB, RegistrationForm);
    else
        RegistrationForm_ErrorResponse(pECB, RegistrationForm);

    Form_Cleanup(RegistrationForm);
    return HSE_STATUS_SUCCESS;
}
```

HttpExtensionProc is invoked by the server when it receives the request containing the form. The first thing we do is initialize our **RegistrationForm**. This definition should match the one in the HTML document (isasample4.htm). We'll then process the request using **RegistrationForm_Request**, which takes as parameters pointers to the ECB and the registration form.

```
BOOL RegistrationForm_Request(EXTENSION_CONTROL_BLOCK *pECB,
                                              FormField *pForm)
/*  Depending on the METHOD defined in the HTML form, process the
    request accordingly. */
{
    BOOL bRetCode = FALSE;

    if (0 == strcmp(pECB->lpszMethod, "get") ||
        0 == strcmp(pECB->lpszMethod, "GET"))
        bRetCode = RegistrationForm_GetRequest(pECB, pForm);

    if (0 == strcmp(pECB->lpszMethod, "post") ||
        0 == strcmp(pECB->lpszMethod, "POST"))
        bRetCode = RegistrationForm_PostRequest(pECB, pForm);

    return bRetCode;
}
```

RegistrationForm_Request will determine whether the request is a GET or a POST by looking at the **pECB->lpszMethod** and calls the appropriate handler—**RegistrationForm_GetRequest** or **RegistrationForm_PostRequest**.

```
BOOL RegistrationForm_GetRequest(EXTENSION_CONTROL_BLOCK *pECB,
                                              FormField
                                              *pRegForm)
{
    /*  Initialise the form data structure with the query string.
        Form_Init()
        will return FALSE if any field marked as Required does not have
        a value entered by the user. */

    return Form_Init(pRegForm, pECB->lpszQueryString);
}
```

RegistrationForm_GetRequest is simple. It uses the **Form_Init** function from our **form** module to break out the field name/value pairs into the **RegistrationForm**. **Form_Init** returns TRUE if all the required fields in the request have a value, otherwise it returns FALSE.

```
BOOL RegistrationForm_PostRequest(EXTENSION_CONTROL_BLOCK *pECB,
                                              FormField
                                              *pForm)
{
```

```
BOOL        bRetCode = TRUE;
DWORD       dwBytesToRead;
LPSTR       lpszBuff;

/* Allocate some space to hold the form data sent in the body of
     the  POST request */
lpszBuff = Mem_Alloc(pECB->cbTotalBytes+1);

/* zero out memory - supposedly done by Mem_Alloc() */
memset(lpszBuff, '\0', pECB->cbTotalBytes);

/* Copy data already stored by the server */
strncpy(lpszBuff, pECB->lpbData, pECB->cbAvailable );

/* Grab any remaining data from the client */
if ((dwBytesToRead=pECB->cbTotalBytes - pECB->cbAvailable) > 0)
    pECB->ReadClient(pECB->ConnID, (LPVOID)(lpszBuff +
                                    pECB->cbAvailable),
                                    &dwBytesToRead);

bRetCode = Form_Init(pForm, lpszBuff);
Mem_Free(lpszBuff);
return bRetCode;
}
```

RegistrationForm_PostRequest is a little more convoluted. The first thing we do is allocate a buffer **lpszBuff** and copy into it the current contents of **pECB->lpbData**. **lpbData** is the buffer the server uses to store the client request. However, the server does not read the request message all at once, as it only has a limited amount of buffer space. The number of bytes the server currently holds in **pECB->lpbData** is **pECB->cbAvailable**. The total number of bytes expected is kept in **pECB> cbTotalBytes**. The difference between these two values is the number of bytes the server has yet to read. Notice that we check this and, if necessary, do a subsequent read, concatenating the rest of the request onto our buffer **lpszBuff**. Once the full request has been read, **Form_Init** is called to initialize the form with the form data we've just read.

The handlers both return TRUE if the form was valid, otherwise FALSE. This return value percolates back up to **HttpExtensionProc**, which then determines which response handler should be called—**RegistrationForm_OKResponse** if all the fields in the request were valid, or **RegistrationForm_ErrorResponse** if any one of the fields was invalid.

```
VOID RegistrationForm_OKResponse(EXTENSION_CONTROL_BLOCK *pECB,
                                                  FormField
                                                  *pForm)

    /* Generate a successful HTML response. */
{
    HtmlPage      *pPage;
    LPSTR          lpszBuff = Mem_Alloc(MAX_BUFF_SIZE+1);

    /* Send HTTP header to client */
    HttpHeader_ExtnWrite(pECB, NULL, "Content-type: text/html\r\n");

    /* Send Body of request to client */

    pPage = HtmlPage_New();
    HtmlPage_Start(pPage, "Registration Form");
    HtmlPage_Append(pPage, "<H1><B>Registration Form</B></H1>\r\n");

    sprintf(lpszBuff, "<HR>\n\r<P><H3><I>Dear %s,"
                "thank you for registering with us.</I></H3>\r\n",
                Form_FindParamValue(pForm, "name"));
    HtmlPage_Append(pPage, lpszBuff);

    sprintf(lpszBuff,
                "<P>We shall email your confirmation in 2 days to %s\r\n",
                Form_FindParamValue(pForm, "email"));
    HtmlPage_Append(pPage, lpszBuff);

    HtmlPage_Append(pPage, "<P><IMG SRC=\"/samples/images/powered.gif\" "
                                    "ALT=\"Microsoft Internet Explorer
                                          for NT\">\r\n");
    HtmlPage_Append(pPage, "<HR>\r\n");
    HtmlPage_End(pPage);
    HtmlPage_ExtnWrite(pECB, pPage);
    HtmlPage_Delete(pPage);

    Mem_Free(lpszBuff);
}
```

RegistrationForm_OKResponse generates an HTML response as per Figure 10.3. Note that the form field values for the customer name and their email address are extracted from the **RegistrationForm** (pointed to by **pForm**) using **Form_FindParamValue**.

```
VOID RegistrationForm_ErrorResponse(EXTENSION_CONTROL_BLOCK *pECB,
                                                          FormField
                                                          *pForm)
{
    /*  Generate an HTML error response - this is probably due to one or
         more required  fields not being completed by the user. */
    FormField    *pField;
    HtmlPage     *pPage;
    DWORD        bFirst=TRUE;

    /* Send HTTP header to client */
    HttpHeader_ExtnWrite(pECB, NULL, "Content-type: text/html\n\r");

    /* Send Body of request to client */

    pPage = HtmlPage_New();
    HtmlPage_Start(pPage, "Registration Form");
    HtmlPage_Append(pPage, "<H1><B>Registration Form</B></H1>\r\n");

    HtmlPage_Append(pPage, "<HR>\r\n<P><H3><I>Input Error</I></H3>\r\n");
    HtmlPage_Append(pPage, "<P>You must enter a value for: ");

    for (pField = pForm; *pField->Name != '\0'; pField++)    {
        if (pField->Value == NULL && pField->Required) {
            if (!bFirst)
                HtmlPage_Append(pPage, ", ");
            bFirst=FALSE;
            HtmlPage_Append(pPage, pField->Name);
        }
    }

    HtmlPage_Append(pPage, "<HR>\r\n");
    HtmlPage_End(pPage);

    HtmlPage_ExtnWrite(pECB, pPage);
    HtmlPage_Delete(pPage);
}
```

RegistrationForm_ErrorResponse is called when the user doesn't fill in one or more required fields. Rather than just informing the user that *some* fields are missing, we iterate through the form looking for fields the user has omitted by making sure that each required field has a non-NULL value. We create a list of any omitted fields and inform the user that they are required. An example of this response is shown in Figure 10.4.

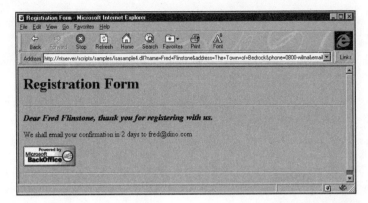

Figure 10.3

A successful registration response.

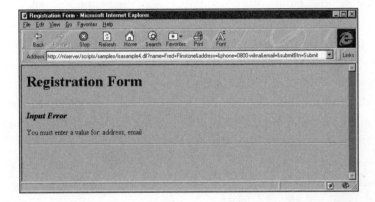

Figure 10.4

An unsuccessful registration response.

Maintaining A User Authentication Database

Having looked at some fairly simple examples, we now illustrate a more complex ISA containing back-end database connectivity. We will actually use the database we construct here in our "Object Connector" filter example in the next section.

There are many different ways of accessing a database from an ISA. In a Windows environment, the normal choice would be to use the ODBC API to manipulate an ODBC-compliant data source such as Microsoft's own SQL Server or a third-party database such as Oracle. Alternatively, the database could be as simple as a flat file containing delimited records.

Here we have chosen the middle ground and elected to implement a database using the public domain Berkeley DB package. Both binary and source code versions of DB have been included on the CD-ROM included with this book with the kind permission of Sleepycat Software Inc. The version we have provided is 1.72 and is not the latest. You are encouraged to send inquiries to **db@sleepycat.com** or visit **www.sleepycat.com/db** for licensing information and the latest source and binary versions.

DB databases are just stored as files in the file system—no fancy servers are required. Three different types of database access method are supported—btree, hash, and sequential record. We have chosen the btree method.

Our database contains user authentication information, which we will use later in our "Authentication Filter" example to map a logical user name and password onto a valid NT name and password that can then be used to authenticate the user to the system. In addition to the two sets of name and password, we also store some additional information including the date and time the user last logged in and an application-specific home directory, which can be used to map the URL onto a user-specific content area. The user data is simply stored as a key/value pair, where the key is the user name and the values are the remaining user attributes, each delimited by a ':' character.

User Interface

Our user interface for the application consists of four predefined HTML pages. A main page lists the maintenance operations available: Add, Find, Delete, and List. Add adds a user to the database, Find finds a specified user, Delete deletes the specified user, and List outputs the list of all users and their associated information.

Each of the operations has its own page for entering appropriate details (except for List, which doesn't require any). Each of these pages calls our ISA http://ntserver/scripts/samples/isasample5.dll. The ISA uses the hidden field **maintop** inside each form to work out which operation to perform.

The HTML source for just the main and user add pages is defined in Listings 10.5 and 10.6. The others are on the CD-ROM enclosed with this book.

Listing 10.5   The main User Maintenance page.

```
<html>
<head>
<title>User Maintenance</title>
</head>
<body>
<h1 align=left>User Maintenance Form</h1>
<h2 align=left>Choose a maintenance operation</h2>
<hr>
<pre>
<A HREF ="/samples/isasample5/isasample5_add.htm">Add User
<A HREF ="/samples/isasample5/isasample5_find.htm">Find User
<A HREF ="/samples/isasample5/isasample5_delete.htm">Delete User
<A HREF ="http://ntserver/scripts/samples/
isasample5.dll?maintop=list">List Users
</pre>
<hr>
</body>
</html>
```

Listing 10.6   The Add User page.

```
<html>
<head>
<title>User Maintenance</title>
</head>
<body>
<h1 align=left>User Maintenance Form</h1>
<h2 align=left>Add User</h2>
<hr>
<pre>Please enter user information below:</pre>
<form action="http://ntserver/scripts/samples/isasample5.dll"
method="POST">
<input TYPE="hidden" NAME="maintop" VALUE="add">
<pre>User Name          <input type=text size=40 maxlength=256
                    name="username"> (Required)</pre>
<pre>User Password      <input type=password size=40 maxlength=256
                    name="userpasswd"> (Required)</pre>
<pre>NT Logon Name      <input type=text size=20 maxlength=256
                    name="ntlogonname"> (Required)</pre>
<pre>NT Password        <input type=password size=20 maxlength=256
                    name="ntpassword"> (Required)</pre>
<pre>Home Directory     <input type=text size=20 maxlength=256
                    name="homedir"> (Required)</pre>
<div align=left>
<pre>
```

```
<input type=submit name="submitBtn" value="Add"><input type=reset
name="resetBtn"
                                                        value="Reset">

</pre>
</div>
<pre><hr></pre>
</form>
</body>

</html>
```

ISA Implementation

We won't go through the whole implementation, rather, we'll just provide the top half of the source code. This will be sufficient to see how the Add operation is implemented. The rest is on the CD-ROM enclosed with this book.

When the ISA gets the request, **HttpExtensionProc** first determines whether the request is a GET or a PUT. This ISA will handle both methods. If it's neither, we generate an HTML error message.

UserMaintForm_HandleResponse is responsible for extracting the "maintop" parameter from the query string to determine which operation should be applied. If it can't find a matching operation it issues an error message. Otherwise it invokes the handler for the operation.

The handler used is expected to totally encapsulate the operation. **UserMaintForm_HandleAdd** is the handler for the add operation. You can see that it uses our simple form abstraction to handle the add maintenance form rather than extracting the form fields from the query string directly.

After extracting the name of the user from the query string, it uses the **User_Add** operation from our user database module to add a new record to the database. Note how it uses **Form_FindParamValue** to get the value of each field from the form in **pForm**.

The rest is pretty self-explanatory, so we'll leave it to you to work through Listing 10.7.

Listing 10.7 Code for isample5.c—Maintaining a user authentication database.

```
/*************************************************************************
 * Name:            isasample5.c
 * Description:     an ISA DLL that is loaded by ISS in response to the URL
 *                  http://ntserver/scripts/samples/isasample5.dll?
 * Function:        Maintains user information stored in the user
 *                      information
 *                  database used for authenticating user credentials.
 * DLL Location:    c:\inetpub\scripts\samples\isasample5.dll
 * HTML Location:   c:\inetpub\wwwroot\samples\isasample5\isasample5.htm
 *************************************************************************/


#define WIN32_LEAN_AN_MEAN
#include <windows.h>
#include <httpext.h>
#include <stdio.h>

/* Imported Library Modules */
#include <debug.h>
#include <mem.h>
#include <http.h>
#include <html.h>
#include <form.h>
#include <user.h>
#include <authdb.h>


/* Defines */
#define EXTN_VERSION MAKELONG(HSE_VERSION_MINOR,
                              HSE_VERSION_MAJOR)
#define EXTN_DESCRIPTION "User Database Maintenance Extension"


#define MAX_MAINT_OP 8

/* Private Prototypes */
BOOL UserMaintForm_Request(EXTENSION_CONTROL_BLOCK *pECB);
BOOL UserMaintForm_GetRequest(EXTENSION_CONTROL_BLOCK *pECB);
LPSTR UserMaintForm_PostRequest(EXTENSION_CONTROL_BLOCK *pECB);

INT  UserMaintForm_HandleResponse(EXTENSION_CONTROL_BLOCK *pECB,
                                  LPSTR lpszQueryString);
INT  UserMaintForm_HandleAdd(EXTENSION_CONTROL_BLOCK *pECB,
                             LPSTR lpszQueryString);
```

```
INT  UserMaintForm_HandleDelete(EXTENSION_CONTROL_BLOCK *pECB,
                                LPSTR lpszQueryString);
INT  UserMaintForm_HandleFind(EXTENSION_CONTROL_BLOCK *pECB,
                              LPSTR lpszQueryString);
INT  UserMaintForm_HandleList(EXTENSION_CONTROL_BLOCK *pECB);


VOID UserMaintForm_AddedOK(EXTENSION_CONTROL_BLOCK *pECB,
                           FormField *pForm);
VOID UserMaintForm_FoundOK(EXTENSION_CONTROL_BLOCK *pECB,
                           LPSTR lpszUserName, PUSER_INFO pUserInfo);
VOID UserMaintForm_DeletedOK(EXTENSION_CONTROL_BLOCK *pECB,
                             LPSTR lpszUserName);
VOID UserMaintForm_Error(EXTENSION_CONTROL_BLOCK *pECB,
                         LPSTR lpszErrMsg);
VOID UserMaintForm_IncompleteResponse(EXTENSION_CONTROL_BLOCK *pECB,
                                      FormField *pForm);


/* Globals */

/* Location of user authentication database */
LPSTR   lpsUserDbPath = "C:\\temp\\user.dbm";


/***********************************************************************/


BOOL WINAPI GetExtensionVersion(HSE_VERSION_INFO *pVersion)
{
    pVersion->dwExtensionVersion = EXTN_VERSION;
    strncpy(pVersion->lpszExtensionDesc, EXTN_DESCRIPTION,
                                         HSE_MAX_EXT_DLL_NAME_LEN);
    Debug((DEST, pVersion->lpszExtensionDesc));
    return TRUE;
}


DWORD WINAPI HttpExtensionProc(EXTENSION_CONTROL_BLOCK *pECB)
{
    DWORD   dwRet = HSE_STATUS_SUCCESS;
    LPSTR   lpszQueryString = NULL;

    /* Process Request and generate appropriate responses */
    if (0 == strcmp(pECB->lpszMethod, "GET"))
    lpszQueryString = pECB->lpszQueryString;
    else if (0 == strcmp(pECB->lpszMethod, "POST"))
        lpszQueryString = UserMaintForm_PostRequest(pECB);

    if (lpszQueryString)
        UserMaintForm_HandleResponse(pECB, lpszQueryString);
```

```
        else
            UserMaintForm_Error(pECB, "Invalid Method - must be GET or
                                POST");

    Mem_Free(lpszQueryString);
    Mem_DumpInUse();
    return dwRet;
}


LPSTR UserMaintForm_PostRequest(EXTENSION_CONTROL_BLOCK *pECB)
{
    LPSTR    lpszRet = NULL;
    DWORD    dwBytesToRead;
    CHAR     *lpszBuff;

    lpszBuff = Mem_Alloc(pECB->cbTotalBytes);
     memset(lpszBuff, '\0', pECB->cbTotalBytes);
    strncpy(lpszBuff, pECB->lpbData, pECB->cbAvailable );
    if ((dwBytesToRead=pECB->cbTotalBytes - pECB->cbAvailable) > 0)
        pECB->ReadClient(pECB->ConnID, (LPVOID)
                        (lpszBuff + pECB->cbAvailable),
                        &dwBytesToRead);


    return lpszBuff;
}


INT UserMaintForm_HandleResponse(EXTENSION_CONTROL_BLOCK *pECB,
                                LPSTR lpszQueryString)
{
    INT         ret = 0;
    LPSTR       lpszMaintOp;

    lpszMaintOp = HttpQueryString_GetParamValue(lpszQueryString,
                                            "maintop");
    if (lpszMaintOp == NULL)
        UserMaintForm_Error(pECB, "Unknown operation");
    else {
        if (0 == strcmp(lpszMaintOp, "add"))
            ret = UserMaintForm_HandleAdd(pECB, lpszQueryString);
        if (0 == strcmp(lpszMaintOp, "find"))
            ret = UserMaintForm_HandleFind(pECB, lpszQueryString);
        if (0 == strcmp(lpszMaintOp, "delete"))
            ret = UserMaintForm_HandleDelete(pECB, lpszQueryString);
        if (0 == strcmp(lpszMaintOp, "list"))
            ret = UserMaintForm_HandleList(pECB);
    }
```

```
    Mem_Free(lpszMaintOp);
    return ret;
}


/***************** ADD USER *********************************************/

INT UserMaintForm_HandleAdd(EXTENSION_CONTROL_BLOCK *pECB,
                           LPSTR lpszQueryString)
{
    INT        ret = 1;
    USER_INFO   UserInfo;

    FormField UserAddForm[] = {
        /* Name           Value    Description                 Required Valid*/
        {"username",      NULL,    "Name of User",             TRUE,    TRUE},
        {"userpasswd",    NULL,    "User Password",            TRUE,    TRUE},
        {"ntlogonname",   NULL,    "User's NT logon name",     TRUE,    TRUE},
        {"ntpassword",    NULL,    "User's NT password",       TRUE,    TRUE},
        {"homedir",       NULL,    "User's home directory",    TRUE,    TRUE},
        {"",              NULL,    NULL,                       FALSE,   TRUE}
    };


    FormField *pForm = UserAddForm;

    if (!Form_Init(pForm, lpszQueryString))
        UserMaintForm_IncompleteResponse(pECB, pForm);
    else {
        /* Initialise the user database */
        User_Init(lpsUserDbPath);

        /* Set the record to be added */
        strncpy(UserInfo.passwd, Form_FindParamValue(pForm,
                    "userpasswd"),
                    MAX_PASSWD);
        strncpy(UserInfo.NTuserName, Form_FindParamValue(pForm,
                    "ntlogonname"),
                    MAX_USERNAME);
        strncpy(UserInfo.NTpasswd, Form_FindParamValue(pForm,
                    "ntpassword"),
                    MAX_PASSWD);
        strncpy(UserInfo.homedir, Form_FindParamValue(pForm, "homedir"),
                    MAX_HOMEDIR);
        setLastLoginTime(UserInfo.lastLoginTime);
```

```
            switch (ret=User_Add(lpsUserDbPath, Form_FindParamValue(pForm,
                      "username"),
                      &UserInfo)) {
        case -1:
            UserMaintForm_Error(pECB, "Internal Error while adding
                                user");
            break;
        case 0:
            UserMaintForm_AddedOK(pECB, pForm);
            break;
        case 1:
            UserMaintForm_Error(pECB, "This user already exists in the
                                database");
            break;
        }
    }
    Form_Cleanup(pForm);
    return ret;
}


VOID UserMaintForm_AddedOK(EXTENSION_CONTROL_BLOCK *pECB,
                                              FormField *pForm)
{
    HtmlPage    *pPage;
    LPSTR       lpBuff = Mem_Alloc(MAX_BUFF_SIZE);

    /* Send HTTP header to client */
    HttpHeader_ExtnWrite(pECB, NULL, "Content-type: text/html\r\n");

    /* Send Body of request to client */
    pPage = HtmlPage_New();
    HtmlPage_Start(pPage, "User Maintenance");
    HtmlPage_Append(pPage, "<H1><B>User Maintenance</B></H1>\r\n");
    sprintf(lpBuff,
      "<HR>\n\r<P><H3><I>User information for %s added</I></H3>\r\n",
      Form_FindParamValue(pForm, "username"));
    HtmlPage_Append(pPage, lpBuff);
    HtmlPage_Append(pPage, "<HR>\r\n");
    HtmlPage_End(pPage);
    HtmlPage_ExtnWrite(pECB, pPage);
    HtmlPage_Delete(pPage);

    Mem_Free(lpBuff);
}
```

```
VOID UserMaintForm_IncompleteResponse(EXTENSION_CONTROL_BLOCK *pECB,
                                                             FormField
                                                              *pForm)
{
    /*  Generate an HTML error response - this is probably due to one or
        more required
        fields not being completed by the user. */
    FormField   *pField;
    HtmlPage     *pPage;
    DWORD        bFirst=TRUE;

    /* Send HTTP header to client */
    HttpHeader_ExtnWrite(pECB, NULL, "Content-type: text/html\n\r");

    /* Send Body of request to client */
    pPage = HtmlPage_New();
    HtmlPage_Start(pPage, "User Maintenance");
    HtmlPage_Append(pPage, "<H1><B>User Maintenance</B></H1>\r\n");
    HtmlPage_Append(pPage, "<HR>\r\n<P><H3><I>Input Error</I></H3>\r\n");
    HtmlPage_Append(pPage, "<P>You must enter a value for: ");

    for (pField = pForm; *pField->Name != '\0'; pField++)    {
        if (pField->Value == NULL && pField->Required) {
            if (!bFirst)
                HtmlPage_Append(pPage, ", ");
            bFirst=FALSE;
            HtmlPage_Append(pPage, pField->Name);
        }
    }
    HtmlPage_Append(pPage, "<HR>\r\n");
    HtmlPage_End(pPage);

    HtmlPage_ExtnWrite(pECB, pPage);
    HtmlPage_Delete(pPage);
}
```

Creating And Deploying A Filter

In this section, we'll look closely at how we build and deploy real filters. We begin with a tutorial and then move on to progressively more complex examples in an attempt to exercise as much ISAPI filter functionality as possible.

Following the tutorial we present three simple custom filter applications:

- A custom logging filter
- A custom authentication filter
- An object connector filter

The logging and authentication filters are commonly cited examples and are similar to others you will see around. We have made the authentication filter slightly more interesting by having it access the user authentication database we created in our last ISA example.

The object connector filter is a little more ambitious and uses some interesting techniques for bending the server to do what we want.

If you are a novice developer, then we suggest you start with the tutorial. In fact, if you haven't already, you should start with the ISA tutorial at the beginning of this chapter as it contains information directly relevant to this one.

Building A Filter—A Step-By-Step Tutorial

In this tutorial, we'll walk through the process of creating a filter from scratch. Because we are creating a DLL, the process we'll follow is very similar to the one we used in our ISA tutorial. Where there is lots of similarity, we won't go into as much detail here—especially details that regard the operation of Developer Studio.

Rather than concentrating on a specific notification type, we will construct a skeleton filter that you could use as the basis for developing your own specific filter applications. Our filter contains simple handlers for each type of notification possible, each illustrating a small aspect of the notification.

The filter will use the **Debug** macro from our **debug** module to provide a trace of the filter's execution path. This will provide some confirmation of the order in which notifications occur within the request life cycle and also the number of times they occur.

Another use for this filter would be to debug *another* filter or ISA. Because it has a passive role, just outputting notification information via a debug window, it could be used to monitor the raw data stream and any other useful request or response information.

Create A New Project

Our first step is to start up Visual C++ and create a new **Project Workspace** of type *DLL* and give the workspace a name—in this example we have used filtersample1. This results in the project directory c:\Msdev\projects\filtersample1 being created.

Project settings should include:

- General: Microsoft Foundation Classes set to Not using MFC.

- C Preprocessor: WIN32 *is* defined, and ../iisutils/ defined in Additional include directories. The latter is only needed for access to our **debug** module and assumes the iisutils project directory has been copied from the CD-ROM enclosed with this book into your projects directory.

- Link: default libraries are *not* ignored, and ../iisutils/libiisutils.lib is included in the list of **Object/library modules**. Once again, the latter is only needed if you want to use our **debug** module and have installed the library and associated header files; otherwise you can omit it.

Define The DLL Entry Points

Defining the DLL entry points uses the same process used for an ISA—except the function names are slightly different. The two entry points that *must* be exported from a filter DLL are **GetFilterVersion** and **HttpFilterProc**. If you want to perform allocation and deallocation of filter-wide resources, you will also want to export **DllMain**, as this is the function invoked by the server when the filter is loaded and subsequently unloaded. We used **DllMain** in our example, so we'll include it as part of the exported DLL interface.

Entry points must be specified in a DEF file. Our example DEF file filtersample1.def looks like this. Create this file and insert it into the project:

```
EXPORTS
GetFilterVersion
HttpFilterProc
DllMain
```

Include Files And Other Preliminary Definitions

Next, create a new text file called filtersample1.c and insert it into the project. Now we're ready to implement our filter. Listing 10.8 shows our preliminary work.

We begin by including windows.h because it contains the myriad of basic Win32 SDK definitions that we take for granted. The good news is that by defining **WIN32_LEAN_AN_MEAN**, you can significantly reduce the size of windows.h and speed up your compilation slightly.

Just as important, you must include httpfilt.h because it contains the definitions and prototypes needed for ISAPI filters—things like **HTTP_FILTER_CONTEXT**, and other things.

Next, we define prototypes for each of the notification handlers (and any support functions we will be implementing). Note that each notification handler is passed a pointer to the **HTTP_FILTER_CONTEXT** for the request along with a data structure containing information specific to the notification.

Listing 10.8 Code for filtersample1.c—Skeleton and Debugging Filter.

```
/*****************************************************************************
* Name:          filtersample1.c
* Description:   an ISAPI filter DLL that is loaded by ISS on startup
and invoked
*                in response to all possible event notifications at the
                 default priority.
* DLL Location:  c:\inetpub\scripts\samples\filtersample1.dll
*****************************************************************************/
#define WIN32_LEAN_AN_MEAN
#include <windows.h>
#include <httpfilt.h>
#include <stdio.h>

/* Imported Library Modules */
#include <debug.h>

/* Defines */
#define FILTER_DESCRIPTION "Skeleton Filter"
#define BUFF_MAX 64

/* Private Prototypes */
DWORD HandleEvent_ReadRawData(HTTP_FILTER_CONTEXT *pFC,
                                               PHTTP_FILTER_RAW_DATA
                                                pReadData);
DWORD HandleEvent_Authentication(HTTP_FILTER_CONTEXT *pFC,
                                               PHTTP_FILTER_AUTHENT
                                                pAuthData);
```

```
DWORD HandleEvent_AccessDenied(HTTP_FILTER_CONTEXT *pFC,
                                              PHTTP_FILTER_ACCESS_DENIED
                                              pAccessData);
DWORD HandleEvent_PreProcHeaders(HTTP_FILTER_CONTEXT *pFC,
                                              PHTTP_FILTER_PREPROC_HEADERS
                                              pPreProcData);
DWORD HandleEvent_UrlMap(HTTP_FILTER_CONTEXT *pFC,
                                              PHTTP_FILTER_URL_MAP
                                              pUrlData);
DWORD HandleEvent_SendRawData(HTTP_FILTER_CONTEXT *pFC,
                                              PHTTP_FILTER_RAW_DATA
                                              pSendData);
DWORD HandleEvent_Log(HTTP_FILTER_CONTEXT *pFC,
                                              PHTTP_FILTER_LOG
                                              pLogData);
DWORD HandleEvent_EndOfNetSession(HTTP_FILTER_CONTEXT *pFC);

/************************************************************************/
```

Define DllMain

In this example, we have illustrated a very basic use of the **DllMain** function. Remember this is called by the server when the DLL is first loaded and then again when the DLL is unloaded. It also called when a thread attaches to or detaches from our DLL. This is the ideal place for allocating and deallocating filter-wide resources such as memory buffers.

```
BOOL WINAPI DllMain(HINSTANCE hinstDLL, DWORD dvReason, LPVOID lpv)
/* DLL main function is executed on DLL loading and unloading. Note
   that if IIS has cached the DLL then this will only be called the first
   time the DLL is loaded and when it is unloaded. */
{
    CHAR    ModuleName[BUFF_MAX+1];

    switch (dvReason) {
        case DLL_PROCESS_ATTACH:
                GetModuleFileName(NULL, ModuleName, BUFF_MAX);
                Debug((DEST, "filtersample1: DLL loaded by - %s",
                        ModuleName));
                GetModuleFileName(hinstDLL, ModuleName, BUFF_MAX);
                Debug((DEST, "filtersample1: DLL module name is - %s",
                        ModuleName));
            break;
```

```
            case DLL_PROCESS_DETACH:
                Debug((DEST, "filtersample1: DLL being unloaded"));
                break;
            case DLL_THREAD_ATTACH:
                Debug((DEST, "filtersample1: Thread entering DllMain"));
                break;
            case DLL_THREAD_DETACH:
                Debug((DEST, "filtersample1: Thread leaving DllMain"));
                break;
    }
    return TRUE;
}
```

Define GetFilterVersion

Next we must define **GetFilterVersion**. This function is called by the server when it *first* loads our filter DLL and is used to set the filter version and description and then to specify the behavior of the filter.

```
BOOL WINAPI GetFilterVersion(HTTP_FILTER_VERSION *pVersion)
/* Entry point for ISAPI filter DLL */
{
            /* Set version */
            pVersion->dwFilterVersion = HTTP_FILTER_REVISION;

            /* Provide a short description of the filter */
            strncpy(pVersion->lpszFilterDesc, FILTER_DESCRIPTION,
             SF_MAX_FILTER_DESC_LEN);

            Debug((DEST, pVersion->lpszFilterDesc));

            /* Set the event we want to be notified about and the
               notification priority */
            pVersion->dwFlags = (SF_NOTIFY_SECURE_PORT |
                    SF_NOTIFY_NONSEURE_PORT |
                    SF_NOTIFY_READ_RAW_DATA |
                    SF_NOTIFY_AUTHENTICATION |
                    SF_NOTIFY_ACCESS_DENIED |
                    SF_NOTIFY_PREPROC_HEADERS |
                    SF_NOTIFY_URL_MAP |
                    SF_NOTIFY_SEND_RAW_DATA |
                    SF_NOTIFY_LOG |
                    SF_NOTIFY_END_OF_NET_SESSION |
                    SF_NOTIFY_ORDER_DEFAULT);
            return TRUE;
}
```

First, we set our filter version to the version of ISAPI supported by our server using the built-in definition **HTTP_FILTER_REVISION**. If we were ever to attempt to run our filter on a server whose ISAPI revision level was incompatible with the version we built the DLL with, then the server could reject the filter.

We then set the filter description we defined in **FILTER_DESCRIPTION**. This is potentially useful to a server administrator who needs to find out via the server which DLLs are currently loaded.

The most important step is to define our filter flags by OR'ing together:

- The kind of connections we want our filter to respond to—**SF_NOTIFY_SECURE_PORT** or **SF_NOTIFY_NONSECURE_PORT**

- The notifications we want to receive—in this case, all possible notifications such as **SF_ NOTIFY_READ_RAW_DATA**, **SF_NOTIFY_AUTHENTICATION**, **SF_NOTIFY_ACCESS_DENIED**, **SF_NOTIFY_PREPROC_HEADERS**, **SF_NOTIFY_URL_MAP**, **SF_NOTIFY_SEND_RAW_DATA**, **SF_NOTIFY_LOG**, or **SF_NOTIFY_END_OF_NET_SESSION**

- The priority our filter should have in the chain of filters capable of responding to these notifications—**SF_NOTIFY_ORDER_DEFAULT**

We have chosen to set our filter at the default priority because the filter is just an observer. We don't really care when our filter gets invoked in the notification chain.

Define HttpFilterProc

We must now define **HttpFilterProc**. This function is the main entry point to our filter. It is invoked for *every* notification we have registered to receive in **GetFilterProc**.

```
DWORD WINAPI HttpFilterProc(HTTP_FILTER_CONTEXT *pFC,
                                 DWORD dwNotificationType, VOID *pvData)
/* Entry point for ISAPI filter DLL—this function is where the work is
   really done */
{
    DWORD dwRet = SF_STATUS_REQ_NEXT_NOTIFICATION;

    switch (dwNotificationType) {
        case SF_NOTIFY_READ_RAW_DATA:
            dwRet = HandleEvent_ReadRawData(pFC,
                                    (PHTTP_FILTER_RAW_DATA)pvData);
```

```
        break;
    case SF_NOTIFY_AUTHENTICATION:
        dwRet = HandleEvent_Authentication(pFC,
                                    (PHTTP_FILTER_AUTHENT)pvData);
        break;
    case SF_NOTIFY_ACCESS_DENIED:
        dwRet = HandleEvent_AccessDenied(pFC,
                                 (PHTTP_FILTER_ACCESS_DENIED)pvData);
        break;
    case SF_NOTIFY_PREPROC_HEADERS:
        dwRet = HandleEvent_PreProcHeaders(pFC,
                               (PHTTP_FILTER_PREPROC_HEADERS)pvData);
        break;
    case SF_NOTIFY_URL_MAP:
        dwRet = HandleEvent_UrlMap(pFC,
                                    (PHTTP_FILTER_URL_MAP)pvData);
        break;
    case SF_NOTIFY_SEND_RAW_DATA:
        dwRet = HandleEvent_SendRawData(pFC,
                                  (PHTTP_FILTER_RAW_DATA)pvData);
        break;
    case SF_NOTIFY_LOG:
        dwRet = HandleEvent_Log(pFC, (PHTTP_FILTER_LOG)pvData);
        break;
    case SF_NOTIFY_END_OF_NET_SESSION:
        dwRet = HandleEvent_EndOfNetSession(pFC);
        break;
    }
    return dwRet;
}
```

The server passes us a pointer to the **HTTP_FILTER_CONTEXT** for the request in **pFC**, followed by the notification type in **dwNotificationType** and a notification-specific data structure in **pvData**.

We switch on **dwNotificationType** to invoke the handler appropriate to the notification. For each handler that needs it, we pass the notification-specific data structure as a parameter—casting it to the correct type for the notification.

Each handler needs **pFC** in order to reference the filter context information and callback functions such as **AllocMem**.

By default, we have set our return status from **HttpFilterProc** to be **SF_STATUS_REQ_NEXT_NOTIFICATION**, which tells the server to pass control to the next filter in the chain for this notification type. This is really just a catch-all, because we let each handler determine what happens next by allowing it to modify the return status. For example, if the handler encounters a fatal error (such as not enough memory), then it will return **SF_STATUS_REQ_ERROR** to the server.

Define Notification Handlers

For each notification we have registered to receive, we define a corresponding handler. You don't have to do this, but we recommend it as it provides some reasonable encapsulation of each notification and makes for a much more readable program.

In this example, we have defined an event handler for every notification type. These handlers are passive observers in that they don't modify the server behavior at all—they just report on it using our **Debug** macro.

Most of the handlers are self-explanatory, so we won't explain them any further here.

```
DWORD HandleEvent_ReadRawData(HTTP_FILTER_CONTEXT *pFC,
                                                    PHTTP_FILTER_RAW_DATA
                                                    pReadData)
{
    DWORD   dwRet = SF_STATUS_REQ_NEXT_NOTIFICATION;
    DWORD   dwBytes;
    LPSTR   lpszBuffer;

    /* Capture no more than BUFF_MAX characters of the raw request */

    lpszBuffer = pFC->AllocMem(pFC, BUFF_MAX+1, 0);
    dwBytes = min(BUFF_MAX, pReadData->cbInData);
    memcpy(lpszBuffer, pReadData->pvInData, dwBytes);
    lpszBuffer[dwBytes]='\0';
    Debug((DEST, "filtersample1: ReadRawData: Request[1-%d]=%s", dwBytes,
            lpszBuffer));
    return dwRet;
}


DWORD HandleEvent_Authentication(HTTP_FILTER_CONTEXT *pFC,
                                                    PHTTP_FILTER_AUTHENT
                                                    pAuthData)
{
    DWORD   dwRet = SF_STATUS_REQ_NEXT_NOTIFICATION;
```

```
    /* Display the user name and password */
    Debug((DEST, "filtersample1:
                Authentication: user = %s, password = %s",
                pAuthData->pszUser, pAuthData->pszPassword));
    return dwRet;
}


DWORD HandleEvent_AccessDenied(HTTP_FILTER_CONTEXT *pFC,
                                             PHTTP_FILTER_ACCESS_DENIED
                                             pAccessData)
{
    DWORD    dwRet = SF_STATUS_REQ_NEXT_NOTIFICATION;
    LPSTR    lpszReason = "Unknown";

    /* Figure out why it was denied */
    switch (pAccessData->dwReason) {
        case SF_DENIED_LOGON:
                lpszReason = "the Logon Failed";
            break;
        case SF_DENIED_RESOURCE:
                lpszReason = "you are not authorized to access this
                             resource";
            break;
        case SF_DENIED_FILTER:
                lpszReason = "the Filter denied access";
            break;
        case SF_DENIED_APPLICATION:
                lpszReason = "the ISA denied access";
            break;
        case SF_DENIED_BY_CONFIG:
                lpszReason = "the server configuration denied access";
            break;
        case (SF_DENIED_BY_CONFIG|SF_DENIED_LOGON):
                lpszReason = "the server configuration denied logon";
            break;
    }

    /* Display some information about the denial */
    Debug((DEST, "filtersample1: AccessDenied: Access denied to URL = %s,
                path = %s",
                pAccessData->pszURL, pAccessData->pszPhysicalPath));
    Debug((DEST, "filtersample1: AccessDenied: The reason is that %s",
                lpszReason));
    return dwRet;
}
```

```
DWORD HandleEvent_PreProcHeaders(HTTP_FILTER_CONTEXT *pFC,
                                            PHTTP_FILTER_PREPROC_HEADERS
                                                pPreProcData)
{
    DWORD    dwRet = SF_STATUS_REQ_NEXT_NOTIFICATION;
    CHAR     HeaderBuff[BUFF_MAX+1];
    DWORD    dwBytes = BUFF_MAX+1;

    /* Display User-Agent header */
    pPreProcData->GetHeader(pFC, "User-Agent:", HeaderBuff, &dwBytes);
    Debug((DEST, "filtersample1: PreProcHeaders: User-Agent = %s",
                                            HeaderBuff));

    return dwRet;
}


DWORD HandleEvent_UrlMap(HTTP_FILTER_CONTEXT *pFC,
                                                PHTTP_FILTER_URL_MAP
                                                pUrlData)
{

    DWORD    dwRet = SF_STATUS_REQ_NEXT_NOTIFICATION;

    /* Display URL and physical path it will be mapped to */
    Debug((DEST, "filtersample1: UrlMap: URL = %s, Physical path = %s",
                pUrlData->pszURL, pUrlData->pszPhysicalPath));
    return dwRet;
}


DWORD HandleEvent_SendRawData(HTTP_FILTER_CONTEXT *pFC,
                                                PHTTP_FILTER_RAW_DATA
                                                pSendData)
{
    DWORD    dwRet = SF_STATUS_REQ_NEXT_NOTIFICATION;
    DWORD    dwBytes;
    LPSTR    lpszBuffer;

    /* Capture no more than BUFF_MAX characters of the raw response */
    lpszBuffer = pFC->AllocMem(pFC, BUFF_MAX+1, 0);
    dwBytes = min(BUFF_MAX, pSendData->cbInData);
    memcpy(lpszBuffer, pSendData->pvInData, dwBytes);
    lpszBuffer[dwBytes]='\0';
    Debug((DEST, "filtersample1: SendRawData: Response[1-%d]=%s",
                dwBytes,
                lpszBuffer));
    return dwRet;
}
```

```
DWORD HandleEvent_Log(HTTP_FILTER_CONTEXT *pFC,
                                            PHTTP_FILTER_LOG pLogData)
{
    DWORD   dwRet = SF_STATUS_REQ_NEXT_NOTIFICATION;

    /* Display client IP address */
    Debug((DEST, "filtersample1: Log: Client IP address = %s",
            pLogData->pszClientHostName));
    return dwRet;
}

DWORD HandleEvent_EndOfNetSession(HTTP_FILTER_CONTEXT *pFC)
{
    DWORD   dwRet = SF_STATUS_REQ_NEXT_NOTIFICATION;

    Debug((DEST, "filtersample1: EndOfNetSession event"));
    return dwRet;
}
```

Build And Install The Filter

Now that the coding part is complete, we must build the DLL.

By default, Developer Studio assumes a debugging configuration. Unless you have changed this, your DLL is generated in the Debug sub-directory of the project directory—c:\Msdev\projects\filtersample1\Debug\filtersample1.dll in our example.

We can test our filter where it stands in our project directory, but it is probably good practice to copy it into a server-specific location. For now we have chosen to use the c:\InetPub\scripts\samples directory because it is already under the regime of the server.

> **Note:** You do not have to register the directory containing the filter DLL using inetmgr as you do for an ISA.
>
> When debugging, you may really not want to have to copy your DLL from your project directory to the server directory. To do this, you need to make sure the DLL is not in use by the server. Remember that by default the server loads the DLL when the server is started and unloads it when the server is stopped. In that time, the DLL is locked by the system and you will not be

able to copy a new version of your DLL on top of it. Therefore, you must stop the server using inetmgr before you build the new copy and restart it again when the build is complete.

Our last installation task is to register the filter in the registry. We do this by using regedit or regedt32 and add the full path of our filter to the registry key:

```
HKEY_LOCAL_MACHINE\SYSTEM\CurrentControlSet\Services\W3SVC\Parameters\
  Filter DLLs
```

As we discussed in Chapter 7, the position of our DLL in the list is important—especially if we want the filter to be invoked at a high priority. However, because we don't really care for this application, we just add the path c:\InetPub\scripts\samples\filtersample1.dll to the end of the comma-separated list.

Run The Filter

Now we're ready to run.

This example relies on our **Debug** macro to trace the path of its execution. This macro is implemented by the **debug** module in our support library libiisutils.lib. By default, this module sends its output to a console window implemented by the **DBMON** utility provided on the Microsoft Win32 SDK CD-ROM. We have included a compiled copy of it on the CD-ROM enclosed with this book for your convenience. For a full discussion on how to use this, please refer to the section later in this chapter "Debugging Techniques For ISAs And Filters." From here, we'll assume that you've got a **DBMON** window up and running.

If you haven't previously stopped IIS, it should still be running. However, we must stop it so that when it is restarted it picks up our newly registered DLL. Use inetmgr to stop and restart the server. If all goes well, our filter has loaded successfully.

You should see the debug messages from **DllMain** and **GetFilterVersion** in the DBMON window. If you don't, you've either compiled without the **debug** module or the DLL has failed to load. Assuming the latter, you can check by using the Event Viewer (**eventvwr**) to see if the server generated an error. You've probably misspelled the name of the DLL or forgot to insert a comma between your DLL path and the path of the previous filter DLL in the **Filters DLL** registry entry.

If you got this far, you can try accessing a resource from your browser. For example, if you built the ISA example isasample1.dll, you might try a request to http://ntserver /scripts/samples/isasample1.dll. The **DBMON** window should show the output of all the Debug messages from our filter giving you a *trace* of all the notifications received for the request (see Figure 10.5).

We suggest you try experimenting with various configurations, such as turning Basic authentication on and off to see how the authentication process works.

Key Points

Here is a reminder of some of the important things you should remember when building a filter DLL.

- Always export the DLL entry points **GetExtensionVersion** and **HttpExtensionProc** (and optionally **DllMain**) in a DEF file.

- Think carefully about the notifications you need to respond to and the priority your filter should be invoked at. Only use **SF_NOTIFY_ORDER_HIGH** if you are sure your filter must be the first to respond to all the notifications you have registered for. If in doubt, choose **SF_NOTIFY_ORDER_DEFAULT**.

- You must register the full path name of the filter in the server's registry entry **Filter DLLs**. Remember to separate entries in the list with a comma.

- Make sure your filter is thread safe by protecting code that accesses global resources with an appropriate synchronization object.

- Do not attempt to call any 16-bit DLLs or libraries from your filter.

Figure 10.5

The **DBMON** window showing a trace of the isasample1.dll request.

Logging Filter

In this example, we'll create a custom logging filter that completely overrides the server's own logging behavior.

IIS Logging Behavior

The server supports two optional logging methods—log to file and log to ODBC data source. You can disable logging completely if you want, however, this is not recommended unless the logging overhead becomes significant. There may be situations in which it is not strictly necessary to maintain a log file—for example, if the server is being front-ended by a proxy server that could take over the logging function. However, usually it's useful, especially for troubleshooting, to be able to record some history of server access.

Use of ODBC-based logging allows for flexible reporting of server activity using a report writer such as Crystal Reports or the use of Microsoft's Internet Database Connector for writing Web-based queries against the log table in the database. File-based logging provides a simple text-based, flat file approach.

By default, the server logs all requests in a file with a date-encoded name in the directory c:\Winnt\system32\LogFiles. You can change this directory path and other logging parameters using inetmgr (see the Logging tab in the properties dialog box for the WWW service). The format of the server's log file names is dependent on the Log Format you configure, such as the NCSA (Common Log Format) format or the standard CERN format.

NCSA-format log files are named NCyymmdd.log and standard-format files are named INyymmdd.log where yy is replaced by the year (not very year-2000-safe), mm the month and dd the day—for example, IN970506.log.

You can configure the server to automatically open a new log file on a daily, weekly, or monthly basis, or when the log file grows to a specified file size.

A Common Log Format record contains the following information:

- The client IP address
- inetd information
- The name of the user

- The date and time the request was logged

- The text of the request, for example, "GET /scripts/samples/isasample1.dll HTTP/1.0"

- The status code generated by the server in the response message

- The number of bytes in the response

Design Considerations

You need to think carefully before you attempt to change the format of a log file because there are many utilities around that facilitate crunching or reporting of logs in these standard formats. However, as with most standards, they're sometimes not sufficient for some purposes—especially if you want to log additional information.

In our filter, rather than attempt to augment the existing log, we'll create a completely new one using our own simple comma-delimited format that contains most of the information provided by the standard log, but adds the type of browser used by the user. This information is available in the **HTTP_USER_AGENT** server variable and is useful for determining the number of Explorer versus Navigator users hitting your site. The format of our record will be:

- Client IP address

- Client user name

- Client Web browser type

- Current date

- Current time

- Server IP address

- Request method

- Request URL

- Status code of the response

- Win32 error status (perhaps giving some extra insight into a failure)

- Request parameters, for example, the query string following a GET request

We will simply call our log file server.log and store it in the directory c:\Winnt\system32\LogFiles along with all the others.

It is important for this filter to be thread safe because it is highly likely that other concurrent server requests on other threads will compete for access to the log file.

To provide the necessary serialization, we'll use a **Mutex** synchronization object provided by the Win32 SDK. A Mutex is one of a range of synchronization objects provided by the system and provides a way of synchronizing threads across multiple processes. This is a bit more than we need, as we are only concerned with synchronization for one instance of the server. Later we will introduce another synchronization object, the **CriticalSection**, which is better suited to our needs. Out of paranoia, we do actually lock the file to protect against concurrent access by some other process.

So how do we actually get the logging information? The crux of the solution is to intercept the **SF_NOTIFY_LOG** notification. You will remember from Chapter 7 that this event is the last event processed by the server before it closes the client session. For this notification, the server passes all the logging information we need in the notification-specific data structure **HTTP_FILTER_LOG**. Each time the notification occurs, we simply extract the log information, write it to our log file, and return control back to the server.

Let's move on to look at the source code.

Preliminary Definitions

Listing 10.9 begins with preliminary definitions for include files, private type definitions, and function prototypes.

Listing 10.9   The code for filtersample2.c—Logging filter.

```
/***********************************************************************
* Name:         filtersample2.c
* Description:  an ISAPI filter DLL that is loaded by ISS on startup
                and invoked
*               in response to the event SF_NOTIFY_LOG. The filter
                completely overrides
*               the server's behaviour for this event.
*               The filter creates a custom log in the file
LOG_FILE_PATH. A mutex is used
*               to serial access to the log from multiple threads.
* DLL Location: c:\inetpub\scripts\samples\filtersample2.dll
***********************************************************************/
```

```
#define WIN32_LEAN_AN_MEAN
#include <windows.h>
#include <httpfilt.h>
#include <stdio.h>
#include <time.h>

/* Imported Library Modules */
#include <debug.h>

/* Defines */
#define FILTER_DESCRIPTION "Custom Log Filter"
#define LOG_FILE_PATH "C:\\winnt\\system32\\LogFiles\\server.log"

/* Private Prototypes */
DWORD HandleEvent_Log(HTTP_FILTER_CONTEXT *pFC,
                                        PHTTP_FILTER_LOG pLogData);
VOID Log_FormatAsCLF(LPSTR lpMsg, HTTP_FILTER_CONTEXT *pFC,
                                        PHTTP_FILTER_LOG pLogData);
```

We begin by including windows.h and httpfilt.h files. Remember, httpfilt.h itself relies on windows.h, which precedes it. We also need stdio.h for **sprintf** support and time.h for date and time function support.

We have also imported one of our libiisutils.lib library modules **debug** to provide some simple progress monitoring for our filter. Following this, we have definitions of **FILTER_DESCRIPTION** and **LOG_FILE_PATH**. The latter determines where our log files will be created.

Finally, we have prototypes for our notification handler function, which will be invoked in response to **SF_NOTIFY_LOG**. We encapsulate the act of writing to the log in **Log_FormatAsCLF**.

GetFilterVersion

The first function we define is **GetFilterVersion**.

```
BOOL WINAPI GetFilterVersion(HTTP_FILTER_VERSION *pVersion)
{
    /* Set version */
    pVersion->dwFilterVersion = HTTP_FILTER_REVISION;

    /* Provide a short description of the filter */
    strncpy(pVersion->lpszFilterDesc, FILTER_DESCRIPTION,
            SF_MAX_FILTER_DESC_LEN);
```

```
    Debug((DEST, "filtersample2: %s", pVersion->lpszFilterDesc));

    /* Set the event we want to be notified about and the notification
       priority */
    pVersion->dwFlags = (SF_NOTIFY_LOG | SF_NOTIFY_ORDER_HIGH);

    return TRUE;
}
```

In **GetFilterVersion**, we set the current ISAPI version level in **pVersion> dwFilterVersion** and copy our concise filter description into **pVersion>lpszFilterDesc**. Finally, we must tell the server that we want to receive the **SF_NOTIFY_LOG** notification and that our filter is to be called at a high priority. This is acceptable because the filter will be responding to and completely overriding any other logging behavior. Finally, we return TRUE, which indicates that the filter was successfully initialized. Returning FALSE would cause the server to unload the filter.

Notice that we call our **Debug** macro to display our own indication that our filter has been loaded. By default, our **debug** module displays such messages to a console window using **DBMON**. Refer to the "Debugging Techniques For ISAs And Filters" section in this chapter for more details on how this works.

HttpFilterProc

Our **HttpFilterProc** function is reassuringly simple.

```
DWORD WINAPI HttpFilterProc(HTTP_FILTER_CONTEXT *pFC,
                            DWORD dwNotificationType, VOID *pvData)
{
    DWORD dwRet = SF_STATUS_REQ_NEXT_NOTIFICATION;

    switch (dwNotificationType) {
        case SF_NOTIFY_LOG:
            dwRet = HandleEvent_Log(pFC, (PHTTP_FILTER_LOG)pvData);
            break;
    }

    return dwRet;
}
```

This function is called whenever an **SF_NOTIFY_LOG** notification is generated by the server. All we do is switch on **dwNotificationType** to invoke our handler function. We pass server-supplied pointers to the **HTTP_FILTER_CONTEXT** for the notification in **pFC** and the event-specific structure **HTTP_FILTER_LOG** in **pvData**. In the unlikely event that our filter gets called for unregistered events, our default return status of **SF_STATUS_REQ_NEXT_NOTIFICATION** will cause the server to call the next filter in the notification chain. Under normal circumstances, however, our handler will yield the appropriate return code.

SF_NOTIFY_LOG Handler

The function **HandleEvent_Log** does the work of handling the notification.

```
DWORD HandleEvent_Log(HTTP_FILTER_CONTEXT *pFC,
                                      PHTTP_FILTER_LOG pLogData)
{
    HANDLE  hFile;
    LPSTR   lpszMsgBuff;
    DWORD   dwBytesWritten;
    DWORD   dwBytesToWrite;
    DWORD   dwPos;
    DWORD   dwRet;
    LPSTR   lpszLogBuff;
    HANDLE  hLogMutex= HANDLE  hLogMutex= CreateMutex (NULL, FALSE,
                                      "filtersample2_mutex");

    /* Format Log Record */
    lpszLogBuff = pFC->AllocMem(pFC, MAX_BUFF_SIZE, 0);

    Log_FormatAsCLF(lpszMsgBuff, pFC, pLogData);

    /* Serialize log file access */
    WaitForSingleObject(hLogMutex, INFINITE);

    /* Open log file */
    hFile = CreateFile(LOG_FILE_PATH, GENERIC_WRITE, FILE_SHARE_WRITE,
                              NULL, OPEN_ALWAYS,
                              FILE_ATTRIBUTE_NORMAL, NULL);
    if (hFile == INVALID_HANDLE_VALUE) {
        FileError_Write("Cannot open log file - ", lpszMsgBuff);
        dwRet = SF_STATUS_REQ_ERROR;
    }
    else {
        /* Append log record to file */
        dwBytesToWrite = strlen(lpszLogBuff);
        dwPos = SetFilePointer(hFile, 0, NULL, FILE_END);
```

```
        LockFile(hFile, dwPos, 0, dwPos + dwBytesToWrite, 0);
        if (!WriteFile(hFile, lpszLogBuff, dwBytesToWrite,
                            &dwBytesWritten, NULL)) {
            FileError_Write("Cannot write to log file - ", lpszMsgBuff);
            dwRet = SF_STATUS_REQ_ERROR;
        }
        else
            dwRet = SF_STATUS_REQ_FINISHED;

        UnlockFile(hFile, dwPos, 0, dwPos + dwBytesToWrite, 0);
    }
    CloseHandle(hFile);

    ReleaseMutex(hLogMutex);
    CloseHandle(hLogMutex);

    return dwRet;
}
```

The first thing our handler does is create a Mutex to protect our writes to the log file. This call returns an opaque handle to the Mutex object, which is then used by subsequent Mutex operations.

We then allocate some memory using the server-supplied **AllocMem** callback to store our formatted log record. Note that we have relied on **MAX_BUFF_SIZE** to be long enough to take the formatted output.

Next we use **Log_FormatAsCLF** (shown in the next code snippet) to extract the logging information in **pLogData** and to format it into our output buffer **lpszMsgBuff**. Once formatted, we then activate the Mutex with **WaitForSingleObject** using the **INFINITE** parameter to indicate that we're prepared to wait for eternity for access to the log file if necessary. Normally, you would check the return code from this function to check that the function did not fail.

Now, suitably protected from competing threads, we can safely operate on the log file. We choose to open, write, and close the log file each time so that the log file is not held open (and locked), preventing access by other tools. We could have opened the log file when the filter started and closed it when the filter was unloaded. To do this we would have needed to make use of the **DllMain** function, which, if defined by our DLL, is automatically activated in response to these load and unload events. We actually use **DllMain** in our next example.

Having appended our record to the log file, we release the Mutex and close its handle. The return status from the handler is **SF_STATUS_REQ_ERROR** if we encountered a problem writing to the file, or **SF_STATUS_REQ_FINISHED** if everything went okay. Returning **SF_STATUS_REQ_FINISHED** will cause the server to stop any other filter (and the server itself) from handling the notification.

Before we close the subject, it is usually a good idea to wrap the code sections we protect using synchronization objects like **Mutex** in a **try-finally** block to ensure that **ReleaseMutex** is called should an exception occur. If we don't do this and an exception occurs midway through the protected region, the application could die, leaving the Mutex in a dangling state.

```
VOID Log_FormatAsCLF(LPSTR lpszLogBuff, HTTP_FILTER_CONTEXT *pFC,
                                        PHTTP_FILTER_LOG pLogData)
{
    CHAR    DateBuff[9];
    CHAR    TimeBuff[9];
    CHAR    AgentBuff[MAX_BUFF_SIZE+1];
    DWORD   dwAgentLen=MAX_BUFF_SIZE;

    /* Also want to log HTTP_USER_AGENT info */
    pFC->GetServerVariable(pFC, "HTTP_USER_AGENT", AgentBuff,
                        &dwAgentLen);

    /* Grab system date and time */
    _strdate(DateBuff);
    _strtime(TimeBuff);

    sprintf(lpszLogBuff, "%s, %s, %s, %s, %s, %s, %s, %s, %d, %d,
                        %s\r\n",
        pLogData->pszClientHostName,
        pLogData->pszClientUserName,
        AgentBuff,
        DateBuff, TimeBuff,
        pLogData->pszServerName,
        pLogData->pszOperation,
        pLogData->pszTarget,
        pLogData->dwHttpStatus,
        pLogData->dwWin32Status,
        pLogData->pszParameters);
}
```

Authentication Filter

In Chapter 7, we briefly discussed how IIS handles user authentication, and in Chapter 1, we described how the Basic authentication scheme worked. In this example, we create a custom authentication filter that authenticates users with the Basic authentication scheme.

Rather than have our scheme apply to all URLs, we restrict it only to URLs that are defined in a list of target resources we maintain in the registry in the key HKEY_LOCAL_MACHINE/SOFTWARE/filtersample3/ResourceList.

In our scheme, we use the user authentication database we constructed in our earlier ISA example. This database stores the following information about a user:

- User name
- Password
- An application-specific NT user name
- An application-specific NT password
- The date and time the user last logged on
- An application-specific home directory

The main purpose of the database is to map a user name and password onto a corresponding NT user name and password. This is a useful technique in situations where you have a large number of users authorized to use a particular application that you want to map onto a much smaller set of application-level or role-level users and corresponding passwords.

For example, you may have a large number of online shopping customers, each with their own user name, to whom you have allocated PIN as a password. When challenged for their name and password, you then want to be able to look up the name and the PIN they respond with and, if valid, transparently log them in to the server as the Windows NT user "onlineshopper" with a suitably obscure password.

We'll briefly recap how the Basic scheme works. When a user's browser requests a protected resource for the first time, the request does not contain any authentication information. At this point, the server challenges the request by sending back a **401 Access Denied** message. The browser will present the user with a dialog box in which he or she then enters a user name and password. When the user clicks on OK, the browser issues the request again, but this time with an Authorization header that specifies the user's credentials and that the Basic authentication scheme is to be used. When the server receives this request, it checks the credentials and, if valid, allows the user access to the resource. If invalid, then another **401 Access Denied** response is issued.

In our filter, we are going to perform both the user authentication and challenge functions. This means that we need to override the default server behavior. We'll take care of this by registering notification handlers for both the **SF_NOTIFY_AUTHENTICATION** and **SF_NOTIFY_ACCESS_DENIED** notifications. When **SF_NOTIFY_ACCESS_DENIED** occurs, we want to issue our own security message to the user.

Subsequently, when **SF_NOTIFY_AUTHENTICATION** occurs, we want to extract the user name and password from the message and use these to search our user authentication database for a matching entry. If we find a match, then we want to use the NT user name and password defined for that user as the credentials to authenticate the user to the server rather than the ones the user entered.

An interesting aspect of this implementation is that because our user authentication database routines are not thread safe, we must attempt to perform thread synchronization explicitly within the filter. We do this using a Win32 synchronization object called a **CriticalSection**.

CriticalSection objects are a slightly faster and more efficient mechanism than some of the other synchronization objects Windows supports, such as **Mutex** and **Semaphore** objects. Unlike the other objects, **CriticalSection**s are restricted to only synchronizing threads within a single process but that doesn't concern us here as we're not attempting to synchronize across multiple server processes.

So let's move on to look at our implementation.

Preliminary Definitions

Listing 10.10 begins with preliminary definitions for include files, private type definitions, and function prototypes.

Listing 10.10   The code for filtersample3.c—Authentication filter.

```
/************************************************************************
* Name:             filtersample3.dll
* Description:      an ISAPI filter DLL that is loaded by ISS on startup
                    and invoked
*                   in response to the event SF_NOTIFY_AUTHENTICATION.
* DLL Location:     c:\inctpub\scripts\samples\filtersample3.dll
*************************************************************************/

#define WIN32_LEAN_AN_MEAN
#include <windows.h>
#include <httpfilt.h>

/* Imported Library Modules */
#include <debug.h>
#include <html.h>
#include <user.h>
#include <resource.h>

/* Defines */
#define FILTER_DESCRIPTION "Authentication Filter"
#define USER_DB_PATH            "C:\\temp\\user.dbm"
#define RESOURCE_KEY            "SOFTWARE\\filtersample3"

/* Private Prototypes */

/* Event Notification Handlers */
DWORD HandleEvent_Authentication(HTTP_FILTER_CONTEXT *pFC,
                                              PHTTP_FILTER_AUTHENT
                                                    pAuthData);
DWORD HandleEvent_AccessDenied(HTTP_FILTER_CONTEXT *pFC,
                                         PHTTP_FILTER_ACCESS_DENIED
                                              pAccessData);

/* Support Functions */
BOOL protectedResource(HTTP_FILTER_CONTEXT *pFC);

/* Globals */
CRITICAL_SECTION csCriticalSection;
LPSTR lpszResourceList = NULL;


/************************************************************************/
```

As usual for our filters, we begin by including the windows.h and httpfilt.h files. We also included header files for modules from our own support library libiisutils.lib.

(Remember, you can get the source code for these from CD-ROM enclosed with this book.) The following modules are needed:

- *debug*—An implementation of **Debug**(). We use judicious placement of these to monitor progress of our filter.

- *html*—A simple HTML wrapper that models an HTML page. We use this to generate an HTML response in **HandleEvent_AccessDenied**.

- *user*—An implementation of our user authentication database.

- *resource*—An implementation of the **ResourceList** stored in the registry containing a list of target URLs we want to apply our custom authentication scheme to.

Following this we have the defines **FILTER_DESCRIPTION** containing a short description of our filter, **USER_DB_PATH**, which contains the physical location of the user authentication database, and **RESOURCE_KEY**, the key in the database where the **ResourceList** value is stored.

We then define prototypes for each of the notification handlers along with support functions we will be implementing.

Finally, we define our global variables. First, we'll use a **CriticalSection** variable called **csCriticalSection**, which will serialize access to the user authentication database, and second, a pointer **lpszResourceList**, which will point to the **ResourceList** values extracted from the registry. Even though we've used a global variable, here it is thread safe because the thread will only read the **ResourceList**—not update it.

DllMain

Our sample illustrates the use of the **DllMain** function to allocate and deallocate filter-wide resources. **DllMain** is called automatically by the system when the DLL is first loaded and provides an ideal place to allocate global resources.

```
BOOL WINAPI DllMain(HINSTANCE hinstDLL, DWORD dvReason, LPVOID lpv)
{
    switch (dvReason) {
        case DLL_PROCESS_ATTACH: /* Initialize our user database */
            lpszResourceList = ResourceList_Init(RESOURCE_KEY);
            return lpszResourceList != NULL && User_Init(USER_DB_PATH);
            break;
        case DLL_PROCESS_DETACH: /* Cleanup the database, release memory
                                    etc. */
```

```
            ResourceList_Cleanup(lpszResourceList);
            User_Cleanup();
            break;
        default:
            break;
    }
    return TRUE;
}
```

When the server loads or unloads a filter DLL or a new server thread attempts to access the DLL, the **DllMain** function is called. The event that instigated the call is reflected in **dwReason**.

The **dwReason** variable can have the values **DLL_PROCESS_ATTACH**, **DLL_THREAD_ATTACH**, **DLL_PROCESS_DETACH**, and **DLL_THREAD_DETACH**. In our case, we are not interested in knowing about the thread-level events so we don't bother to intercept them. We are only concerned with initializing and cleaning up our global resources when the DLL first loads and when it unloads.

Consequently, we switch on **dwReason**. On **DLL_PROCESS_ATTACH**, we must initialize our target URL list using **ResourceList_Init** and also initialize our user authentication database. On **DLL_PROCESS_DETACH**, we do the converse and invoke the clean-up routines for each to ensure that any memory is deallocated.

GetFilterProc

The first function we define is **GetFilterProc**.

```
BOOL WINAPI GetFilterVersion(HTTP_FILTER_VERSION *pVersion)
{
    /* Set version */
    pVersion->dwFilterVersion = HTTP_FILTER_REVISION;

    /* Provide a short description of the filter */
    strncpy(pVersion->lpszFilterDesc, FILTER_DESCRIPTION,
            SF_MAX_FILTER_DESC_LEN);

    Debug((DEST, "FilterSample3: %s", pVersion->lpszFilterDesc));

    /* Set the event we want to be notified about and the notification
       priority */
```

```
pVersion->dwFlags = (SF_NOTIFY_SECURE_PORT |
                     SF_NOTIFY_NONSECURE_PORT |
                     SF_NOTIFY_AUTHENTICATION |
                     SF_NOTIFY_ACCESS_DENIED |
                     SF_NOTIFY_ORDER_DEFAULT);

    return TRUE;
}
```

After setting the filter version and description, we define our filter flags by OR'ing together:

- The kind of connections we want our filter to respond to— **SF_NOTIFY_SECURE_PORT** or **SF_NOTIFY_NONSECURE_PORT**.

- The notifications we want to receive—**SF_ NOTIFY_AUTHENTICATION** or **SF_ NOTIFY_ACCESS_DENIED**.

- The priority our filter should have in the chain of filters capable of responding to these notifications—**SF_NOTIFY_ORDER_DEFAULT**.

HttpFilterProc

By now you should be aware that **HttpFilterProc** is the *main* function of the filter and that it is called by the server each time an event notification we have registered to receive occurs.

```
DWORD WINAPI HttpFilterProc(HTTP_FILTER_CONTEXT *pFC,
                            DWORD dwNotificationType, VOID *pvData)
{
    DWORD dwRet = SF_STATUS_REQ_NEXT_NOTIFICATION;

    switch (dwNotificationType) {
        case SF_NOTIFY_AUTHENTICATION:
            dwRet = HandleEvent_Authentication(pFC,
                                          (PHTTP_FILTER_AUTHENT)pvData);
            break;
        case SF_NOTIFY_ACCESS_DENIED:
            dwRet = HandleEvent_AccessDenied(pFC,
                                      (PHTTP_FILTER_ACCESS_DENIED)pvData);
            break;
    }
    return dwRet;
}
```

There are only two notifications of interest: **SF_NOTIFY_AUTHENTICATION** and **SF_NOTIFY_ACCESS_DENIED**. We switch on **dwNotificationType** to work out which notification has occurred and invoke the corresponding handler. Each handler returns a status code capable of overriding our default of **SF_STATUS_REQ_NEXT_NOTIFICATION**, which allows the server to call the next filter that has registered to receive this notification.

SF_NOTIFY_AUTHENTICATION Handler

Our function **HandleEvent_Authentication** does the work of handling the notification.

```
DWORD HandleEvent_Authentication(HTTP_FILTER_CONTEXT *pFC,
                                                 PHTTP_FILTER_AUTHENT
                                                     pAuthData)
{
    DWORD           dwRet = SF_STATUS_REQ_NEXT_NOTIFICATION;
    CHAR            UserName[SF_MAX_USERNAME];
    CHAR            Password[SF_MAX_PASSWORD];
    PCACHE_INFO     pCacheEntry;

    if (strlen(pAuthData->pszUser) != 0) { /* Not anonymous user */

        /*  First check we want to authenticate the resource by checking
               against our
            list of protected URLs */
        if (protectedResource(pFC)) {
            /* It's one of our URLs so authenticate user */
            strcpy(UserName, pAuthData->pszUser);
            strcpy(Password, pAuthData->pszPassword);
            __try {
                EnterCriticalSection(&csCriticalSection);

                switch (User_Find(USER_DB_PATH, pAuthData->pszUser,
                                                &pCacheEntry)) {
                    case -1: /* An error */
                        dwRet= SF_STATUS_REQ_ERROR;
                        break;
                    case 1:  /* User is not in the database */
                        Debug((DEST, "Invalid user: %s", UserName));
                        break;
                    case 0:  /* User IS in the database */
```

```
                    /*  Copy correspondng NT name and NT password back
                            into pAuthData
                        for the server to use to complete authentication
                            of the user */
                    strcpy(pAuthData->pszUser,
                            pCacheEntry->UserData.NTuserName);
                    strcpy(pAuthData->pszPassword,
                            pCacheEntry->UserData.NTpasswd);

                    Debug((DEST, "Valid user: %s mapped to %s,
                            passwd: %s mapped to %s",
                            UserName,
                            pAuthData->pszUser,
                            Password, pAuthData->pszPassword));

                    dwRet = SF_STATUS_REQ_HANDLED_NOTIFICATION;
                    break;
                }
            }
            __finally {
                LeaveCriticalSection(&csCriticalSection);
            }
        }
    }
    return dwRet;
}

BOOL protectedResource(HTTP_FILTER_CONTEXT *pFC)
{
    CHAR    ResName[MAX_BUFF_SIZE];
    DWORD   dwSize = MAX_BUFF_SIZE;
    BOOL    bRet = TRUE;

    if (pFC->GetServerVariable(pFC, "URL", ResName, &dwSize)) {
        Debug((DEST, "URL = %s", ResName));
        bRet = ResourceList_Find(lpszResourceList, ResName);
    }
    return bRet;
}
```

SF_NOTIFY_AUTHENTICATION occurs regardless of the authentication schemes implemented or configured on the server. We need to cope with two possible scenarios:

- Anonymous login, where the server is configured to transparently authenticate a user who requests access to resources that are accessible by the anonymous login user configured in the server.

- Basic authentication, where the server is configured to challenge a request using a **401 Access Denied** message that contains a WWW-Authenticate header.

When anonymous login occurs, the user name passed to us in **pAuthData->pszUser** is the empty string "", consequently it suffices to check for an anonymous user by seeing if the string has a zero size. If so, then we allow the server to handle the response. Otherwise, we handle the response ourselves . We call our **protectedResource** function, which uses the **GetServerVariable** callback kindly supplied to us as part of the **HTTP_FILTER_CONTEXT** to extract the request URL to determine if it matches one of the URLs in our ResourceList. If there is no match, then we'll hand control back to the server and let its authentication machinery process the request.

Assuming there is a match, we save a copy of the user name and password supplied by the server in the notification-specific structure **HTTP_FILTER_AUTHENT**. We then look up the name of the user in our authentication database.

> **Note:** *Because our database management functions are not thread safe, we have encapsulated our call to **User_Find** in a **CriticalSection**. User_Find manipulates a cache of the most recently accessed users, and if we did not serialize, access to it would result in the cache becoming corrupted. We let the critical section extend to the point where there are no more cache entries being referred to.*

If the user is not in the database, we again let the server apply its default authentication semantics by using **SF_STATUS_REQ_NEXT_NOTIFICATION** to pass back control. If a database error occurs, then we return an error status back to the server. However, if the user is in the database, **User_Find** passes back a valid cache entry from which we extract the corresponding NT user name and NT password necessary for the server to correctly authenticate the user.

So, we our final act is to use these NT credentials to *replace* the original credentials supplied by the user and stored by the server. Because we do not want any other filter to intercept this notification, we hand back **SF_STATUS_REQ_HANDLED_NOTIFICATION**, which will tell the server *not* to invoke any other filter that has registered to receive this notification.

Notice how we have used Microsoft's **try..finally** language extension to guarantee that **LeaveCriticalSection** will be called if the block of code protected by the **try** statement is interrupted due to an exception occurring.

SF_NOTIFY_ACCESS_DENIED Handler

Our handler for this notification needs to do two things. First, it needs to ensure that a **401 Access Denied** header is returned in the response message, and second, it needs to generate appropriate security text to include in the message body.

To send the header, we use our utility function **HttpHeader_FiltWrite** (this is shown in the next code snippet). This function wraps a call to the **SF_REQ_SEND_RESPONSE_HEADER** form of **pFC->ServerSupportFunction**, which allows us to send back our own header and define the status code and any other additional headers. In this case, there are no extra headers so we'll simply pass in NULL, which, when passed to **ServerSupportFunction**, will cause it to generate an extra "\r\n", which indicates the end of the header.

To send the security message, we again use our HTML wrapper functions to create an HTML response.

```
DWORD HandleEvent_AccessDenied(HTTP_FILTER_CONTEXT *pFC,
                            PHTTP_FILTER_ACCESS_DENIED pAccessData)
{
    HtmlPage *pPage;

    HttpHeader_FiltWrite(pFC, "401 Access Denied", NULL);

    pPage = HtmlPage_New();
    HtmlPage_Start(pPage, "Access Denied");
    HtmlPage_Append(pPage, "<H1><B>Access Denied</B></H1> <HR>"
        "<H3><I>Sorry you do not have access to this area</I><H3> ");
    HtmlPage_FiltWrite(pFC, pPage);
    HtmlPage_Delete(pPage);

    return SF_STATUS_REQ_FINISHED;
}


BOOL HttpHeader_FiltWrite(HTTP_FILTER_CONTEXT *pFC, LPSTR lpStatusLine,
                                            LPSTR lpHeader)
/* Sends the header of a response message back to the client. If
    lpStatusLine is NULL then
    200 OK sent by default. If lpHeader is NULL then "\r\n" appended to
    header by default. */
{
```

```
CHAR     lpBuff[MAX_BUFF_SIZE];
DWORD    dwBytes;
DWORD    dwRet;

sprintf(lpBuff, "%s\r\n", lpHeader);
dwBytes = MAX_BUFF_SIZE;
dwRet   = pFC->ServerSupportFunction(pFC,
                                     SF_REQ_SEND_RESPONSE_HEADER,
                                     lpStatusLine,
                                     0, (DWORD)lpBuff);
return dwRet;
}
```

Object Connector Filter

Now that you have cut your teeth on some simple examples, we present a more complex example to illustrate some of the less intuitive events generated by the server and some of the common techniques used when writing filters.

Specifically, we illustrate how you can use the following event notifications to create an "object connector" filter.

- SF_NOTIFY_READ_RAW_DATA

- SF_NOTIFY_SEND_RAW_DATA

- SF_NOTIFY_PREPROC_HEADERS

- SF_NOTIFY_URL_MAP

- SF_NOTIFY_END_OF_NET_SESSION

In the process, we'll present some tricks for fooling the server into performing some unnatural acts.

So, just what do we mean by such a grandiose section title? Well, a connector is basically a gateway to some back-end service or data source implemented as an ISAPI filter DLL inside the Web server. Microsoft's Internet Database Connector (IDC) is the most well known of these. We'll digress for a moment to look at how IDC works and then look at how this approach compares with our own.

Microsoft IDC

IDC provides a way of specifying SQL operations to be executed against an ODBC-compliant database such as SQL Server or Oracle, and converting the database response to an HTML document.

The client issues an IDC request by specifying the name of an IDX file in the request URL as shown in the following HTML form definition:

```
<FORM METHOD="POST" ACTION="/myapp/queries/customer.idc">
```

The IDX file located on the server contains a specification of the SQL query to be performed. When the server gets this request, the IDC filter (httpodbc.dll) intercepts it, locates the IDX file, connects to the data source specified within the file, and issues the SQL operation against the data source via the ODBC driver for that data source. The results returned from the ODBC call are formatted according to layout rules specified in a companion file to the IDX file called an HTX file. This file contains an HTML template document containing place holders for the fields specified in the SQL query, for example, a reference to <%fieldname%> would be expanded to the actual data for this field returned by the SQL statement. The HTX file also allows other macros to be specified including <%if%><%else%><%endif%> to specify formatting alternatives based on data returned by the SQL statement.

A Simple Object Model

We will use some of the techniques employed by the IDC to build a simple connector for expanding references to "objects" embedded within an HTML template document.

For our purposes, an object is simply a *thing* capable of yielding a value. Our connector architecture provides a way of specifying a reference and a mechanism for invoking an object handler. The task of the object handler is to instantiate the object and to yield a value from the specified *attribute* or invocation of the specified *method*. This sounds more impressive than it really is, and is a little contrived as well, but it provides an interesting (and object-oriented) landscape against which to explore some contemporary ideas. Back to reality.

The syntax of an object reference is:

```
<!=object.attribute>
```

or

```
<!=object.method param=value,param=value,...>
```

Notice the vague similarity to IDC field references.

Our scheme does not consist of anything as elegant as IDX and HTX files—we simply embed references in an HTML document that can be static or dynamically generated by an ISA or a CGI application. Because our connector is a filter, it doesn't care where the request comes from or what generates the response.

Our simple scheme relies on the filter instantiating an object model from which the object references will be satisfied. The model we have implemented includes the following objects:

- Intrinsic objects **date** and **time**. The references to **<!=date.value>** and **<!=time.value>** are converted to textual representations of the current server date and time respectively—formatted as **DD/MM/YY** and **HH.MM.SS**.

- An example of an external object—**userauthlist**. The references to **<!=userauthlist.getlogintime username=***name*****>** access the user authentication database we created in one of our ISA examples. The method called **getlogintime** searches the database for a name matching the **username** parameter and returns the user's last login time formatted as **DD/MM/YY[HH.MM.SS]**.

- The intrinsic object **form**. The references to **<!=form.***fieldname*****>** are expanded to contain the value of the field *fieldname* entered by the user into an HTML form. The form object is instantiated on every GET or POST request that contains form data. It is up to the ISA or CGI script processing the form data to construct an HTML template containing the form field references.

Connector Design Considerations

Before we move on into implementation, let's take a moment to consider some elements of the filter design.

At a high level, this type of problem is basically one of macro expansion where, given a response message containing object references, we expand each reference and generate an expanded response.

The hard part of the problem is that we don't know how many object references we have in advance, and even if we did, we wouldn't know what size they would expand to. This means we cannot calculate the size of the expanded response in advance. Ordinarily this wouldn't be an issue, except for the fact that the way the server operates is to send the header of a response back to the client before it has processed the response body. As we will see, this not only means we need to do some sort of buffering, but we also need to delay *when* the server sends back the header for the expanded response. In fact, we must actually prevent the server from sending anything at all until we've buffered and expanded the entire document!

Note that when we say unexpanded response, we mean the document that the server would ordinarily send back to the client without our intervention. We don't care where this document comes from—it could be a static HTML page or dynamically generated by an ISA or CGI script. When we say expanded response, we mean a new document generated by our connector filter containing the same content as the unexpanded response but with all its object references expanded.

A general outline of the solution follows:

1. Because there can be multiple **SF_NOTIFY_SEND_RAW_DATA** notifications per request—one when the server sends the header of the unexpanded response, and the rest when it sends the body parts of the unexpanded response, we must be able to distinguish between these two states.

2. When we receive an **SF_NOTIFY_SEND_RAW_DATA** notification for the unexpanded response header, we need to take a copy of this header and remember the value of its **Content-Length** field. We must then dupe the server into *not* transmitting the header because we want to transmit it later once we've processed the entire response.

3. When we receive **SF_NOTIFY_SEND_RAW_DATA** notifications for unexpanded body parts, we must scan each body part for object references, copying data as we go to an output buffer. For each object reference, we must expand the reference using a corresponding object handler. The expanded object should then be formatted into the output buffer. We again must prevent the server from sending the unexpanded body part to the client. Remember, we should be accumulating all the output ourselves so that we can write it out in one fell swoop along with the saved header once we've processed all the unexpanded body parts.

4. We should keep receiving **SF_NOTIFY_SEND_RAW_DATA** notifications and processing the associated responses until the number of unexpanded response characters we've processed equals the **Content-Length** value we extracted when we saved the header before.

5. When this condition occurs, (when there is no more response left to process), we should output the saved header followed by our expanded response. Since the **Content-Length** of the expanded response will likely be greater than that of the unexpanded response, we must change the **Content-Length** header field in the stored header before we send the header.

Other considerations are:

- We will only expand documents for URLs that match a list of target URLs stored in the registry. We can use the **SF_NOTIFY_URL_MAP** notification for this task.

- We must maintain our own state information about the request and the response for the lifetime of the request. For example, we must keep the saved header, the expanded response, the **Content-Length** value of the unexpanded response, how far through the input document we are, and so on. Therefore, we must allocate and initialize this data at the start of the request and then we must deallocate it at the end. We can use the **SF_NOTIFY_READ_RAW_DATA** notification as the place to perform the initialization and **SF_NOTIFY_END_OF_NET_SESSION** to deallocate these data structures.

- To maintain our **form** object model, we must intercept every client request. For GET or POST requests containing form data, we must scan the field name and value information into our form model. Both the **SF_NOTIFY_READ_RAW_DATA** and **SF_NOTIFY_PREPROC_HEADERS** notifications can do this. When **SF_NOTIFY_READ_RAW_DATA** occurs, we must save a copy of the complete request for later processing by **SF_NOTIFY_PREPROC_HEADERS**.

Implementing The Connector

We will now walk sequentially through the filter code, commenting as we go. The code is structured in a modular fashion and basically follows the temporal flow of execution. Because there is quite a lot of code to look at, we have broken it up into sections to help maintain some context. The full code for this example is contained on the CD-ROM enclosed with this book, in the filtersample4 project directory.

Note that this filter, like our previous examples, uses modules from our support library. (Please refer to the module source code provided on the CD-ROM.)

Preliminary Definitions

Listing 10.11 begins with preliminary definitions for include files, private type definitions, and function prototypes. In this section, we'll briefly describe each of these before discussing the actual implementation of each function.

Listing 10.11   The code for filtersample4.c—Object connector filter.

```
/************************************************************************
* Name:              filtersample4.c
* Description:       Object Connector
* DLL Location:      c:\inetpub\scripts\samples\filtersample4.dll
*************************************************************************/
#define WIN32_LEAN_AN_MEAN
#include <windows.h>
#include <httpfilt.h>
#include <stdio.h>

/* Imported Library Modules */
#include <debug.h>
#include <mem.h>
#include <http.h>
#include <user.h>
#include <resource.h>
#include <formmodel.h>
#include <response.h>

/* Defines */

#define FILTER_DESCRIPTION "Object Connector"

/* Maximum number of object references in a document */
#define MAX_REFS 32

/* Maximum length of an object name */
#define MAX_OBJECT_NAME 32

/* Maximum length of an attribute name */
#define MAX_ATTRIB_NAME32
```

```
/* Maximum length of a parameter string */
#define MAX_PARAMS 32

/* Types */

/*  REQUESTINFO holds extra information about the request/response that
    we keep for the duration of the request. A pointer to this is
    stored in the HTTP_FILTER_CONTEXT->pFilterContext. */
typedef struct _REQUESTINFO {
  LPSTR             lpszHeader;         /* A pointer to a saved request
                                           header */
  DWORD             cbOrigContentLength; /* Content length of original
                                           response */
  DWORD             cbAccumRespLength;  /* Amount of response processed
                                           so far*/
  PRESPONSE         pResponse;          /* The expanded response */
  enum SEND_STATE   eRespState;         /* The response state */
  LPSTR             pRequest;           /* A copy of the request
                                           message */
  DWORD             bTargetUrl;         /* TRUE if the URL matches our
                                           target list */
  LPSTR             lpszResourceList;   /* A target list of URLs to be
                                           expanded */
  PFORMINFO         pForm;              /* Information about any form
                                           embedded in the pRequest */

} REQUESTINFO, *PREQUESTINFO;

/*  A page can contain object references. For each reference
    we allocate a REF_PAIR to keep track of the start and the
    end of the reference. i.e. RefStart points to the '<' and
    RefEnd to the '>'. */
typedef struct _REF_PAIR {
              LPSTR   RefStart;
              LPSTR   RefEnd;
              } REF_PAIR, *PREF_PAIR;

/* Object handler dispatch table entry */
typedef struct _DISPATCH_ENTRY {
      CHAR ObjectName[MAX_OBJECT_NAME+1];
      BOOL (*ObjectHandler)(PREQUESTINFO pReq,
                                        LPSTR lpszAttrName,
                                        LPSTR lpszParamList);
} DISPATCH_ENTRY, *PDESPATCH_ENTRY;

/* Private Prototypes */
```

```
/* Server event handlers */
DWORD HandleEvent_UrlMap(HTTP_FILTER_CONTEXT *pFC,
                                            PHTTP_FILTER_URL_MAP
                                               pUrlData);
DWORD HandleEvent_SendRawData(HTTP_FILTER_CONTEXT *pFC,
                                            PHTTP_FILTER_RAW_DATA
                                               pSendData);
DWORD HandleEvent_ReadRawData(HTTP_FILTER_CONTEXT *pFC,
                                            PHTTP_FILTER_RAW_DATA
                                               pReadData);
DWORD HandleEvent_PreProcHeaders(HTTP_FILTER_CONTEXT *pFC,
                                         PHTTP_FILTER_PREPROC_HEADERS
                                            pHeaderData);
DWORD HandleEvent_Terminate(HTTP_FILTER_CONTEXT *pFC);


/* Support functions */
DWORD   HandleResponseHeader(HTTP_FILTER_CONTEXT *pFC,
                                            PHTTP_FILTER_RAW_DATA
                                               pSendData);
DWORD   HandleResponseBody(HTTP_FILTER_CONTEXT *pFC,
                                            PHTTP_FILTER_RAW_DATA
                                               pSendData);
INT          ContainsReferences(PREFSTART pRefs, LPVOID lpvBuff, DWORD
                                                        cbSize);
BOOL         ExpandReferences(PREQUESTINFO pReq, PREFSTART pRefs,
                                            DWORD *cbRefs,
                                            HTTP_FILTER_CONTEXT *pFC,
BOOL         ExpandObject(PREQUESTINFO pReq, LPSTR lpszObjName,
                              LPSTR lpszAttrName,
                              LPSTR lpszParamList);
LPSTR        ExpandHeader(PHTTP_FILTER_CONTEXT pFC, LPSTR lpszHeader,
                                            DWORD cbNewLength);
INT          ExtractContentLength(LPSTR lpszHeader);
PHTTP_FILTER_RAW_DATA pSendData);

/* Object handlers - one for each type of object reference */
BOOL    DateObjectHandler(PREQUESTINFO pReq, LPSTR lpszAttrName,
                                         LPSTR lpszParamList);
BOOL    TimeObjectHandler(PREQUESTINFO pReq, LPSTR lpszAttrName,
                                         LPSTR lpszParamList);
BOOL    UserAuthListObjectHandler(PREQUESTINFO pReq, LPSTR lpszAttrName,
                                         LPSTR lpszParamList);
BOOL    FormObjectHandler(PREQUESTINFO pReq, LPSTR lpszAttrName,
                                         LPSTR lpszParamList);


/* Globals */
```

```
/* An entry for each object handler supported by the connector's object
   model */
DISPATCH_ENTRY ObjectDespatchTable[] = {
        {"date", DateObjectHandler},
        {"time", TimeObjectHandler},
        {"userauthlist", UserAuthListObjectHandler},
        {"form",  FormObjectHandler},
        {"", NULL}};


/**********************************************************************/
```

In addition to the httpfilt.h and windows.h include files, we have again included relevant header files of modules from our utility library libiisutils.lib. The modules we include are:

- *debug*—Debugging support. Implements the **Debug** macro.

- *mem*—Memory allocation. Wherever possible, we have used the **AllocMem** function provided as part of **HTTP_FILTER_CONTEXT**, however, the support library (which is largely filter/ISA independent) simply allocates memory out of the local heap.

- *http*—Models an HTTP message. We use this module to scan an HTTP GET or PUT request for form data.

- *user*—Models a user authentication database. This is used by the **UserAuthListObjectHandler**, which currently just implements a simple query against the user authentication database we constructed in a previous example.

- *resource*—Models a resource list maintained in the registry. We use this to maintain a list of target URLs. Only input documents whose request URLs are in the target list will be expanded.

- *formmodel*—Models a server-side representation of an HTML form. The form is implemented as a double-linked list of field/value pairs.

- *response*—Models a response message. We use this module to implement our output document. The documented is implemented as a double- linked list of document parts. As we receive each part, we add it to the list. Later, when we've got all the parts, we compact the response into a single buffer ready for sending back to the client.

Our design also requires us to maintain a significant amount of extra *state* information about the request. We must maintain this through the lifetime of the request. We can do this safely without the need for any global data by making use of the **pFilterContext** member of the **HTTP_FILTER_CONTEXT** the server allocates to our request. We use **pFilterContext** to store a pointer to our own state information structure **REQUESTINFO**.

REQUESTINFO keeps track of the following elements:

- **lpszHeader**—The header of the unexpanded response. We need to keep track of this so we can modify its **Content-Length** header field later and then send the header with the buffered output document.

- **cbOrigContentLength**—The integer value of the **Content-Length** header field. This determines the size of the unexpanded response and is needed to work out when we're at the end so we can then send the buffered expanded response instead.

- **cbAccumRespLength**—The amount of the input document processed so far. When this equals **cbOrigContentLength**, we've reached the end of the input document.

- **pResponse**—A pointer to the buffered output document. The output document is buffered using the Reponse module that represents the response as a linked list for easy appending and prepending of output document fragments.

- **bRespHeader**—TRUE if we're processing a response header within an **SF_NOTIFY_SEND_RAW_DATA** notification, FALSE if we're processing the body of a response.

- **pRequest**—A copy of the client request message. We keep this so we can parse the message for form fields to be stored in our form model.

- **bTargetUrl**—A boolean flag that is TRUE if the request URL matches one of the URLs in our target resource list.

- **lpszResourceList**—A list of target URLs that are extracted from the SOFTWARE\FilterSample4\ResourceList entry in the registry.

- **pForm**—A pointer to our form model. This model maintains a list of the fields and corresponding values it extracted from the form associated with the current GET or POST request.

Our next type definition is the structure **REF_PAIR**. When we scan the unexpanded response, we keep track of each object reference we find in an array of **REF_PAIRs**. Each **REF_PAIR** contains a pointer to the start and the end of the reference. We use this information later when we actually expand the references.

Next we have a bunch of function prototypes for:

- event notification handlers
- support functions
- object handlers

Each event notification generated by the server is handled by a separate event handler:

- **SF_NOTIFY_URL_MAP** is handled by **HandleEvent_UrlMap**
- **SF_NOTIFY_SEND_RAW_DATA** is handled by **HandleEvent_SendRawData**
- **SF_NOTIFY_SEND_READ_RAW_DATA** is handled by **HandleEvent_ReadRawData**
- **SF_NOTIFY_PREPROC_HEADERS** is handled by **HandleEvent_PreProcHeaders**
- **SF_NOTIFY_END_OF_NET_SESSION** is handled by **HandleEvent_Terminate**

Where necessary, each notification handler is passed a pointer to a corresponding notification-specific data structure.

Our support functions provide the following:

- **HandleResponseHeader**—This is called by **HandleEvent_SendRawData** to handle the notification when the server is about to send a response *header*.
- **HandleResponseBody**—This is called by **HandleEvent_SendRawData** to handle all remaining notifications for sending raw data, such as all notifications relating to sending the *body* of a response message.
- **ContainsReferences**—This determines whether an input document passed in **lpvBuff** has object references in it. If it does, then for each reference it allocates a **REF_PAIR** entry in a list maintained by **HandleEvent_SendRawData**.

- **ExpandReferences**—This takes the list of **REF_PAIRs** and uses **ExpandObject** to expand each object in the list into the output document.

- **ExpandObject**—This takes the name and the attributes of the object reference and uses the **ObjectDespatchTable** to invoke the appropriate object handler for the specified object name.

- **ExpandHeader**—This function inserts a new **Content-Length** value into the header passed as a parameter and yields a new header.

- **ExtractContentLength**—This extracts the value of the **Content-Length** header field from the specified header.

Last, but certainly not least, are the object handlers themselves and the **ObjectHandlerDespatch** table. In this table, we must provide a handler for each type of object reference that can occur. Currently we support:

- "date" objects handled by **DateObjectHandler**

- "time" objects handled by **TimeObjectHandler**

- "userauthlist" objects handled by **UserAuthListObjectHandler**

- "form" objects handled by **FormObjectHandler**

That completes the discussion of the preliminary definitions. Now we review each of the function implementations roughly in order of execution.

GetFilterProc

We begin, as always, by defining our **GetFilterVersion** version.

```
BOOL WINAPI GetFilterVersion(HTTP_FILTER_VERSION *pVersion)
{
    /* Set the filter version */
    pVersion->dwFilterVersion = HTTP_FILTER_REVISION;

    /* Provide a short description of the filter */
    strncpy(pVersion->lpszFilterDesc, FILTER_DESCRIPTION,
            SF_MAX_FILTER_DESC_LEN);

    Debug((DEST, "FilterSample4: %s", pVersion->lpszFilterDesc));

    /* Set the event we want to be notified about and the notification
       priority */
```

```
        pVersion->dwFlags = (SF_NOTIFY_SECURE_PORT |
                             SF_NOTIFY_NONSECURE_PORT |
                             SF_NOTIFY_READ_RAW_DATA |
                             SF_NOTIFY_SEND_RAW_DATA |
                             SF_NOTIFY_URL_MAP |
                             SF_NOTIFY_PREPROC_HEADERS |
                             SF_NOTIFY_END_OF_NET_SESSION |
                             SF_NOTIFY_ORDER_HIGH);
        return TRUE;
}
```

First, we set our filter version and filter description and then we define our filter flags by OR'ing together:

- The kind of connections we want our filter to respond to—
  SF_NOTIFY_SECURE_PORT or **SF_NOTIFY_NONSECURE_PORT**

- The notifications we want to receive—**SF_ NOTIFY_READ_RAW_DATA,
  SF_NOTIFY_SEND_RAW_DATA, SF_NOTIFY_URL_MAP,
  SF_NOTIFY_PREPROC_HEADERS,** or
  SF_NOTIFY_END_OF_NET_SESSION

- The priority our filter should have in the chain of filters capable of responding
  to these notifications—**SF_NOTIFY_ORDER_HIGH**

We have chosen to set our filter at a high priority so that we can expand each object reference in the response message before other filters get see the output document.

HttpFilterProc

Next, our **HttpFilterProc** function is used to map server notifications to corresponding notification handlers.

```
DWORD WINAPI HttpFilterProc(HTTP_FILTER_CONTEXT *pFC,
                            DWORD dwNotificationType, VOID *pvData)
{
    DWORD dwRet = SF_STATUS_REQ_NEXT_NOTIFICATION;

    switch (dwNotificationType) {
        case SF_NOTIFY_READ_RAW_DATA:
            dwRet = HandleEvent_ReadRawData(pFC,
                                            (PHTTP_FILTER_RAW_DATA)pvData);
            break;
        case SF_NOTIFY_URL_MAP:
            dwRet = HandleEvent_UrlMap(pFC,
                                       (PHTTP_FILTER_URL_MAP)pvData);
```

```
        break;
    case SF_NOTIFY_SEND_RAW_DATA:
        dwRet = HandleEvent_SendRawData(pFC,
                                    (PHTTP_FILTER_RAW_DATA)pvData);
        break;
    case SF_NOTIFY_PREPROC_HEADERS:
        dwRet = HandleEvent_PreProcHeaders(pFC,
                                (PHTTP_FILTER_PREPROC_HEADERS)pvData);
        break;
    case SF_NOTIFY_END_OF_NET_SESSION:
        dwRet = HandleEvent_Terminate(pFC);
        break;
    default:
        /* Instruct server to call next filter in the chain for this
            event type */
        dwRet = SF_STATUS_REQ_NEXT_NOTIFICATION;
        break;
    }
    return dwRet;
}
```

In this example, our handlers will only return either
SF_STATUS_REQ_NEXT_NOTIFICATION or **SF_STATUS_REQ_ERROR**.
There are no circumstances in which the handler needs to completely handle a notification (by returning **SF_STATUS_REQ_HANDLED_NOTIFICATION** or
SF_STATUS_REQ_FINISHED) because we want our filter to appear as transparent as possible, so that other filters will work correctly.

SF_NOTIFY_READ_RAW_DATA Handler
Our first handler function looks after the notification generated once the server has read the request from the client.

```
DWORD HandleEvent_ReadRawData(HTTP_FILTER_CONTEXT *pFC,
                                    PHTTP_FILTER_RAW_DATA pReadData)
{
    /* Here we scan the body of raw request */

    DWORD          dwRet = SF_STATUS_REQ_NEXT_NOTIFICATION;
    PREQUESTINFO   pReqInfo;

    Debug((DEST, "filtersample4: ReadRawData"));
```

```
/* Allocate some space to save our own request context information */
pFC->pFilterContext = pFC->AllocMem(pFC, sizeof(REQUESTINFO), 0);

if (pFC->pFilterContext == NULL)
    dwRet = SF_STATUS_REQ_ERROR;
else {
    /*  Initialize our request information to be saved across
        notifications
        for this request. */
    pReqInfo = (PREQUESTINFO)pFC->pFilterContext;
    pReqInfo->bTargetUrl=FALSE;
    pReqInfo->lpszResourceList=NULL;
    pReqInfo->bRespHeader=TRUE;
    pReqInfo->pResponse=Response_New();
    pReqInfo->lpszHeader = NULL;
    pReqInfo->pRequest=NULL;
    pReqInfo->cbAccumRespLength=0;
    pReqInfo->cbOrigContentLength=0;

    /* Create a form model - assuming in advance this request has
       form content! */
    pReqInfo->pForm = pFC->AllocMem(pFC, sizeof(FORMINFO), 0);
    if (pReqInfo->pForm == NULL) {
        SetLastError(ERROR_NOT_ENOUGH_MEMORY);
        dwRet = SF_STATUS_REQ_ERROR;
    }
    else {
        /* Now we keep a copy of the request so we can analyze it in
           PREPROC_HEADERS */
        LPSTR lpszBuff;

        if ((lpszBuff = pFC->AllocMem(pFC, pReadData->cbInData + 1,
            0)) == NULL) {
            SetLastError(ERROR_NOT_ENOUGH_MEMORY);
            dwRet = SF_STATUS_REQ_ERROR;
        }
        else {
            memcpy(lpszBuff, pReadData->pvInData,
                            pReadData->cbInData);
            lpszBuff[pReadData->cbInData]='\0';
            pReqInfo->pRequest = lpszBuff;
        }
    }
}
return dwRet;
}
```

This handler is the first to be called because **SF_NOTIFY_READ_RAW_DATA** is the first notification generated by the server in the request life cycle.

The first thing we do is create and initialize a **REQUESTINFO** structure that we will use throughout the request to maintain our own state information. Note that we use the **AllocMem** callback supplied in the **HTTP_FILTER_CONTEXT** structure to allocate the memory for this structure. Where possible, we use **AllocMem** in our filter implementation because the server will deallocate the memory for us when the request finishes — after the **SF_NOTIFY_END_OF_NET_SESSION** notification has been processed.

This state information is held for the duration of the request only and is therefore private to the request. Consequently, there are no issues with respect to multi-threaded access to the filter.

As part of the initialization, we also create a new form model and keep a pointer to it in **REQUESTINFO**. This form model will be filled in later. The last thing we do is read the raw request sent by the client and make a copy of it for use in **SF_NOTIFY_PREPROC_HEADERS**. Notice also that we use the **pvInData** and **cbInData** members of the notification-specific data structure **HTTP_FILTER_RAW_DATA** to get access to the raw request data and its length.

We are careful throughout our filter about how we copy memory. It is very easy to overwrite server memory. To make life easy for ourselves when it comes to copying and searching buffers, wherever possible we create NULL-terminated buffers, which means that we must always allocate one more byte than the size of the object we're trying to copy.

Our initialization done, and assuming no memory allocation errors occur, our handler returns **SF_STATUS_NEXT_NOTIFICATION** and hands back control through **HttpFilterProc** to the server.

SF_NOTIFY_PREPROC_HEADERS Handler

The next notification we handle is when the server is about to process the headers in the request message.

```
DWORD HandleEvent_PreProcHeaders(HTTP_FILTER_CONTEXT *pFC,
                                 PHTTP_FILTER_PREPROC_HEADERS
                                     pHeaderData)
{
```

```
DWORD           dwRet = SF_STATUS_REQ_NEXT_NOTIFICATION;
PREQUESTINFO    pReqInfo;
CHAR            buffer[MAX_BUFF_SIZE];
DWORD           dwSize = MAX_BUFF_SIZE;

pReqInfo = (PREQUESTINFO)pFC->pFilterContext;

Debug((DEST, "filtersample4: PreProcHeaders"));

/* Determine if this is a GET or a POST request */
pHeaderData->GetHeader(pFC, "method", buffer, &dwSize);

/* Create a form model to store form fields in the request */
FormModel_Init(&pReqInfo->pForm->FieldListHead);

if (strcmp(buffer, "GET") == 0) {
    /* It's a GET */
    LPSTR lpszQueryPos;
    dwSize = MAX_BUFF_SIZE;

    /*  Parse the QUERY_STRING and load param/value pairs into the
        form model */
    pHeaderData->GetHeader(pFC, "url", buffer, &dwSize);
    lpszQueryPos=strchr(buffer, '?');
    if (lpszQueryPos != NULL)
        FormModel_Load(pReqInfo->pForm, lpszQueryPos+1,
                    strlen(lpszQueryPos+1));
}
if (strcmp(buffer, "POST") == 0) {
    /* It's a POST */
    LPSTR lpPtr = pReqInfo->pRequest;
    LPSTR lpEnd = lpPtr + strlen(lpPtr);

    /* Find the beginning of the message body */
    while (lpPtr < lpEnd && *lpPtr     != '\r' && *(lpPtr+1) != '\n'
                                && *( lpPtr+2) !='\r' &&
                                *(lpPtr+3) != '\n') lpPtr++;

    /* Parse the message body and load param/value pairs into the
        form model */
    if (lpPtr < lpEnd)
        FormModel_Load(pReqInfo->pForm, lpPtr, strlen(lpPtr));
}
    return dwRet;
}
```

This is where things become more interesting. Our aim here is to determine whether we have a GET or POST request and to extract from it any HTML form data contained in the request and load it into our form model.

We first determine the request method by using

```
pHeaderData->GetHeader(pFC, "method", buffer, &dwSize);
```

to extract the *method* name from the request and store it in buffer. Along with "url" and "version", "method" is a predefined name you can use to get at the method component of the request.

Next, we initialize an instance of our form model. The form only exists for the lifetime of the request. We don't do anything fancy like trying to maintain form state across multiple requests—we'll leave that up to the application.

Having created a model to hold our form information, we must extract the form data from the request differently, depending on the method.

For a **GET** method, we must get the data from the query string encoded at the end of the request URL. We use **GetHeader** again to extract the URL from the request header and look for the telltale '?' character in the URL, which will identify the presence of form data. If a query string exists, it is passed to **FormModel_Load**. **FormModel_Load** parses and decodes the string, breaking out each parameter and value pair before storing it in the form **pForm**. Refer to iisutils project on the CD-ROM enclosed with this book for the implementation of **FormModel_Load**.

For a **POST** request, form data is not encoded in the URL but is contained in the body of the request. Because the server does not provide access to the raw request as part of this notification, we must use the copy we saved in our **REQUESTINFO** structure during **SF_NOTIFY_READ_RAW_DATA** at **pReqInfo->pRequest**. We must first find the start of the message body and do this by searching from the beginning of the request for the sequence "\r\n\r\n". Remember that a blank line always separates the message header and message body—even if there is no body. Having found a blank line with something following it, we then pass a pointer to the beginning of the body to **Form_Load**, which decodes and stores the form data.

Last, we hand back control via **HttpFilterProc** to the server by returning an **SF_STATUS_REQ_NEXT_NOTIFICATION** status.

SF_NOTIFY_URL_MAP Handler

The **SF_NOTIFY_URL_MAP** notification occurs just before the server maps the URL to a physical path on the server. The handler for this notification is given below.

```
DWORD HandleEvent_UrlMap(HTTP_FILTER_CONTEXT *pFC,
                                              PHTTP_FILTER_URL_MAP
                                                  pUrlData)
{
    DWORD           dwRet = SF_STATUS_REQ_NEXT_NOTIFICATION;
    PREQUESTINFO    pReqInfo;

    Debug((DEST, "filtersample4: UrlMap: URL = %s", pUrlData->pszURL));

    /* Create a resource list to store target URL's kept in the
       registry */
    pReqInfo = (PREQUESTINFO)pFC->pFilterContext;
    pReqInfo>lpszResourceList=
        ResourceList_Init("SOFTWARE\\FilterSample4");
    if (pReqInfo->lpszResourceList == NULL)
        dwRet = SF_STATUS_REQ_ERROR;
    else {
        /* Check to see if the request URL is one we need to process */
        pReqInfo->bTargetUrl =
            ResourceList_Find(pReqInfo>lpszResourceList,
            (LPSTR)pUrlData->pszURL);
    }
    return dwRet;
}
```

Intercepting this event gives you the opportunity to interrogate the path or to translate it to something else. In this example, we are just interested in looking at the physical path to see if it matches one of the resource paths we maintain in the registry for this filter.

To start off, we use our iisutils utility function **ResourceList_Init** to access the registry entry SOFTWARE\FilterSample4\ResourceList, where we keep the list of resource paths we want to process. **ResourceList_Init** creates an in-memory list of these paths and returns a pointer to the list, which we then store in our **REQUEST_INFO** structure for later use (as it turns out we don't actually use it again outside this handler).

We extract the physical path from the notification-specific structure **HTTP_FILTER_URL_MAP** using the **pUrlData->pszURL** and use this to search our resource list for a match using **ResourceList_Find**. (The source code for the Resource module is on the CD-ROM enclosed with this book.)

The **pReqInfo->bTargetUrl** flag is set, depending on the outcome of the find. If the **pszURL** matches one of our target resources, **bTargetUrl** will be set to TRUE, otherwise it will be FALSE.

We actually interrogate **bTargetUrl** in our **SF_NOTIFY_SEND_RAW_DATA** handler to decide whether or not we should translate the outgoing response message. If we didn't do this, the overhead of our conversion process would slow down every request. We choose a simple flag to allow the test to occur as quickly as possible—especially as a single request may generate many **SF_NOTIFY_SEND_RAW_DATA** notifications.

Once again, we return **SF_STATUS_REQ_NEXT_NOTIFICATION** and yield control back to the server.

SF_NOTIFY_SEND_RAW_DATA Handler

Well, now we're finally at the heart of the matter. The transformation of an unexpanded response to an expanded one. We must process the unexpanded response before the server has a chance to send it back to the client. Consequently, in our handler for the **SF_NOTIFY_SEND_RAW_DATA** notification below, we must process the unexpanded response by expanding any references and saving the expanded version until we are ready for the server to send the whole thing back to the client.

```
DWORD HandleEvent_SendRawData(HTTP_FILTER_CONTEXT *pFC,
                                              PHTTP_FILTER_RAW_DATA
                                              pSendData)
{
    DWORD           dwRet = SF_STATUS_REQ_NEXT_NOTIFICATION;
    PREQUESTINFO    pReqInfo;

    pReqInfo = (PREQUESTINFO)pFC->pFilterContext;

    Debug((DEST, "filtersample4: SendRawData"));

/* Only process responses for URLs in our target list */
    if (pReqInfo->bTargetUrl)
```

```
        /* See if a header or the body of a response */

        if (pReqInfo->bRespHeader)
            dwRet = HandleResponseHeader(pFC, pSendData);
        else
            dwRet = HandleResponseBody(pFC, pSendData);

    return dwRet;
}
```

For ease of understanding, we've split this handler into two logical pieces—one to handle header responses and the other body responses.

To determine whether we should handle the response at all, we'll test the flag **pReqInfo->bTargetUrl**. Remember, we set this back in our handler for **SF_NOTIFY_MAP_URL** when we compare the request URL against our list of target URLs.

If this tests TRUE, the request is being made against one of the resources in our target list. If it tests FALSE, we do nothing and delegate processing of the request back to the server.

Assuming there is a match, we next determine whether we're processing a header or a body part. We do this by keeping track of where we are in the cycle of processing the response **pReqInfo->bRespHeader**. This is initialized to TRUE at the beginning of every request (by **HandleEvent_ReadRawData**). After we have processed the response header, we flip this flag to FALSE to indicate we are processing the response body.

So, we test **bRespHeader** and invoke either **HandleResponseHeader** or **HandleResponseBody** and return a status code back to **HttpFilterProc**.

HandleResponseHeader

The overall aim of **HandleResponseHeader** is to take a copy of the response header so it can be sent later along with our expanded response. In addition to saving the header, we also have to stop the server from sending it once we pass control back to it from our handler.

```
DWORD HandleResponseHeader(HTTP_FILTER_CONTEXT *pFC,
                                            PHTTP_FILTER_RAW_DATA
                                                pSendData)
{
```

```
DWORD           dwRet = SF_STATUS_REQ_NEXT_NOTIFICATION;
PREQUESTINFO    pReqInfo;

pReqInfo = (PREQUESTINFO)pFC->pFilterContext;

/* We're only interested in 200 OK headers */
if (strstr(pSendData->pvInData, "200 OK")) {
    /* Allocate a buffer to store the header */
    pReqInfo->lpszHeader = pFC->AllocMem(pFC,
                        pSendData->cbInData+1, 0);
    if (pReqInfo->lpszHeader == NULL) {
        SetLastError(ERROR_NOT_ENOUGH_MEMORY);
        dwRet = SF_STATUS_REQ_ERROR;
    }
    else {
        /* Save the header until we're ready to send the whole
            response */
        memcpy(pReqInfo->lpszHeader, (char*)pSendData->pvInData,
                    pSendData->cbInData);
        pReqInfo->lpszHeader[pSendData->cbInData]='\0';

        /*  Save the Content-Length of the document so we can work
            out when we've seen the send of it. */
        pReqInfo->cbOrigContentLength =
          ExtractContentLength(pReqInfo->lpszHeader);

        /* In the meantime convince the server not to send its
            header */
        pSendData->cbInData = pSendData->cbInData = 0;
        pSendData->pvInData = NULL;
    }
    pReqInfo->bRespState = FALSE;
}
return dwRet;
}
```

First, we are only interested in responses that actually contain data, and furthermore, we are only interested in successful responses. Therefore we check that the header contains a **200 OK** status code. If it doesn't, we let the server send the response back to the client by returning **SF_STATUS_REQ_NEXT_NOTIFICATION**.

Otherwise, we go on to store a copy of the header. Again, we use the notification-specific data structure **HTTP_FILTER_RAW_DATA** (which is also used by **SF_NOTIFY_READ_RAW_DATA**) to access the response data. The pointer

pSendData->pvInData points to the buffer where the server has put the response into and **pSendData->cbInData** contains the size of the response in bytes.

Having made a copy of the header and stored a pointer to it in our **REQUESTINFO** structure at **pReqInfo->lpszHeader**, we extract from the header the value of the **Content-Length** header field using **ExtractContentLength** (see the following code snippet) and store this in **REQUESTINFO** also. We will use this value in the **HandleResponseBody** function coming up soon to determine when we've reached then end of our input document.

```c
INT ExtractContentLength(LPSTR lpszHeader)
{
    LPSTR    pContLenPos;
    CHAR     Length[12];
    INT      i=0;
    INT      cbLength=0;

    pContLenPos=strstr(lpszHeader, "Content-Length:");
    if (pContLenPos) {
        /* Find the end of the header - should be a \r\n */
        while (*pContLenPos >= ' ') {
            if (isdigit(*pContLenPos))
                Length[i++]=*pContLenPos;
            ++pContLenPos;
        }
        Length[i]='\0';
        cbLength = atoi(Length);
    }
    return cbLength;
}
```

These tasks done, our penultimate act is to convince the server not to send the response header. We do this by zeroing out the address of the server buffer and the byte count fields the server set in **pSendData** prior to invoking our notification handler. When we yield control back to the server, it will see the empty buffer and will not write anything back to the client.

Please note that for this technique to succeed, we assume that the server will free the buffer originally allocated at the end of the request and that, apart from this, the server does not reference the buffer from anywhere else.

Finally, we set our **pReqInfo->bRespHeader** variable to FALSE indicating *to us* that we have processed the header and are about to begin processing the response body.

We can return **SF_STATUS_NEXT_NOTIFICATION** because we want the server to keep on handling the remainder of the response. The very next thing the server does after we return control back to it is to grab the body of the response and issue another **SF_NOTIFY_SEND_RAW_DATA** notification.

HandleResponseBody

HandleResponseBody is where the work of expanding the response occurs. This handler will be called for every **SF_NOTIFY_SEND_RAW_DATA** notification *following* that of the header.

```
DWORD HandleResponseBody(HTTP_FILTER_CONTEXT *pFC,
                                            PHTTP_FILTER_RAW_DATA
                                                pSendData)
{
    DWORD                   dwRet = SF_STATUS_REQ_NEXT_NOTIFICATION;
    PREQUESTINFO            pReqInfo;
    DWORD                   cbRefs=0;
    REF_PAIR                RefStarts[MAX_REFS];

    pReqInfo = (PREQUESTINFO)pFC->pFilterContext;

    /* See if the body contains any object references */
    cbRefs=ContainsReferences(RefStarts, pSendData->pvInData,
                                    pSendData->cbInData);

    if (cbRefs == 0)
        Response_Append(pReqInfo->pResponse, pSendData->pvInData,
                                    pSendData->cbInData);
    else
        ExpandReferences(pReqInfo, RefStarts, &cbRefs, pFC, pSendData);

    /* See if we're at the end of the content yet */
    pReqInfo->cbAccumRespLength += pSendData->cbInData;

    if (pReqInfo->cbAccumRespLength < pReqInfo->cbOrigContentLength) {

        /* Still data to be processed so dupe the server into sending
            nothing */
        pSendData->cbInData = pSendData->cbInBuffer = 0;
        pSendData->pvInData = NULL;
```

```
        }
        else {
            /* We've reached the end so write out the expanded header and the
               expanded body */
            LPSTR         lpszNewResponse;
            LPSTR         lpszNewHeader;
            DWORD  cbHeaderLen;

            /*  Must adjust the Content-Length in the saved header
                   to reflect the size of the expanded document */
            lpszNewHeader = ExpandHeader(pFC, pReqInfo->lpszHeader,
                         pReqInfo->pResponse->cbTotalRespSize);

            /* Now prepend the header to our new content */
            if (lpszNewHeader != NULL) {
                cbHeaderLen = strlen(lpszNewHeader);
                Response_Prepend(pReqInfo->pResponse, lpszNewHeader,
                              cbHeaderLen);
            }
            else
                return SF_STATUS_REQ_ERROR;

            /* Get the server to write out our expanded content */
            if (lpszNewResponse=Response_Compact(pFC, pReqInfo->pResponse)) {
                pSendData->cbInBuffer = pReqInfo->pResponse->cbTotalRespSize;
                pSendData->cbInData = pReqInfo->pResponse->cbTotalRespSize;
                pSendData->pvInData = lpszNewResponse;
            }
            else
                return SF_STATUS_REQ_ERROR;
        }
        return dwRet;
}
```

We first check to see if the server response buffer contains any references by calling **ContainsReferences** (see the next code snippet). This is a simple routine that just looks for the reference pattern <!=...> and for each reference found, it adds a **REF_PAIR** entry into the **RefStarts** array. Each **REF_PAIR** defines the starting and ending position of the pattern in **pSendData->pvInData**.

```
INT ContainsReferences(PREF_PAIR pRefs, LPVOID lpvBuff, DWORD cbSize)
{
    LPSTR  lpvStart,  lpvEnd;
    INT    refCount=0;
```

```
    lpvStart = lpvBuff;
    lpvEnd = lpvStart + cbSize;

    while (lpvStart < lpvEnd && refCount < MAX_REFS) {
        lpvStart = strstr(lpvStart, "<!=");
        if (lpvStart == NULL) break;
        pRefs[refCount].RefStart=lpvStart;
        while (lpvStart < lpvEnd && *lpvStart != '>') lpvStart++;
        pRefs[refCount++].RefEnd=lpvStart;
    }
    return refCount;
}
```

If no references are found, all we need do is take a copy of the server's response buffer and append it to the buffered response we are accumulating.

> **Note:** *Our output buffer is not just a linear chunk of memory, but is a double-linked list maintained by our **Response** utility module from libiisutils.lib. We chose to use a list so that we could easily add expanded body parts to the end of it and once they had all been accumulated, prepend the saved header to the start of the list without having to **realloc** memory all over the place. As it turns out, we have to morph our list-based response back into a lump of memory when it eventually comes time to write the whole response (header and all) back to the client.*

If references are found, the **ExpandReferences** function (in the next code snippet) is used to expand each reference and copy the result into the output buffer.

Either way, we keep track of the amount of the response we have processed using **pReqInfo->cbAccumRespLength** by adding to it the length of each response we process.

Once the references in the current response have been expanded, we compare **pReqInfo->cbAccumRespLength** against the **pReqInfo->cbOrigContentLength** to see if any more response data will be forthcoming. If there is still response data to come, then once again we zero out the server's own response buffer to prevent it from sending the current response before we relinquish control back to the server. If, however, there are no more responses left to come, we'll prepend our saved header to the output buffer using **Response_Prepend**. Before we do this we must change the **Content-Length** of the saved header to reflect the length of the expanded document using **ExpandHeader**.

We'll then compact **pResponse** back into a single chunk of memory using **Response_Compact**. Instead of zeroing out the server's buffer this time, we point the server buffer at our compacted response and then return control back to the server. This causes the server to send our buffer to the client rather than its own.

ExpandHeader

The **ExpandHeader** function searches **lpszHeader** for the **Content-Length** header field and replaces the value directly following it with **dbNewSize**. The function allocates and then returns a completely new header **lpszNewHeader** containing the new **Content-Length** header field.

```
LPSTR ExpandHeader(PHTTP_FILTER_CONTEXT pFC, LPSTR lpszHeader,
                                    DWORD cbNewSize)
{
    LPSTR       pContLenPos;
    LPSTR       lpszNewHeader;
    DWORD       cbContLen;
    CHAR        Length[12];

    pContLenPos=strstr(lpszHeader, "Content-Length:");
    if (pContLenPos) {
        /* Calc number of bytes before the header */
        *pContLenPos='\0'; ++pContLenPos;

        /* Find the end of the header - should be a \r\n */
        while (*pContLenPos >= ' ') ++pContLenPos;

        /* Insert length for new header */
        sprintf(Length, "%d", cbNewSize);
        cbContLen=strlen(lpszHeader) +
                strlen("Content-Length: ") +
                strlen(Length) +
                strlen(pContLenPos);

        /* Create the new header */
        lpszNewHeader=pFC->AllocMem(pFC, cbContLen+1, 0);
        if (lpszNewHeader != NULL)
            sprintf(lpszNewHeader, "%sContent-Length: %s%s", lpszHeader,
                    Length,
                    pContLenPos);
        else
            SetLastError(ERROR_NOT_ENOUGH_MEMORY);
```

```
        return lpszNewHeader;
    }
    return NULL;
}
```

ExpandReferences

Here is the code for the **ExpandReferences** function, in which we walk through
pRefs, expanding each reference and copying it into the buffer that holds our accumulated expanded response.

```
BOOL ExpandReferences(PREQUESTINFO pReq, PREF_PAIR pRefs,
                                        DWORD *cbRefs,
                                        HTTP_FILTER_CONTEXT *pFC,
                                        PHTTP_FILTER_RAW_DATA
pSendData)
{
    DWORD    i;
    LPSTR    lpBufStart, lpBufEnd;
    LPSTR    lpRefStart, lpRefEnd;
    LPSTR    lpDot=NULL;
    LPSTR    lpRef;
    CHAR     ObjectName[MAX_OBJECT_NAME+1];
    CHAR     AttribName[MAX_ATTRIB_NAME+1];
    CHAR     Parameters[MAX_PARAMS+1];
    DWORD    dwLen;
    DWORD    dwBytes;
    DWORD    dwNRefs = 0;

    lpBufStart = (LPSTR)pSendData->pvInData;
    lpBufEnd = (LPSTR)pSendData->pvInData + pSendData->cbInData;

    /* Iterate over the references in the pRefs array */
    for (i=0; i<*cbRefs; i++) {
        lpRefStart=pRefs[i].RefStart+3; /* Skip over <!= */
        lpRefEnd=pRefs[i].RefEnd;

        /* Find the '.' in "object.attribute" */
        for (lpRef=lpRefStart, lpDot=NULL; lpRef<lpRefEnd; lpRef++)
            if (*lpRef == '.') {
                lpDot = lpRef;
                break;
            }
```

```
            /* Ignore references with no attribute */
            if (lpDot == NULL) {
                /* Write back response preamble */
                dwBytes=pRefs[i].RefStart-lpBufStart;
                Response_Append(pReq->pResponse, lpBufStart, dwBytes);
            }
            else {
                dwNRefs++;

                /* Break out the object name */
                dwLen=min(MAX_OBJECT_NAME, lpDot-lpRefStart);
                strncpy(ObjectName, lpRefStart, dwLen);
                ObjectName[dwLen]='\0';

                /* Find the end of the attribute */
                while (++lpRef < lpRefEnd && *lpRef != ' ' && *lpRef != '>');

                /* Break out the attribute name */
                dwLen=min(MAX_ATTRIB_NAME, lpRef-lpDot-1);
                strncpy(AttribName, lpDot+1, dwLen);
                AttribName[dwLen]='\0';

                /* Break out the parameters if there are any */
                if (lpRef < lpRefEnd && *lpRef == ' ') {
                    dwLen=min(MAX_PARAMS, lpRefEnd-lpRef-1);
                    strncpy(Parameters, lpRef+1, dwLen);
                }
                else
                    dwLen=0;
                Parameters[dwLen]='\0';

                /* Buffer the response preamble */
                dwBytes=pRefs[i].RefStart-lpBufStart;
                Response_Append(pReq->pResponse, lpBufStart, dwBytes);

                /* Expand the object - ignore failures */
                ExpandObject(pReq, ObjectName, AttribName, Parameters);
            }
            lpBufStart = pRefs[i].RefEnd+1;
    }

    /* Buffer the remainder of the response */
    dwBytes=lpBufEnd - lpBufStart;
    Response_Append(pReq->pResponse, lpBufStart, dwBytes);
```

```
    /* Actual number of references processed */
    *cbRefs = dwNRefs;
    return TRUE;
}
```

In **ExpandReferences**, we walk through the array of **REF_PAIRs** passed in as a parameter, and for each reference specified we break out the **ObjectName**, **AttributeName**, and optional **Parameters**.

> Note: **AttributeName** is mandatory. References of the form **<!=object>** are ignored and not expanded.

Before expanding each reference, we'll copy all characters in the server's response buffer (**pSendData->pvInData**) between the current reference and end of the previous one (or the beginning of the response if there was no previous reference) into the output buffer (**pResponse**). We then expand the object reference using **ExpandObject** and copy the expanded version into the output buffer. We repeat this process until we've processed all the references (or have hit our reference limit **MAX_REFS**). The last thing we must do is copy the balance of the unexpanded response (all characters after the last reference) into the output buffer.

ExpandObject

ExpandObject is a simple routine called by **ExpandReferences**, which takes the **ObjectName** and **AttributeName** as parameters and then it searches the **ObjectHandlerDespatchTable** for a matching object name. If it finds a match, it invokes the corresponding handler, which is responsible for expanding objects of the type specified.

```
BOOL ExpandObject(PREQUESTINFO pReq, LPSTR lpszObjName, LPSTR
                                    lpszAttrName,
                                 LPSTR lpszParamList)
{
    BOOL                          ret = FALSE;
    PDESPATCH_ENTRY pEntry;

    for (pEntry=ObjectDespatchTable; *pEntry->ObjectName != '\0';
                                 pEntry++) {
```

```
        if (strcmp(lpszObjName, pEntry->ObjectName) == 0) {
            ret = pEntry->ObjectHandler(pReq, lpszAttrName,
                    lpszParamList);
            break;
        }
    }
    return ret;
}
```

Object Handlers

Below, we list the currently supported object handlers:

- **DateObjectHandler**

- **TimeObjectHandler**

- **UserAuthListObjectHandler**

- **FormObjectHandler**

Each object handler is responsible for expanding a particular object type into the output buffer **pReq->pResponse**. Each handler is passed the object attribute or method in **lpszAttribute** (it is up to the object to distinguish) and an optional parameter in **lpszParameter**.

The handler performs an object-specific operation to yield a result that it must format based on its own rules and then copy into the output buffer.

Our example handlers simply output text representations of their results, however, more complex handlers could generate HTML or other more complex media types.

DateObjectHandler simply formats the current server date as a DD/MM/YY string into the output buffer. It does not use an attribute, but one must be supplied for the object reference to be syntactically correct. We suggest using "date.value".

```
BOOL DateObjectHandler(PREQUESTINFO pReq, LPSTR lpszAttrName,
                                        LPSTR lpszParamList)
{
    SYSTEMTIME  Time;
    CHAR               FormattedDate[10+1];

    GetSystemTime(&Time);
    sprintf(FormattedDate, "%02d/%02d/%04d", Time.wDay, Time.wMonth,
            Time.wYear);
```

```
    Response_Append(pReq->pResponse, FormattedDate, 10);
    return TRUE;
}
```

TimeObjectHandler again just formats the current server time as an HH.MM.SS string into the output buffer. The time object does not have a specific attribute either, but once again one is needed for the reference to be syntactically correct. We use "time.value".

```
BOOL TimeObjectHandler(PREQUESTINFO pReq, LPSTR lpszAttrName,
                                           LPSTR lpszParamList)
{
    SYSTEMTIME   Time;
    CHAR                 FormattedTime[8+1];

    GetSystemTime(&Time);
    sprintf(FormattedTime, "%02d.%02d.%02d", Time.wHour, Time.wMinute,
            Time.wSecond);
    Response_Append(pReq->pResponse, FormattedTime, 8);
    return TRUE;
}
```

FormObjectHandler treats the **lpszAttrName** as the field name from a form embedded in the current request and searches for its current value in the form model constructed during the **SF_NOTIFY_PREPROC_HEADERS** notification. For example, if the string "Fred Flintstone" had been entered by the user into an HTML form with a "username" field, then <!form.username> would yield "Fred Flintstone".

```
BOOL FormObjectHandler(PREQUESTINFO pReq, LPSTR lpszAttrName,
                                          LPSTR lpszParamList)
{
    BOOL        ret=FALSE;
    LPSTR       lpszFieldValue;
    PFIELDINFO  pField;
    DWORD       dwBytes;

    pField=FormModel_Find(&pReq->pForm->FieldListHead, lpszAttrName);
    if (pField)
        lpszFieldValue=pField->FieldValue;
    else
        lpszFieldValue="";
```

```
    dwBytes = strlen(lpszFieldValue);
    Response_Append(pReq->pResponse, lpszFieldValue, dwBytes);
    return ret;
}
```

The **UserAuthListObjectHandler** is a wrapper for the user authentication database we constructed in one of our ISA examples. It expands objects of the form **<!=userauthlist.getlogin user=username>**. In its present form, it implements a simple query **getlogin** against the database, which gets the last login time of the user specified in the parameter.

```
BOOL UserAuthListObjectHandler(PREQUESTINFO pReq, LPSTR lpszAttrName,
                                                  LPSTR lpszParamList)
/* Description:
    Handles references like: <!=userauthlist.getlogin user=username>

    Attributes/Methods defined:
    getlogintime: gets the last login date/time for the specified user */
{
    BOOL          ret=FALSE;
    PCACHE_INFO   pCacheEntry;
    LPSTR         lpszParamValue, lpszSavedParam;
    LPSTR         UserDbPath="C:\\temp\\user.dbm";
    DWORD         dwBytes;
    PFIELDINFO    pField;

    /* Process specified attribute */
    if (strcmp(lpszAttrName, "getlogintime") == 0) {

        /* Must be a parameter */
        if (strlen(lpszParamList) == 0)
            return ret;

        /* The parameter must have a value */
        if ((lpszParamValue = GetParamValue(lpszParamList, "username",
                                            ',')) == NULL)
            return ret;

        /* Remember this so we can deallocate later */
        lpszSavedParam=lpszParamValue;

        /* The value could be a field reference in the current form */
        if (strstr(lpszParamValue, "form.")) {
            /* Looks like it might be */
```

```
            pField=FormModel_Find(&pReq->pForm->FieldListHead,
                                lpszParamValue+5);
        if (pField)
            lpszParamValue=pField->FieldValue;
    }

    User_Init(UserDbPath);
    switch(User_Find(UserDbPath, lpszParamValue, &pCacheEntry)) {
    case -1: /*Error */
        break;
    case 1:     /* User not found */
        break;
    case 0: /* User found so format results and send back to
                client */
        dwBytes = strlen(pCacheEntry->UserData.lastLoginTime);
        Response_Append(pReq->pResponse,
                        pCacheEntry->UserData.lastLoginTime,
                                        dwBytes);
        ret = TRUE;
        break;
    }
    User_Cleanup();

    Mem_Free(lpszSavedParam); /* Allocated by GetParamValue() */
    return ret;
}

    return ret;
}
```

SF_NOTIFY_END_OF_NET_SESSION Handler

This handler is called just before the server terminates the session with the client and is the place where we deallocate the resources we created at the beginning of the request (in **HandleEvent_ReadRawData**). Much of the memory we have allocated during the request was created using the server-supplied **AllocMem** callback, which guarantees that the memory it allocates will be automatically deallocated at the end of the request, so we only have to explicitly clean up resources where we've allocated our own memory from the local heap. This only applies to our generic modules **Resource**, **FormModel**, and **Response**.

```
DWORD HandleEvent_Terminate(HTTP_FILTER_CONTEXT *pFC)
{
    DWORD           dwRet = SF_STATUS_REQ_NEXT_NOTIFICATION;
    PREQUESTINFO    pReqInfo;

    pReqInfo =(PREQUESTINFO)pFC->pFilterContext;
    Debug((DEST, "filtersample4: Terminate"));

    if (pReqInfo->lpszResourceList != NULL)
        ResourceList_Cleanup(pReqInfo->lpszResourceList);

    if (pReqInfo->pForm != NULL)
        FormModel_Cleanup(&pReqInfo->pForm->FieldListHead);

    if (pReqInfo->pForm != NULL)
        Response_Cleanup(pReqInfo->pResponse);

    return dwRet;
}
```

Connector Event Sequence

Let's briefly recap on the sequence of events that occurs:

1. The client requests a resource that yields a document containing one or more object references.

2. When the server notifies us of **SF_NOTIFY_READ_RAW_DATA**, we initialize our own state information we maintain about the request and keep a copy of the request itself.

3. When **SF_NOTIFY_PREPROC_HEADERS** header occurs, we scan any form data out of our saved request into our form model.

4. When **SF_NOTIFY_URL_MAP** occurs, we check to see if the URL is one we should process by looking it up in the list we keep in the registry.

5. When **SF_NOTIFY_SEND_RAW_DATA** first occurs, this will be to advise us that the server is about to send the response header. We save the header and prevent the server from sending it.

6. When **SF_NOTIFY_SEND_RAW_DATA** next occurs, it will be to advise us that the server is about to send the response body. We search the response for references and expand the response into our output buffer by calling the ap-

propriate object handler for each reference. We again prevent the server from sending its response.

7. When subsequent **SF_NOTIFY_SEND_RAW_DATA** notifications occur, we repeat step 6 until we've processed the whole response, whereupon we create a new response consisting of the saved header and the expanded response in our output buffer. This new response is handed back to the server (effectively replacing its original response), which it then sends to the client.

8. When **SF_NOTIFY_END_OF_NET_SESSION** occurs, we deallocate all heap-based resources we explicitly allocated during the course of handling the request.

Extending The Connector

There are obvious ways we can improve and extend our Object Connector (at least in concept, if not in practice). For example:

- The connector relies on using the server's **AllocMem** memory allocation routines. Although convenient for us, it places a burden of memory management on the server for every request. A better approach would be to modify the connector so that it manages and reuses memory from its own pool of memory buffers allocated inside a separate heap.

- Implementation of an HTX file-like interface for formatting the object values including more sophisticated macros—for example, macros for if-then-else for selecting different output formats based on an object value.

- Registration and dispatch of object handlers through some external interface rather than through a built-in dispatch table and built-in functions.

- Inclusion of more useful intrinsic objects, for example, an HTTP object that yields the value of server variables like http.server_name.

- Re-architecting of the connector so that it uses a proper object model and implementation in C++ to allow connection to "real" objects.

We're sure you can think up lots of other ideas, too.

Common Errors With Filters

There are a few traps that always seem to trip you up when developing a filter. The two main traps to watch out for are incorrect filter registration and entry point declarations.

Incorrect Filter Registration

Make sure you register your DLL correctly in the registry. Remember, you need to define the full path name and use commas to separate it from the other entries in the list.

Incorrect Entry Point Declarations

Make sure you define **GetFilterVersion** and **HttpFilterProc** correctly in your DEF file. If these aren't provided, the server will not be able to load your DLL correctly. If in doubt, look in the event viewer for errors from the **W3SCV** service.

Tips For Easier And Safer Development

Here are some useful tips for making development of server extensions a little safer and easier.

Developing On The Same Machine As The Server

It is a whole lot easier to develop on the same machine as the server. If you don't, you will find it very frustrating to have to continually copy code from one machine to another. Ideally, you want to keep the coding through debugging loop as tight as possible.

It is important that you do not develop ISA or ISAPI filter software on your production Web server. Remember that the DLLs you create are loaded by IIS itself, and can easily corrupt the server, causing it to crash or perform erratically.

Using A Debugging Version Of A Memory Allocator

In situations where you must allocate your own memory from the heap, such as in an ISA or in a filter where it's not convenient to use the **AllocMem** callback, it can be useful to use a memory allocator with some built-in debugging support. At the minimum, memory allocation routines that keep track of the total number of bytes currently allocated are useful so that before you terminate your application you can check if there is still memory that has not been returned to the system. Our **mem** utility module on the CD-ROM included with this book implements this simple scheme.

Using A Separate Heap For Allocating Memory

By default, when your DLL requests memory using **malloc** or **LocalAlloc**, the request is satisfied from the heap of the server process. There are plenty of advantages to allocating a separate heap for allocating memory for use by your DLL. The main one is memory space protection. Memory exceptions are probably the most common problem you will have when developing your DLLs. It is all too easy for a rogue pointer to go wandering through the server's heap, and worse if it's overwriting server data. These sorts of problems are sometimes extremely hard to track down and often take some time to manifest themselves. Even after you've solved any memory exception problems, it is sometimes difficult to trust your application's behavior thereafter.

Windows provides **HeapCreate**, **HeapAlloc**, **HeapFree**, and **HeapDestroy** functions, which allow you to create your own heap that will be isolated from that of the server's. It is not hard to create a set of simple wrapper functions that use such a heap for allocating and deallocating memory.

Using a separate heap can also improve performance, especially if the heap is small, because there will be less chance that it will be swapped out to disk.

Checking Return Codes

Be diligent about checking the return codes from all ISAPI functions (and Win32 functions also). Most of the ISAPI functions return a boolean value, indicating success or failure. Quite often you will be able to obtain a more detailed error status using Win32's **GetLastError**, which should shed light on the underlying Win32 error.

An example of this is the **GetServerVariable** callback function in the **EXTENSION_CONTROL_BLOCK**, which uses **SetLastError** to return a more detailed error status. Refer to the **GetServerVariable** description in Chapter 8 for the list of applicable error codes.

Ensuring Your ISA Or Filter Is Thread Safe

Thread safety is an extremely important issue. IIS is a multi-threaded process where each request from a client is dispatched onto a separate thread. These threads operate concurrently and independently. If your DLL needs to access global resources, whether statically or dynamically allocated, then you must ensure that any updating of these resources is properly serialized. If not, it's possible for your resource to become inconsistent and either cause your application to behave strangely, or worse still, completely crash the server.

Win32 provides a set of thread synchronization objects that allow you to serialize access to global resources. In this chapter we have already used the two most commonly used objects—**CriticalSections** and **Mutexes**.

Both **CriticalSection** and **Mutex** objects are used to protect a resource from simultaneous access from multiple threads. Each of these objects can only be owned by one thread at a time. Other competing threads must wait until the CriticalSection has been "left" or **Mutex** has been "released" before one of them can take ownership of the object.

The **CriticalSection** object is one of the more commonly used synchronization objects in ISA and filter development. It is also faster and more efficient than a **Mutex**. Note, however, that a **CriticalSection** is only able to synchronize threads within the current process. **Mutex** objects will actually synchronize threads across multiple processes.

The other synchronization objects provided by Win32 are the traditional **Semaphore** and the **Event**.

A **Semaphore** is usually used to limit the number of threads accessing a shared resource to a particular number. The value of the semaphore starts at a certain number and is decremented each time a shared resource is allocated and incremented each time it is freed. When the value of the semaphore reaches zero, any thread that requests access to the resource is blocked until another thread releases a resource and increments the semaphore count.

As its name implies, an **Event** object is useful for notifying a waiting thread when a particular event has occurred—typically, the completion of some operation. An **Event** is often used in a situation when a master thread initializes a shared resource, blocking access to it from other worker threads by setting the **Event** to a nonsignalled state until it has completed the initialization. When the master thread completes its job, it sets the **Event** to a signalled state, causing the other threads to wake up and gain access to the resource.

When implementing any of these synchronization schemes you should use exception handling support such as the **try-except** and **try-finally** block statements that Microsoft has added to its C compiler (or if you're using C++, the **try-catch-throw** statements) to ensure that the synchronization object is always released before the exception terminates your application. This is necessary because most synchronization objects are created by and within the operating system, and if not cleaned up correctly, will consume resources even after your program has terminated. We gave a very simple example of **try..finally** usage in Listing 10.11.

Debugging Techniques For ISAs And Filters

In this section, we look at some useful techniques for debugging both filters and DLLs. At best, debugging is a painful process, so the more weapons we have in our arsenal, the better.

Here we look at two different types of debugging techniques—interactive debugging and non-interactive debugging.

Visual C++ provides excellent interactive debugging facilities that allow us to debug our DLLs by attaching the debugger to an already running IIS server or running the server manually.

However, there are situations in which interactive debugging is not possible, or is too cumbersome—this is where non-interactive techniques are useful.

We should really distinguish between debugging, error reporting, and logging. Often it is tempting to roll these things together, however, they each meet quite different needs.

Debugging is typically a set of ad hoc techniques used to resolve bugs in code while developing. This usually involves a mixture of interactive (such as the interactive debugger) and non-interactive techniques (such as the judicious use of output statements to display values of key variables or to trace the execution path of the application). You should also think about how you will debug your DLL once it has been put into production. If something does go wrong, you'll need a reliable way of debugging to try and track down the problem while the DLL is still in service. This is not always easy, however, if you've thought about it in advance, it can save your life (or at least your patience!). Typically, a mixture of error reporting and logging techniques will be applicable.

Error reporting is not an ad hoc process, it's something that should be designed into an application from day one. Every application should implement an error reporting and recovery mechanism that reports the error through an appropriate mechanism and then, if possible, recovers. If recovery is not possible, the application should die as gracefully as it can. How the error is reported is also an important issue, especially for a server application. You could use a log file, however, these are only useful if they are monitored by someone; too often applications create log files that are unknown to the system administrator.

In a Windows NT environment, the best approach for this type of reporting is to use the NT Event Log, because it offers a secure and centralized service for handling events from both local and remote Windows services.

We've kind of jumped the gun on logging. By logging, we mean execution tracing and data structure monitoring. This is useful both during development and when an application is moved into production. To be able to turn on a multilevel trace while the application is running can be extremely useful when you have no option but to debug the application live. This is where logging to a plain old log file is okay (using the NT Event Log for this purpose is not appropriate). Although you must think about the quantity of log data you generate and the rate at which it is generated, there's no point in developing a logging solution that's going to generate huge amounts of data and just fill up the disk. Any permanent logging scheme should include a management regime such as treating the log file as a circular buffer or iterating through a fixed set of numbered files.

In our experience, this management aspect is often overlooked and can rear up and bite you down the road. NT's Event Log has some basic management capability that allows you to set the maximum log file size and then control the way events wrap around inside the file when the size maximum is reached; for example, it allows you to select between overwriting events as needed, overwriting events older than a specified period, or clearing out the log manually.

So, after that sermon, we're going to focus on *debugging* and leave the other two areas for you to think more about on your own.

Disabling Server Extension Caching

We mentioned this earlier, but it is directly relevant our discussion: By default, IIS caches ISAs in memory so that the penalty of loading the DLL is only incurred when it is first used. However, during developing and debugging, having the DLL cached is not convenient because you have to stop the server each time you want to deploy a new version of your ISA, and then restart it. You can disable caching by changing the server's Extension Caching flag in the registry from 1 to 0. The fully qualified registry entry name is:

```
HKEY_LOCAL_MACHINE/SYSTEM/CurrentControlSet/Services/W3SVC/Parameters/
   CacheExtensions
```

Remember, however, to set it back to 1 once you've completed your development, especially if the server is going to be migrated to a production environment. Otherwise, you will incur the performance penalty of loading and unloading the DLL on every request to it.

Displaying Output From Your DLL

Because it is so easy to do, writing debug messages to the screen is traditionally the most common way of debugging an application. For years programmers have spread output statements of various kinds throughout the code (and, to their embarrassment, have sometimes forgotten to remove them) to keep track of variable values, or to find out where execution falls into the great abyss.

Outputting debug messages in a server environment is a bit of a challenge because there is no standard input/output or error stream to write to as in a console application. Similarly, in the case of the IIS, there is no desktop context for you to display messages in a window.

OutputDebugString And DBMON

Thankfully, Windows provides some support for this type of non-interactive debugging via the **OutputDebugString** function, which writes a string to the debugger that is attached to the current application. If you are using Visual C++'s interactive debugger, these messages will be sent to its debug window. However, this is not of much use for non-interactive debugging. Thankfully, the Win32 SDK contains a wonderfully useful utility called **DBMON**, which creates a console debug window and displays the output of **OutputDebugString** from any process. The messages from each process are automatically distinguished because **DBMON** prepends the task ID to the string. Of all the non-interactive approaches, this is the most useful—as long as you're not generating too much output.

In situations where you are generating more output than can be displayed in the **DBMON** window, it is best to send your messages to a log file.

The **debug** module used throughout this chapter (and available on the CD-ROM enclosed with this book) actually provides a common interface to both **OutputDebugString** and to a log file (the name of which is currently hardwired to be c:\temp\debug.log). This is useful because it allows you to flip between the various methods without changing your code.

In fact, this module implements a third mechanism, useful for outputting much smaller amounts of information. It does this using a Windows **MessageBox** and uses NT's **MB_SERVICE_NOTIFICATION** flag, which allows the **MessageBox** to be used within a service context.

The module implements both a function **DebugOutput(enum DebugType eDebugType, LPSTR lpDebugMessage)** and a wrapper macro **Debug()**, which cunningly implements a **varargs** interface using **sprintf**.

We have already discussed the problems of logging messages to an unmanaged file. There are other issues to do with concurrency. Any logging scheme must be thread safe because it is possible for multiple threads to write to the log at once. Our implementation uses a **Mutex** object that will actually synchronize access to the log across multiple processes. Out of paranoia, it also locks the file so that access to the log by processes not participating in the synchronization scheme is also managed.

Running IIS Interactively

If your environment allows you to debug your DLL interactively, it's pretty hard to beat the Visual C++ debugger. Using this debugger, it is a cinch to debug your DLL. In order to do this, however, you need to take complete control of IIS. In this section, we'll briefly describe the steps you take to do this.

Remember from our discussion in Chapter 7 that IIS is actually implemented as a wrapper program inetinfo (found in the directory c:\Winnt\system32\inetsrv), which implements three services—Gopher, FTP, and WWW services—each implemented in separate DLLs. We are only interested here in the WWW service. You can actually start this service only by using the following command line:

```
inetinfo -e W3SVC
```

This causes inetinfo to load the DLL W3svc.dll. Follow these steps to run IIS interactively from the debugger:

1. Make sure that you have the correct permissions to run the service. To run inetinfo, you should become a member of the administrator group and then add the following two rights assigned to you using usermgr: "Act as part of the operating system" and "Generate security audits." Once these rights have been assigned, you will need to log out and log back in again for them to take effect.

2. Next, go into Visual C++ and open the project for your DLL.

3. Bring up the Project Settings dialog box using Build|Settings, and select the Debug tab. Select the General category from the drop-down list and enter the

full path of inetinfo into the Executable For Debug Session field. On our system this path is c:\Winnt\system32\inetsrv\inetinfo.exe. Then, in the Program arguments field, enter *-e W3SVC*.

4. If you are debugging a filter DLL, you need to make sure that the **FilterDLLs** registry key points to your DLL. It is probably easiest for the registry entry to point directly to the DLL in your project's Debug directory—either that, or it should point to an identical copy of the DLL that you're debugging.

5. Similarly, if you are debugging an ISA DLL, you must make sure that the logical path you use in your request maps to the physical development directory containing your DLL—either that or the DLL being referred to in the request must be an exact copy of the version you are debugging.

6. Set break points in your code as usual.

7. Make sure that the server is not running using inetmgr.

8. Now you're ready to go. Select Build|Debug|Go to start the server. It takes a few seconds to load (even on a 166 MHz Pentium).

9. Activate your DLL by sending a request to the server from your client application, for example, your Web browser.

Attaching A Debugger While IIS Is Running

Starting IIS manually is not really reflective of real life. If you need to debug a DLL while the server is running, Windows NT provides the ability to attach your debugger to an executing task using taskmgr. Here's how:

1. Start taskmgr and select the Processes tab.

2. Search down the list of running processes for inetinfo, select it with your mouse, and bring up the right-button menu.

3. Choose the Debug option from the menu. This will start your the Visual C++ debugger (assuming it is the default debugger).

4. Go into Developer Studio and bring up the Project Settings dialog box by selecting Build|Settings. Choose the Debug tab and then select Additional DLLs from the Category list.

5. Enter the full path name of your DLL into the list and make sure the entry is checked.

6. Load your source file and set break points as required.

7. When you initiate a client request that causes your DLL to do something, execution should stop when one of your break points is reached, and you can then use all the facilities of your debugger as usual.

Summary

In this chapter, we have covered a lot of ground and looked at how to develop and deploy both ISA and filter DLLs. By now you should be quite familiar with the advantages and some of the disadvantages of an ISAPI approach to application development. Although ISAPI provides a means of developing high performance server applications, it also requires fastidious attention to detail, especially in areas such as memory management and thread safety. Developing applications at this level is not for the novice developer. If you want to develop server applications at a much higher level, we recommend looking into some of the other components of Microsoft's ActiveX server framework, such as Active Server Pages (ASP) and the Internet Database Connector.

Advanced developers specifically targeting a Microsoft environment may also like to look at MFC's ISAPI wrapper classes for a more object-oriented approach to developing extensions.

If you are developing for a multivendor, multiplatform environment, searching for the Microsoft grail won't help you (at least not in the short-to-medium term). This is one of the main motivations behind using our own object-oriented server extension framework *SEREF*. With this in mind, take a close look at Chapters 11 through 14, the SEREF chapters.

Object Orientation: A Brief Overview

CHAPTER

11

Object orientation is one of the buzz phrases of the computer industry, complete with its own arcane vocabulary. In this chapter we delve into Object Orientation (OO, as we'll refer to it) and possibly debunk some myths along the way. We'll provide enough information here to successfully read the chapter that describes the OO Web server extension framework.

Object Orientation: A Brief Overview

For those of you who are already skilled or experienced OO practitioners, we suggest that you skip this chapter and move on to the description of the framework architecture, which begins in Chapter 12. First we'll describe some of the important theoretical underpinnings of OO.

Basic OO Concepts

The purpose of OO, in all its guises, is ultimately to enable the creation of software systems and architectures that are robust, extensible, simple, and stable. Though the genesis of any system that fulfills all those criteria remains a somewhat utopian ideal, OO certainly aids and supplements the natural creative process of the human mind.

The two most fundamental concepts in OO are the *class* and the *object.* A class is the description of the structure, interface, and implementation of some entity that exists in the problem or solution domain. Some commentators view a class as a template for object instantiation. An object is an instance of a class. This is to say that it is a distinct instantiation of a class and thus, has a discrete existence in whatever execution environment it resides. Grady Booch, chief scientist at Rational and renowned OO guru, describes objects as having *state*, *identity*, and *behavior.*

In OO languages, classes are declared and described using plain ASCII source files (like C++ and Java) or created and manipulated via a browser-based IDE (Smalltalk). Objects are instantiated implicitly, on the stack, or explicitly, by heap allocation. C++ supports both stack and heap-resident objects, whereas Smalltalk and Java

463

support heap-allocated objects only. Depending on the language, objects may be automatically garbage collected or may have to be explicitly destroyed.

We have patterned the next section in a similar manner to the seminal OO publication *Object Oriented Analysis And Design—With Applications*, Grady Booch, (Publisher Benjamin/Cummings). We also offer some simple language examples to demonstrate the concrete realization of the concepts described.

Abstraction

The human mind uses abstraction to simplify ideas and concepts to a level of understanding and personal, cognitive comfort. It allows the essence—the basic nature of some thing—to be captured, classified, and possibly disseminated. This is the Booch definition, "An abstraction denotes the essential characteristics of an object that distinguish it from all other kinds of objects and thus provides crisply defined conceptual boundaries relative to the perspective of the viewer."

The last phrase is interesting because it states that an abstraction depends upon your frame of reference. To a large extent, this is empirically true. For example, different analysts may create different abstractions given the same problem domain during analysis and design. As Booch describes in detail, this is also a matter of classification.

To illustrate, C++ provides the notion of abstract classes, which may define a protocol (and potentially some state) for sub-classes to implement (because an abstract class may not be instantiated). Here is a much simplified abstract class for a plotting surface:

```
class Surface {
public:
    Surface() { }
    virtual ~Surface() { }
    virtual Plot * newPlot() = 0;
    virtual void render() = 0;
    virtual void clear() = 0;
}
```

As you can see, the class itself offers no implementation, but defines the protocol discovered as essential for plotting surfaces.

Other languages, such as Java, provide an *interface* construct that allows the definition of an interface only—as in no state.

Encapsulation

The primary function (if you'll excuse the term) of encapsulation is to clearly separate the interface of an object from its implementation. Encapsulation may sometimes be called *information hiding*, implying that some portion or portions of the object under consideration are invisible. This is a basic *black box* approach to objects and classes; you can see certain parts of the entity under consideration, but not others.

Encapsulation is an important concept in OO. It allows the implementation of objects to change without affecting or requiring the modification of other parts of the software system that use the services of the object whose implementation is altered. Clients of a particular supplier object are bound by and dependent upon only the interface of the supplier. In this manner, we never need to know or make assumptions about the implementation of some service. This has the desirable effect that we may create software that is relatively immune to change—with respect to separate abstractions—even though it's dependent upon them contractually.

To illustrate this, Java provides for different *access* restrictions in a class definition in a similar manner to C++. Consider the following class:

```
public class TextCookie extends AttributedCookie {
private String rText;
private void drawSelected() {
    embolden();
    draw();
}
protected Font rFont;

public TextCookie() { }
public TextCookie(String rText, Rectangle rBounds) {
        super(rBounds);
        this.rText = rText;
}
public String getText() { return rText; }
public String setText(String rText) { this.rText = rText; }
}
```

The **TextCookie** class offers an interface of at least four public methods (the lines prefixed by the *public* keyword). We say *at least* because it has probably inherited more from the immediate super-class **AttributedCookie**. There is one private **String** variable **rText**, and one private method **drawSelected**. These are implementation-only concerns and may not be accessed by any client of the **TextCookie** class.

Hierarchy

In Booch's words, "Hierarchy is the ranking or ordering of abstractions." A ranking of abstractions will normally have as its end result some form of factored taxonomy that is representative of the commonality discovered during analysis and design. Effectively, once design has reached some form of equilibrium, there will be (in most systems) an inheritance lattice that is the development effort's representation of the abstractions discovered and invented. This lattice is not necessary similar to the real world structure of the system under consideration—but that should not be viewed as problematic.

Factoring is a technique applied predominantly during design to enable the common behavior of abstractions to migrate to other (usually super) classes. With common behavior and attributes migrating to a single place in the hierarchy, duplication is reduced and bug fixes are instantly transitive. The closer you get to the root of a hierarchy, the more general the abstractions become. The converse is also true as one navigates away from the root. Inheritance relationships are, for this reason, sometimes called *generalization/specialization relationships*—depending upon the direction from which the relationship is described.

The use and abuse of inheritance has been the subject of many debates. On the one hand, inheritance provides an intelligible and sometimes natural OO decomposition for certain problems and allows sharing of behavior across subordinate classes. On the other hand, it has been abused in projects, usually by inappropriate use. The most common mistakes are using inheritance to model the value of an attribute or creating hierarchies when the use of delegation would be more appropriate. Inheritance also introduces the problem of the *fragile base class,* where the same advantages that lead to the use of inheritance are also its downfall.

Inheritance is often classified as *white box reuse* because sub-classes of a particular class are in fact dependent upon its implementation. It is, however, fair to say that inheritance, if used properly, is a valuable concept.

As a C++ example, consider Listing 11.1, which shows heavily elided declarations for a network hierarchy.

Listing 11.1 The NetworkObject partial class hierarchy.

```
class NetworkObject {
private:
    NetworkNode * pNode;
public:
    NetworkObject();
    virtual ~NetworkObject();
    Node & getNode();
    virtual unsigned int  isInService() = 0;
+.
};

class Port : public NetworkObject{
private:
        PtrArray<Connection> * pVirtualConnections;
public:
        Port();
        ~Port();
+.
};
class FrameRelayPort : public Port {
+.
public:
        FrameRelayPort();
        ~FrameRelayPort();
        unsigned int  isInService();
++
};
```

The abstract class **NetworkObject** asserts some basic characteristics of a network object in the problem domain we have modeled. The elided class **Port** specializes **NetworkObject** and is in turn specialized by the class **FrameRelayPort**. This is an excerpt from a real problem domain, in which the design suggested this hierarchy. The behavior is distributed reasonably evenly through the lattice and in turn calls upon other abstract entities (such as class **Connection**) to model the domain.

Polymorphism

Although polymorphism is not mentioned separately in Booch (though discussed), it deserves special mention. Simply, this concept describes the existence of objects that have a common interface but a different implementation. As these objects present the same interface to clients or (more rarely) suppliers, they may be used in the same scenarios but with potentially different results.

Languages such as C++ achieve polymorphism using inheritance and virtual member functions. In C++, a derived class should be able to be used by methods that expect instances of its base class without problems. If not, inheritance is being improperly used. C++ also provides *parameterized types*, which exhibit untyped polymorphic traits but do not necessarily rely upon the existence of virtual functions.

Refer back to Listing 11.1, and then examine this C++ member function for an alerter class:

```
void Alerter::sendAlert(NetworkObject & rObject) {
    if (rObject.isInService())
        errorLogger << "Object In Service" <<
                        << rObject << endl;
}
```

The argument to the function is a **NetworkObject** that declares a pure virtual function in its public interface, as shown here:

```
virtual unsigned int  isInService() = 0;
```

It's obvious that a concrete sub-class of **NetworkObject** must provide an implementation for the **isInService** member function. So, in the previous code snippet, the call to

```
if (rObject.isInService())
```

references an implementation (via a virtual table associated with the particular instance) in some sub-class of **NetworkObject**. The exact type of this instance of **NetworkObject** is unknown to the **sendAlert** member function. But that's just as it should be. Because we know that all concrete classes will provide an implementation, the **sendAlert** member function will operate for all descendants of **NetworkObject**.

Typing

We define the *type* of a class or object we define more loosely than Booch. We see a type as the observable interface of a class or object. In some ways, type is almost synonymous with the notion of abstraction. Type is a restricted view of the overall structure and composition of a class.

OO programming languages enforce typing differently. C++ and Java offer both static and dynamic typing, whereas Smalltalk has almost no notion of typing—with the notable exception that everything is an object.

In a language such as Java, type is partially separated from the notion of class via the existence of the *interface* construct. In C++, a similar effect can be achieved with the use of multiple inheritance and completely abstract classes.

Relationships Between Classes And Objects

Objects, as we've said before, do not exist in isolation. They have to collaborate with others to achieve the utility of the system they model. Here are some of the possible relationships:

- *Association*—A semantic dependency between one class and another. Associations may be uni- or bidirectional, and have a specified cardinality, navigability, and so on.

- *Aggregation*—A whole/part relationship, in which one object aggregates another. Such aggregation may be as per *composition*, in that the life of the part is the same as the life of the aggregate (ownership) or it may potentially be longer, if the containment is via reference, pointer, or is defined in that way.

- *Generalization*—The relationship between a super-class and a sub-class (base class and derived class). A class C generalizes class D if class C is a super-class of class D.

- *Specialization*—The relationship between a sub-class and a super-class (derived class and base class). A class D specializes class C if class D is a sub-class of class C.

- *Instantiates*—Shown in Booch to be the relationship between a concrete class and a *parameterized type*. In C++, for example, this is the relationship between a particular instance of a template and the template definition itself.

- *Dependency*—Denotes the dependence of a client object on a supplier object to supply certain services, such as implementing a particular interface.

Booch also defines a *has* relationship, which is basically aggregation, and a *uses* relationship, which is similar to a *dependency*, in that it provides some service to the source. The *metaclass* relationship is used to denote the relationship between a class and *its* own class. Such relationships cannot be represented natively in C++, but are part of a language such as Smalltalk. Of course, the notion of metaclass does not, in and of itself, admit the possibility of the infinite regress of classes and objects.

OOA, OOD, And OOP

Even though OO presents a differently *focused* approach to system decomposition, it still requires analysis, design, and implementation phases. The major difference with an OO approach here is that these phases are to be regarded as *iterative*, rather than the big bang cycle typically employed by non-OO methods (for example, the waterfall cycle).

The purpose of object-oriented analysis (OOA), like most other forms of analysis, is to gain an understanding of the problem domain. Thus, in analysis, we seek to understand *why*, not *how*. An OO analysis will seek to capture a reasonable and accurate, but not usually exhaustive, understanding of the domain. Most OO methods place a strong emphasis on capturing the behavior of a system, and ignore the potential design and/or implementation. To this end, this domain analysis usually focuses on discovering the primary and secondary scenarios in a system. A scenario is somewhat akin to a business process or task, wherein some input stimulus results in a sequence of actions that create a corresponding output. It is becoming common to front-end scenarios using Use Case diagrams, which can simply depict a business process in such a manner that the client can verify the processes discovered are *correct*. Use cases may also be fed directly into the story-boarding phase of analysis and design.

It is very common to capture this domain understanding using the notation of whatever OO method is employed. Popular methods that have an accompanying notation include Booch, OMT, SOMA, and OOSE. Currently in vogue, and at release 1.0, is the Unified Modeling Language (UML), which we use in our examples.

Using UML terminology, some of the static, logical diagrams created during OOA include use cases and class diagrams. Some of the dynamic diagrams include state transition diagrams and sequence diagrams.

Object-oriented design (OOD) seeks to map, discover, abstract, or amplify the models, scenarios, and behaviors discovered in analysis, into a coherent and self-consistent design that builds on the implied partial architectural vision of the analyst. If you're using the Booch method, design (and, to a certain extent, analysis) has the following abbreviated *iterative* cycle:

- Identification of class and objects.

- Identification of class and object semantics.

- Discover/invent inter-class/object relationships and mechanisms.

- Specify class interfaces and manufacture implementations.

These phases are intensely creative and not easily automated. The design of a system is, among other things, a matter of taste, experience, time, and interest. Booch gives a full treatment of the heuristics that may be applied strategically and tactically during design.

The results of the analysis (the *Macro Development Phase* in Booch parlance) usually feed into the *Micro Development* phase, which usually encompasses design and implementation. Design, as described generically, is viewed as layered into at least *tactical* and *strategic* versions, which often require different mind sets and experience levels. Using UML terminology, some of the static, logical diagrams created or augmented during OOD include class diagrams and collaboration diagrams. We also usually define modules, subsystems, and categories. Some of the dynamic diagrams created include state transition diagrams and sequence diagrams.

OOP is an acronym for object-oriented programming, which is the construction of the actual software, the implemented result of OOA and OOD. The choice of an OO programming language is normally made early—not that that is necessarily the best time. Clients have often made their choice in advance, or have a preferred language or set of tools to use. Whatever language is used, it should be able to represent all the relationships and mechanisms we have discovered or specified during analysis and design.

Object-Oriented Frameworks

Objects, clearly, do not exist in a vacuum. They collaborate and have relationships with other objects, have their own threads of control, act as clients, servers, brokers, and more. An object may have different roles depending upon the context—in fact, there is not enough space here to describe all the different scenarios and objects that may exist. Different methods exist by which classes and objects may be shared, and we'll describe them in the following sections.

Class Libraries

For each distinct application or system there may be classes in common. Such classes are typically utility classes, such as string classes, network classes, and so on. It would be a singularly bad idea to duplicate code across these systems or reinvent the abstractions required.

To aid in the sharing of classes, some form of *library* system may be used. This is usually a simple packaging of classes into a described (manifested) and basic reusable form. Such a collection is called a *class library*. These libraries are considered to be at the lower level of the reuse spectrum, because they usually encourage the reuse of single abstractions. Class libraries are not to be frowned upon at all because they provide a vehicle for reuse that leverages development investment.

A different embodiment of the notion of sharing is the *framework*.

What Is A Framework?

We state that a framework has a predefined and encapsulated set of objects and inter-object collaborations that cooperate to provide the basis for a *templated* solution to some problem. We use templated to mean pro forma and complete, yet void of defining and specific behavior. We could also say that a framework embodies some mechanism that is sufficiently abstracted for reuse. Note that in our discussions we consider only OO frameworks.

There is thus an implied coarser grain of reuse present when a framework is used, as compared to a class library. When leveraging from an existing framework, we are not reusing a single class, but potentially many classes and their relationships. This is not to say we are reusing more than one abstraction, just more than one entity.

Using (and, for that matter, developing) a framework is difficult at first because you cede control, by and large, to the framework. The framework calls you—you don't call it. For those not experienced in OO, this can be something of a shock at first.

White Box Frameworks

A *white box* framework is probably the most common form of framework available today. The term white box is used similarly to the way it is used for inheritance. In fact, a white box framework uses inheritance as the mechanism by which framework extension and the creation of derived utility is achieved.

Such a framework is usually designed so that the classes—whose observable behavior may or should be altered to facilitate the creation of useful software—declare accessible methods in an appropriate manner. For example, in C++, member functions that are candidates for overriding would be declared as virtual. In some cases, a member function may be declared abstractly, forcing a sub-class implementation.

If you are interested in examining a commercial and high-quality white box framework, consider perusing the documentation for the zApp GUI framework, accessible at the URL **www.roguewave.com**.

Black Box Frameworks

A *black box* framework is not a common type of framework. The term black box is used to signify that the framework does not rely solely on inheritance to allow for the extension or use of the framework. Instead, reuse is achieved by delegation and composition, which, as we mentioned previously, some practitioners believe allows the creation of more reusable and flexible software.

Such a framework is normally designed so that the classes whose observable behavior should be implemented to facilitate the creation of useful software are declared as an appropriate abstract interface. Concrete implementers of such interfaces may then be instantiated and provided to the framework. The framework will delegate responsibility as appropriate to the supplied objects.

Vertical And Horizontal Frameworks

Both white and black box frameworks may also be further categorized as either *vertical* or *horizontal*.

A *horizontal* framework has potential utility across a number of domains. One example is a GUI framework, because a GUI may front many different types of systems in many domains. Horizontal frameworks are not tied to any specific problem domain.

A *vertical* framework may sometimes be referred to as a *domain* framework. This type of framework provides the necessary behavior to allow the implementation of a number of applications specific to a particular domain. An example of this type of framework is an accounting framework that finds utility in the accounting domain. Such frameworks often embody valuable, prized domain expertise that is important to capture and reuse.

Application And System Frameworks

In a similar manner to the preceding section, frameworks may also be categorized as *application* or *system* frameworks.

An *application* framework provides the same mechanisms and predefined behavior that we expect of a framework but at a reasonably high level of abstraction. This means that an application framework deals in concepts that typically have an identifiable corollary in the problem or solution domain, and have been isolated as such. As their name implies, they find use in the direct construction of applications. An example of an application framework is a GUI framework.

A *system* framework also provides the same mechanisms and predefined behavior that we expect of a framework but at a lower level of abstraction. This means that a system framework deals in concepts that typically do not have a directly visible and identifiable corollary in the problem or solution domain. Thus, they provide an implementation blueprint for lower-level services such as device drivers, shells, communication abstraction layers, and so on. Therefore, such a framework could enable the construction of Vxds for Windows 95, a hard disk driver for Solaris, and many others.

If you are interested in papers at a higher level concerning frameworks, visit Taligent's site at **www.taligent.com**.

Advantages Of Using Object-Oriented Frameworks

Because we have described some of the different types of frameworks, it must be obvious that we see utility and advantage in using (or should we say, re-using) them. To help summarize the chapter, we list the main advantages in the following sections.

Leverage Expertise

This much should be self-evident: Because a framework provides a template for many solutions to some problem, in a way that uses multiple objects and their relationships, there is implied expertise captured in the framework and its mechanisms. Thus, when you reuse or extend the framework, you are reusing the work of the framework's architects, designers, and implementers who encountered a problem or problems and solved them in such a way that a reusable skeleton resulted.

The undertaking to design and implement a framework is significant. When complete, and if the architectural vision was strong, consistent, and clear, a thing of use and even beauty may result.

Reduce Development Time

With the extension of a framework, we are building upon the work of other developers, and therefore, we are surely saving the time that they invested in the construction of the framework.

In some cases, this can actually be a phenomenal amount of time, even though you may not realize it during development. Consider a GUI framework, for example. The event-driven model of most GUIs is reasonably simple to understand. However, the proliferation of events and data structures that underpin most GUI implementations (at the low, base level) do mount up and become difficult to manage effectively. Additionally, the portability of applications designed to address one particular GUI model is normally very poor.

A GUI framework such as the C++ framework zApp or the AWT of Java provide a common model of a GUI that is cross-platform portable and hides many of the obscenities patched over low-level GUI implementations. Important events, in most cases, are mapped to behavior via some well-defined interface that is normally defined somewhere in a rich and varied framework structure.

With a well-designed and debugged framework, some of the finer nuances of the problem domain may be abstracted away, which in most scenarios is a blessing in disguise.

Improved Maintenance

Certainly for white box frameworks, a number of maintenance issues are soothed. The most important advantage can also be the downfall of some frameworks. We refer, of course, to the alteration of core behavior and its transitive propagation upon alteration.

If basic implementation details of some distant super-class are altered, this may detrimentally affect the derived classes. As you can see from that statement, it pays to be sure of your framework.

Summary

In this chapter, we described, in coarse detail, the basic concepts of the OO model. We enumerated and gave detail for the elements of a simple object model. We explained the concepts of object and class and showed that a number of relationships may exist between them.

We mentioned the areas of OOA, OOD, and OOP, giving brief and informal definitions of them. The reference section of this book lists some valuable references we used for this area.

Last, we covered the topics of class libraries and frameworks. This subject leads to the next chapter, in which we'll describe an OO framework created to specifically address and solve the issues in creating cross-platform and cross-API portable Web server extensions.

HIGH PERFORMANCE

Toward A Web Server Extension Framework

CHAPTER

12

Chapter 11 outlined basic OO concepts and provided a brief introduction to OO frameworks. In this chapter, we'll begin to examine a framework designed to provide an extensible and vendor-independent set of cohesive and collaborative abstractions for the construction of Web server extensions.

Toward A Web Server Extension Framework

A Web server extension framework will provide a focused and readily extensible object-oriented framework that will allow software developers to create Web server extensions with minimum effort. Further, extensions that are created should be source code portable across at least the ISAPI and NSAPI APIs, and therefore also portable across all API-supported operating systems. Finally, the framework will operate in such a manner that the performance of generic extensions will not be adversely affected.

Any endeavor must have a basic rationale that drives it. The first section of this chapter enumerates some of the reasons that led us to create a Web server extension framework.

What Use Is A Server Extension Framework?

As we hoped that this framework potentially had a commercial existence, it was necessary for us to at least list some basic advantages that such a software system might offer. Such advantages, though no guarantee of commercial success, would demonstrate our understanding of the utility that such a system might offer to the extension development community. Note that we do not describe commercial or business objectives for this product, as this is beyond the scope of this work.

Portability

Portability is one of the most difficult goals to achieve with respect to software. This goal is made that much harder to achieve by the use of proprietary APIs such as

ISAPI and NSAPI, which also introduce the notion of vendor portability. Put simply, if you write an extension that depends upon ISAPI, it can be tedious and time consuming to port that extension across to NSAPI. Furthermore, if you want your NSAPI extension to port back to ISAPI, you may face platform issues as well as basic API differences, which make the task that much harder.

It became obvious that a write-once, port-many philosophy would be quite valuable. Even if you ignored the cross-platform issues, API vagaries would render most development efforts time consuming.

We were aware of the basic approaches in languages such as C, which enable such portability to occur. These are inferior to those that can be offered and embodied by a well-designed OO framework.

Common Code Base

If a well-designed and complete framework were to exist for Web server extensions, it would be possible therefore to create extensions that could be used with different vendor APIs and across various platforms with a common code base. The advantage here is obvious—the maintenance effort is dramatically reduced.

Additionally, the focus for the extension developer returns to the task at hand, and is not concerned with the possible API/platform issues.

Single Model

One of the problems we found with ISAPI and NSAPI was the subtly different models they used to describe the processing of an Internet request. Although not that onerous to handle, this provides an unnecessary distraction.

We felt a framework could provide a simplified and consistent OO model of the temporal progression of a request as it was handled. If a further API became apparent or important, it was also our hope that it could be decomposed such that it could fit into the existing framework behavior.

Simplify Extension Creation

Extension creation in either ISAPI or NSAPI is not impossible to do. We felt that we could simplify the process further with a small and focused OO framework. This would reduce development time, as there would be less to learn to create an extension—the framework would do the hard stuff for the developer.

Basic Comparison Of ISAPI And NSAPI

At the highest level, we compared the execution model of the two APIs. As we discussed in Chapter 2, both APIs achieve server extension using the shared object support (DLL under Windows NT, shared libraries under flavors of Unix) of the target operating system. As a natural extension of this method, they both utilize C linkage callback functions in the shared object that provide entry points that the Web server will call at various times. A call-back will occur for each event or events in which an interest has been registered by the extension software. The common method of extension deployment simplifies matters greatly. If there had been significant differences, this may have rendered the configuration for the framework problematic. This commonality also suggests that the framework, if feasible in other areas, can leverage off this shared philosophy to simplify the deployment model. This is a lower level concern, but gives one hope of success.

To help decide how to approach the framework's overall functionality and anticipate what problems might arise, we decided to examine the behavior sets of these two APIs and focus upon their intersection. We hoped to identify the core behavior of the APIs: those that must be supported and those that may be problematic. Table 12.1 is an abbreviated comparison.

There is potentially a large degree of common functionality across both APIs. This is to be expected given the simple nature of HTTP and the domain under examination. We decided that, given Table 12.1, there is virtually nothing that cannot be either directly implemented or simulated reasonably well.

Each server provides, for each request, session, or at the server global level, a number of working variables. These variables mostly represent transient information. We examined the most commonly useful information provided by ISAPI, as this appeared to be the largest set, and compared it with NSAPI. This comparison is shown in Table 12.2. Note that the variable names shown are as per ISAPI.

Table 12.1 ISAPI and NSAPI feature set comparison.

Feature/Information	NSAPI	ISAPI	Comments
Version of filter	Redundant	Required	Of minor importance.
Secure port Yes/No	Can be simulated	Available	No problem.
Callback function used for notification	No, data structure approach	Yes, single callback for each event type	Can be hidden.
Assign a priority to filter functions	Yes/No	Yes	In NSAPI, you imply priority by the placement of the directive in the obj.conf file.
Add header(s) to response to be sent	Yes	Yes	Has standard behavior.
Write raw data to Client	Yes, as an event normally	Yes	Has standard behavior.
WWW-Authenticate headers on server denial	Yes	Yes	
Add general headers for denial of service	Yes	Yes	
Filter raw data (or access to the raw data) as sent	Not as an event	Yes	For NSAPI, the full request is available after reading. It is unlikely that this will work as required, though.
Preprocessing headers	No, but simulation might be possible	Yes	
Modify, Delete, and Add headers	Yes	Yes	
URL translation, virtual to physical	Yes	Yes	
Physical path check	Yes	No	For ISAPI to be simulated, this should be able to follow an event from URL mapping.
Object typing	Yes	No	It would be possible to simulate this behavior in ISAPI.
Service request	Yes	No	This is not filter behavior, but rather an ISA function.
With some			foresight, this could be addressed, however.

continued

Table 12.1 ISAPI and NSAPI feature set comparison (continued).

Feature/Information	NSAPI	ISAPI	Comments
Log event	Yes	Yes	NSAPI version does not encourage altering what is sent to the access log. ISAPI, on the other hand, is quite liberal.
Session ending with Client	No	Yes	Can simulate, by augmenting the log event and stipulating one request per session.

Table 12.2 Transient variables available.

Variable Name	NSAPI	ISAPI
AUTH_TYPE	Only Basic is defined	Basic/NTLM/Custom; NTLM is NT specific
CONTENT_LENGTH	Yes	Yes
CONTENT_TYPE	Yes	Yes
GATEWAY_INTERFACE	No, can be simulated	Yes
PATH_INFO	Yes	Yes
PATH_TRANSLATED	Yes	Yes
QUERY_STRING	Yes	Yes
REMOTE_ADDR	Yes	Yes
REMOTE_HOST	Yes	Yes
REMOTE_USER	Yes	Yes
REQUEST_METHOD	Yes	Yes
SCRIPT_NAME (CGI)	Yes	Yes
SERVER_PORT	Yes	Yes
SERVER_PROTOCOL	Yes	Yes
AUTH_PASSWORD	Yes	Yes
SERVER_SOFTWARE	Yes	Yes
HTTPP_ACCEPT	Yes	Yes

Of course, we did consider other more esoteric (and again, some more basic) details before we finally decided that the creation of an extension framework was possible. Even at this stage though, you can see that there is a reasonable chance of success for a framework that seeks to fulfill the goals outlined at the beginning of this chapter.

So, given the broadly similar model, same problem domain, and identified behavioral intersection, we decided to proceed and build the framework. We have omitted in our explanation portions of the analysis and design that would only lengthen the description and not amplify the intent and philosophy.

SEREF

SEREF (**SER**ver Extension Framework) is the acronym by which we'll refer to the extension framework. In this chapter, we'll use SEREF also to mean a generalized Web server extension framework. First, we'll discuss why we chose C++ as the implementation language for SEREF.

The Choice Of An OOPL

Even though this is regarded, to a certain extent, as a mere implementation detail, we knew that it was necessary to decide upon a target OOPL. All things considered, C++ lent itself best to the task. We used a number of criteria to reach this decision, some of which are performance, platform support, stability, and closeness to the APIs that we would have to effectively wrap up. This would also be possible in a language such as Java. We could not compromise performance to that extent (even with the existence of a JIT compiler), nor could we introduce a risk that the imminent change (from JDK 1.0.2 to JDK 1.1) would necessitate an instant port/rewrite.

We also had to determine which features of C++ might be problematic. By far the worst supported or implemented features of C++ are templates and nested classes. (Remember that the platforms we consider here are Windows NT and Unix only.)

From past experience with a variety of flavors of Unix, templates were often poorly implemented. However, with the improvement of public domain software such as GNU C++, this support and quality are growing rapidly. So, at least for flavors of Unix, there should be no major problem with the use of templates. Likewise, the support for nested classes, which is a basic feature of C++, should be okay.

Windows NT presents somewhat of a quandary. We know that all popular Win32 implementations of C++ are similar in their level of support for nested classes—that is, adequate. However, virtually all compilers have a problem exporting template instantiations from a DLL.

Under Win32, it is possible to define the implementation of a class in one DLL, and export its interface so that other clients (DLL-based or otherwise) can instantiate it, derive from it, and so on. The problem is this: If you wish to derive a class from a class defined in a DLL, it must be marked as exported (normally in a compiler-specific way). If you fail to do this, then derivation is not possible. As you know, inheritance is a reasonably common relationship in OO systems. So what is the problem with templates? Well, not all compilers support a means by which a template instance can be exported. With our Visual C++ 4.x initial target compiler under Win32, this was definitely the case. This means that any template instance we create could not be exported from the DLL in which it was instantiated.

In itself, this issue with templates was not a significant problem for the type of classes we expected to be templated (specialized collection classes), because we could just as effectively (but not as nicely) use delegation techniques. But it's important to be aware of the limitations.

The Basic SEREF Architecture

Now it's time to look at the architecture of the framework. The most important aspect to consider in designing a framework such as SEREF is how the events and their progression should be modeled.

If we cast aside all notions of implementation, we can note that every event:

- Needs to have its own specific default and expected behavior.

- Is interested in only a portion of the total state space of a requests processing.

- Must be multi-thread safe.

- Should have clear and well-defined semantics.

- Should share certain characteristics.

The previous list shows some basic qualities of a *generic* event. But what other, more abstract qualities does an event have?

A Dependency Mechanism

Each concrete instance of an event *depends* on some other entity for its existence. In the case of a Web server extension, whatever internal mechanism is employed to create each event can be generalized to a form of *event manager*.

Let's consider event notification further. If we accept that an event manager exists, how does it create events? If you turn this argument and put the burden on the developer to imply what is of interest, there's the possibility that instead of creating events, an event manager merely notifies events or the transition of events to interested parties (*dependents*). This is the idea used in SEREF—*event handlers* are created by third-party code during the initialization phase and the handlers register their interest in events with the SEREF event manager, which acts as the model of the framework. The SEREF event manager presents an abstract interface to the real event-driving machinery of the Web server. To simplify this idea, you can think of the event handlers as the simple extension functions discussed in the ISAPI (Chapters 7 through 10) and NSAPI (Chapters 3 through 6) specific parts of this book. Aside from interfacing with the Web server internals, the event manager is responsible for keeping a list of dependents that have informed it that they are interested in certain *aspects* (event types). These dependents are notified when the server triggers the aspect.

If you are familiar with the Model-View-Controller (MVC) paradigm first employed in Smalltalk, you will see the similarities with our description and the basic MVC mechanism.

The MVC Triad

The MVC mechanism is a classic design pattern commonly used in Smalltalk. Its basic intention is to separate the Model (information) from View (presentation of some information from the model) and Controller (responsible for interfacing with user input and external stimuli). In classic MVC, a model is only aware that it has dependents, which can attach and detach themselves from the model. Obviously, as entropy increases, aspects of the model may change. When this happens, the model informs dependents of this change by broadcasting a message (of potentially different forms) to its dependents. If they are interested in the change that has occurred, they can ask the model for the information they are interested in. This is the simplest form of MVC.

A slightly more advanced form of MVC in Smalltalk lets dependents register with the model by supplying an aspect in which they are interested and a message that they desire to be sent when this aspect alters. The dependency update process is then stream-lined because the dependent has a specific message sent to it when change occurs, and does not need to filter from the many potential states that a model may pass.

*Some Smalltalks have an even more advanced mechanism. This method uses objects called **ValueHolders**, which actually wrap attributes of the model and keep their own dependent list. This streamlines the propagation of change notification to dependents and also aids in the creation of software that has consistent and easy-to-maintain notification semantics. Refer to the many Smalltalk resources on the Internet for more information.*

So, these are the basics of the notification. The event manager exists once SEREF is loaded, and allows external event handlers to attach to it during the SEREF boot-strap process. An event handler registers interest in predefined event types. These event types have a parallel structure to the event types that the framework supports. When there is a change to the event manager that interests dependents, a general mechanism notifies the dependents in order of their registration. More abstract parts of the event-handling mechanism must translate this generic notification to a specific, understandable message or set of messages. During this translation, certain core request or session objects may also be created to streamline event processing.

What Type Of Framework?

We discussed in Chapter 11 the types of framework that you can create. SEREF falls into the category of a *white box, horizontal-domain, application-level framework.*

Why white box? Well, as inheritance is the mechanism of reuse in this scheme, this fits in with our goal of making SEREF easy to understand. Delegation, while some-times a superior technique, sometimes leads to collections of objects that appear disconnected in such a way that the system appears more complex than it really is. A framework must be simpler than the problem it tries to solve, or why would a developer choose to use it?

In fact, this choice also fits in with the dependency mechanism we discussed. Remember that we said that abstract parts of the event handling mechanism must translate generic notifications into specific and understandable messages or message sets. If we keep our basic dependent generic (for example, if it receives a very general message), then a related object has to perform the translation. The easiest way to do this is to polymorphically override the generic message and perform appropriate actions to make it fit in with our needs.

We hoped that adopting this approach would achieve another goal. This goal has loftier ideals—that we'd have a large core of reusable and closed-for-modification objects, with system, event, and platform specifics relegated to an easily manageable and abstract periphery. We'll discuss how we modeled this approach as we progress.

Supporting Classes

All frameworks require classes that support their general operation. SEREF was no different in this regard—it became obvious that if we wanted the framework to operate at maximum efficiency, we'd need specialized support classes.

We identified these as necessary:

- String
- Vector
- Dictionary (associative array)
- Associations (that could be placed in the dictionary)

and, as we got further in the design process, we defined:

- Pool
- Cloning container

We examined the Standard Template Library (STL) as a possible candidate but felt that, as it could only support polymorphic containers in a clumsy manner (via wrapping techniques, which we don't want to use), it would not suffice. Polymorphic containers hold pointers, not values, and are generally more efficient because the overhead in pointer copying is minimal. They suffer from weaker and less obvious ownership semantics, but because these classes are private to SEREF, it's not too important an issue.

So we're ready to design, create, and test our initial container classes. The string class **OptString** already exists in our class library. Fortunately, the container classes we require at first are quite simple to design and implement. The next sections illustrate the classes involved.

The Class IVector

As we mentioned, our containers should be polymorphic (holding pointers) and also template based. Figure 12.1 shows the UML notation diagram for our polymorphic vector class, **IVector**. **IVector** allows the addition to, removal from, and location of members in itself, as well as simple integer-based subscripting.

As you can see, **IVector** is always an unbounded vector (it resizes automatically) and presents a simple but basically complete interface to vector users. Interestingly, it uses a nested class called **Iterator** to provide an iterator over itself. This iterator is created by calling the **begin** member function—this was our one concession to the STL. We liked the use of nested classes to model iterators, and thus adopted it. Listing 12.1 shows an abbreviated listing of **IVector**.

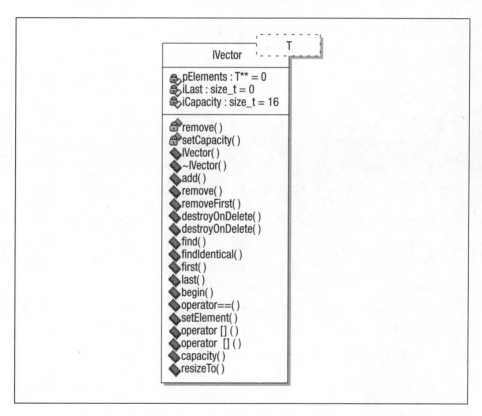

Figure 12.1
Class **IVector** UML diagram.

Listing 12.1   Partial source code for **IVector**.

```
#if !defined(IVECTOR_H_)
#define IVECTOR_H_
#include <sys/types.h>

template <class T>
class IVector {
private:
   T ** pElements;
   size_t iCapacity, iLast, iDelete;

   T * remove(size_t iIndex) {
      T * pReturn = (T *) NULL;
      if (iIndex != (size_t) -1 && size()) {
         pReturn = pElements[iIndex];
         for (; iIndex<capacity() - 1; iIndex++)
            pElements[iIndex] = pElements[iIndex+1];
         pElements[size()-1] = (T*) 0;
         iLast--;
      }
   return pReturn;
   }
    void initFromTo(size_t i) {
      initFromTo(i, capacity() -1);
   }

   void initFromTo(size_t i, size_t j) {
      for ( ; i<=j ; i++)
         pElements[i] = (T *) 0;
   }

   void setCapacity(size_t iNewCap) { iCapacity = iNewCap; }

public:
   IVector(size_t iCap=16) : pElements(new T*[iCap]),
                                 iCapacity(iCap==0 ? 1 : iCap),
                                 iLast(0), iDelete(0) {
      initFromTo(0);
   }

   virtual ~IVector() {
      if (destroyOnDelete()) destroy();
      delete [] pElements;
   }
```

```
size_t add(T * pObject) {
    int iReturnCode=0;
    if (size() < capacity() || resizeTo(capacity() * 2)) {
        pElements[iLast++] = pObject;
        iReturnCode = size();
    }
    return iReturnCode;
}

T * remove(T * pObject) {
    return remove(findIdentical(pObject));
}

T * removeFirst() {
    return remove((size_t) 0);
}

size_t find(T const * pObject) {
    for (size_t i=0; i<size() ; i++)
        if ((* ((T * )pObject)) ==(*(pElements[i])))
            return i;
    return (size_t) -1;
}

size_t findIdentical(T const * pObject) {
    for (size_t i=0; i<size() ; i++) {
    if (pObject == pElements[i])
            return i;
    }
    return (size_t) -1;
}

T * first() { return pElements[0]; }

T * last() {
    return (size() == 0) ?
                (T*) 0 : pElements[size() - 1]; }

void destroy() {
    for (size_t i=0; i<size(); i++) {
        delete pElements[i];
        pElements[i] = (T*) 0;
    }
    iLast = 0;
}
```

```
size_t destroyElementAt(size_t iIndex) {
    size_t iRetCode = 0;
    if (iIndex < size()) {
        T * pElement = remove(iIndex);
        delete pElement;
        iRetCode = 1;
    }
    return iRetCode;
}

size_t size() const { return iLast; }

int destroyOnDelete() const { return iDelete; }

void destroyOnDelete(size_t i) { iDelete = i; }

class Iterator {
private:
    typedef IVector<T> CONTAINER;
    CONTAINER * pOwner;
    size_t iIndex, iStart;
public:
    Iterator(CONTAINER * pOwn = (CONTAINER *) 0,
             size_t iStrt = 0)
             : pOwner(pOwn), iIndex(iStrt), iStart(iStrt) {
    }
    ~Iterator() { }
    T * operator++() {
        return (!pOwner) ?
                (T*) 0 : (*pOwner)[iIndex++]; }
    T * current() {
        return (!pOwner) ?
                (T*) 0 : (*pOwner)[iIndex]; }
    int more() { return (!pOwner) ? 0 : iIndex < pOwner->size(); }
    void reset() { iIndex = iStart; }
};

Iterator begin(size_t iIndex = 0) {
        return Iterator(this, iIndex);
}

int operator==(IVector<T> const & rhs) {
    int iReturnCode = 0;
    if (rhs.size() == size()) {
        iReturnCode = 1;
```

```
            for (size_t i = 0; i<size() && iReturnCode; i++) {
                T * pObject = rhs[i];
                T * pElement = (*this)[i];
                if (pObject && pElement && *pElement == *pObject)
                        ;
                else
                        iReturnCode = 0;
            }
        }
    return iReturnCode;
    }


    T * setElement(size_t i, T * pObject) {
        if (i>=capacity() && !resizeTo(i+1))
            return (T*) 0;
        if (i>=size())
            iLast=i+1;
        return (pElements[i] = pObject);
    }

    T * operator[](size_t i) {
            return (i<size()) ? pElements[i] : (T *) 0; }

    T * operator[](size_t i) const {
            return (i<size()) ? pElements[i] : (T *) 0; }

    size_t capacity() const { return iCapacity; }

    size_t resizeTo(size_t iNewSize) {
        if (iNewSize > capacity()) {
            T ** pNewElements = new T*[iNewSize];
            for (size_t i = 0; i<iNewSize ; i++)
                pNewElements[i] = (i<size()) ? pElements[i] : (T*) 0;
            setCapacity(iNewSize);
            delete [] pElements;
            pElements = pNewElements;
        }
        return capacity();
    }

};

#endif
```

If you examine the source code closely, you can see we've made some other decisions. With regards to the use of exceptions, we found that during benchmarking, under Windows NT, exceptions incurred an unacceptably large performance penalty (up to 15 percent for certain compilers). We decided to use basic tests to detect errors, and not throw exceptions. Again, because the support classes should be private to SEREF, this will not be problematic.

Another subtle design aspect is that **IVector**'s destructor is defined as virtual. As you may know, destructors are declared virtual to enable the correct and complete destruction sequence to occur for derived types. But didn't we say that our template classes suffered a problem under Win32 compilers with respect to inheritance and exported template instances? Well, we did—but this won't always be the case. So, we'll declare the destructor virtual and accept the increase in size due to the virtual table pointer, so we don't have to worry about it later.

Finally, we'll allow the client of the **IVector** instance to inform it (**IVector**) what its action should be when destroyed—that is, whether it should destroy its contained elements or just free the space it used to hold the pointer value. This is achieved by calling the member function **destroyOnDelete** with a non-zero flag.

The Class IIDictionary

The notification method of the framework involves dependents that register interest in certain aspects of the model that may change. At a lower level, a dictionary class (associative array, if you prefer) would be useful in supporting this idea. This is because the aspects of the model could be the keys of associations in the dictionary. Each association would have a value of the dependent that has interest. As with most container classes, a dictionary class is most easily a template class. For efficiency, we decided again that the framework dictionary class would be a polymorphic container.

Most dictionary implementations are based around a hash table mechanism. Each key that is added to the table is used to generate a hash value, which is an index into the hash table. The associated value of the key will be placed at this hash table index. Of course, it is possible for two different keys to generate the same hash value—schemes are normally in place to handle these types of collisions. This typically involves some form of chain that hangs off the hash table location. For most dictionary implementations, the following conditions are important:

- The hash value is easy to calculate.

- The loading factor of the hash table is high (better than 80 percent).

- There is a uniform distribution of hash values for a set of keys.

(This was taken from *IEEE Software*, November 1985, pages 38-53, "An Interactive System For Finding Perfect Hash Functions.")

The choice of the hash function is therefore most important. For older systems, there was typically a global function with a specialized implementation that took care of this. In our experience, an OO system will delegate the responsibility for hash value calculation to objects. Although this is in the spirit of OO, it can make it more difficult to provide for intervention by an external agent to help in the management of hash table loading factor.

In our case, we'll require that each object implement a *HashValue* member function that we would query to ascertain the hash for an object acting as a key. This name is in uppercase format for historical reasons concerned with backward compatibility and versions of the Borland C++ compiler.

The **IIDictionary** template places few other restrictions on the objects that may act as keys. Figure 12.2 shows an incomplete UML notation class diagram for **IIDictionary**.

For maximum flexibility in the use of the dictionary, we allow the client to dictate many facets of its operation. The parameters to the template are shown in Table 12.3.

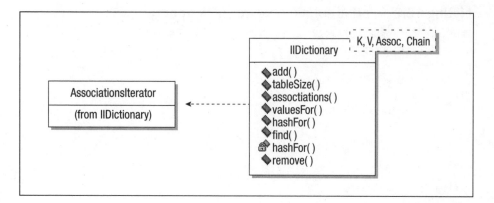

Figure 12.2
The UML notation class diagram for **IIDictionary**.

Table 12.3 The available Transient variables.

Template Parameter	Use
K	The key type.
V	The value type.
Assoc	The association type. Some association of K and V.
Chain	The chain collection type. Used to hold objects of type Assoc when collisions occur and ordinarily. The Chain type must implement a nested iterator that is exposed by the dictionary for value iteration purposes.

Thus, a client can instantiate an **IIDictionary** object, in such a way that the dictionary appears as a dictionary to external view and acts as expected. But internally, via the use of the **Chain** type, it acts in a highly specific manner that has been decided by policy or requirement external to the dictionary. This sounds like a violation of encapsulation in some ways, but it allows the **IIDictionary** class to be used in unanticipated situations, which is always advantageous. SEREF does, in fact, allow an excellent opportunity to demonstrate this adaptability and allow a simple solution to the problems that accompany—the attempt to make multi-thread issues invisible to the dependency mechanism.

Listing 12.2 shows the *public interface* method implementations for **IIDictionary**. You'll find the include file that holds this class on the CD-ROM enclosed with this book.

Listing 12.2 Partial source code for **IIDictionary**.

```
template <class K, class V, class Assoc, class Chain>
class IIDictionary {
public:
// Construct with hash table size default
IIDictionary(size_t iTabSize = 64) :
    iNumberOfAssociations(0) {
        rTable.destroyOnDelete(1);
        setHashTableSize(iTabSize);
    }

virtual ~IIDictionary() { }
```

```
// Add a key and associated value
virtual size_t add(K * pKey, V * pValue) {
      size_t iIndex = hashFor(pKey);

      Chain * pVector;
      if ((pVector = rTable[iIndex]) == (Chain *) 0) {
        pVector = new Chain();
        rTable.setElement(iIndex, pVector);
        pVector->destroyOnDelete(1);
       }

      pVector->add(new Assoc(pKey, pValue));
      iNumberOfAssociations++;
      return 1;
   }
// Remove a key
   virtual size_t remove(K * pKey) {
      return remove(pKey, (V *) NULL);
   }
// Remove a key that has a particular value
   virtual size_t remove(K * pKey, V * pValue) {
      Chain * pChain = chainAt(pKey);
      size_t iDestroyed = 0;
      if (pChain) {
         for (size_t i = 0; i<pChain->size() ; i++) {
            Assoc * pAssoc = (*pChain)[i];
            if (*pKey == *(pAssoc->key())) {
               if (!pValue || (*pValue == *(pAssoc->value()))) {
                  if (pChain->destroyElementAt(i))
                     iDestroyed++;
                  --iNumberOfAssociations;
               }
            }
         }
      }
      return iDestroyed;
   }
// Hash table size
   size_t tableSize() const { return rTable.capacity(); }
// Redefines the iterator of the Chain type to be the ValuesIterator
   typedef Chain::Iterator ValuesIterator;

/**
 * Returns a ValuesIterator (defined in this class) that may be used
 * to iterate over the values for a particular key. The key search is
 * based upon equality and not identity.
```

```
*/
    virtual ValuesIterator valuesFor(K const * pKey) {
        size_t iIndex;
        size_t iHashIndex = hashFor((K *) pKey);
        if ((iIndex = find(pKey)) != (size_t) -1)
            return rTable[iHashIndex]->begin(iIndex);
        return ValuesIterator();
    }

    class AssociationsIterator {
    private:
        typedef IIDictionary<K,V,Assoc,Chain> DICT_OWNER;
        DICT_OWNER * pOwner;
        Chain * pCurrentChain;
        Chain::Iterator rCurrentIterator;
        size_t iIndex;

        Chain * findNextChain() {
            for ( pCurrentChain = (Chain *) 0;
                  iIndex < pOwner->tableSize() &&
                    !pCurrentChain; iIndex++)
                if (pOwner->chainAt(iIndex))
                    pCurrentChain = pOwner->chainAt(iIndex);
            return pCurrentChain;
        }

        int moveToNextAssociation() {

            if (pCurrentChain == (Chain *) 0 ||
              !rCurrentIterator.more())
                if (findNextChain())
                    rCurrentIterator = pCurrentChain->begin();

            }
            return (pCurrentChain == (Chain *) 0) ? 0 : 1;
        }
    public:
        AssociationsIterator(DICT_OWNER * pOwn = (DICT_OWNER *) 0) :
                        pOwner(pOwn),
                        pCurrentChain((Chain *) 0),
                        iIndex(0) {
        }
        AssociationsIterator(AssociationsIterator const & rhs) {
            *this = rhs;
        }
```

```
        AssociationsIterator & operator=
            (AssociationsIterator const & rhs) {
            if (this != &rhs) {
                pOwner = rhs.pOwner;
                pCurrentChain = rhs.pCurrentChain;
                rCurrentIterator = rhs.rCurrentIterator;
                iIndex = rhs.iIndex;
            }
            return *this;
        }


        ~AssociationsIterator() {
        }
        Assoc * operator++() {
         moveToNextAssociation(); return ++rCurrentIterator; }
        Assoc * current() {
         moveToNextAssociation(); return rCurrentIterator.current(); }
        int more() {
          moveToNextAssociation(); return rCurrentIterator.more(); }
        void reset() { iIndex = 0; moveToNextAssociation(); }
    };

// Returns an iterator over ALL the associations of the receiver
    virtual AssociationsIterator associations() {
        return AssociationsIterator(this);
    }


/**
 * Returns (size_t) -1 if the key supplied cannot be
 * located, else >=0.
 */
    virtual size_t find(K const * pKey) {
        unsigned int iIndex = hashFor((K *) pKey);
        Chain * pAssocs = rTable[iIndex];
        if (pAssocs) {
           for (size_t i=0 ; i<pAssocs->size() ; i++) {
               Assoc * pCurrent = (*pAssocs)[i];
               if (*(pCurrent->key()) == *pKey) {
                   return i;
               }
           }
        }
        return (size_t) -1;
    }
```

```
/**
 * Returns the total number of keys in the receiver.
 */
    virtual size_t numberOfAssociations() const
    { return iNumberOfAssociations; }

    virtual size_t numberOfElements() const {
            return numberOfAssociations();
    }

/**
 * Destroys the contents of the dictionary
 */
    virtual void destroy() {
        rTable.destroy();
    }

/**
 * Returns the Chain collection at an index
 */
    Chain * chainAt(size_t iIndex) const
        { return (iIndex < rTable.size()) ?
                rTable[iIndex] : (Chain *) 0; }
/**
 * Returns the Chain collection at a key
 */
    Chain * chainAt(K const * pKey) const {
        return chainAt((size_t) hashFor((K *) pKey));
    }
};
```

Notice the declaration of class **AssociationsIterator** as a nested class of **IIDictionary**. This class provides the association iteration service that any dictionary should provide. When it's instantiated, using, for example, the member function **associations**, it provides a means of navigating through the associations held in the dictionary. Typical forward iterator services are provided via an increment operator. The member function **current** allows access to the currently visible association. The member function **more** returns zero when the end of the iterative sequence is reached.

Also, we expose the **Iterator** class of the **Chain** parameter as a values iterator. We do this so that when, for example, a find operation is executed on an **IIDictionary** object, the appropriate iterator is returned to the client. This is demonstrated in Listing 12.3, an extract from the SEREF event manager delegate, which is a templated type.

Listing 12.3 An example find and iterate sequence
on a IIDictionary.

```
C::ValuesIterator rIterator = dependents().valuesFor(rAspect);
        int iReturn = 0;
        iNumberNotified = 0;
        while (rIterator.more()) {
                ASSOC * pAssoc = rIterator.current();
                D * pDependent = pAssoc->value();
                iNumberNotified++;
                iReturn = pDependent->update(rAspect, pHolder);
                if (pDependent->terminateNotification(iReturn))
                    break;
                ++rIterator;
        }
```

In Listing 12.3, the call to **dependents** returns an **IIDictionary** reference. This object is sent the **valuesFor** message, with a particular key. This returns an iterator that has the type **C::ValuesIterator**. The template parameter **C** is the dictionary used by SEREF for dependent management. The iterator is then traversed, each association in the iterator has its **value** extracted, and this is sent the message **update**. We'll cover this in more detail in the "SEREF Event Manager" section of this chapter, but this gives you an idea of how the **IIDictionary** class is used.

The Class IIAssoc

We noted that the keys and values of **IIDictionary** are held as associations—that is, key/value pairs. To model this, we initially created the class **IIAssoc** (later, we show another association class, **IICloningAssoc**). This is a very simple class, which holds the key=value pairs as pointers and provides access to them. It also provides copy, assignment, and equality behavior. The full source code for **IIAssoc** is shown in Listing 12.4.

Listing 12.4 The IIAssoc class.

```
template <class K, class V>
class IIAssoc {
private:
      K * pKey;
      V * pValue;
protected:
/*
 * Delete the contained key and value
```

```
*/
     void deleteState() {
          if (pKey) delete pKey;
          if (pValue) delete pValue;
     }
public:
/*
* Constructor
*/
     IIAssoc(K * pK, V * pV) : pKey(pK), pValue(pV) { }
/*
* Copy constructor
*/
     IIAssoc(IIAssoc<K,V> const & rhs) : pKey(0), pValue(0) {
          *this = rhs;
     }
     ~IIAssoc() { deleteState(); }
     V * value() const { return pValue; }
     K * key() const { return pKey; }
/*
* Provide equality operator through contained  key and value
*/
      int operator==(IIAssoc<K,V> const & rhs) {
              return *(rhs.value()) == *((V *) value()) &&
                     *(rhs.key()) == *((K *) key());
     }
/*
* Handle asignment
*/
     IIAssoc<K,V> & operator=(IIAssoc<K,V> const & rhs) {
          if (this != &rhs) {
               deleteState();
               pKey = new K(*(rhs.key()));
               pValue = new V(*(rhs.value()));
          }
          return *this;
     }
};
```

The Dependency Mechanism

We have described how a basic dependency mechanism that is a variant of the MVC triad underpins the event manager. We know that its primary purpose is to provide a semantically strong infrastructure that will allow the propagation of the processing phases of an HTTP request to interested parties. In the following sections, we'll describe the dependent and model interfaces. Distilled to its essence, the system means that a dependent object tells the model it is interested in a known aspect of the model. When that aspect changes, the dependent is informed.

The SEREF event manager and event handlers are implemented over the top of the more abstract mechanisms described here.

The Dependent Interface

Therefore, the most basic (atomic, if you will) behavior of a dependency-based model is the registration of dependents upon a model type object. Because we cannot, and probably don't even want to attempt to, predict in advance the type of dependents a model may have to service, we'll define a **Dependent** abstract class. Figure 12.3 is a UML notation class diagram of the most interesting properties of **Dependent**.

For creators of a **Dependent** sub-class, there are two pure virtual functions that must be implemented. These are shown here:

```
virtual int update(EncodedEvent const *, VoidHolder *) = 0;
virtual Dependent * clone() = 0;
```

The first of these, **update**, provides a hint as to how the dependency mechanism works. When a model in which the dependent has a registered interest changes, it may send a message to the dependent with the signature given. The **EncodedEvent** is a simple class that has an event name and an associated protocol, and indicates to the dependent what aspect of the model has changed. The **update** implementation may therefore provide behavior for whatever occurs.

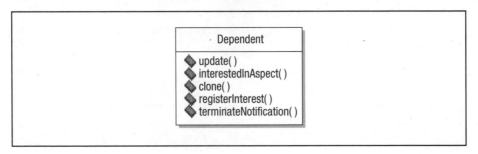

Figure 12.3

The **Dependent** abstract class.

*Note: The **Dependent** class is not modeled as a template due to problems with inheritance and exported template instantiations under many Win32 compilers. Otherwise, we would have defined at least the event type (**EncodedEvent**) as a parameter to a **Dependent** template.*

The second required member function is **clone**. This member function, when executed, must provide a new, heap-allocated instance of the object whose **clone** method is called. We use this tortuous phrase because the use of a virtual-cloning member function implies that the object may have potentially many different types. Clone type methods are also known as *virtual constructors* or *factory methods*. Listing 12.5 shows a partial listing of the **Dependent** class, not including some minor public member functions.

Listing 12.5   A partial listing of the **Dependent** class.

```
class Dependent {
private:
/**
 * The aspect in which we are interested
*/
        EncodedEvent *pAspect;
public:
        Dependent() { }
        Dependent(Dependent const & rhs) : pAspect(0) {
                *this = rhs;
        }
        Dependent & operator=(Dependent const & rhs) {
                if (this != &rhs) {
                        if (pAspect != NULL)
                                delete pAspect;
                        pAspect =
                          new EncodedEvent(*(rhs.pAspect));
                }
        return *this;
        }
/**
 * Register interest in the aspect supplied with the given model.
*/
        Dependent(EncodedEvent * pAsp) : pAspect(pAsp) { }
/**
 * Virtual destructor
*/
        virtual ~Dependent() { delete pAspect; }
```

```
/**
*The interface member function. An update message is sent when
* the dependency controller undergoes a change that is of interest
* to the dependent.
* Both the aspect and a VoidHolder are sent.
*/
        virtual int update(EncodedEvent const *, VoidHolder *) = 0;
/**
* Clone "this"
*/
        virtual Dependent * clone() = 0;
};
```

The Skeleton Model Template

A corollary to the dependent is the model that the dependent *depends on*. Models potentially take an infinite number of forms, but, if the **Dependent** class is involved, must follow a particular protocol.

We decided that the most basic model behavior entails the following:

* Adding and removing dependents

* Keeping track of dependents

* Providing methods to notify dependents of change

To this end we provide a templated model class called **SkeletonModel**. The behavior listed is all that the **SkeletonModel** templated class provides. We modeled this class as a template so that it could easily:

* Use different container classes for maintaining lists of dependents

* Use different aspects in notification

* Use different dependent interfaces as required

You may be wondering why **SkeletonModel** is a template. This is because it would seem that inheritance would be required to make this class useful, because on its own it provides no domain-specific behavior. We have already noted the problems with inheritance when attempting to export concrete template instances with some Win32 compilers. Well, in the case of **SkeletonModel**, there are mitigating circumstances. One is that it defines no pure virtual member functions, which makes delegation feasible. Another is that the public interface of **SkeletonModel** is very small, which makes it possible to wrap it up and use delegation techniques. We didn't want to compromise the design to the extent that a very generally applicable class, a simple dependency model, was made specific and tied to a particular implementation. With the **Dependent** class, we had no such qualms as it was of much less general utility. Figure 12.4 shows a UML notation class diagram of **SkeletonModel**.

The template parameters for **SkeletonModel** are described in Table 12.4.

To help explain how the registration scheme works, Listing 12.6 shows an interface-only listing for the **SkeletonModel** template.

Listing 12.6   The **SkeletonModel** interface listing.

```
template <class D, class A, class C, class ASSOC>
class SkeletonModel {
private:
        C rDependents;
        C & dependents();
        SkeletonModel(SkeletonModel<D,A,C,ASSOC> const &);
        SkeletonModel &
            operator=(SkeletonModel<D,A,C,ASSOC> const &);

public:
        SkeletonModel();
        virtual ~SkeletonModel();
        int addDependent(D * pDependent,  A * rAspect);
        int removeDependent(D * pDependent,  A * pAspect) ;
        int notifyDependents(A const * rAspect);
        int notifyDependents(A const * rAspect,
                                    VoidHolder * pHolder,
                                    int & iNumberNotified);
        int getExitCode() const;
        void setExitCode(int iNewCode);
        size_t numberOfDependents();
};
```

Table 12.4   **SkeletonModel** template parameters.

Template Parameter	Use
D	The dependent type.
A	The aspect type.
C	The collection type to hold instances of D.
ASSOC	The association type, whose key is of type A and value of type D.

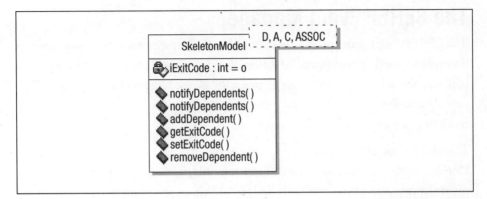

Figure 12.4

UML notation class diagram for the **SkeletonModel** template.

When an object wishes to register as a dependent on an instance of **SkeletonModel**, it sends an **addDependent** message to the model, with itself (the dependent) as the first parameter and the aspect in which it is interested as the second parameter. When a change in the model occurs, it sends a **notifyDependents** message to itself. This causes the location of all dependents that are interested in the aspect that has altered. This set of objects is then sent an **update** message with the same signature as that defined for the **Dependent** abstract class. Here is that signature again:

```
int update(EncodedEvent const *, VoidHolder *)
```

So, dependents are sent the aspect that has changed, along with a pointer to a class called **VoidHolder**. This class is used to pass any opaque pointers that may have been defined externally to the model and form part of some specific but unelaborated protocol for dependents. This use of opacity has a specific application in SEREF; that is covered in depth in Chapters 13 and 14.

As you will note from the extended **notifyDependents** signature, the number of dependents notified is returned via an integer reference. Note that the number returned does not necessarily equal the number of dependents registered as interested in the aspect change being notified. This is because **SkeletonModel** expects dependents to provide a member function called **terminateNotification**. Just after it has processed an **update** call, this member function is used (by the model) to query the dependent for the meaning of its return code. Again, we shall see that this method of controlling dependent notification is used by SEREF.

The SEREF Event Manager

The SEREF event manager and event handlers are implemented over more abstract dependency mechanisms described earlier in this chapter. Basically, the SEREF event manager should act as a mediator between its dependents and the low-level Web server extension API. In fact, even this is somewhat of a simplification, but we'll cover this in more detail in Chapter 14.

The event manager's dependents are *event handlers*. These are derived classes of the **Dependent** abstract class we described earlier in this chapter. As such, they will implement the two pure virtual methods **update** and **clone** previously mentioned. In the framework, there is a complete and separate hierarchy of event handlers that provide encapsulations of all the supported events. Each event handler translates the generic **update** message received during notification into another virtual member function call that best represents the nature of the behavior that is desired.

As a matter of fact, the event manager class is little more than a concrete wrapper of an instance of a **SkeletonModel**. Why is this? Well, when you examine the essential nature of notifying temporal event flow for HTTP requests, it requires little more than knowing that an event has occurred and informing your dependents (the event handlers). As you notify each one, you should ask it if its return code after **update** means that it wants to signal complete processing of the event. If so, the model should not continue notifying dependents. As you know, this is remarkably similar to what happens when a Web server notifies callback functions that have been registered with it—except at a higher level of abstraction and with far greater opportunity for reuse. Listing 12.7 is a partial listing of the SEREF event manager source code.

Listing 12.7   The SEREF event manager wrapper.

```
class EventManager {
private:
        typedef SEREFEvent DEPTYPE;
        typedef IICloningAssoc<EncodedEvent, DEPTYPE> MASSOC;
        typedef IVector<MASSOC> CDEPS;
        typedef IPool<MASSOC, SEREFMutex> POOL;
        typedef IVector< POOL > POOLVEC;
        typedef ICloningContainer<MASSOC, CDEPS,
                                            POOLVEC, POOL,
                                            SEREFMutex> VALUE;
        typedef IIDictionary<EncodedEvent, DEPTYPE,
                        MASSOC, VALUE> DICTIONARY;
```

```
            SkeletonModel<DEPTYPE, EncodedEvent,
                            DICTIONARY, MASSOC > rModel;
        EventManager(EventManager const & rhs);
        EventManager & operator=(EventManager const & rhs);
public:
    EventManager() { }
    virtual ~EventManager() { }
    int dispatchEvent(EncodedEvent const * rAspect) {
            return rModel.notifyDependents(rAspect);
        }
    int dispatchEvent(EncodedEvent const * rAspect,
                        VoidHolder * pVoidHolder,
                        int iDefaultReturnCode = 0)
    {
            int iNumberNotified;
            int iReturnCode=
                rModel.notifyDependents(
                                    rAspect,
                                    pVoidHolder,
                                    iNumberNotified);
            return !iNumberNotified ? iDefaultReturnCode :
                                            iReturnCode;
        }
    int addEventHandler(DEPTYPE * pDependent,
                            EncodedEvent * rAspect) {
            return rModel.addDependent(pDependent, rAspect);
        }
};
```

The **EventManager** class wraps the addition and notification of dependents, and changes the interface vocabulary along the way, to be in accordance with the responsibilities of the event manager. Interestingly, it does not expose the removal of dependent's functionality implemented by **SkeletonModel**. This is primarily because of the current nature of Web server extension deployment—it is not dynamic in nature and does not provide this behavior. It could, however, be shown to clients of the **EventManager** class at a later date.

The **typedef** definitions in the private section of **EventManager** define a number of template instances that are used to implement the dictionary that will track dependents. Note that the definitions become quite complex, as specialized containers are used to provide custom behavior that is multi-thread safe.

Discussion of how the framework is glued into the lower level API is deferred to Chapter 14. However, we'll now discuss how SEREF handles issues of multi-threading and why two new container classes are required.

Multi-Threading Issues In SEREF

Most Web servers service client requests using threads—a lightweight and efficient solution under most contemporary operating systems. This raises the question: How do you dispatch events through a centralized event dispatcher without compromising the integrity of dependents?

The major problem that occurs in a multi-threaded, shared object is synchronization. This is because threads will have access to all global and static data simultaneously. Instance data falls into this category when using the simple dependency scheme implemented in SEREF.

The registration of dependencies on the event manager allows a simplistic dependency mechanism to be implemented. However, the event that the (singly instantiated) dependent is interested in can be notified multiple times in a threaded model. Because the per-instance data for a dependent is essentially *global* for multiple threads of control (allocated from the heap and accessible through a single pointer), some means of protecting this data is required. You could do the following:

- Serialize access through each dependent. This basically rules out any notion of efficiency.

- Dictate that each shared object allocate as many *duplicate* dependents as required. This is clumsy.

- Service requests by *cloning* a new object from the dependent and using the clone to service the request. This probably implies that an object will be passed as an argument to the virtual function subdispatcher in the clone so that each thread will get its own thread (that is, in the case of SEREF, request) specific data.

Cloning is the method used to implement a thread-safe approach in SEREF. To avoid the overhead of repeated heap allocation and deallocation, the event manager, or rather, a specialized collection class, **IPool**, implements a simple scheme that will allocate N clones of each dependent upon its registration. Clones are then doled out immediately as the need arises, allocating new ones only when absolutely necessary. Using preallocated clones and lazy instantiation means an efficient and extensible mechanism is in place.

Now we'll side-step design issues. We are going to introduce the classes to support cloning and then briefly note how the implementation works in **EventManager**.

The IPool Class

The purpose of the **IPool** template class is to provide a thread-safe pool of polymorphic objects. It is thread safe because when it is asked for an object, it will ensure that (to the best of its knowledge) it has never been requested before and is therefore not in use somewhere. An **IPool** is aggressive in ownership; it owns and will delete all objects that are supplied to it for the purposes of cloning and clone management.

An **IPool** is populated by supplying the pool with a prototypical object that implements a member function called **clone**. This member function will return a new heap-allocated instance of the prototype. Internally, the pool keeps two vectors, one for unused (that is, nonallocated objects) and the other for used (that is, passed out) objects. Listing 12.8 shows the partial source code listing for class **IPool**.

Listing 12.8   The partial source code for **IPool**.

```
template <class T, class L>
class IPool {
private:
        typedef IVector<T> PoolContainer;
        PoolContainer * pUsedObjects, *pUnusedObjects;
        T * pPrototype;
        size_t iSize, iLoaded;
        L * pLock;
        IPool<T,L> & operator=(IPool<T,L> const &);
        IPool(IPool<T,L> const &);
protected:
        void lock() { if (pLock) pLock->lock(); }
        void unlock() { if (pLock) pLock->unlock(); }
public:
        IPool(size_t iSz = 16) :
                    pUsedObjects(new PoolContainer(iSz)),
                    pUnusedObjects(new PoolContainer(iSz)),
                    pPrototype((T *) 0), iSize(iSz),
                    iLoaded(0) {
        }

        ~IPool() {
                destroy();
                delete pUsedObjects;
                delete pUnusedObjects;
        }
```

```
size_t populate(T * pCloneableObject) {
        if (iLoaded || !pCloneableObject) return 0;

        pUnusedObjects->
            add((pPrototype=pCloneableObject));

        for (; iLoaded<iSize-1 ; iLoaded++) {
                T * pClone = pCloneableObject->clone();
                if (!pUnusedObjects->add(pClone))
                        break;
        }
        if (!pLock)
                pLock = new L();
        return pUnusedObjects->size() == iSize - 1;
}


T * getPrototype() { return pPrototype; }

T * next() {
        if (!available()) return (T *) 0;
        lock();
        T * pObject = pUnusedObjects->removeFirst();
        pUsedObjects->add(pObject);
        unlock();
        return pObject;
}

size_t release(T * pObject) {
        if (pUsedObjects->findIdentical(pObject)
                == (size_t) -1)
                return 0;
        lock();
        pUsedObjects->remove(pObject);
        pUnusedObjects->add(pObject);
        unlock();
        return 1;
}

size_t destroy() {
        lock();
        if (iLoaded && pUsedObjects->size() == 0) {
                pUsedObjects->destroy();
                pUnusedObjects->destroy();
                iLoaded = 0;
                delete pLock;
                pLock=0;
```

```
                    }
                    unlock();
                    return !iLoaded;
            }

            size_t available() const {
                    return pUnusedObjects->size();
            }
};
```

To populate the pool, the member function **populate** is called with the prototype object. When a guaranteed unique instance is required, a client calls **next**, which returns either a pointer to an object or a null object.

> **Note**: In the demo version of SEREF, from which this source code is excerpted, no automatic resizing of pools ever occurs. You'll find SEREF on the CD-ROM enclosed with this book.

Once finished with an object accessed using **next**, the client is expected return it to the pool using the member function **release**. Nearly all member functions of **IPool** are guaranteed atomic. This is dependent upon the class supplied as parameter **L** when the template is instantiated. SEREF provides a standard platform-independent **Mutex** class that is used internally.

Figure 12.5 shows the UML notation class diagram for **IPool**, noting its dependence upon class **IVector**.

The ICloningContainer Class

The **ICloningContainer** template class provides almost vectorlike operations and iterative services over a polymorphic element collection. A nested class of **ICloningContainer** provides iterative services that return exclusive-use members during iteration.

When we were implementing SEREF, we saw the need to create this type of collection to support our requirements for thread safety. The template parameters that **ICloningContainer** supports are shown in Table 12.5.

An instance of **ICloningContainer** collects elements of type **T**. When an element is added to the container, a new pool of type **P** is created and added to the internal

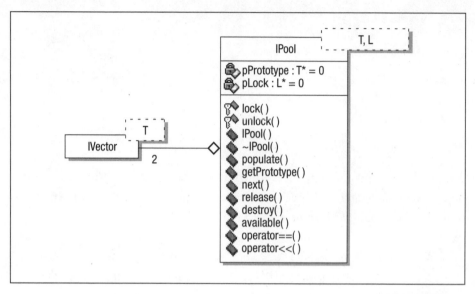

Figure 12.5

The UML notation class diagram for **IPool**.

collection of type **CP**. The new element is then used to populate the pool. As noted in Table 12.5, the type **T** must implement a public member function with appropriate duplicative behavior.

When an array type operation is used, such as subscripting or an operation that asks for the first element of the container, the element returned is for reference only (or is read only) and may not be assumed to be for the exclusive use of the client.

ICloningContainer provides an interesting behavior for iteration. When simple containers such as vectors, sets, and the like have an iterator created on them, it is not normally assumed that the elements accessed during iteration are for the exclusive use of the client. In the case of **ICloningContainer**, however, this is not true.

An iterator is created on an instance of **ICloningContainer** typically by calling the **begin** member function. The **ICloningIterator::Iterator** instance returned by this member function has "best effort" semantics with respect to guaranteed exclusivity of use. This means that the objects that may be accessed by iterator navigation are not in use elsewhere. Refer to Listing 12.9, which shows the source code for the **ICloningContainer::Iterator**.

Table 12.5   ICloningContainer template parameters.

Template Parameter	Use
T	The type of elements that are collected. Whatever type is used must support a clone method that returns a heap-allocated instance of the receiver.
CT	The container type that the clones will be returned in.
CP	The container of pools type.
P	The basic pool type.
L	The lock type to use.

Listing 12.9   The source code for ICloningContainer::Iterator.

```
class Iterator {
private:
    typedef ICloningContainer<T,CT,CP,P,L> PARENT;
    PARENT * pOwner;
    CT * pCont;
    size_t iIndex, iStart;
    void getClones() {
        if (iIndex == (size_t) -1) {
            if (pOwner) pCont = pOwner->clone(iStart);
            else       pCont = new CT();
            iIndex = 0;
        }
    }
    void uncloneObjects() {
        if (pOwner) {
            pOwner->unclone(pCont, iStart);
            delete pCont;
            pCont = (CT *) 0;
        }
    }
public:
    Iterator(PARENT * pOwn  = (PARENT *) 0, size_t i = 0) :
                    pOwner(pOwn),
                    pCont((CT *) 0),
                    iIndex((size_t) -1), iStart(i) {
    }

    Iterator(Iterator const & rhs) : pOwner(0), pCont(0),
                            iIndex((size_t) -1), iStart(0) {
        *this = rhs;
    }
```

```
        Iterator & operator=(Iterator const & rhs) {
            if (this != &rhs) {
                uncloneObjects();
                pOwner = rhs.pOwner;
                if (pOwner && rhs.pCont)
                    getClones();
                iIndex = rhs.iIndex;
                iStart = rhs.iStart;
            }
            return *this;
        }

        ~Iterator() {
            uncloneObjects();
        }
        T * operator++() { getClones(); return (*pCont)[iIndex++]; }
        T * current() { getClones(); return (*pCont)[iIndex]; }
        int more() { getClones();  return iIndex < pCont->size(); }
        void reset() { getClones(); iIndex = 0; }
    };
```

The key to providing thread-safe use is in the **getClones** member function. When the iterator is used, it always checks its state to see whether the container over which it is to iterate is not null. The container over which it iterates has a special meaning, however—it is not the pointer to the **ICloningContainer** parent that is passed in upon construction. Rather, it is the container that results from calling the **clone** member function in the parent. The **clone** member function in **ICloningContainer** is shown in Listing 12.10.

Listing 12.10 The clone protected member function of ICloningContainer.

```
CT * clone(size_t iStart=0) {
        CT * pCont= new CT();
        for (size_t i=iStart,j=0; i<size() ; i++) {
            pCont->add((*pContainer)[i]->next());
        }
    return pCont;
}
```

As you can see, the **clone** of **ICloningContainer** is rather simple. It returns a heap-allocated container of type **CT** (refer back to Table 12.5) that holds the clones returned from repeated calls to the **next** member function of the pool object. Note that the **pContainer** object is of type **CP**. There is a similar function called **unclone**, which returns the clones from an object of type **CT** to the pools as required. This function is called in the destructor of **ICloningIterator::Iterator**.

The UML notation diagram for **ICloningContainer** is shown in Figure 12.6.

Detailed Operation Of The Event Manager

We finally have supplied enough background information to illustrate the operation of the event manager. To illustrate again, the **EventManager** class is shown in its relationship with the **SkeletonModel** template in Figure 12.7.

As you will recall, we stated that one of the objectives for making the **SkeletonModel** class a template was to be able to use different container classes for maintaining lists of dependents. This, as it turned out, was a key decision, as was the implementation of class **IIDictionary** as a template class that could have its internal collection classes externally specified. The decision bears fruit in the **typedef** definitions and template specification in **EventManager** and shown again in Listing 12.11.

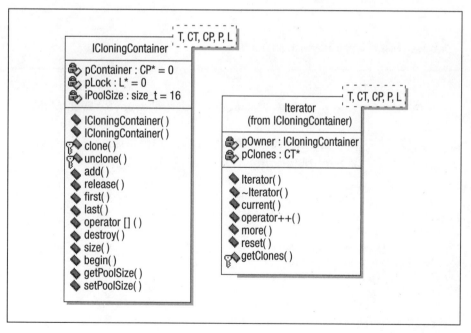

Figure 12.6

The UML notation class diagram for **ICloningContainer**.

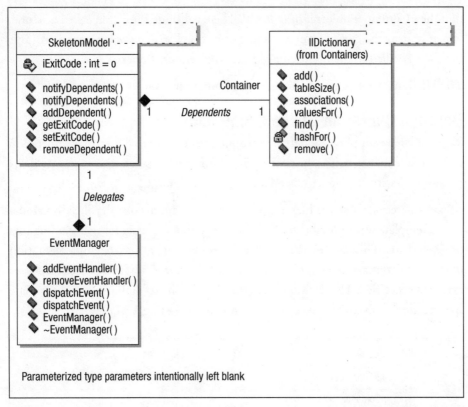

Figure 12.7
The UML notation class diagram for **EventManager**.

Listing 12.11   The **SkeletonModel** contained instance
               of **EventManager**.

```
typedef SEREFEvent DEPTYPE;
typedef IICloningAssoc<EncodedEvent, DEPTYPE> MASSOC;
typedef IVector<MASSOC> CDEPS;
typedef IPool<MASSOC, SEREFMutex> POOL;
typedef IVector< POOL > POOLVEC;
typedef ICloningContainer<MASSOC, CDEPS,
                          POOLVEC, POOL,
                          SEREFMutex> VALUE;
typedef IIDictionary<EncodedEvent, DEPTYPE,
                     MASSOC, VALUE> DICTIONARY;

SkeletonModel<DEPTYPE, EncodedEvent,
              DICTIONARY, MASSOC > rModel;
```

Here we create a model whose dependents are maintained in a dictionary. The slightly tricky twist is the specification of the **Chain** type of the dictionary to be an **ICloningContainer**. Any dependent added to the dictionary is automatically added to a cloning container. The semantics of element addition in **ICloningContainer** are as we specified before—that is, the newly added element is cloned a certain number of times. This is initially how we populate the pool of dependent event handlers along with their registered interest in a specific aspect.

So how does this model provide for thread safety? If you re-read the **IIDictionary** description, you will see that it exposes the iterator of its **Chain** type as an iterator over a set of values queried by calling its **valuesFor** method. To explain, we'll display the dependent notification logic in **SkeletonModel** (which **EventManager** effectively wraps as **dispatchEvent**) in Listing 12.12.

Listing 12.12 The **notifyDependents** member function of **SkeletonModel**.

```
int notifyDependents(A const * rAspect,
                                VoidHolder * pHolder,
                                int & iNumberNotified) {
        C::ValuesIterator rIterator =
             dependents().valuesFor(rAspect);
        int iReturn = 0;
        iNumberNotified = 0;
        while (rIterator.more()) {
             ASSOC * pAssoc = rIterator.current();
             D * pDependent = pAssoc->value();
             iNumberNotified++;
             iReturn = pDependent->
                             update(rAspect, pHolder);
             if (pDependent->terminateNotification(iReturn))
                  break;
             ++rIterator;
        }
    return iReturn;
}
```

The call to **valuesFor** is at the beginning of the function, which returns an **ICloningContainer::Iterator**, which does its best to provide exclusive clones of certain objects. In this case we know that the objects in question are SEREF event handlers. After this call is executed, we iterate over the collection of event handlers, sending each an **update** message, which the dependents registered in **SkeletonModel** must implement. The value returned is captured, and the dependent is asked if this means the end of processing (for whatever reason). If the answer is non-zero, the dispatch terminates and the **while** loop is executed. Otherwise, dispatch continues.

At the end of **notifyDependents**, the automatic variable **rIterator** will be destroyed. The **EventManager class** contains an instance of a **SkeletonModel**, so the type of **C::ValuesIterator** is an **ICloningContainer::Iterator**. Therefore, the action of the **rIterator** destructor means that clones will be returned to their parent container. So, for any thread executing the **notifyDependents** member function of the single instance of the event manager, thread safety is guaranteed.

To better illustrate the complete sequence, consider Figures 12.8 and 12.9, which show the UML sequence and collaboration diagrams applicable to the dispatch of a single event.

Portability

The final part of this chapter describes and identifies some of the portability issues of concern to SEREF. One of the target APIs, Netscape's NSAPI, offers Unix support in addition to Windows NT availability. Thus we had to neatly cater to the platform differences in a way as unobtrusive to SEREF developers as possible, as well as allow for certain core services, such as the provision of mutual exclusion locks, to be used within the framework in a platform-insulated manner.

Of course, the solution to the portability dilemma is quite simple. The most obvious solution is to create abstract classes that model the service, facility, or entity in question. Then, create and use a *factory* at runtime that instantiates the required implementation on demand. The factory is just an abstract class possessing the appropriate protocol—it is created in SEREF at shared-object load time by a small piece of bootstrapping code.

During the course of development, we identified a number of abstract concepts that should be modeled, and thus provided by factory implementations. Table 12.6 identifies the main factories and their purpose.

We'll examine the latter two factories (the gate and condition factories) in the next chapter. The system services factory we examine in more detail now.

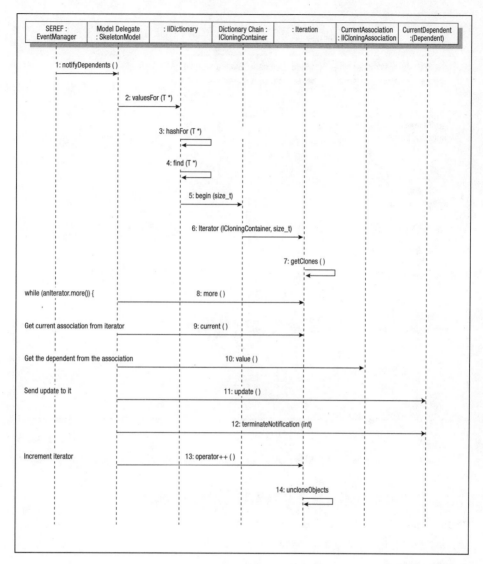

Figure 12.8

The UML notation sequence diagram for **EventManager**.

Table 12.6 SEREF factories.

Factory Class Name	Purpose
SystemServicesFactory	Provide instances of system service type objects.
SEREFGateFactory	Provide delegate gates upon request.
SEREFConditionFactory	Return condition objects upon request.

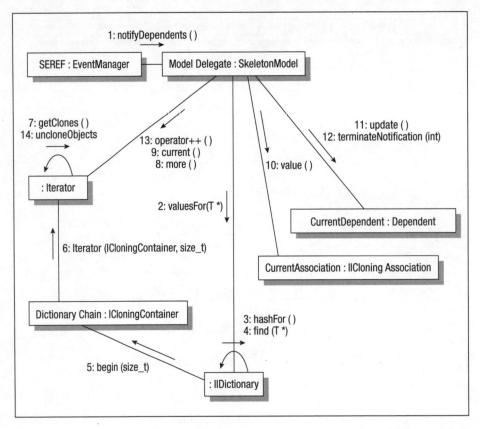

Figure 12.9

The UML notation collaboration diagram for **EventManager**.

The Provision Of System Services

SEREF has a very specific focus, and thus requires a very small subset of the total services normally provided by an operating system to applications. We identified the following services as essential to the framework:

- Mutual exclusion locks (mutexs)

- Runtime shared-object loading

The second of these, shared-object loading, is of great importance—its necessity is discussed in the sidebar.

Attaching Framework Extensions To SEREF

Chapter 13 thoroughly discusses the event handler boilerplate classes that provide a solid and semantically consistent base upon which to build portable and vendor-independent Web server extensions. The following question will arise: How does the framework ever use these extensions? The answer is shared objects.

*Developer extensions must be packaged into a shared object (DLL or shared library) to be loaded by the framework. In the demo SEREF copy included on the CD-ROM enclosed with this book, this is an object with a specific name (simple.so or simple.dll). At runtime, when the SEREF master shared object is loaded by whatever server is used (the configuration is discussed in Chapter 14), it in turn tries to load this shared object. (Note: In the full version of SEREF, a separate configuration file describes 1 to N shared objects that may be loaded.) If it can open this object, it tries to locate the C linkage function **initialise**. If it can locate that symbol, it executes it. This function is expected to register event handler dependencies upon the event manager pointer that is passed to it. Thus, each event handler that is to be registered is attached to the event manager using the **addEventHandler** member function of the SEREF event manager. After this, each event handler is cloned N times, and after all handlers have been registered, the event manager is ready to dispatch incoming events to its new dependents.*

Because we have concluded that these two basic services are required, we have to provide a factory protocol to support them. This is, of course, the purpose of the **SystemServicesFactory** class, whose interface is shown in Listing 12.13.

Listing 12.13   The **SystemServicesFactory** abstract class.

```
class SystemServicesFactory {
private:
   static SystemServicesFactory * pInstance;
protected:
   SystemServicesFactory() {}
   static void setFactory(SystemServicesFactory * pFactory) {
                   pInstance = pFactory;
           }
public:
   SystemServicesFactory * factory() { return pInstance; }
   virtual Mutex * mutex() = 0;
   virtual Mutex * newMutex() = 0;
```

```
    virtual Mutex * newMutex(OptString const &) = 0;
    virtual SharedObject * sharedObject(char const *) = 0;
};
```

As you can see, the public interface is quite small. Concrete factories for each appropriate operating system are created at runtime by the bootstrap code. Only one factory per operating system is required. When the factory is constructed, it calls the protected member function **setFactory** with its **this** pointer to set the factory for the particular framework implementation.

An object requiring a service, such as the creation of a shared object instance, may call the **factory** static member function of **SystemServicesFactory** and send it the message **sharedObject**. Such a scenario is shown in Listing 12.14.

Listing 12.14   Loading a shared object in the SEREF shared object.

```
SharedObject * pSharedObject =
                    SystemServicesFactory::factory()->
                    sharedObject(DEP_LIB);
    int iReturnCode = pSharedObject->load();
    if (iReturnCode <= 0) {
        serefErrorLogger <<
            "Fatal error: could not load shared object #" <<
                    iReturnCode << "\n";
        serefErrorLogger << "Error: " <<
            pSharedObject->errorDescription() << "\n";
    }
    else {
        int (WCDECL *pAddress)(void *) =
            (int (WCDECL *)(void *))
                (pSharedObject->getSymbolAddress("initialise"));
        if (pAddress) (*pAddress)((void *) pEventDispatcher);
        else serefErrorLogger <<
                "Fatal error: could not load symbol address" << "\n";
    }
```

The source code in Listing 12.14 is part of the function used to load the SEREF demo's single shared library (in the SEREF demo, only one shared library is loaded with a fixed name). This shared library implements developer extensions for trial use.

To explain the concept further, we show in Listing 12.15 the **SystemServicesFactory** implementation for Windows NT.

Listing 12.15 A Win32 system services factory.

```
class WIN32Services : public SystemServicesFactory {
public:
   WIN32Services() { setFactory(this); }
   ~WIN32Services() { delete factory(); }
   virtual Mutex * mutex() { return new WIN32Mutex(); }
   virtual Mutex * newMutex() { return new WIN32Mutex(); }
   virtual Mutex * newMutex(OptString const & rName) {
           return new WIN32Mutex(rName);
   }
   virtual SharedObject * sharedObject(char const * pName) {
           return new WIN32SharedObject(pName);
   }
};
```

By dint of its public inheritance from **SystemServicesFactory**, and the fact that it considers itself a leaf class, the **WIN32Services** class must provide a complete factory implementation. Each pure virtual function of its base class is thus implemented, and returns a pointer to a concrete class through an abstract base class pointer. For example, a call to **sharedObject** returns a pointer to a **SharedObject** instance. However, the class **SharedObject**, as shown in Listing 12.16, is yet another abstract class. The concrete class **WIN32SharedObject**, shown in Listing 12.17, is a concrete implementation of **SharedObject** for the Win32 platform. In a similar fashion, **WIN32Mutex** is a concrete implementation of the abstract **Mutex** class, which we do not illustrate.

Listing 12.16 The **SharedObject** abstract class.

```
class SharedObject {
private:
   OptString rObjectName;
   int iLoaded;
protected:
   void setLoaded(int i) { iLoaded = i; }
   int getLoaded() const { return iLoaded; }
public:
/**
 * Standard constructor. The string supplied is interpreted
 * as the path name of the shared object to be accessed.
 */
   SharedObject(OptString const & rName) :
       rObjectName(rName), iLoaded(0) { }
```

```
/**
 * Virtual destructor
 */
    virtual ~SharedObject() { }
/**
 * Pure virtual function that derived classes implement to
 * load the shared object.
 */
    virtual  int load() = 0;
/**
 * Pure virtual function that ids the last error
 */
    virtual  OptString errorDescription() = 0;
/**
 * Pure virtual function that derived classes implement to
 * unload the shared object
 */
    virtual  int unload() = 0;
/**
 * Inline accessor. Returns the "loaded" status of the
 * receiver. !=0 is assumed to mean
 * loaded.
 */
    int isLoaded() const { return getLoaded() > 0; }
/**
 * Returns the path name of the shared object
 */
    OptString const & getName() const { return rObjectName; }
/**
 * @param
 * pString - the name of the symbol to locate
 * @return
 * A valid or NULL void * pointer to the symbol supplied
 */
    virtual void * getSymbolAddress(char const * pString) = 0;
/**
 * @param
 * rString - the name of the symbol to locate
 * @return
 * A valid or NULL void * pointer to the symbol supplied
 */
    virtual void * getSymbolAddress(OptString const & rString) = 0;
};
```

Listing 12.17   The **WIN32SharedObject** concrete class.

```
class WIN32SharedObject : public SharedObject {
private:
   HINSTANCE hObject;
   WIN32SharedObject & operator=(WIN32SharedObject const &);
   WIN32SharedObject(WIN32SharedObject const &);
public:
   WIN32SharedObject(OptString const & rName) :
                            SharedObject(rName),
                            hObject((HINSTANCE) NULL) { }

   ~WIN32SharedObject() { if (isLoaded()) unload();}

   int load()  {
     if (getName().length() > 0) {
        hObject = ::LoadLibrary(getName().c_str());
        setLoaded(hObject != NULL ? 1 : (::GetLastError() * -1));
     }
     return getLoaded();
   }

   OptString errorDescription() {
      return OptString("None available");
   }

   int unload() {
     int iRetCode = isLoaded() ? ::FreeLibrary(hObject) : 0;
     hObject = (HINSTANCE) NULL;
     setLoaded(0);
     return iRetCode;
   }

   void * getSymbolAddress(char const * pName) {
     void * pAddr = (hObject == NULL) ? (void *) NULL :
                          (::GetProcAddress(hObject, pName));
     return pAddr;
   }

   void * getSymbolAddress(OptString const & rName) {
              return getSymbolAddress(rName.c_str());
   }
};
```

Under POSIX-compliant systems (most flavors of Unix), we implement and provide a **POSIXSystemServicesFactory**, which for the Unix version of SEREF is just dropped in by the bootstrap code. All classes that reference member functions of **SystemServicesFactory** don't need to know or care about this.

So by means of the system services' factories, we provide *interface-driven* access to specific implementations, which insulates our classes and the framework from a dependence upon any particular operating system. The only requirement of the operating system is that it must support mutex locks and dynamic shared objects. Because these are the only operating systems we are interested in, there is no issue to address.

Summary

In this chapter we discussed the basic requirements and operation of an object-oriented framework to provide an abstracted view of Web server extension development. We justified our choice of C++ as an implementation language and described the white box reuse philosophy used in the SEREF framework.

The supporting classes of SEREF were introduced and described in detail, as was the event manager and its implementation of a dependency mechanism, which could be used to notify extension software of request processing stages. This mechanism is, after all, the real purpose of the framework. We noted that object pools and cloning containers collaborated to provide thread-safe, efficient object location and assignment.

Last, we discussed the portability approach that SEREF uses, and how object factories are used to insulate the framework classes from the particular platform on which they exist.

Chapter 13 builds upon these ideas to illustrate the events that SEREF supports and their semantics and implementation.

The SEREF Event Model

CHAPTER

13

In the previous chapter, we briefly mentioned that the event hierarchy in the SEREF framework abstracted the temporal progression of an HTTP request. This chapter will describe the event hierarchy in greater detail.

The SEREF Event Model

The model we'll present allows all the important phases that a request passes through to be implemented in such a way as to be extension API and platform independent with the same source.

This chapter assumes that you are reasonably familiar with at least one of the APIs described in this book, HTTP 1.x, C++, and general object-oriented principles.

The Event Hierarchy

As we mentioned in Chapter 12, there is a complete and separate hierarchy of event handlers that provide encapsulations of all the normal supported events for a (HTTP) request. The UML notation class diagram in Figure 13.1 illustrates this hierarchy.

As you can see, the **Dependent** class forms the root of our event hierarchy. The reason for this is because all events in SEREF are modeled as dependents of the event manager. When anything occurs with respect to the event (such as when it actually *fires*), the effect is that the **update** message is sent to the event through its **Dependent** interface. Each event is modeled as a particular aspect of the event manager.

We'll now describe the next class down in the hierarchy, **SEREFEvent**. In this chapter we'll continue to use the phrase *event handler* to denote a sub-class of **SEREFEvent**.

> **Note:** We do not describe the trivial implementation of the **LogEvent** class in this chapter.

The SEREFEvent Class

This class exists as a result of a factoring exercise that occurred later in the development process—it holds a **SEREFEventCondition** object for each event handler. This particular class has a special and discrete role in allowing for vendor API insulation.

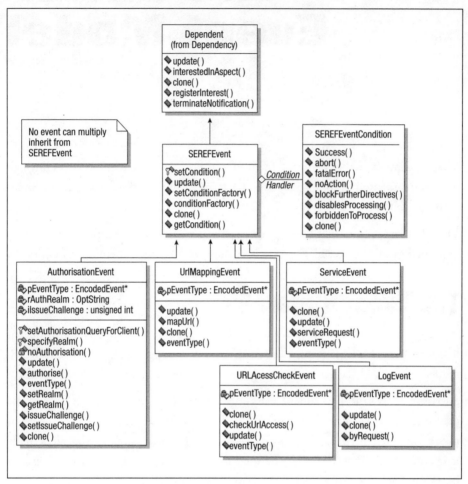

Figure 13.1

The SEREF event hierarchy UML class diagram.

As we developed, we discovered that whatever action the event handler wished to signal to the server had to be returned to the server, so that it could be acted upon. To explain this further, if the event handler wishes to inform the server that it has performed the definitive event processing for a particular request, it must return an appropriate API-specific value.

Each Web server extension API has different manifest constants, with different values to signal the same actions. One way around this is to create an entirely new set of integer codes. However, an integer is semantically weak—What does the literal integer -1 actually mean?

To compound the issue, one of the supported APIs, NSAPI, has manifest constants that produce different results depending upon the event being processed. This can be very confusing.

So, as a means of providing stronger semantics and insulating ourselves from API vagaries, we encapsulated the return code in an interface. We call this interface **SEREFEventCondition**, as it provides a defined protocol that is used to signal the condition of an event handler upon return. Listing 13.1 shows the basic condition interface.

Listing 13.1 The **SEREFEventCondition** abstract class.

```
class SEREFEventCondition {
public:
   SEREFEventCondition() { }
   virtual ~SEREFEventCondition() { }
   virtual int success() = 0;
   virtual int abort() = 0;
   virtual int fatalError() = 0;
   virtual int noAction() = 0;
   virtual int blockFurtherDirectives() = 0;
   virtual int disablesProcessing(int i) = 0;
   virtual int forbiddenToProcess() = 0;
   virtual SEREFEventCondition * clone() = 0;
};
```

As you can see, all member functions are defined as pure virtual. Table 13.1 describes very briefly the semantics of each one. Each member function still, however, returns an integer code that must be returned to the event manager.

If you consider this idea further, it should be apparent that each event has a different condition type, to allow for each to signal a condition in its own way. Also, each API must have its own set of condition objects. The UML class diagram in Figure 13.2 shows a partial hierarchy for a set of NSAPI condition classes for the authorization, service, and URL mapping events.

Condition objects have to be created by some mechanism that does not negate their API independence. This is the point of the **SEREFConditionFactory** that we first mentioned in Chapter 12. Employing a similar mechanism to the system services factory, the condition factory manufactures condition objects upon request. The interface of the **SEREFConditionFactory** allows condition objects to be

Table 13.1 Condition member function semantics.

Member Function	Semantics
success	Implies that the event handler successfully processed the event. This does not imply that further event handlers should be ignored.
abort	Requests an attempt to abort the request.
fatalError	Signals that event handler has encountered a fatal error.
noAction	Implies that further event handlers may run.
blockFurtherDirectives	Instructs the event manager to attempt to block further processing of this event by any other installed event handlers. This return is an implied success as well.
disablesProcessing	Asks: Does the supplied parameter imply that further event handler processing should be disabled?
forbiddenToProcess	Returns a code that informs the event manager that we have forbidden ourselves from processing a request.

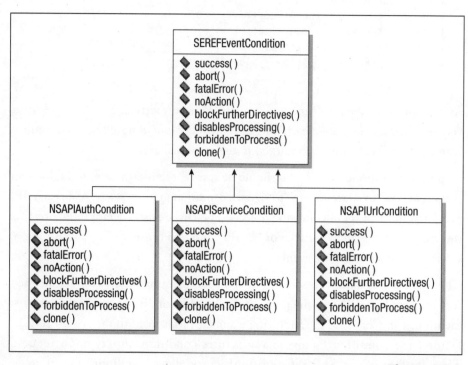

Figure 13.2

UML class diagram for the NSAPI condition partial hierarchy.

requested for each event type. The **SEREFEvent** class holds a static pointer to a **SEREFConditionFactory**, the real (but unknown to **SEREFEvent**) type of which will be that of an extension API-specific condition factory.

> **Note:** A piece of framework glue sets up this static member variable when the framework is loaded. The set up code is highly platform- and API-specific but is very, very small (less than 200 lines per API/platform combination). Some aspects of the set up code are described in Chapter 14.

Because the aim of this scheme is to allow an event handler, a concrete sub-class of **SEREFEvent**, to return an integer code upon completion, the **getCondition** member function of **SEREFEvent** allows access to the current condition object. This access allows the event handler to send one of the messages identified in Table 13.1 to the object, thus returning a specific but *hidden* return value. Listing 13.2 shows a very abbreviated **SEREFEvent** class.

Listing 13.2   The abbreviated **SEREFEvent** listing.

```
class SEREFEvent : public Dependent {
private:
    SEREFEventCondition * pCondition;
    static SEREFConditionFactory * pConditionFactory;
protected:
/**
* Accessor, setting the condition object for the receiver.
* This does not need to be called normally.
*/
    void setCondition(SEREFEventCondition * pNewConHandler) {
        if (pCondition) delete pCondition;
        pCondition = pNewConHandler;
    }

public:
    typedef Dependent super;
    SEREFEvent() : pCondition((SEREFEventCondition *) 0) { }

    SEREFEvent(SEREFEvent const & rhs) {
        *this = rhs;
    }
```

```
    SEREFEvent & operator=(SEREFEvent const & rhs) {
        if (this != &rhs) {
            super::operator=(rhs);
            setCondition(rhs.pCondition->clone());
        }
        return *this;
    }

    virtual ~SEREFEvent() { if (pCondition) delete pCondition; }

/**
 * Static accessor, setting the condition factory for the receiver.
 * Note that this value may only be set once.
 */
static void setConditionFactory(SEREFConditionFactory * pFactory) {
        if (!pConditionFactory)
            pConditionFactory = pFactory;
    }
/**
 * Static accessor, returning the condition factory for the receiver.
 */
    static SEREFConditionFactory * conditionFactory() {
        return pConditionFactory;
    }
/**
 * Accessor, returning the current condition object of this sub-type.
 * Note that this object should be the one used to return an appropriate
 * API-independent error code when an event is processed by a developer's
 * specialized derived class.
 */
    SEREFEventCondition * getCondition() const { return pCondition; }

    int terminateNotification(int iCode) {
        return getCondition()->disablesProcessing(iCode);
    }
};
```

We'll now discuss the events modeled by the framework.

HTTP Authorization Event

As Chapter 1 illustrated, HTTP requests may be authenticated using a simple challenge/response mechanism that allows the exchange of authorization information between a client and server. Each supported API of the framework allows this to be performed in a different manner.

With Netscape's NSAPI, the authorization information has to be decoded by the developer. This requires a BASE64 decoder and knowledge of the lower-level operation of HTTP.

With the Microsoft ISAPI, much less work is required. The authorization event notified in ISAPI already possesses a decoded user name and password. What is less clear in ISAPI is how to control a challenge to a client who presents invalid or no authorization for access to a controlled resource.

The authorization event is an example of how an OO framework can help to alleviate the problems in providing a vendor-independent piece of extension software. Our model of authorization provides clear and consistent semantics across both APIs and all supported platforms. The UML notation class diagram in Figure 13.3 shows the **AuthorisationEvent** class.

Generic Dependency Transform Method

We have discussed in the "Event Hierarchy" section, previously in this chapter, how the **update** method of class **Dependent** is abstract. Sub-classes of **Dependent** must

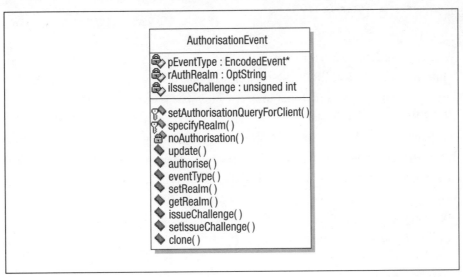

Figure 13.3
The **AuthorisationEvent** class.

implement this method to provide custom behavior that reflects their interest in the dependency mechanism.

The **AuthorisationEvent** class overrides **update** and implements some basic behavior using virtual functions that further sub-classes (as in developer-supplied code) can override to implement a real authentication policy. To show what we mean, consider the actual **update** method shown in Listing 13.3. The behavior supplied is just another template upon which a developer can build extension software. SEREF makes extensive use of a layered architecture to simplify its work.

Listing 13.3   The **update** member function of **AuthorisationEvent**.

```
int AuthorisationEvent::update(
                                EncodedEvent const * rAspect,
                                VoidHolder * pHolder
                                )
{
    SEREFEvent::update(rAspect, pHolder);
    SEREFUser rUser(pHolder);
    WebClient * pClient = conditionFactory()->webClient(pHolder);
    InternetRequest * pRequest = pClient->getRequest();
    int iReturnCode = (rUser.getUserName().length() == 0) ?
                        noAuthorisation(*pRequest) :
                        authorise(rUser,*pRequest);
    delete pClient;
    return iReturnCode;
}
```

When the **update** member function is called, an authorization event has occurred. Thus we'll construct a **SEREFUser** object with the API-specific information that has been wrapped up in a **VoidHolder** object. (This class is covered in the description of the **SEREFUser** class in the "SEREFUser Class" section, later in this chapter.) Next we'll construct a Web client and obtain its HTTP request (the **WebClient** and **InternetRequest** abstract classes are discussed fully when we describe the **ServiceEvent** class in this chapter) from it. We'll then check to see if this object contains a decoded, significant user name. If so, we'll call the virtual function **authorise**, otherwise, we'll call the **noAuthorisation** member function. Each of these scenarios is covered in the following sections.

Adding An Authorization Event Handler

The sidebar in this chapter, "Revisiting Adding Event Handlers To The Framework," describes the generic method by which event handlers are added as dependents of the framework. To demystify the description somewhat, Listing 13.4 shows an example **initialise** C function for Win32 that registers a basic authorization event handler whose type is **BasicAuthenticator**.

Listing 13.4 An example **initialise** function for event handler registration.

```
extern "C" {
int __declspec( dllexport ) initialise(void * pDispatcher) {
   EventManager * pManager =
            static_cast<EventManager *>(pDispatcher);
   if (!pManager) serefErrorLogger <<
                    "Could not get address of event dispatcher"
                    << endl;
   else {
      pManager->addEventHandler(
                    new BasicAuthenticator(),
                    AuthorisationEvent::eventType()
                    );
   return 1;
}
}
```

The **BasicAuthenticator** class (not shown) is expected to implement at least a **clone** method, as described in Chapter 12. Once the call to **initialise** has returned control to the framework (as the sidebar explains, SEREF itself calls **initialise**), at least one event handler for authorization has been added to the frameworks list of registered handlers.

> **Note:** Under Unix implementations, the __declspec(dllexport) is, of course, not required.

Revisiting Adding Event Handlers To The Framework

Up until now, we have not fully discussed how an event handler is added into SEREF. The mechanism employed is, as you know, an extension of the dependency mechanism.

In Chapter 12, we provided a description as to how SEREF searches a shared object identified to it as containing event handlers.

*For each shared object that SEREF is aware of, it will try to locate the C linkage function **initialise** in that shared object's symbol space. If it can locate this symbol, it executes it. This function is expected to register event handler dependencies upon the event manager pointer that is passed to it. Thus, each event handler that is to be registered is attached to the event manager using the **addEventHandler** member function of the SEREF event manager. After this, each event handler is cloned N times. After all handlers have been registered, the event manager is ready to dispatch incoming events to its new dependents.*

*Each boilerplate event handler (**AuthorisationEvent**, **UrlMappingEvent**, and so on) has a static **EncodedEvent** pointer that represents its aspect as notified by the event manager. This pointer is accessed by calling the static member function **eventType** defined for each event class. These pointers are created by the server glue at SEREF load time and should be used by developers as the aspect of the event.*

Note again that this simple mechanism is common across all supported platforms.

Basic Encapsulated Behavior

Next we'll describe the behavior supplied by the basic **AuthorisationEvent** class and how it may be used to create an extension. As we identified, there are two basic scenarios to consider.

Authorization Credentials Supplied

You might consider this the most important scenario that you would have to deal with. When a client supplies credentials, it is asking for permission to access a protected resource. Any extension must decide, based upon the authorization details supplied and the target resource, whether the request should be allowed.

When you sub-class **AuthorisationEvent**, certain virtual functions are defined to allow this determination to be performed and the response to the client formulated. Consider again Listing 13.3, and how the member function **authorise** is called when a user name (the name held by the **SEREFUser** instance) exists—as in it has a length greater than zero characters. If we have a user name, this does in fact mean that the client has supplied some authorization information. So the semantics of the pro forma **authorise** function, shown in Listing 13.5, are that the user object supplied as a parameter contains the credentials for the current request.

Listing 13.5 The **authorise** virtual function of **AuthorisationEvent**.

```
virtual int AuthorisationEvent::authorise(
                                    SEREFUser & rUser,
                                    InternetRequest &
                                    )
{
     return getCondition()->noAction();
}
```

As you can see, the supplied **authorise** does nothing special, it simply returns a *no action* value to the event manager, which signals that nothing has been done with respect to the validation of the credentials supplied via the **SEREFUser** object. Subclasses may override this virtual function to provide specific behavior.

Figure 13.4 shows a UML notation sequence diagram that succinctly shows the defined object interactions for the basic authorization sequence. We have omitted the construction of the Web client object to simplify the diagram.

Nonsupplied Authorization Credentials

The other scenario we might encounter is a request that needs authentication but provides no credentials. The HTTP 1.0 means of dealing with this is to challenge the requester by supplying a realm (some opaque description that may be used as a prompt if the client is part of an interactive session with a human user) and waiting for an appropriately encoded response.

Once again, virtual functions provide the device by which we'll enable custom extension building for this synopsis. If you consider Listing 13.3 again, you will notice that when the **SEREFUser** object has no user name (as in credentials supplied or decoded), the member function **noAuthorisation** is called. The standard implementation for this member function is shown in Listing 13.6.

Listing 13.6 The standard **noAuthorisation** member function.

```
int AuthorisationEvent::noAuthorisation(InternetRequest & rRequest) {
          specifyRealm();
          if (issueChallenge())
                    setAuthorisationQueryForClient(rRequest);
return getCondition()->abort();
}
```

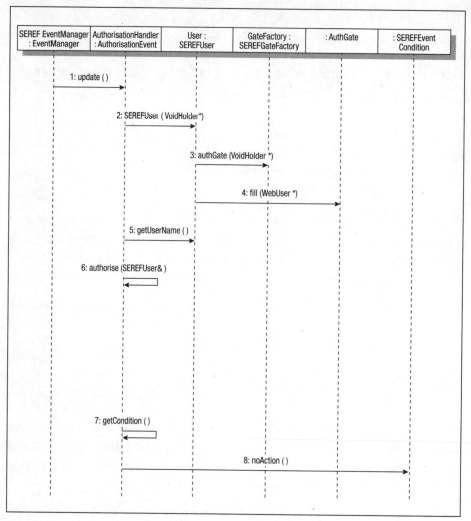

Figure 13.4

The UML notation sequence diagram for basic authorization behavior.

There are two virtual member functions potentially called in **noAuthorisation** (which is declared as private to **AuthorisationEvent**). These are **specifyRealm** and **setAuthorisationQueryForClient**.

The first of these, **specifyRealm**, enables a custom authorization handler to set the realm to be used when challenging the client. The default realm is unspecified but may be altered by supplying an appropriate string to the **setRealm** protected member function of **AuthorisationEvent**. Assuming a challenge is issued to the client, this realm will be returned as the value of the WWW-Authenticate header. (Notice that we said *if* a challenge is issued.) Alternately, **specifyRealm** may call the protected member function **setIssueChallenge** with the integer value zero. This has the effect of disabling the challenge to the client—meaning that authorization will fail, and miserably. This is useful for disallowing *any* access to some superrestricted object.

If we assume that the challenge is being issued, then the other virtual function, **setAuthorisationQueryForClient**, may be overridden to supply extra or different headers to the client. The standard, supplied implementation of this member function is shown here:

```
virtual void
AuthorisationEvent::setAuthorisationQueryForClient
                            (InternetRequest & pRequest)
{
     pRequest.addResponseHeader(
                    "status",
                    "401 Unauthorized");
     pRequest.addResponseHeader(
                    "WWW-Authenticate",
                     getRealm());
}
```

The default implementation just sets a **401 Request** status along with the realm as specified by the developer (or the default of unspecified). This is congruent with HTTP 1.0 behavior.

By far the most prevalent behavior here would be the specification of just a realm. The framework provides all other necessary behavior to set the appropriate headers and challenge the client.

We'll again use a UML notation sequence diagram, in Figure 13.5, to depict the standard object interactions that occur when a client authentication challenge is issued. We have omitted the construction of the Web client object to simplify the diagram.

Example Implementation

The simple example shown in Listing 13.7 implements an authorization extension class **SimpleAuthorization** by extending the **AuthorisationEvent** class. When an unauthorized request is received, a fixed realm is set. If authorization credentials are present, these are checked against the URI accessible by the public member function getUri of the **InternetRequest** class. The URI corresponds to the format as dictated by HTTP 1.0. The check is simple: If the authorization user name appears in the URI, access is granted, otherwise it's denied.

Listing 13.7   The **SimpleAuthorization** class.

```
class SimpleAuthorization : public AuthorisationEvent {
public:
int authorise(SEREFUser & rUser, InternetRequest & rRequest) {
    size_t i = rRequest.getUri().find(rUser.getUserName());
    return (i != (size_t) -1) ?
        getCondition()->success() :
        getCondition()->abort();
}
void specifyRealm() {
    setRealm("High Performance");
}
Dependent * clone() { return new SimpleAuthorization(); }
};
```

As you can see, this is a very simple class. As is, this extension will work in the same manner for both ISAPI and NSAPI, under Windows NT and Unix, without source code alteration.

Notice how the **getCondition** member function (that the **SEREFEvent** class implements) is used to signal success or abort in the **authorise** member function. The condition object is created in the **AuthorisationEvent** constructor. This snippet shows the constructor code:

```
AuthorisationEvent ::AuthorisationEvent()
                                    : iIssueChallenge(1) {
   setCondition(conditionFactory()->authCondition());
}
```

As we discussed in the "SEREFEvent Class" section earlier in this chapter, the condition factory of the **SEREFEvent** class is used to create the appropriate condition object.

We'll mention a final point of interest: the inclusion of the **clone** member function. If you recall our discussion in Chapter 12 of the mechanism employed to ensure thread safety in SEREF, you will remember that the **clone** member function was an essential feature of any framework-extending class. Its implementation is as simple as expected—simply instantiate a new instance of the class.

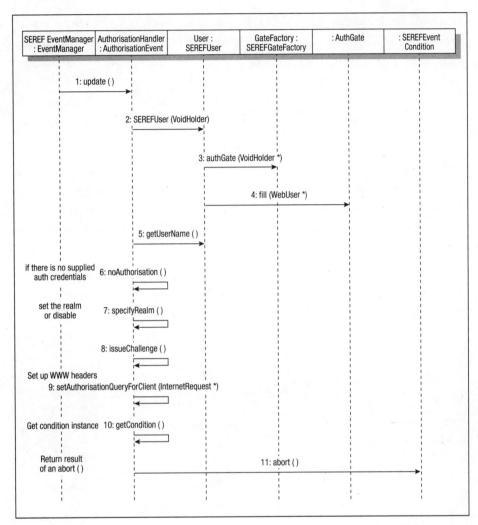

Figure 13.5

The UML notation sequence diagram for no credentials authorization behavior.

API Gates And The Provision Of Independence

At this juncture, we'll diverge from our description before we move on with the discussion of further events. The topic of API gates and how they relate to SEREF is important to understanding how the framework maintains its API independence for some key classes.

As we saw for the **AuthorisationEvent** class, an object of type **SEREFUser** is created that encapsulates the user, password, and group possibly found in a request's credentials. An API gate, which we'll refer to as a gate, is used by this concrete class to actually decode this information in a manner that does not compromise API insulation. Through the gate idiom, the **SEREFUser** class looks the same for both the ISAPI and NSAPI versions of the framework.

So what is a gate, really? Simply put, a gate provides a mediating interface between the lower level API and the higher level, abstracted view that the framework maintains. The word *interface* is the key here, because a gate is defined by an abstract class that has no implementation or state. When passed API-specific information via a generic mechanism, a gate can unwrap the parochial information. In a complementary fashion, a gate can be asked to rewrap the information with changes dictated by some client (for example, the **SEREFUser** class) and propagate them as appropriate.

There are two gate interfaces defined in the framework; they are shown Figure 13.6 along with their ISAPI and NSAPI concrete sub-classes.

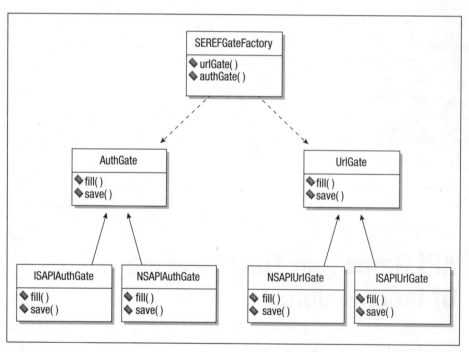

Figure 13.6

The gate classes of SEREF.

The **UrlGate** class mediates for URL type events, whereas the **AuthGate** class mediates for authorization events. Also shown is the **SEREFGateFactory** abstract class, which is responsible for serving up the appropriate gates upon demand. The serve glue is responsible for creating the appropriate concrete gate factory at runtime and setting up the instance associated with the class concerned via a pointer to the abstract class. Separate instances are used in SEREF for factories, as we are currently unsure if there is a need for dynamic factory instances per factory-dependent class.

The SEREFUser class

Now we'll move on to the description of this class. The UML notation class diagram in Figure 13.7 shows the hierarchy of user classes in SEREF.

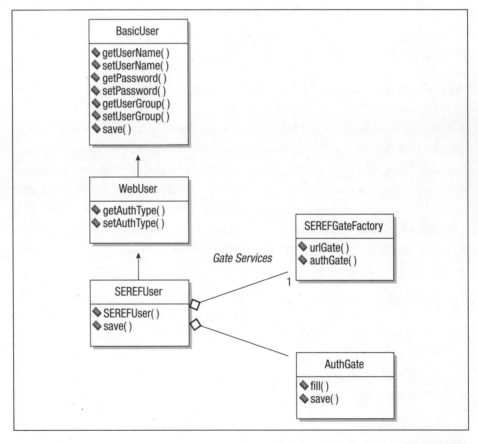

Figure 13.7
The user class hierarchy.

To really understand how the class collaborates with the **AuthGate** class we'll need to consider and explain the partial **SEREFUser** class in Listing 13.8.

Listing 13.8   Partial **SEREFUser** class listing.

```
class SEREFUser : public WebUser {
public:
        static void setFactory(SEREFGateFactory * pNewFactory) {
                if (!pFactory) pFactory = pNewFactory;
        }
private:
        static SEREFGateFactory * pFactory;
        AuthGate * pGate;
public:
   SEREFUser(VoidHolder * pHolder) : pGate(NULL), WebUser() {
                pGate = pFactory->authGate(pHolder);
                if (pGate) pGate->fill(this);
   }
   ~SEREFUser() { if (pGate) delete pGate; }
   void save() { if (pGate) pGate->save(this); }
};
```

We'll assume that some external code has set up the appropriate factory, as defined by the static member variable **pFactory**. When a **SEREFUser** object is created, a pointer to a **VoidHolder** object is passed as an argument. In SEREF, a **VoidHolder** is used to pass (in an opaque manner) API-specific parameters to a mapping class that can decode the enclosed pointers. The discussion of this method is beyond the scope of this book, but it is sufficient to think of this type of object as a simple carrier of opaque information that can be decoded by a more intelligent (and API-specific) object. If we repeat the definition of the **update** function of class **AuthorisationEvent**, you will see that a **VoidHolder** is passed by the framework event manager during notification

```
int AuthorisationEvent::update(
                              EncodedEvent const * rAspect,
                              VoidHolder * pHolder
                              )
{
     SEREFEvent::update(rAspect, pHolder);
     SEREFUser rUser(pHolder);
.....
```

and is subsequently used to construct the user object.

When a **SEREFUser** is created, the **VoidHolder** is passed to an **AuthGate** created by asking the gate factory to manufacture one. Following this, the gate is asked to fill the object by whatever means is necessary. This is the method used to decode user information from a request and place it in a **SEREFUser** object where it can be easily altered. If alterations are made to the **SEREFUser** object, they may be written back to the request by calling the **save** member function, which calls the **save** member function of **AuthGate**.

To illustrate this idea further, Listing 13.9 shows the implementation of a concrete (remember that the **SEREFUser** class only sees the abstract class interface) authorization gate for the NSAPI of Netscape.

Listing 13.9 NSAPI **AuthGate** implementation.

```
NSAPIAuthGate::NSAPIAuthGate(VoidHolder * pParameter) {
   rMap.setHolder(pParameter);
}

void NSAPIAuthGate::save(WebUser * pUser) {
   Request * pRequest = rMap.getRequest();
   if (pUser->getUserName().length() > 0) {
      pblock_nvinsert("auth-user",
                     (char *) pUser->getUserName().c_str(),
                     pRequest->vars);
      pblock_nvinsert("auth-type", "basic", pRequest->vars);
      OptString rGroup(pUser->getUserGroup());
      if (rGroup.length() > 0)
         pblock_nvinsert("auth-group",
                        (char *) rGroup.c_str(),
                        pRequest->vars);
   }
}

void NSAPIAuthGate::fill(WebUser * pUser) {
   if (!rMap.isNull()) {
      char * cpName = pblock_findval(
                           "auth-user",
                           rMap.getRequest()->vars);
      if (cpName) {
         pUser->setUserName(cpName);
         pUser->setUserGroup(
                           pblock_findval(
                           "auth-group",
                           rMap.getRequest()->vars);
```

```
        }
        else {
            BasicHTTPCredentials rAuthObject(
                                 pblock_findval("authorization",
                                 rMap.getRequest()->headers),
                                 new Base64Decoder());
            int iRetCode = rAuthObject.validate();
            if (iRetCode) {
                pUser->setUserName(rAuthObject.getUser());
                pUser->setPassword(rAuthObject.getPassword());
            }
        }
    }
}
```

The **rMap** instance variable referenced is an API-specific object that can translate the opaque pointers of the **VoidHolder** to appropriate API-specific types. There is one such map type for each API.

As you can see, the **fill** operation attempts to populate a **WebUser** instance (**WebUser** is a super-class of **SEREFUser**) with information extracted by decoding a BASE64 encoded string, if found. Conversely, the **save** operation attempts to set the credentials of the supplied **WebUser** object in the requests state space. Please see Chapter 6 for a full description of the semantics of NSAPI.

A slightly more complex aspect of the concrete gate implementations is that they are aware of the temporal changes in request parameters. This knowledge allows, in the specific case of the **SEREFUser** class, a user object to be constructed at any time during *and* after authorization that has the correct user credentials encapsulated, with the possible exception of the password. Both supported APIs provide access by different means during the progression of a request's processing.

The authorization gate illustrates this, particularly in the **fill** method of the NSAPI implementation. Its simple logic tries to detect the existence of a user name associated with a request before trying to decode a BASE64 string (if available). This is not only the correct behavior; it is also more efficient in the case of an identity mapping between the authenticated and supplied user name.

*Note: For both ISAPI and NSAPI, any **SEREFUser** object, if constructed after the authorization event has occurred, will contain only the user name and possibly the user group. This is because the APIs behave differently with respect to the availability of a password. The password is probably best left invisible after authorization has occurred.*

URL Mapping Event

As we noted in the chapters on ISAPI and NSAPI (Chapters 3 through 10), one of the common behaviors of extension APIs is the provision of a *hook* to enable the alteration of the logic behind virtual URI to physical path mapping for an HTTP request. This is the basic purpose of the **UrlMappingEvent** class.

The UML notation class diagram in Figure 13.8 shows the **UrlMappingEvent** class.

Generic Dependency Transform Method

The **UrlMappingEvent** class overrides the **update** of **Dependent** and implements some behavior using virtual functions that sub-classes can override to implement a real mapping policy. The **update** method is shown in Listing 13.10. In a similar vein to the authorization class, the behavior supplied is just a template upon which a developer can build URL mapping extension software.

Listing 13.10   The **update member** function of **UrlMappingEvent**.

```
int UrlMappingEvent::update(EncodedEvent const * rAspect,
                                    VoidHolder * pVoidHolder) {
    SEREFEvent::update(rAspect, pVoidHolder);
    SEREFUrl pUrl(pVoidHolder);
    int i = mapUrl(pUrl);
  return i;
}
```

The **update** implementation does little more than create a **SEREFUrl** object with the API-specific information (again, wrapped up in a **VoidHolder** object) and call a virtual function, **mapUrl**, passing the constructed URL object by nonconstant refer-

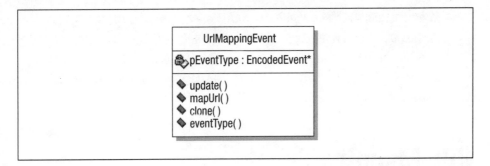

Figure 13.8

The UrlMappingEvent class.

ence. Sub-classes are free to modify the physical path encapsulated by the URL object and commit these changes back to the request. The **SEREFUrl** class is discussed next.

The SEREFUrl Class

Modeling a URL is a relatively simple affair. In our framework, a **LogicalUrl** anchors the base of the hierarchy, and provides accessors and a parser for URLs encoded as strings. It also implements accessors that can be used to alter the state of the known components of the URL. These are, however, declared as protected, and the **EditableUrl** class exposes these state-changing methods for public use. This allows us to provide truly immutable URL objects when required.

The final and most derived class in the hierarchy is **SEREFUrl**. This class parallels the use of gates seen in the **SEREFUser** class, using an object called a **UrlGate** to provide the API translation services as required. The URL hierarchy is depicted in the UML notation class diagram in Figure 13.9.

The **SEREFUrl** class provides a **save** member function, which is used to commit any changes made to the physical URL back to the request. Notice that in this discussion we have only discussed the alteration of the physical URL—this should come as no real surprise because the physical path is the only one we can modify that has any effect.

The earlier section, "API Gates And The Provision Of Independence," discusses the way gates are used to provide API insulation. We won't go into exhaustive detail concerning what a **UrlGate** abstract class models, apart from saying that it defines the protocol used to extract URL data from and write URL changes to the currently considered API, *whatever* that may be. To illustrate, Listing 13.11 is the URL gate implementation for the ISAPI of Microsoft's IIS.

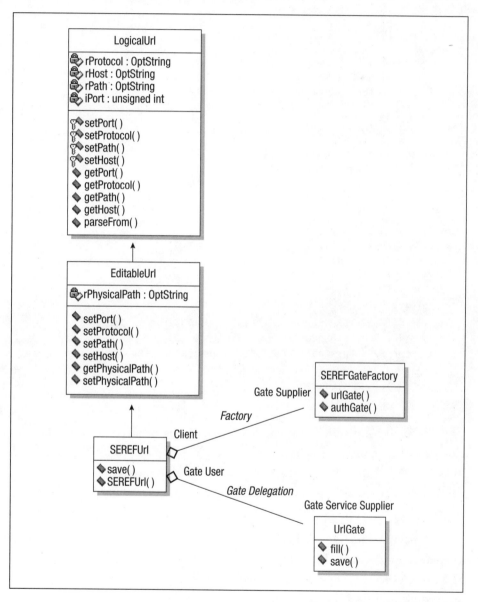

Figure 13.9
The SEREF URL hierarchy.

Listing 13.11   The **UrlGate** class for the ISAPI.

```
ISAPIUrlGate::ISAPIUrlGate(VoidHolder * pParameter) {
    rMap.setHolder(pParameter);
}


void ISAPIUrlGate::save(EditableUrl * pUrl) {
    if (pUrl != NULL &&
        pUrl->getPhysicalPath().length() > 0 && !rMap.isNull()) {
        LPEXTENSION_CONTROL_BLOCK
            pBlock = rMap.getExtensionBlock();
        if (pBlock)
            return;
        PHTTP_FILTER_URL_MAP pContext = rMap.getUrlContext();
        ::strcpy(pContext->pszPhysicalPath,
                pUrl->getPhysicalPath().c_str());
    }
}


void ISAPIUrlGate::fill(EditableUrl * pUrl) {
    if (!rMap.isNull()) {
        LPEXTENSION_CONTROL_BLOCK pBlock = rMap.getExtensionBlock();
        if (pBlock)
            pUrl->setPhysicalPath(pBlock->lpszPathTranslated);
        else {
            PHTTP_FILTER_URL_MAP pContext = rMap.getUrlContext();
            pUrl->setPath(pContext->pszURL);
            pUrl->setPhysicalPath(pContext->pszPhysicalPath);
        }
    }
}
```

The **fill** member function is responsible for transferring details from the API to the **EditableUrl** pointer. Thus, **save** transfers the physical path from the **EditableUrl** object to the API-specific data structures. Remember that the **save** function has to be deliberately called by a client extension to mandate the transfer of any physical changes to the API.

The **fill** member function is called in the constructor of the **SEREFUrl** class, after a **UrlGate** heap-allocated object is created by calling the **urlGate** member function of **SEREFGateFactory**. The call to **fill** is passed the **this** pointer of the **SEREFUrl** object and then filled with whatever information the gate object can find.

It is interesting to note that, in Listing 13.11, both the **fill** and **save** member functions have to be aware of the context in which they are called. If they are called as an ISAPI filter, they have to deal with a different ISAPI structure than if they are called as part of an ISA DLL (which may be used to implement service event handlers). We felt that separating the behavior for these APIs would detract from understandability.

Adding A URL Mapping Event Handler

We previously showed, in Listing 13.4, an example **initialise** C function that attached an authorization event handler to SEREF. The addition of the event handler for a URL event handler is achieved in a similar manner, as in Listing 13.12:

Listing 13.12   An example **initialise** function for URL mapping
                       event handler registration.

```
extern "C" {
int __declspec( dllexport ) initialise(void * pDispatcher) {
EventManager * pManager =
            static_cast<EventManager *>(pDispatcher);

   if (!pManager) serefErrorLogger <<
                      "Could not get address of event dispatcher"
                      << endl;
   else {
      pManager->addEventHandler(
                    new UrlMapper(),
                    UrlMappingEvent::eventType()
                    );
   return 1;
}
}
```

We'll assume that the class **UrlMapper** exists and is derived from the **UrlMappingEvent** class. This nonillustrated class directly registers interest in URL mapping events by using the aspect of the basic URL mapping event, dereferenced by calling the static member function **eventType** of **UrlMappingEvent**. This returns a pointer to an **EncodedEvent** class whose event type is the one notified by the event manager during URL mapping.

Basic Encapsulated Behavior

Again, we'll describe the behavior supplied by the basic event class **UrlMappingEvent** and how it is used to create an extension. The behavioral flow is really quite simple.

When you sub-class **UrlMappingEvent**, the virtual member function **mapUrl** is the only one visible to your sub-class that is designed to be overridden. If you refer back to Listing 13.10, you can see that this function is called after the **SEREFUrl** object is constructed and with this object as a parameter. Like other framework-supplied events, the **UrlMappingEvent** class does provide a default implementation for this function, shown in this code snippet:

```
virtual int UrlMappingEvent::mapUrl(SEREFUrl &) {
return getCondition()->noAction();
}
```

The supplied **mapUrl** does nothing useful, it simply returns a *no action* value to the event manager, which signals that nothing has changed with respect to the **SEREFUrl** object. Any sub-class should provide an implementation for this virtual function that implements the appropriate mapping. As we noted previously, sub-classes are free to modify the physical path encapsulated by the URL object and commit these changes back to the request.

Figure 13.10 shows a UML notation collaboration diagram that shows the defined object interactions for URL mapping.

Example Implementation

Our example implementation is a very simple and specific URL-mapping class that provides a framework-based implementation of the NSAPI function described in the "Sample Name Translation Function" section of Chapter 6.

The extension looks for a + sign followed by a user name in the current URI and, if found, translates it to a physical path that cannot be derived by the default rules of the server. When such a mapping occurs, the resulting physical path is constructed by concatenating a statically stored *partial* physical path and the portion of the URI that appears after the plus sign (if it is detected). The **EncodedUrlMapper** class in Listing 13.13 shows the complete implementation for this scheme.

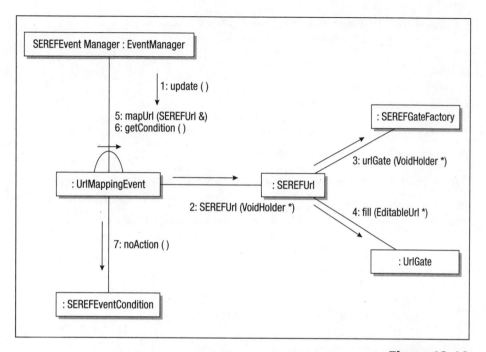

Figure 13.10

A UML notation collaboration diagram for basic URL mapping.

Listing 13.13   The **EncodedUrlMapper** class.

```
class EncodedUrlMapper : public UrlMappingEvent {
public:
    virtual int mapUrl(SEREFUrl & rUrl) {
        size_t iIndex;
        OptString rPath(rUrl.getPath());
        if ((iIndex=rPath.rfind("+")) != (size_t) -1) {
            OptString rString(getUserBase());
            rString.append(rPath.substr(iIndex+1));
            rUrl.setPhysicalPath(rString);
            rUrl.save();
            return getCondition()->blockFurtherDirectives();
        }
        return getCondition()->noAction();
    }

    Dependent * clone() { return new EncodedUrlMapper(); }

    static OptString const & getUserBase()
                { return rBase; }
```

```
static void setUserBase(OptString const & rNewBase)
            { rBase = rNewBase; }

private:
   static OptString rBase;
};
```

We'll provide a standard implementation of the **clone** factory method that is used by the framework to ensure thread safety.

The **mapUrl** member function is called when a URL is being mapped from a virtual to physical path. In our **mapUrl**, we look at the **rUrl** that is passed to us to see if it contains the plus symbol. If this is the case, we execute these lines:

```
OptString rString(getUserBase());
      rString.append(rPath.substr(iIndex+1));
      rUrl.setPhysicalPath(rString);
      rUrl.save();
      return getCondition()->blockFurtherDirectives();
```

First, we'll construct a temporary object that holds the partial physical path as accessed by calling the static member function **getUserBase**. We'll assume that this path has been set up somewhere else.

> **Note:** As befits the illustrative status of this class, there are better ways of defining a base path name for use in this extension class, such as using an externally configurable source.

To this string, **rString**, we'll then append every character in the URI that appears after the plus sign. The next two lines are crucial. First, we'll set the physical path of the **SEREFUrl** object, **rUrl**. Remember that this has changed the current, transient view of the physical path. Now, because we are confident that the change should be committed to the request, we'll call the **save** member function of **SEREFUrl**. As we described in "The SEREFUrl Class" section earlier in this chapter, **save** transfers the physical path from the **EditableUrl** object to the API-specific data structures via an encapsulated **UrlGate**. Of course, we'll see none of this externally.

The return value, when mapping has occurred, shows another face of the **SEREFEventCondition** object. As we have altered and saved the physical path that the request maps to, we should inform the server that we have performed the definitive translation. The **return** statement

```
return getCondition()->blockFurtherDirectives();
```

does this by calling the **blockFurtherDirectives** member function of the condition object instance held by the **SEREFEvent** super-class. Regardless of the API that is used, the value returned indicates that any other handlers should not be given a chance to handle this event.

URL Access Check Event

The **UrlAccessCheckEvent** class allows the creation of extensions to verify the accessibility of the target resource of an HTTP request. As you may have anticipated, the implementation of this event is similar to the **UrlMappingEvent** class.

The UML notation class diagram in Figure 13.11 shows the **UrlAccessCheckEvent** class.

> *Note: ISAPI does not provide an access check event. For the ISAPI deployed framework, this event is simulated by the framework entry-point, glue code that we'll discuss in Chapter 14.*

Generic Dependency Transform Method

The **UrlAccessCheckEvent** class overriding of **Dependent::update**, as shown in Listing 13.14, uses hooks and template methods to facilitate a real access check

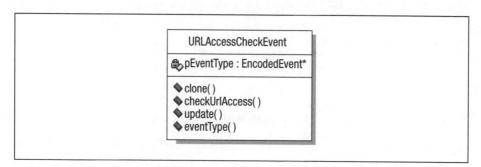

Figure 13.11
The **UrlAccessCheckEvent** class.

implementation. The purpose of such an event is to allow a request to be further checked for permission to access a resource—recognizing that even an authenticated user cannot access everything with impunity. We'll note again the template nature of this method—in its embodiment of abstract processing logic.

Listing 13.14 The **update** member function of **UrlAccessCheckEvent**.

```
int UrlAccessCheckEvent::update(
                        EncodedEvent const * rAspect,
                        VoidHolder * pVoidHolder)
{
    SEREFEvent::update(rAspect, pVoidHolder);
    SEREFUser rUser(pVoidHolder);
    SEREFUrl pUrl(pVoidHolder);
    return checkUrlAccess(pUrl, rUser);
}
```

The **update** implementation creates a **SEREFUser** object and **SEREFUrl** object (using the method we have described previously) before calling a specially defined virtual function, **checkUrlAccess**. Both constructed objects are passed by reference as arguments to this function.

Adding An Access Check Event Handler

We have previously noted the form of the **initialise** method that is used by external extension software to attach event handlers to the event manager. The addition of the event handler for URL access checking is achieved in an almost identical fashion to a URL mapping event handler. To avoid repetition, we'll show only the addition of an event handler to the event manager in this code extract:

```
pManager->addEventHandler(
                new UrlAccessChecker(),
                UrlAccessCheckEvent::eventType()
                );
```

See Listing 13.12 for the full body of an **initialise** function.

We'll assume class **UrlAccessChecker** specializes the **UrlAccessCheckEvent** class. In common with other SEREF notified events, the **UrlAccessCheckEvent** class provides a public static member function that returns a pointer to a static **EncodedEvent** pointer, which is the aspect of the event that the event manager will notify.

Basic Encapsulated Behavior

When a developer specializes **UrlAccessCheckEvent**, the virtual member function **checkUrlAccess** must be overridden. In common with other events, the **UrlAccessCheckEvent** class provides a default implementation, shown in the next code snippet:

```
virtual int UrlAccessCheckEvent::checkUrlAccess(
                                    SEREFUrl &,
                                    SEREFUser &) {
    return getCondition()->noAction();
}
```

The default **checkUrlAccess** function does nothing particularly useful, returning a *no action* value to the event manager, deferring access checks to any other registered handlers. The URL object parameter has passed through the mapping stage and a physical path should be present. The **SEREFUser** object *may* have at least the name of the authenticated user if the client has been challenged. This is installation-dependent in that, if the resource is not access controlled, there is no real way to protect it. The combination of a user name and a physical resource name should usually be enough to allow event handlers to make a policy decision regarding accessibility.

Example Implementation

We'll show a very simple access verification event handler in Listing 13.15.

Listing 13.15   A simple access check class.

```
class SimpleAccessChecker : public UrlAccessCheckEvent {
public:
   virtual int checkUrlAccess(SEREFUrl & rUrl,
                                    SEREFUser & rUser) {
      if (rUser.getUserName().length() == 0)
         return getCondition()->noAction();
      else
         return
         (rUrl.getPath().find(rUser.getUserName())
             != (size_t) -1)?
            getCondition()->success() :
            getCondition()->abort();
   }

   Dependent * clone() { return new SimpleAccessChecker(); }
};
```

Again, we'll provide a standard **clone** implementation for **SimpleAccessChecker,** as required by the framework.

This terse class implements an access checker that complements the URL mapper given in Listing 13.13. When it receives event notification through the virtual **checkUrlAccess** function, it first checks that there is a user name in the **SEREFUser** reference passed to it. If there is not, then no sensible access check can occur, and the value obtained by calling the **SEREFEventCondition** member function **noAction** is returned to the event manager. This should allow other access check event handlers to receive the notification.

The alternate scenario is when a user name is present. When this happens, the URL path held in the **SEREFUrl** reference is searched for the presence of the user name. If found, **SimpleAccessChecker** returns a success message, which *may* block other event handlers. If the user name is not found, the abort error notification is returned, which should abort the request.

The Service Event

As we know all too well by now, each HTTP request expects a response. This may be just a simple document, a complex image, an octet stream—the possibilities are unbounded. The **ServiceEvent** class exists to provide appropriate semantics to allow request servicing.

The UML notation class diagram in Figure 13.12 shows the **ServiceEvent** class.

Generic Dependency Transform Method

The **ServiceEvent** class overrides the **update** method of **Dependent** and, in keeping with the general mechanisms used by the framework, creates certain key objects and calls a virtual function, specifically designed to be overridden. This virtual function, **serviceRequest**, is expected to perform appropriate servicing actions. We'll show the **update** method in Listing 13.16. Note again that this is boilerplate code only—it requires a sub-class to build upon it to provide interesting behavior.

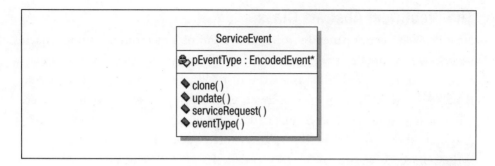

Figure 13.12
The **ServiceEvent** class.

Listing 13.16   The **update** member function of **ServiceEvent**.

```
int ServiceEvent::update(EncodedEvent const * rAspect,
                              VoidHolder * pVoidHolder) {
    SEREFEvent::update(rAspect, pVoidHolder);
    SEREFUrl rUrl(pVoidHolder);
    WebClient * pClient =
                    conditionFactory()->
                        webClient(pVoidHolder);
    int i = getCondition()->noAction();
    if (pClient) {
        i = serviceRequest(rUrl, *pClient);
        delete pClient;
    }
    return i;
}
```

To allow request servicing to be performed, the **serviceRequest** virtual function logically requires (at least) a reference to the request's URL and a connection to the client. The former is required to figure out what resource to access or query to perform; the latter must actually write the response to the client. If you examine Listing 13.16, you will see that the **SEREFUrl** object is created first, followed by an object of type **WebClient**.

Once these objects have been created, the **serviceRequest** function is called with both objects supplied as parameters. The **WebClient** pointer is dereferenced to provide reference (as opposed to pointer) semantics to implementers of **serviceRequest**. The **WebClient** abstract class is crucial to our understanding of the operation of the **ServiceEvent** class and we'll describe it next.

The WebClient Abstract Class

Now there's an entity patiently sitting at the end of a connection during request processing—we decided to call it a **WebClient**. This type of object has a name, can provide streams to read from and write to itself, and has an associated request. Because the **WebClient** class is abstract, each API provides a specific concrete implementation of the Web client interface. Figure 13.13, a UML notation class diagram, shows the **WebClient**, **InternetRequest**, **ReadConnection**, and **WriteConnection** classes, and an API-specific class, **ISAPIWebClient**.

Derived classes of **WebClient** must implement the member functions shown in Table 13.2.

WebClient offers a few other features, such as accessing the DNS-resolved name of the client and starting the response to the client in a protocol-independent manner. In most instances, however, the request and I/O connections to the client will be the most used.

To avoid compromising our API independence, instances of a **WebClient** are served up using a factory approach. The **SEREFConditionFactory** is, by dint of a historical mistake, responsible for this.

The next few sections explain the utility of the other classes in Figure 13.13. First we'll look at the **InternetRequest** abstract class and then the **ReadConnection** and **WriteConnection** interfaces.

Table 13.2   Pure virtual functions of the **WebClient** class.

Virtual Function	Semantics
InternetRequest * makeRequest( )	Returns a pointer to an InternetRequest that the WebClient class stores and is responsible for deleting.
WriteConnection & getWriteConnection( )	Returns a reference to a writeable connection to the client.
ReadConnection & getReadConnection( )	Returns a reference to a readable connection to the client.

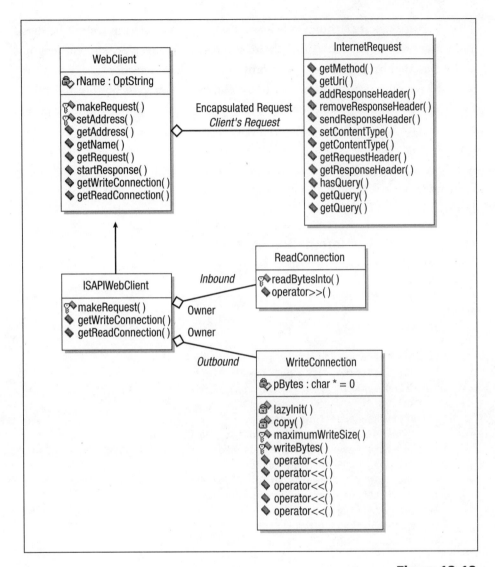

Figure 13.13

The UML notation class diagram for **WebClient** and associated classes.

The InternetRequest Class

This abstract class encapsulates the detail of a request and is not necessarily limited to HTTP. However, because HTTP is the most interesting protocol from our perspective, we'll limit our discussion to this area only.

The **InternetRequest** class thus provides an *interface* for accessing request headers and setting response headers. Such headers include content-type, content-length, and so on. Member functions are also provided that allow detection of whether the request has a query associated with it (for example, if it was possibly a form). If so, forms can be parsed into dictionary objects on request or the raw query can be accessed. The **InternetRequest** class takes care of (and hides) lower-level, specific detail through the use of other interfaces such as **ReadConnection**, which is described next. For each API there is defined a concrete Internet request class—**InternetRequest** defines a number of pure virtual functions that are shown in Listing 13.17.

Listing 13.17   The **InternetRequest** class.

```
class InternetRequest {
private:
    OptString rUri;
protected:
    InternetRequest() { }
public:
    virtual ~InternetRequest() { }
    virtual OptString getMethod() = 0;
    OptString const & getUri() const;
    virtual void
      addResponseHeader(OptString const & rKey,
                                    OptString const & rValue) = 0;
    virtual void removeResponseHeader(OptString const &) = 0;
    virtual int sendResponseHeaders() = 0;
    virtual void setContentType(OptString const & rType) ;
    virtual OptString getContentType();
    virtual OptString
        getRequestHeader(OptString const & rKey) = 0;
    virtual OptString
        getResponseHeader(OptString const & rKey) = 0;
    virtual int hasQuery() = 0;
    virtual QueryDictionary * getQuery() = 0;
    virtual QueryDictionary * getQuery(ReadConnection &) = 0;
};
```

The concrete implementations of **WebClient** are responsible for creating the appropriate **InternetRequest** sub-class upon request. They do this by implementing the pure virtual function **makeRequest**, as described in Table 13.2. Note that only the concrete **WebClient** knows the real class of the **InternetRequest** that it creates—all other references are through the **InternetRequest** interface. The description of the **QueryDictionary** class, seen in the latter portion of Listing 13.17, is described after our example service handler implementation.

We'll now show an example of the use of this class in conjunction with **WebClient**. The example is a an elided implementation of the **ServiceEvent** class's **serviceRequest** virtual function, which sets the content type of the response to the associated client:

```
int SomeClass::serviceRequest(SEREFUrl & rUrl,
                                      WebClient & rClient) {
   InternetRequest * pRequest = rClient.getRequest();
   pRequest->setContentType("text/html");
```

The ReadConnection And WriteConnection Interfaces

A client does not live in isolation. It is connected by some network conduit (typically a socket) to the server that can be read from and written to. The **WebClient** abstract class defines two pure virtual functions to provide access to these routes, shown in Table 13.2 as **getReadConnection** and **getWriteConnection**.

To facilitate the creation of new API support, there are two abstract classes that define the read and write interfaces to a client, called **ReadConnection** and **WriteConnection**. Because we decided it would be useful to provide some common behavior in the classes themselves, using the concrete sub-classes to implement only the essential transport of information between client and server, they are less abstract than some of the other classes in the framework. To explain further, consider Listing 13.18, which shows the partial listing of the **WriteConnection** interface.

Listing 13.18   The abbreviated **WriteConnection** abstract class definition.

```
class WriteConnection : public ClientConnection {
private:
     char * cpBuffer;
     void lazyInit();
     void copy(WriteConnection const &);
protected:
     virtual unsigned int maximumWriteSize() = 0;
     virtual int writeBytes(char const *) = 0;
public:
     WriteConnection();
     WriteConnection(WriteConnection const &);
```

```
WriteConnection & operator=(WriteConnection const &);
~WriteConnection();
WriteConnection & operator<<(char const * pString);
WriteConnection & operator<<(OptString const & rString);
WriteConnection & operator<<(int i);
WriteConnection & operator<<(double d);
WriteConnection & operator<<
            (WriteConnection &
            (*_pFunction)(WriteConnection&));
};
```

The **WriteConnection** provides a fairly standard **iostream**-like interface to clients as well as copy constructor and assignment operator implementations. The stream insertion operators are written in terms of the pure, virtual functions **maximumWriteSize** and **writeBytes**. Thus, the implementation of the operator to insert an integer into the stream (write an integer as a string to the client) is as shown here:

```
WriteConnection & WriteConnection::operator<<(int i){
    lazyInit();
    ::sprintf(cpBuffer, "%d", i);
    writeBytes(cpBuffer);
    return *this;
}
```

The important parts of the implementation, from an API implementer's perspective, are **maximumWriteSize** and **writeBytes**. The first of these returns an unsigned integer that indicates the maximum number of bytes that can be written atomically by the API, the second actually writes the bytes using (probably) API-specific routines. To see this in action, consider Listing 13.19, which is an NSAPI sub-classed implementation of a **WriteConnection**.

Listing 13.19   An NSAPI **WriteConnection**.

```
NSAPIWClientConnection::NSAPIWClientConnection
                (VoidHolder * pHolder) {
    rMap.setHolder(pHolder);
}

NSAPIWClientConnection::~NSAPIWClientConnection() {
}
```

```
int NSAPIWClientConnection::writeBytes(char const * cpBuffer) {
      if (getErrorCode() == 0 && *cpBuffer != '\0') {
            Session * pSession = rMap.getSession();;
            if(net_write(pSession->csd,(char *) cpBuffer,
                                  strlen(cpBuffer)) == IO_ERROR)
                  setErrorCode(-1);
      }
      return getErrorCode();
}

unsigned int NSAPIWClientConnection::maximumWriteSize() {
      return (unsigned int) NET_BUFFERSIZE;
}

NSAPIWClientConnection::NSAPIWClientConnection
                     (NSAPIWClientConnection & rhs) {
      *this = rhs;
}

NSAPIWClientConnection &
      NSAPIWClientConnection::operator=(
            NSAPIWClientConnection const & rhs) {
      if (this != &rhs) {
            super::operator=(rhs);
            rMap = rhs.rMap;
      }
      return *this;
}
```

The NSAPI implementation uses API-specific function calls and manifest constants to provide an appropriate service. For example, the **writeBytes** implementation uses the **net_write**, low-level function call to provide the *write to client* behavior required (see Chapter 6 for the NSAPI description). Also, the **maximumWriteSize** is defined in NSAPI by a manifest constant, **NET_BUFFERSIZE**, which we'll use in our implementation.

If we were to consider ISAPI, then the **WriteClient** function pointer of the **HTTP_FILTER_CONTEXT** structure is used to implement **writeBytes**, with the **maxiumWriteSize** just returning the maximum value of an unsigned integer. See Chapter 10 for full details on this.

The concrete implementations of **WebClient** are responsible for creating the appropriate **WriteConnection** sub-class upon request. In a similar manner to the

InternetRequest class, only the concrete **WebClient** knows the real class of the **WriteConnection** that it creates—all other references are through the **WriteConnection** interface. Our API independence continues to be preserved by this mechanism.

The **ReadConnection** abstract class, implemented using a similar philosophy, requires one pure virtual function to be implemented, which reads the entire contents of the client-supplied information into a string class. This implementation is not shown.

Adding A Service Event Handler

We have mentioned a number of times that a shared object added to SEREF is expected to expose a C linkage function called **initialise**, which registers all handlers present in the shared object as dependents upon the event manager of the framework. These dependents are expected to register interest in a specific aspect of the event manager, which, for each defined event, is held in a static **EncodedEvent** pointer of the base event handler class. The registration of a service handler is shown in Listing 13.20:

Listing 13.20   An example **initialise** function for service event handler registration.

```
extern "C" {
int __declspec( dllexport ) initialise(void * pDispatcher) {
EventManager * pManager =
            static_cast<EventManager *>(pDispatcher);
   if (!pManager) serefErrorLogger <<
                      "Could not get address of event dispatcher"
                      << endl;
   else {
      pManager->addEventHandler(
                      new FormEcho(),
                      ServiceEvent::eventType()
                      );
   return 1;
}
}
```

We'll assume that the class **FormEcho** exists and is derived from the **ServiceEvent** class. Notice again that we'll call the static member function **eventType** of the **ServiceEvent** class to access the **EncodedEvent** aspect for the service type event.

Basic Encapsulated Behavior

When you sub-class **ServiceEvent**, ostensibly to create a service type function, the virtual member function **serviceRequest** is the only one visible to your sub-class that is designed to be overridden. Like other framework-supplied events, the **ServiceEvent** class does provide a default implementation for this function, shown in this code snippet:

```
virtual int
ServiceEvent::serviceRequest(SEREFUrl &, WebClient & rClient) {
    return getCondition()->noAction();
}
```

Meaningful sub-classes of **ServiceEvent** must reimplement the **serviceRequest** and return **getCondition()->noAction()** if they decline to offer service, or **getCondition() ->success()** for successful request service. A full example showing how to utilize the **WebClient** and **SEREFUrl** references is shown in the next section.

Figure 13.14 shows a UML notation sequence diagram that shows the defined object interactions for service events.

Example Implementation

Our example service implementation looks for the word FORM in the physical path that the request URI was mapped to. If it finds it, it will assume that the client is sending encoded form contents as part of the request. The **FormEcho** class will read and parse the form and echo the parsed key/value pairs back to the client with some narrative. The **FormEcho** class in Listing 13.21 shows the complete implementation.

Listing 13.21   The **FormEcho** class.

```
class FormEcho : public ServiceEvent {
private:
int processForm(WebClient & rClient) {
   if (!rClient.startResponse())
      return getCondition()->noAction();
   InternetRequest * pRequest = rClient.getRequest();
   QueryDictionary * pDictionary;
   if (!pRequest->hasQuery())
      pDictionary = pRequest->getQuery(rClient.getReadConnection());
```

```
   else
      pDictionary = pRequest->getQuery();
   QueryDictionary::AssociationsIterator rIterator =
                                   pDictionary->associations();
   WriteConnection & rConnx = rClient.getWriteConnection();
   rConnx << "Processing form, contents: <p>";
   while (rIterator.more()) {
      IIAssoc<OptString,OptString> * pCurrent = rIterator.current();
      rConnx << "Key: " << *(pCurrent->key()) << " == ";
      rConnx << "Value: " << *(pCurrent->value()) << "<br>";
      ++ rIterator;
   }
   delete pDictionary;
   return getCondition()->success();
}


public:
int serviceRequest(SEREFUrl & rUrl, WebClient & rClient) {
   if (rUrl.getPhysicalPath().find("FORM") != (size_t) -1)
      return processForm(rClient);
return getCondition()->noAction();
}


Dependent * clone() { return new FormEcho(); }
};
```

Again, we'll provide a standard implementation for **FormEcho** of the **clone** factory method that is used by the framework to ensure thread safety.

As you expected, the **serviceRequest** virtual function is overridden to provide the implementation. Our first action is to check the **SEREFUrl** object's physical path for the word FORM. If this isn't found, the **noAction** member function returns the required value to return to the server, to indicate that the extension did not do anything. Otherwise, the **processForm** private member function is called.

The **processForm** method is a little more complex than some of our other examples. We included it, however, to show the means by which forms can be processed using the framework. We'll now step through **processForm**, explaining it in detail.

Our first action is to call the **startResponse** member function of the supplied **WebClient**. This step is essential—it allows concrete Web client implementations to perform whatever startup or initialization is required by the *hidden* API:

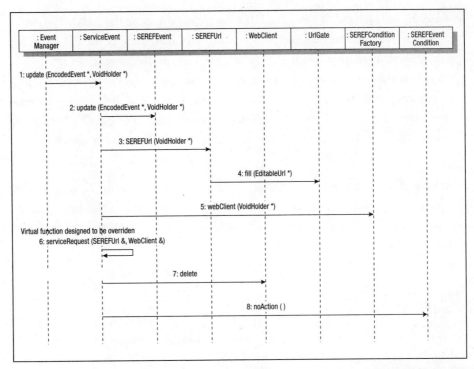

Figure 13.14

A UML notation sequence diagram for service type events.

```
int processForm(WebClient & rClient) {
   if (!rClient.startResponse())
      return getCondition()->noAction();
```

If **startResponse** returns a zero value, it has failed and we'll return from **processForm** with a **noAction** value. If this step proceeds as expected, we'll then get the **InternetRequest** from the **WebClient** reference like this:

```
InternetRequest * pRequest = rClient.getRequest();
```

The next few lines declare a **QueryDictionary** pointer, and point it at a parsed version of the client's form:

```
QueryDictionary * pDictionary;
if (!pRequest->hasQuery())
   pDictionary = pRequest->getQuery(rClient.getReadConnection());
else
   pDictionary = pRequest->getQuery();
```

We determine if the client has a GET transmitted form using the **hasQuery** member function of **InternetRequest**, which returns zero if there is no HTTP GET query present. If there is, we'll simply ask the **InternetRequest** to return it as a **QueryDictionary**. Otherwise, we must assume that there is a POST form waiting that requires access to the client's read connection. To successfully retrieve and process this type of form, we'll pass the **ReadConnection** reference from the **WebClient** to the request by passing the result of calling its **getReadConnection** member function.

The **QueryDictionary** class is described fully in the next section. To help in this explanation, for now consider it to be just an **IIDictionary** that holds keys and values as strings. The **IIDictionary** class is thoroughly described in the section "The Class IIDictionary," in Chapter 12.

To process the retrieved and parsed form, we'll first get an iterator over the associations of the dictionary:

```
QueryDictionary::AssociationsIterator rIterator =
                         pDictionary->associations();
```

This will allow us to walk through both the key and its associated value at the same time. Next we'll grab a reference to the **WriteConnection** to the client, so we can write information to it:

```
WriteConnection & rConnx = rClient.getWriteConnection();
rConnx << "Processing form, contents: <p>";
```

Now we'll begin iteration and get a pointer to the association we are currently looking at:

```
while (rIterator.more()) {
   IIAssoc<OptString,OptString> * pCurrent = rIterator.current();
```

Because we have the key and value in the association, we'll write their values to the client using the insertion operators of the **WriteConnection** interface with some qualifying text:

```
rConnx << "Key: " << *(pCurrent->key()) << " == ";
rConnx << "Value: " << *(pCurrent->value()) << "<br>";
```

Finally, we'll increment the iterator to move to the next association:

```
++ rIterator;
}
```

To wrap up the form processing, we'll delete the dictionary we asked for and return the result of calling the **success** member function of the condition object held by the **ServiceEvent** class:

```
delete pDictionary;
return getCondition()->success();
}
```

> **Note:** The commercial version of SEREF includes an HTML class library that can be used to create HTML documents, effects, and so on. The demo framework, as you'll find on the CD-ROM enclosed with this book, does not include this library—hence our use of raw HTML tags in the response sent to the client.

The QueryDictionary Class

The **QueryDictionary** class provides a repository for the associations present in a form sent from a client and an ancillary service, specifically the tokenization and parsing of raw, encoded forms into such associations. It was initially presumed to be a candidate sub-class of some **IIDictionary** instance that had, as its associations, string keys and values.

As we mentioned in Chapter 12, certain problems arise when you attempt to export template instances from a DLL under Win32, especially when you try to use inheritance. Because of this, the **QueryDictionary** class, instead of inheriting from some more concrete instance of an **IIDictionary** (which is a template class), has to wrap the target **IIDictionary** class instead and delegate to it.

As it turns out, this method is in fact superior to the use of inheritance. Why? Well, the **QueryDictionary** class should not provide any public interface functions that allow keys and values to be removed from it. If we used inheritance to model this relationship, the **QueryDictionary** would have to restrict the **IIDictionary** super-class implementation (which allows key removal), which is not desirable. Using delegation, the **QueryDictionary** merely does not provide a **remove** method—neatly sidestepping the problem. The **QueryDictionary** class is shown in Listing 13.22.

Listing 13.22   The **QueryDictionary** class.

```
class QueryDictionary {
private:
typedef IIAssoc<OptString, OptString> ASSOC;
typedef IIDictionary<OptString, OptString,
                              ASSOC, IVector<ASSOC > > QDICT;
QDICT rDictionary;
QueryDictionary(QueryDictionary const &);
QueryDictionary & operator=(QueryDictionary const &);
public:
QueryDictionary() { }
     virtual ~QueryDictionary() { }
void add(OptString * pKey, OptString * pValue) {
   rDictionary.add(pKey, pValue);
}
typedef QDICT::AssociationsIterator AssociationsIterator;
typedef QDICT::ValuesIterator ValuesIterator;
AssociationsIterator associations() {
         return rDictionary.associations();
     }
 ValuesIterator valuesFor(OptString const * pKey) {
         return rDictionary.valuesFor(pKey);
     }
 size_t find(OptString const * pKey)
         { return rDictionary.find(pKey); }
 size_t numberOfAssociations() const {
                   return rDictionary.numberOfAssociations();
}
void destroy() {
         rDictionary.destroy();
}
int parse(char  const * pQueryString) {
     return parse(OptString(pQueryString));
}
int parse(OptString const & rQueryString) {
     int iCount=0;
     OptString rKey, rValue;

     size_t iLastPos = 0, iNextEquals = 0;

     while (iLastPos < rQueryString.length() &&
             iNextEquals != NPOS) {
         iNextEquals = rQueryString.index("=", iLastPos);
         if (iNextEquals != NPOS) {
             size_t iNextAmpersand =
```

```
                         rQueryString.index("&", iNextEquals + 1);
            rKey = rQueryString.
                        substr(iLastPos, iNextEquals-iLastPos);
            iNextAmpersand = (iNextAmpersand == NPOS) ?
                  rQueryString.length() -1:
                     iNextAmpersand-1;
            rValue=rQueryString.
                        substr(iNextEquals+1,
                                    iNextAmpersand - iNextEquals);
            iLastPos = iNextAmpersand + 2;
            rDictionary.add(new OptString(rKey),
                                   new OptString(rValue));
            iCount++;
         }
      }
   return iCount;
}

};
```

As you can see, only the **parse** member function provides any new functionality, showing a simple means of iterating over an encoded form represented as a string, and adding each discovered key and value to the encapsulated dictionary.

As a quick aside, it is interesting to note the type of dictionary used. Here are the **typedef** statements that define its type again:

```
typedef IIAssoc<OptString, OptString> ASSOC;
typedef IIDictionary<OptString, OptString,
                           ASSOC, IVector<ASSOC > > QDICT;
```

As we mentioned in Chapter 12, the **IIDictionary** class provides a very flexible template, even to the extent of allowing the collision container (called the **Chain** by the template) to be externally specified. In the case of **QueryDictionary**, the **Chain** we'll use (again, fully described in Chapter 12) is just a simple vector, as opposed to the event manager's use of the more complex cloning container.

Summary

This chapter described all the events, except one, of the SEREF event model. The simple framework model presents a flexible, efficient, and vendor/API-independent model to the extension developer.

The root of the framework event hierarchy, **SEREFEvent**, has one descendent for each discrete event type. These types are authorization, URL mapping, URL access checking, service, and logging. Each event type implemented by a class provides a transformation mechanism that mutates the generic dependency message (generated by the dependency mechanism) into a virtual function designed to be overridden.

The use of abstract classes as interfaces enables a loosely coupled, factory-based approach to API and platform portability. The framework's fundamental tenet is notion of programming to an *interface*, not a concrete implementation. We also described the use of *gates* as a simple technology for implementing some of this behavior.

For each event, an example was provided to demonstrate a simple extension. All the source code presented is portable across both of the supported APIs and all the supported platforms.

The next chapter presents the low-level integration required to glue the framework to each API.

The API-Framework Connection

CHAPTER

14

No matter how much we abstract the behavior of an extension framework, it still is required to communicate with the lower level API.

The API-Framework Connection

This chapter shows the simple means by which this is achieved in SEREF and how the underlying C procedural APIs are glued to the framework mechanisms. We do not describe the C APIs in detail, as these are covered fully in Chapters 3 through 6 (NSAPI) and 7 through 10 (ISAPI). We assume that a reasonable knowledge of one or other API will enable you to understand this chapter quite easily.

We'll use the term *inter-paradigm* in this text to describe the process of mapping between the procedural API view and the OO perspective of the framework.

> **Note:** *It is not necessary for you to read this chapter to understand how to extend the framework, as this is covered adequately in Chapters 12 and 13. This chapter is for those of you who would like to know how our OO framework is bolted onto a procedural API. As such, the explanations of some aspects of the framework are sometimes obtuse and will most likely require reading some of the SEREF source code that you'll find on the CD-ROM enclosed with this book.*

Objectives

The inter-paradigm code had far fewer constraints and conditions placed upon it than the rest of the framework. The following is a list of the main objectives:

- *Small*—The amount of connecting code must be as small as possible. This is mainly because it is comprised of API-specific and low-level code, which is parochial, not easily portable, and more difficult to maintain—but its existence is unavoidable.

- *Efficient*—The inter-paradigm code should, if possible, impose virtually zero overhead on extension processing.

- *Complete*—All necessary functionality must be provided to allow the event manager to perform its job without undue or unfair constraint.

Basic API Connectivity

The framework event management mechanism has been illustrated in some detail. But how does the C, API-specific view that we wrap get *massaged* into our framework's abstracted notion of events?

This question can be answered quite easily. Remember that the framework is realized for each platform/API combination by a shared object that is loaded by the Web server. The Web server must be made aware of the framework's interest in its events. So, it becomes obvious that this API/platform combination shared object must contain the necessary code to expose itself to the server *and* perform the translation. This will then allow the event manager to notify dependents—a developer's framework extensions. All we really have to do then, for each deployed framework shared object, is ensure that the required inter-paradigm code exists to perform this translation.

The inter-paradigm code itself is, by necessity, written *to* the API specifications. It must impersonate a simple event handler to the API, and then perform its more complex behavior, event dispatch, invisibly to the server API. This recursive model is quite simple conceptually and allows for simpler configuration of the framework when it is installed. This is because only *one* handler has to be registered with the Web server for an event—the framework inter-paradigm code.

Event Handler Registration In Review

The connection between the framework and whatever API it happens to be cooperating with is one part of the picture. Remember that the framework itself does not know or care of the API that is being used.

One of the obvious facets of the general server extension model is that *multiple* extensions may be registered for events. The SEREF model allows for this via its dependency mechanism (described fully in Chapter 12)—but of course, some means must be provided by the framework to allow the event handler registration to take place.

We have said that one to many shared objects may be loaded by the framework, and that each shared object, if it is to be considered by the framework, must export the C linkage function **initialise**. This function has the signature shown here for Win32

```
extern "C" { int __declspec( dllexport ) initialise(void * pDispatcher);}
```

and likewise for Unix variants

```
extern "C" { int initialise(void * pDispatcher); }
```

The **initialise** function is provided with a pointer to **void**, which is the SEREF event manager. This pointer can be statically cast into an **EventManager** type; after which event handlers may be registered using the event manager's **addEventHandler** method. Here is a simple, example code segment, which registers four event handlers:

```
extern "C" {
int __declspec( dllexport ) initialise(void * pDispatcher) {
  EventManager * pManager =
      static_cast<EventManager *>(pDispatcher);
  if (!pManager)
      serefErrorLogger
        << "Could not get address of event dispatcher"
        << endl;
  else {
    pManager->addEventHandler(
      new DeveloperUrlMapping(), UrlMappingEvent::eventType());
    pManager->addEventHandler(
      new DeveloperAuthClass(), AuthorisationEvent::eventType());
    pManager->addEventHandler(
      new ServiceClassExample(), ServiceEvent::eventType());
    pManager->addEventHandler(
      new MemoryStatus(), ServiceEvent::eventType());
  }
return 1;
  }
}
```

Part of the inter-paradigm code includes using the SEREF configuration file to load as many shared objects as are defined when the framework itself is loaded by the Web server it is connected to. Each shared object is searched for the **initialise** symbol, which is executed if found. The SEREF abstracted view of shared objects is discussed in Chapter 12's "The Provision Of System Services" section. We do not show or discuss the initialization code in this book.

> **Note:** *The demo version of the framework you'll find on the CD-ROM enclosed with this book does not include the ability to load more than one shared object. Further, it only allows a shared object with a fixed name to be attached to itself. This limitation is not present in the commercial product.*

API-Specific Code

This section shows excerpts from the actual inter-paradigm code for both the ISAPI and NSAPI mappings. The excerpts show how the framework impersonates extensions for each API and the way in which the event manager is used to notify framework-extending objects. Each section also highlights the more important aspects considered when the mapping was created. It may be of interest to know that this is the only procedural code *anywhere* in the framework, everything else is either abstract, object oriented, or both.

We do not show or cover issues of configuration in this chapter. These are fully discussed in the CD-ROM documentation files.

Netscape's NSAPI

The API model of NSAPI, covered in Chapters 3 through 6, uses individual callback functions associated with directives. The directives are simple strings that indicate the event type. When a request is processed, each event handler may be called for the request and is passed a number of parameters that describe the request and session.

SEREF Integration

The integration of SEREF with NSAPI is easily achieved. We expose C linkage generic functions in the inter-paradigm code, which are the event handlers that are registered with the Netscape Web server as server extensions. One function is exposed by SEREF for each event that the framework supports. Part of the Netscape bootstrap code is shown in Listing 14.1.

Listing 14.1   The partial NSAPI bootstrap code.

```
#include "nsapiconditionfactory.h"
#include "nsapigatefactory.h"

SEREFConditionFactory *
    SEREFEvent::pConditionFactory = new NSAPIConditionFactory();
SEREFGateFactory * SEREFUrl::pFactory = new NSAPIGateFactory();
SEREFGateFactory * SEREFUser::pFactory = new NSAPIGateFactory();

extern "C" {
static
VoidHolder * newVoidHolder(pblock * pServer,
                                       Session * pSession,
                                       Request * pRequest)
{
  VoidHolder * pHolder = new VoidHolder(3);
  pHolder->add(pServer);
  pHolder->add(pSession);
  pHolder->add(pRequest);
  return pHolder;
}

static
int routeEntryPoint(pblock * pBlocker,
                          Session * pSession,
                          Request * pRequest,
                          EncodedEvent * pGenericEventType)
{
  VoidHolder * pHolder =
          newVoidHolder(pBlocker, pSession, pRequest);
  pb_param * pProtocol = pblock_find("protocol", pRequest->reqpb);
  EncodedEvent rEvent(pGenericEventType->event(),
              pProtocol->value);
  int i = pEventDispatcher->dispatchEvent(&rEvent, pHolder);
  delete pHolder;
  return i;
}

SEREFCLQ int nameTranslation(pblock * pServer, Session * pSession,
Request * pRequest) {
  return routeEntryPoint(pServer, pSession, pRequest,
  UrlMappingEvent::eventType());

}
```

```
SEREFCLQ int nameCheck(pblock * pServer, Session * pSession, Request *
  pRequest) {
  return routeEntryPoint(pServer, pSession, pRequest,
  UrlAccessCheckEvent::eventType());
}

SEREFCLQ int authCheck(pblock * pServer, Session * pSession, Request *
  pRequest) {
  return routeEntryPoint(pServer, pSession, pRequest,
  AuthorisationEvent::eventType());
}

SEREFCLQ int serviceRequest(pblock * pServer, Session * pSession, Request
  * pRequest) {
  return routeEntryPoint(pServer, pSession, pRequest,
  ServiceEvent::eventType());
}

SEREFCLQ int logRequest(pblock * pServer, Session * pSession, Request *
  pRequest) {
  return routeEntryPoint(pServer, pSession, pRequest,
  LogEvent::eventType());
}
}
```

Let's consider one specific example, URL mapping. The framework implements the **nameTranslation** function as the necessary NSAPI hook, as shown here:

```
SEREFCLQ int nameTranslation(pblock * pServer,
                                        Session * pSession,
                                        Request * pRequest) {
  return routeEntryPoint(pServer, pSession, pRequest,
                            UrlMappingEvent::eventType());
}
```

The **SEREFCLQ** token is a manifest constant that is defined in a platform-specific way in a SEREF header file. It represents the text required to be prepended to a function name to export it for dynamic linking purposes.

If you are familiar with NSAPI, you will see instantly that this function has the usual NSAPI extension function signature. It defers the real implementation to the **routeEntryPoint** function, passing its NSAPI-supplied parameters as well as an **EncodedEvent** pointer accessed by calling a static member function of the

UrlMappingEvent class. This base SEREF event type represents the OO view of the URL mapping event. The **EncodedEvent** pointer that it exposes via the **eventType** member function denotes the aspect of the URL mapping event in the framework event manager. This feature is used in all the SEREF-supplied, generic functions for NSAPI, as you will see by examining the other callbacks in Listing 14.1.

The **routeEntryPoint** function, shown again here, creates, as its first action, a **VoidHolder** and places the NSAPI-supplied parameters into it:

```
static
int routeEntryPoint(pblock * pBlocker,
                     Session * pSession,
                     Request * pRequest,
                     EncodedEvent * pGenericEventType)
{
  VoidHolder * pHolder =
          newVoidHolder(pBlocker, pSession, pRequest);
  pb_param * pProtocol = pblock_find("protocol", pRequest->reqpb);
  EncodedEvent rEvent(pGenericEventType->event(),
              pProtocol->value);
  int i = pEventDispatcher->dispatchEvent(&rEvent, pHolder);
  delete pHolder;
  return i;
}
```

As we discussed in Chapter13, a gate class uses the **VoidHolder** object to provide mapping services. It is invisible to developer extensions.

It then creates, on the stack, an **EncodedEvent** that has the current request's protocol and aspect to be notified by the framework **EventManager**. In the following statement

```
int i = pEventDispatcher->dispatchEvent(&rEvent, pHolder);
```

the event manager is asked to dispatch the current event (the one we have just constructed) along with the opaque **VoidHolder** pointer. The dispatch of an event to interested dependents is described fully in the section of Chapter 12 titled "The Dependency Mechanism."

Finally, we should note the creation of the appropriate NSAPI factories at the top of Listing 14.1 and shown again in the following:

```
SEREFConditionFactory *
    SEREFEvent::pConditionFactory = new NSAPIConditionFactory();
SEREFGateFactory * SEREFUrl::pFactory = new NSAPIGateFactory();
SEREFGateFactory * SEREFUser::pFactory = new NSAPIGateFactory();
```

We fully discussed the factory operation in Chapters 12 and 13. As you can see, our NSAPI inter-paradigm code creates concrete factory types as one of its responsibilities. Remember that the API-specific factories implement abstract interfaces, so that the **NSAPIGateFactory** is referenced as the **SEREFGateFactory** type.

Implementation Difficulties And Tradeoffs

All things considered, the NSAPI implementation was remarkably easy to achieve. Other than the usual bugs and glitches that accompany any software development, the NSAPI did not impede progress in any way. We only encountered slight difficulties using shared libraries under Solaris 2.5, but this was an issue with the LD_LIBRARY_PATH environment variable rather than NSAPI.

Because there was no corollary in ISAPI, we had to make a trade-off and deny the use of the **pblock** parameter that is passed as the first argument to any NSAPI function. This is a good example of when a framework (OO or otherwise) limits the behavior of a vendor-specific API. Ironically, in the production framework, the **pblock** parameter is used by the framework initialization function to access an externally defined parameter—the SEREF configuration file, which contains the list of shared objects to be loaded by the framework. We do not, however, consider this constraint to be more than a minor irritation. Future versions of SEREF will probably provide a vendor-independent means of achieving the same service.

The framework does not provide an implementation for the **ObjectType** directive allowed by NSAPI. We decided that the function of this event, which allows the media type of the response to be set, could be reasonably subsumed by other events, most probably during request servicing. In addition, ISAPI provides no native event for this behavior.

Microsoft's ISAPI

You will notice in this section that the vocabulary is Windows NT-oriented due to the single platform availability of IIS.

The ISAPI filter API, covered in Chapters 7 through 10, is used to provide event notifications for all supported ISAPI events, with the exception of the request servicing. The filter API uses a single callback function when a request is processed, this function is executed with a filter context, which is specific to the request, a notification type, and a notification structure. The value of the notification type changes, as does the notification structure for each supported event that the request will pass through. Developers have to cast the pointer to void by which the notification structure is passed according to the type of notification.

For the service phase of a request, the ISA specification is normally used. The use of ISA DLLs is again covered in Chapters 7 through 10. Implementing an ISA DLL is pretty similar to writing a CGI program, except that an ISA resides in a DLL that is dynamically loaded as necessary by IIS. A single C linkage function is exported from the DLL to be called by the server whenever a request has a URL that includes the DLL name in its path.

SEREF Integration With ISAPI Filters

The integration of SEREF with the ISAPI filter API is, again, quite a simple matter. A single C linkage function, the ISAPI standard **HttpFilterProc**, is used in the inter-paradigm code as the filter registered with IIS. This filter registers interest in all the events that can be notified by IIS that have a corresponding SEREF mapping. Part of the ISAPI filter bootstrap code is shown in Listing 14.2.

Listing 14.2   The partial ISAPI connector code.

```
SystemServicesFactory *
  pSystemFactory = new WIN32Services();
SystemServicesFactory *
  SEREFMutex::pFactory = new WIN32Services();
SEREFConditionFactory *
  SEREFEvent::pConditionFactory = new ISAPIConditionFactory();
SEREFGateFactory *
  SEREFUrl::pFactory = new ISAPIGateFactory();
SEREFGateFactory *
  SEREFUser::pFactory = new ISAPIGateFactory();

extern "C" {
static
VoidHolder * newVoidHolder(PHTTP_FILTER_CONTEXT pContext,
                           DWORD iType,
                           LPVOID pNotification)
```

```
{
  VoidHolder * pHolder = new VoidHolder(3);
  pHolder->add(pContext);
  pHolder->add((void *) iType);
  pHolder->add(pNotification);

return pHolder;
}


static
int dispatchEvent(VoidHolder * pHolder,
                        char const * cpProtocol,
                        OptString const & rEventName)
{
EncodedEvent rEvent(rEventName, cpProtocol);
return
   pEventDispatcher->
          dispatchEvent(&rEvent,
                              pHolder,
                              SF_STATUS_REQ_NEXT_NOTIFICATION);

}

BOOL  WINAPI GetFilterVersion(PHTTP_FILTER_VERSION pVersion)
{
  ::strcpy(pVersion->lpszFilterDesc,
    "SEREF Master Dispatcher: (c) Optimation NZ Ltd 1996,1997");
  pVersion->dwFilterVersion = HTTP_FILTER_REVISION;
  pVersion->dwFlags = (SF_NOTIFY_ORDER_DEFAULT |
            SF_NOTIFY_AUTHENTICATION | SF_NOTIFY_URL_MAP |
            SF_NOTIFY_LOG | SF_NOTIFY_NONSECURE_PORT);
  return TRUE;
}


DWORD WINAPI HttpFilterProc(PHTTP_FILTER_CONTEXT pContext,
                                    DWORD iType,
                                    LPVOID pNotification)
{
int iReturnCode = SF_STATUS_REQ_NEXT_NOTIFICATION;
VoidHolder * pHolder = newVoidHolder(pContext, iType, pNotification);
char cProtocol[128];
DWORD lSize = 128;

  (*(pContext->GetServerVariable))
        (pContext, "SERVER_PROTOCOL", cProtocol, &lSize);
```

```
  switch(iType) {
  case SF_NOTIFY_AUTHENTICATION:
    iReturnCode =
          dispatchEvent(
                pHolder, cProtocol,
                AuthorisationEvent::eventType()->event());
    break;
  case SF_NOTIFY_URL_MAP:
    iReturnCode =
          dispatchEvent(
                pHolder, cProtocol,
                UrlMappingEvent::eventType()->event());
    if (iReturnCode == SF_STATUS_REQ_HANDLED_NOTIFICATION)
      iReturnCode =
          dispatchEvent(
                pHolder, cProtocol,
                UrlAccessCheckEvent::eventType()->event());
    break;
  case SF_NOTIFY_LOG:
    iReturnCode =
          dispatchEvent(
                pHolder, cProtocol,
                LogEvent::eventType()->event());
    break;
  }
delete pHolder;
return iReturnCode;
}
```

The ISAPI-specified **GetFilterVersion** function is implemented in the inter-paradigm code and registers SEREF as a normal priority filter that needs to be informed of the authentication, URL mapping, and logging events that ISAPI triggers for requests.

To consider the means by which SEREF maps raw ISAPI events, we extract one of the actions from **HttpFilterProc** in the following code:

```
case SF_NOTIFY_AUTHENTICATION:
    iReturnCode =
          dispatchEvent(
                pHolder, cProtocol,
                AuthorisationEvent::eventType()->event());
    break;
```

The notification type of **SF_NOTIFY_AUTHENTICATION** corresponds to the authentication event. As a preamble to the event manager's dispatch of this event to dependents, a **VoidHolder** is created that contains a pointer to the filter context, the notification type, and the notification structure. This action is performed for all trapped events. The **VoidHolder** will eventually be passed to a framework gate, as we showed in Chapters 12 and 13, which can use such contextual information to interrogate the API and propagate changes to it with respect to a request.

To dispatch the event via the event manager, the C function **dispatchEvent** is called with a pointer to the **VoidHolder**, the protocol of the request, and the aspect of the event to be notified by the event manager. The actual **dispatchEvent** function simply constructs an **EncodedEvent** with the supplied event aspect and protocol, shown again in the following:

```
int dispatchEvent(VoidHolder * pHolder,
                      char const * cpProtocol,
                      OptString const & rEventName)
{
EncodedEvent rEvent(rEventName, cpProtocol);
return
   pEventDispatcher->
         dispatchEvent(&rEvent,
                            pHolder,
                            SF_STATUS_REQ_NEXT_NOTIFICATION);
}
```

The event manager is then asked to dispatch the event by calling its member function **dispatchEvent**. This will transmit the event notification to all dependents that are registered with the event manager as having interest in this event.

From a cursory examination of Listing 14.2, one of the ISAPI events, URL mapping, is augmented to provide the URL access check event, which ISAPI does not natively provide. NSAPI generates this event and we felt that ISAPI should too—and, because of our framework view of the world, we could simulate this event.

The following piece of code shows the method by which SEREF simulates access checking:

```
case SF_NOTIFY_URL_MAP:
    iReturnCode =
          dispatchEvent(
```

```
                pHolder, cProtocol,
                UrlMappingEvent::eventType()->event());
    if (iReturnCode == SF_STATUS_REQ_HANDLED_NOTIFICATION)
      iReturnCode =
          dispatchEvent(
                pHolder, cProtocol,
                UrlAccessCheckEvent::eventType()->event());
  break;
```

After the normal URL map has occurred (the first calls to **dispatchEvent** in the code excerpt), we check the status code returned by the last URL mapping dependent to see if it signaled that it performed a definitive mapping. This will be the case if the return code from event dispatch is **SF_STATUS_REQ_HANDLED_NOTIFICATION**. A dependent will have returned this value if it called the **success** member function of the **SEREFEventCondition** instance associated with the **URLMappingEvent** class and then returned the integer code from that call to the event manager. If this is the return code, then the framework *fakes* an access check event, by calling the **dispatchEvent** with the **UrlAccessCheckEvent** aspect.

One of the difficulties with this approach is that the construction of the **SEREFUser** object, used during access checking to verify access, internally uses an authentication gate. The ISAPI instance of this gate normally uses an ISAPI authentication structure to query the API for the user name and password of the client. However, this type of structure is passed during an authentication event, not a URL mapping event. To surmount this potential problem, the ISAPI authorization gate will use an alternate route to the user name if this is deemed necessary (for example, if the construction of the user object takes place during an event in which the authentication structure is not defined). This route is, in fact, to use the server variables REMOTE_USER or UNMAPPED_REMOTE_USER, which are the mapped (Windows NT user name) and unmapped names of the requesting client.

To aid in this process, the **ISAPIParameters** object (of the ISAPI authorization gate), which contains the **VoidHolder** and provides strongly typed access to the opaque pointers therein, knows how to query the holder object for the notification type of the event with which it is associated. If the notification type does not match the type requested via one of the map's member functions, a null pointer will be returned. So, if the authorization gate asks for an authentication structure during URL mapping, it will receive a null pointer. When the gate encounters this condition, it will revert to the secondary route identified before.

It is interesting to note that there is nothing in the ISAPI filter specification that disallows the service of a request from a filter. In fact, the beta version of the framework extended the URL map handling even further to allow the service of a request after the URL access check. We decided to omit this from the commercial release because this behavior is potentially confusing for those used to ISAPI, who will want to use the framework. Pending further user input, we may reintroduce this feature, as it provides an attractive symmetry with the NSAPI approach.

> **Note:** *The demo copy of SEREF on the CD-ROM included with this book re-introduces this feature.*

SEREF Integration With ISA Applications

The integration of SEREF with the ISA API is easy and indirect. The standard ISA callback functions, **HttpExtensionProc** and **GetExtensionVersion**, are exported by the inter-paradigm code. Part of the ISA bootstrap code is shown in Listing 14.3.

Listing 14.3   The partial ISA connector code.

```
extern "C" {
BOOL WINAPI GetExtensionVersion( HSE_VERSION_INFO  *pVer )
{
    pVer->dwExtensionVersion = MAKELONG( HSE_VERSION_MINOR,
                                         HSE_VERSION_MAJOR );
    lstrcpyn( pVer->lpszExtensionDesc,
    "SEREF ISA Implementation: (c) Optimation New Zealand 1996,1997",
            HSE_MAX_EXT_DLL_NAME_LEN );
    return TRUE;
}


extern int __declspec( dllexport ) initialise(void * pDispatcher);

DWORD WINAPI HttpExtensionProc( EXTENSION_CONTROL_BLOCK  *lpEcb )
{
return (!initialise(pEventDIspatcher))
            ? HSE_STATUS_ERROR : serviceRequest(lpEcb);
}


static int serviceRequest(EXTENSION_CONTROL_BLOCK  *lpEcb)
```

```
{
  VoidHolder * pHolder = new VoidHolder(3);
  pHolder->add(lpEcb);
  pHolder->add((void *) SF_REQ_SEND_RESPONSE_HEADER);
  EncodedEvent rEvent(ServiceEvent::eventType()->event(), "HTTP");
  int i = pEventDispatcher->
            dispatchEvent(&rEvent, pHolder, HSE_STATUS_ERROR);
  delete pHolder;
return i;
}
}
```

When the extension procedure **HttpExtensionProc** is called, the server has parsed a URL whose path includes the name of the DLL in which the ISA application resides. The framework implements the extension procedure to call the **initialise** function *directly*—this means that no other shared object is loaded and that the **initialise** function *must* be declared in the current DLL. The **initialise** function has the same semantics as described in the "Event Handler Registration In Review" section earlier in this chapter, with the exception that it will usually only register handlers created to service requests.

After the service event handler has been registered, the static function **serviceRequest** is called, which creates an **EncodedEvent**, a **VoidHolder**, and finally directs the event manager to dispatch the service event to interested dependents. For most ISA deployments, there will only be one such dependent. This dependent then does whatever is necessary to fulfill the request—it writes back to the client, and so on. The extension procedure returns with its exit code notified by the event handler.

Because of the nature of ISA applications, the framework code is normally statically linked in with the single event handler and deployed as a DLL in the normal ISA manner. This wastes storage space and some memory, but does allow the same model to be realized for both filters and ISA DLLs. This is of greater value to most developers than a few hundred kilobytes of memory. Note that all the same abstractions and design are in place for an ISA application—allowing a solid OO approach to ISAs and filters.

Finally, we should note that the same source code for service event handlers may be used for NSAPI, ISAPI filters, and ISA applications in combination with the framework—there is no reason why this cannot occur successfully unless the developer introduces a platform or API dependency.

Implementation Difficulties And Tradeoffs

The integration of SEREF with the ISAPI filter API was reasonably easy to achieve. One of the problems we faced was how far to go in simulating events for compatibility with NSAPI (or any other API, for that matter). Some events were easy to simulate—the NSAPI-defined URL access check event, for example. Others, such as the ISAPI event for reading raw data, were much harder to simulate with respect to NSAPI.

So, only the events defined implicitly by the SEREF event hierarchy are captured or simulated. Those supported are:

- Authentication

- URL mapping

- URL access check

- Service

- Logging

Of these, only the URL access check needs simulation, for ISAPI. Additionally, the service event can be implemented a little differently at the deployment level for IIS—but this is a developer choice.

The following ISAPI events are therefore not part of the framework event family:

- Notify secure port

- Read raw data

- Write raw data

- Preprocess headers

- End of net session

- Notify access denied

The *notify access denied* event is in fact subsumed by the framework authentication model as an alternate authorization scenario. Of the remaining events, only the read and write of raw data would prove difficult to implement with consistent semantics in an NSAPI environment. Of course, the nature of the event hierarchy is such that any number of events may be added over time. The current hierarchy allows the majority of extensions to be modeled successfully.

Finally, the ability of ISAPI filters to service requests was included and then excluded from the framework. The initial inclusion of this facility enabled a completely consistent model to operate, from a developer's viewpoint. However, the two-perspective view, in which an ISA is deployed separately, is currently back in place, allowing ISAPI and ISA developers to more easily understand the framework actions. Pending further research, this may alter in the future. In fact, as we mentioned before, the demo copy of SEREF on the CD-ROM included with this book reintroduces the ISAPI filter service ability.

Summary

This technically oriented chapter illustrated the ways in which the SEREF OO framework is connected to the various APIs with which it operates. Each API has its own mapping, which reflects the different implementations and specifications that vendors have in this area. We declared our objectives for this inter-paradigm code to be that it was small, efficient, and complete.

Both the NSAPI and ISAPI mappings were described and the inter-paradigm code shown. A brief walk-through of the behavior of each, with respect to server notified events, was given. We also noted that the great majority of the framework's activity actually occurs in an abstracted, OO view of events, requests, and sessions.

Finally, the compromises required to support the behavioral intersection of the currently supported APIs were stated and the rationale for the event hierarchy presented.

Index

Netscape server, 76, 127-129
phases of, 19, 61-63
Request messages
See also Request methods; Request/
response paradigm.
example sessions
GET request, Navigator-generated,
25-26
GET request to compressed
resource, 32-33
HEAD request, 36
POST request, Navigator-generated,
38-39
HTTP_FILTER_CONTEXT
structure, 303-305
InternetRequest class, 565-568
request headers, 24-25
server operation, 61-63
syntax, 23
Request methods
See also Request messages.
Allow header, 30
GET method, 35-36
HEAD method, 36-37
method key, Netscape server, 129
POST method, 37-40
PUT method, 40
specifying, 23
Request phase, request life cycle, 19
Request processing
Authenticate Transaction phase
(Authentication phase), 76, 92-93, 131
Check Path phase (Path Check phase),
76, 93-94, 128-120, 131
Determine Object Type phase
(Object type phase), 76, 94, 129, 131
filters, ISAPI, 263-265
obj.conf configuration file, 91, 98-103
object directives, 103
overview, 91-92
Perform Service phase (Service phase),
76, 94, 129, 131
service functions, 206-208
threaded operation, 141
Translate URL phase
(Name Translation phase), 76, 93,
128, 131

Update Logs phase (Add Log phase;
Logging phase), 76, 95, 129, 131
Request structure
add log functions, 242
in authentication functions, 163
headers member, 130
in initialization functions, 154
in name translation functions, 184
object type functions, 202
overview, 126-127
path check function, 194
reqpb member, 129-130
senthdrs member, 131
service functions, 210
srvhdrs member, 131-132
stat_path member, 133
thread safety, 148
vars member, 127-129
Request types, **ServerSupportFunction**
callback, 288-290
Request/response paradigm
See also Request processing.
overview, 15
phases, 60
REQUESTINFO structure, 423-424
REQUEST_METHOD environment
variable, CGI, 67, 278, 280
reset method, **ICloningContainer::Iterator**
class, 516
resizeTo method, **IVector** class, 493
resource library module, 407, 422
RESOURCE, SF_DENIED_ flag, 319
ResourceList_Init function, 432
Resources
See also Objects.
caching, 33, 59
Last-Modified header, 34
proxying, 59
and request/response paradigm, 15
static vs. dynamic, 35-36
Response headers
See also Message headers; Response
messages.
AddResponseHeaders function, 307-308
convincing server not to send, 436
HandleResponseHeader function,
424, 434-436